THE DECLINE AND FALL OF PRACTICALLY EVERYONE

THE DECLINE AND FALL OF PRACTICALLY EVERYONE

OR, WE BLEW IT REAL GOOD

Victor G. Novander Jr.

The History of the Human Race has been one of the Devolution of Original Consciousness into Unconscious Self-Awareness.

Library of Congress Control Number: 2005907637
ISBN: Hardcovver 978-1-59926-531-5
Softcover 978-1-59926-530-8

This book was printed in the United States of America.

To order additional copies of this book, contact:
Xlibris Corporation
1-888-795-4274
www.Xlibris.com
Orders@Xlibris.com
30232

ACKNOWLEDGEMENTS

Every experience in my life had to have happened just the way it did, otherwise I wouldn't be where I am today. And where I am today is where I want to be. Consequently, I am grateful for all of my "teachers" along the way. All of them were indispensable. I single out the one who is solely responsible for unlocking the trap door in my head that allowed the real me to emerge to whatever extent I have. That person is Arthur Janov, the discoverer of primal pain and the developer of Primal Therapy. By my going through therapy at The Primal Institute and becoming a lifelong primal person, I've been able to set my feet upon the path that leads to the restoration of my childhood consciousness, of my becoming like a little child—able to give and to receive love.

DEDICATION

This book is dedicated to Arthur Janov who discovered the hidden correlation between the false self, that is, the self of everyday unconscious self-awareness, and the real self, that is, the self of childhood consciousness, suppressed into the subconscious because of overwhelming primal pain.

DISCLAIMER

I am not a Primal Therapist. I am not qualified to practice as a Primal Therapist. I speak only for myself as having been a primal person since 1974. The Primal Foundation has not evaluated any statement in this book. If what is in this book motivates anyone to become a primal person, I urge anyone so inclined to contact The Primal Foundation. Even if one is inclined to become a self-primaler, with or without the aid of a primal buddy, I urge consulting with The Primal Foundation.

The Primal Foundation
1205 Abbot Kinney Blvd., Venice, CA 90291
Telephone: (310) 392-2003
Fax: (310) 392-8554
E-mail: primalctr@earthlink.net

The body does not lie; it always tells the truth. If the body's truth is too overwhelming, the mind will lie to itself to preserve itself from disintegration. That's why we are unconscious.

CONTENTS

INTRODUCTION

WHY I'VE WRITTEN THIS BOOK

WAKE UP! Unless enough people know that what they experience as the self is nothing but a robot preprogrammed by primal pain, our species and our planet are failure-fated. I've written this book as an alarm bell to arouse us from our present state of unconscious self-awareness and to point the way toward restoring ourselves to consciousness.

Without the restoration of consciousness, all the attempts of self-awareness to reverse the deplorable condition into which humanity has fallen and to safeguard the ecology of our home, planet Earth, will only make matters worse. Without descending through self-awareness and experiencing the primal pain that lies below it and controls it, self-awareness can only continue to seek symbolic, substitute satisfaction of the organism's subconscious, unmet, infantile needs. It is the unconscious self's substitution of an infinite number of insatiable wants or desires for unmet, infantile needs that has driven humanity to the brink of destroying itself and the life-sustaining nurture of Earth. Without the systematic dismantling of self-awareness through connecting the self's insatiable wants and desires with the underlying primal pain, regardless of one's political persuasion, religion, or philosophy, every solution of self-awareness for humanity's problems will only make the problem more insoluble.

I've written this book because I feel that if a reader senses that my experience of history has the ring of reality to it, he will be able to connect it to his own history. He will be motivated to seek to restore his own consciousness.

I've written this book to lead my readers into an awakening or into a spontaneous first primal, bringing to life an inextinguishable spark of consciousness smoldering in the tinder of their self-awareness, ready to burst into flame when the commitment has been made to become a primal person.

Today we are often reminded to "think outside the box." That is what I would like you to do as you read this book. What you have been taught most likely will tell you to reject offhand what is written here.

For those of you familiar with the books of Carlos Castaneda, particularly *Journey to Ixtlan*, I am trying to do the same thing here that Don Juan did with

Carlos. I am attempting to get you to "stop your world" and jump into another dimension. For Don Juan, it was the world of sorcery. For me, it is the world of primal consciousness. It is the world we all knew as conscious children before primal pain forced us to become unconsciously self-aware. It is the world that is again possible to us through the process of resolving the primal pain that made us unconsciously self-aware in the first place.

I am writing for every person who wants to be a parent and make a home for his children. It is those who have primaled, who have altered their genes, that is, made them less crazy with primal pain, who can pass on less unconscious genes to their children. And, being less unconscious themselves, will cause less primal pain in their children.

Finally, I've written this book for myself. I wanted to have the experience of feeling the entire flow of human history the same way I experienced in my childhood the devolution of my consciousness into unconscious self-awareness. For, after all, it is only an author's discovery of essential humanity in himself that makes it possible for his readers to discover their own truths.

Please, avoid the tendency to dismiss what I'm going to say here on a variety of academic disciplines because I don't have Ph.D. behind my name. That requirement for qualification to speak is just another way by an element within the academic elite to marginalize the rest of us. You decide whether or not what I've written makes sense. One doesn't need special qualifications to make sense.

I am not asking you to accept what I've written as being "the Gospel Truth." What I am asking is that you really think and feel *for yourself* whether or not what I'm saying resonates with *your childhood* and *your life*. If it does, and only then, act appropriately on that knowledge.

In large measure, I share with everyone else being unconsciously self-aware. What sets me and thousands of others apart is having experienced unconscious self-awareness for what it is—a defense system holding back primal pain—and that we have begun the journey toward the restoration of childhood consciousness.

I apologize to my readers for consistent use of the male pronoun when I intend the context to mean either or both sexes. No satisfactory solution to this problem has been found. The use of "they" or "them" causes awkward constructions. The use of "he or she" or "his or her" interferes with the flow of the sentence. Even James Kilpatrick, an acknowledged expert on the English language, has thrown up his hands and uttered his exasperated "Aaargh" to every solution that has been proposed.

PART I

PRELIMINARY CONSIDERATIONS

CHAPTER 1

WHERE I'M COMING FROM

The Book's Proposition

What I know of our most ancient ancestors reveals that they were in a state of unconscious self-awareness. What I have learned of all of their descendants, as one millennium followed upon another, is that humanity has continued to devolve from an initial state of a consciousness-in-pain into a state of ever-increasing unconscious self-awareness.

What I mean by a consciousness-in-pain is a state of being in which the person has been subjected to primal pain, whether he be a young child today or an ancient adult. What I mean by unconscious self-awareness is a state of being in which the person has been subjected to so much primal pain as to have found it necessary to suppress any experience of his consciousness-in-pain and in the process to have substituted self-awareness, which is unconscious of the primal pain that controls its every thought, emotion and deed. By primal pain, I mean the pain that results from the needs not being met of a fetus, child, or adolescent and is too traumatic to experience and is, therefore, suppressed, becoming unconscious.

One example here from my own life will suffice to show what I mean by a primal pain and how I suppressed it. The need is for one's parents to be honest in what they tell their children. The primal pain is being lied to about something important enough to cause too much pain to handle. In the example that follows, the means of suppression was intellectual rationalization.

I was about twelve years old and wanted a full-sized, two-wheeled bicycle for my birthday. I had saved up what in those days was a huge sum of money: ten dollars. I gave it to my father and asked him to put it toward a bicycle. He did buy for me a shiny, new, red bicycle. He said he paid twenty-eight dollars for it. I was overjoyed that I had a new bicycle and that I had helped to pay for it.

Some days later I was in the basement of our house. My mother was one flight up the stairs at the back door, talking to a neighbor. She mentioned that my dad had been able to buy the bicycle for fourteen dollars. She didn't know that I overheard her. I was devastated. They had lied to me. I had paid for most of the cost of the bicycle out of my own money. I was in deep pain. I felt I could never trust them again about anything.

I suppressed the pain by rationalizing about what a good deal my dad had made and bragging to my friends about how much I'd contributed toward buying the bicycle. Rationalizing my primal pain was one of the main ways I used to excuse my parents for hurting me.

Since my experience is, and my research points to, that no one has ever been in a state of pain-free consciousness, I cannot say that there was a time in our past when our ancestors were pain-free and fully conscious. Nevertheless, it will help to contrast, side by side what a state of pure consciousness would be like with what a state of pure unconscious self-awareness would be like. Subsequent chapters will explore the devolution of the traits of consciousness into the traits of self-awareness.

Consciousness	**Self-Awareness**
A state of being in which:	A state of being in which:
One's world is an indivisible whole.	One's world is one of dualities, i.e., mind and matter, inner and outer, self and other.
One has free will.	One's will is controlled by one's suppressed, unmet, infantile needs to be met symbolically in the present.
What is real are experiences.	What is real are subjects and objects.
Time is an ongoing present moment.	Time is either cyclical or linear, which has both a beginning and an ending.
All is interconnected.	There are causes and effects.
One is a living, interconnected being in an alive, interconnected cosmos.	One is a living being separate from the cosmos, which is either animate or inanimate.
One's three-level brain is interconnected.	The three levels of one's brain are disconnected.
One's sense of consciousness permeates the whole organism.	One's sense of self-awareness has a specific location in the body.
One attends to one's needs.	One seeks to satisfy insatiable wants.
One ends one's suffering by primaling one's primal pain.	One ends one's suffering through placation, reimmersion, the use of power and transcendence.

I base the proposition of this book on thirty-five years of experience as a primal person. My experience is that what is commonly referred to today as self-consciousness is actually an unconscious self-awareness. My experience is that prior to becoming a primal person, I was unaware that all my thoughts, emotions and deeds were totally controlled by subconscious primal pain.

My experience as a primal person makes clear to me that from my conception to the crystallization of my self-awareness around the age of four, I encapsulated the entire history of the incremental crystallization of self-awareness in all of my ancestors, generation by generation. In the span of four years, I lost as much consciousness as did all of my ancestors over hundreds of thousands of years. The effects of primal pain are cumulative. The consequences of primal pain are passed down from generation to generation, each succeeding one more unconscious than the previous. Part III of this volume explores a number of different aspects of religion that illustrate how, through the millennia, the effects of primal pain are cumulative.

Further, my experience is that as I have resolved my primal pain in primals, my thoughts, emotions and acts have become less controlled and more spontaneous. Incrementally, I have been divesting myself of an unconscious self-awareness and restoring original consciousness.

What led me to the formulation of the proposition for this book was the development of an interest in the oral traditions of Native Americans. I was struck by the high degree of harmony demonstrated in their personal and tribal lives and in their harmonious relationship with the natural world. As I worked to restore my childhood consciousness, I recognized that there was a direct connection between the harmony I was experiencing and the harmony experienced by Native Americans prior to any contact with Europeans. For example, it is simply a given that young children relate to what unconscious self-awareness refers to as a stuffed animal as being alive. I found that primaling was creating a state of being in me in which there was no such thing as a thing; the whole cosmos was alive and in harmony with himself. (Of course, I don't mean maleness here.) This state of being is characteristic of Native Americans prior to the European invasions. My returning childhood consciousness was their adult consciousness. Since, according to Native Americans, their oral traditions go back many thousands of years, it came to me that childhood consciousness is the original consciousness of humankind. It followed then that human history primarily is about the devolution of consciousness into unconscious self-awareness.

Today, the condition of most of humankind is one of being unconscious. Also, today, the condition of most of humankind is one of suffering. The scourge of war is everywhere. Human rights abuses abound. Among the more technological nations, emotional and mental illness permeate society. It is a condition that accompanies self-awareness. The child who suffers because his needs are not being met not only becomes self-aware, which is a defense system to keep his pain from consciousness, but he continues to suffer. His organism is neurotic, becomes ill and, as an adult, he creates the kinds of societies that perpetrate and perpetuate suffering.

Further, on the subject of suffering, it is important to note that in a significant number of the oral traditions of Native Americans, the first people had no illnesses. That is to say that in an ideal state of consciousness there is health. In present-day, isolated, aboriginal societies, suffering is at a minimum compared to the terrible suffering that is in all the "civilized" areas of the world where humankind is unconscious. With the experience of my self-awareness as having been totally unconscious and with my own suffering, it is easy to see why there is so much suffering on a suffering planet.

This brief history of our species, then, is the first one to be written from an entirely different perspective from that of unconscious self-awareness, the state of being in the "civilized" world. Therefore, because even a newly developing state of less consciousness among us is a relatively unknown one, these introductory remarks must be comprehensive enough to give as complete a picture as possible of what it means to be on the path of restoring one's own consciousness.

Furthermore, because I have not arrived at full consciousness, whether I know it or not, I am still crying out through this book for my mommy and daddy to please listen to me. Accordingly, I've sought to be alert throughout the whole process of writing this book for the surfacing of pain relating to the fact that my mother and father never really listened to me. Over the past thirty-five years, I've primaled many times on that feeling: "Please listen to me, Mommy" or "Please listen to me, Daddy."

What I am also saying here is that there are no objective histories. All historians write from some subjective point of view, and I am making mine as clear as I can. Not only are all histories subjective but, with regard to prehistoric times, they are purely conjectural. Artifacts from prehistory cannot speak. Oral traditions are modified through the millennia to fit current conceptions. This is also true after writing ushered in the historical period—no one can help but recast the past within the framework of the current status of the devolvement of consciousness into unconscious self-awareness.

Writing came about during the 4th millennium BCE in the Middle East when Stage II of unconscious self-awareness was being replaced by Stage III, which centers on the use of power. Hence, the writing of histories from the outset concentrated on how power was exercised in human and heavenly affairs. And, as we know, histories are written by the victorious. Prior to writing, oral traditions had all sorts of motifs, but when writing came about in Stage III of self-awareness, oral traditions began to be written down with a power motif, modifying whatever motifs had prevailed to that point. This history is written from the point of view of a consciousness that is in the process of being restored. Hence, I'm going to see history as a two-way street. One way leads to the continued devolution of consciousness into unconscious self-awareness. The other, through the practice of primaling, leads to the evolution of self-awareness back into the normative consciousness of early childhood and of our most ancient ancestors.

Since I can no longer accept historical points of view that have arisen out of an uninformed self-awareness, I have to reinterpret what others have said happened. I have to read between the lines with primal eyes. This means discarding the nineteenth century view that our paleolithic ancestors were much less conscious than we are and that our species has evolved a consciousness superior to all others. It means dismissing the view that the story of humanity is one of progress.

Reading with primal eyes also means challenging the prevailing opinion that our paleolithic ancestors were as conscious as we are today. My experience suggests that they were far less unconscious than we are. Human history is neither evolution toward greater consciousness nor is it static in regard to consciousness but is a devolution toward greater unconsciousness.

In this history, I shall make liberal use of the evolution of religious and philosophical ideas and of changing worldviews because they reveal in discrete steps the degeneration of the quality of human life. This history is not a history of religion nor of philosophy but of what they reveal about the human condition, about the devolution of consciousness into unconscious self-awareness.

My experience indicates that the role of religious and philosophical belief systems for self-awareness is to shield us from unbearable primal pain. All religious belief systems in their rituals, ceremonies, customs and dogmas and all philosophical rationalizations are reactions to, and symbolizations of, the suppressed primal pain of our own deprivation as embryo-fetuses, as infants and as children. For instance, the ancient, annual sacrificial rituals to satisfy the deities are reflective of the sacrifices a child has to make of himself in order to satisfy his parents. It is not my intent at all, however, to debunk religion. It is as necessary to life for some as breathing. As long as the primal world remains outside of their experience, some effective means of suppressing primal pain is necessary to mitigate suffering. I accept that any religious person is going to experience human history through his own worldview.

Some religious historians, for example, Mircea Eliade, postulated that to be religious is innately human. He reasons that this is so because some of the earliest "hard" evidence of what life was like in paleolithic times implies a belief in either/or both male and female deities. My experience as a primal person shows me that our ancient ancestors became religious as a consequence of becoming self-aware. Consistent with the dualism that is part of the nature of self-awareness, the inner world of the self is mirrored in the outer world with deities created in the self's own image.

We admonish ourselves to remember our history in order not to be condemned to everlastingly repeating our mistakes. No history that I know of has succeeded in that endeavor. Consciousness continues to decrease, suffering to increase. At this stage, it seems to me that the only kind of history that will help us toward more consciousness and less suffering is one that exposes the so-called progress of humanity from bestiality to civilization as being little more than a desperate attempt to escape from ever-increasing levels of primal pain. Perhaps such a history will enable us to stand back from ourselves and to experience self-awareness for what it is: a defense system holding back the primal pain that caused self-awareness to come into being when we were children. That is its primary function. It comes into existence to shield the organism from unbearable pain and continues to do so throughout life.

The formation in us of self-awareness when we were children took place in discrete jumps. To illustrate, I see a picture of myself around four years of age. With both arms, I'm holding a large number of small toy cars and trucks. What is clear to me about that image is that by that time I had given up trying to get my needs met and had jumped to the Stage of substituting wants for needs. I was now hopelessly trying to fill the emptiness in my life with things, having given up on receiving love. It was much in the manner that electrons jump orbit in an atom. A certain amount of energy has to be gained or lost before the electron jumps to a different orbit. In like manner, when the unconsciousness of a certain, critical mass of people devolves to a different level, the society as a whole jumps to that higher level of unconsciousness. It is not necessary for everyone to jump to that higher level to cause the character of the society to become more unconscious.

That consciousness declines in a society in discrete jumps means that all of its history occurs in discontinuous stages. In addition, it means that cognizance of all earlier stages of less unconsciousness is lost. The corollary to that is that the current state of unconsciousness is now considered to be normative, past states being considered more primitive.

Hence, what I have looked for in my research are evidences of discrete jumps in the formation of self-awareness. I have found the clues primarily in religion and in philosophy, but the arts, education, language, warfare, economics, medicine, science and indeed every kind of human endeavor has provided its share of the signs of the changes. The subject area is so vast that I cannot be comprehensive of every nuance of discrete jumps in self-awareness. I have had to limit myself to the most obvious connections between childhood consciousness and original human consciousness and between the loss of both childhood consciousness and original consciousness to unconscious self-awareness.

Aside from the vastness of the subject of the devolution of consciousness into unconscious self-awareness, there is the difficulty in describing any one aspect of a primal understanding of life because each aspect implies all the others. An understanding of one aspect is not possible apart from an understanding of the whole. Consequently, as various aspects are singled out for treatment, of necessity, there will be a repetition of how the other aspects relate to the one in question with regard to the whole.

I've also asked myself the question as to why, since the origin of primal pain is lost in antiquity, primal pain was not discovered until Janov did so around 1970. Actually, primal pain has been alluded to ever since self-awareness began to replace consciousness. Oral traditions referred to it in their recitation of the events of the origin of the cosmos and of humanity and of humanity's fall from an initial state of health and wholeness. Oral traditions also spoke of it in connection with the work of shamans who treated persons who were experiencing a loss of self-awareness, perhaps because it was stolen by an evil shaman or by a vengeful deity. Loss of self-awareness suggests a nervous breakdown or a psychotic break due to uncontrollable rising primal pain.

Indeed, symbolic primals were occurring as early as the beginnings of Buddhism and Christianity. Enlightenment in Buddhism is most certainly a primal in a religious context. Enlightenment as the experience of the self being controlled by desire is parallel to, and symbolic of, the self being controlled by primal pain. In Christianity, Paul's conversion was a primal masked as a religious experience. The Christian experience of the self as being in a state of sinfulness, like enlightenment, is parallel to, and symbolic of, self-awareness being totally permeated with primal pain.

When secularism began, most likely in the 1st millennium BCE, principally with Greek philosophy, and subsequently up to our own day, if a person experienced a spontaneous primal, the usual diagnosis was that the person was experiencing a psychotic regression to childhood. (A primal is to be distinguished from psychoanalysis in that a primal is a reliving of the past, while psychoanalysis is self-awareness remembering the past.) A secular setting, plus the intuitive insight of Arthur Janov, has given us primal therapy, the cure for what ails us.

More About Where I'm Coming From, But Personally

Nothing I've written so far or will write in this book will amount to anything unless my life shows that I have become less unconscious and less self-aware. At times that is not easy. Some people, for whatever reasons, are unable to see the changes. In general, the psychiatric profession discounts personal, anecdotal evidence. Regardless of what other people might think about me, I know that the changes in me have been so profound that the pre-primal person I used to be has changed fundamentally. I am a new person.

After several years of being a primal person, I started to notice a change taking place in me. At that time, I conceptualized the change as that my mind was becoming reunited with my body and my emotions. The process of the dissolution of self-awareness and the restoration of consciousness had exceeded a certain threshold so that now I was cognizant of what was happening.

This change was of particular significance to me because of what I had to do at age thirteen in order to protect myself from pain I could no longer handle.

What I did was to say to myself that I didn't want to feel any more pain. Instantly, I felt a trapdoor closing in my head, shutting myself off from experiencing any more pain. Once closed, the door disappeared. There was no way to open it again then, even if I had wanted to.

When the trapdoor slammed shut in my head, I went dead inside. At the same time, the outside world became dead as well. Later on, I adopted what became known in Christianity as Death of God theology. A dualistic, dead self-awareness was mirrored by a God who was dead also. They were accurate reflections of each other.

In retrospect, I am cognizant that what I had done was to complete my defense system, cutting off any remaining access of primal pain to self-awareness. The last vestige of consciousness was now suppressed into subconsciousness and self-awareness had become totally unconscious. The connections among the thinking, feeling and sensing portions of my brain were now so effectively blocked that I might be angry and not even know it. Self-awareness now had no clue that there was a hidden part of me that was screaming in pain and that would continue to seek the resolution of that pain.

As the years went by and I continued to make primal connections, thus continuing to become less unconscious, I knew I was becoming as I was as a small boy. My consciousness as a small boy was returning. The connections among the thinking, feeling and sensing portions of my brain were becoming reestablished. The sensation of where "I" was located was descending through my body and becoming less localized. Incrementally, consciousness was pervading and permeating all of "my" organism.

As more and more of childhood consciousness returned through the years, I found that my whole worldview was changing. I discovered that part of the very essence of self-awareness is to think solely in terms of dualities. Conversely, in a returning consciousness, I was experiencing the absence of dualities and the presence of an interconnected oneness. Instead of the experience of the duality of an inner world and an outer world, I found that distinction vanishing. Replacing the duality of mind and matter was the experience of life everywhere. The duality of cyclical and linear time was fading into the experience of an ever-changing present moment.

After thirty-five years of primaling and the restoration of a sufficient amount of consciousness, dualities have become much less a part of my experience. In a more childlike manner, consciousness is diffused throughout my organism. My present state of unconsciousness has fewer boundaries. What is more real now than subjects and objects are events, experiences, interconnections and relations. Now, more than ever before, all events are living and the time is NOW.

The fruit of the year-by-year cultivation of connections has been an ever-lengthening present moment. It is as if my present is ever less elusive and is expanding, crowding out the past and the future. The closer I come to reestablishing all connections, the closer I am to living in a NOW in which time has no meaning. This is an attribute of childhood consciousness. The young child has no conception of time because sufficient primal pain has not built up enough to create a self-awareness that can't let go of the past because of unfulfilled infantile needs.

Self-awareness is preoccupied with attachments to the past and expectations of the future. These preoccupations prevent it from living in the present. When I reflect upon the period of my life before I became a primal person, I realize that I was so attached to my past and had such expectations of the future that I lived my life without ever experiencing it; I was always somewhere else during the present moment. That is now all changed. Now I live much more in the present moment.

In my evolving, new worldview, there is a universal consciousness of whom I am an interconnected member. My primal experience is that it is in the nature not only of humans but of the entirety of universal consciousness to be whole. My experience is that the means to restore wholeness is for each person to resolve his primal pain in primals.

Perhaps the most significant change for me has been the feeling that I am much more the person I was intended to be. I am a grown-up Sonny Boy—what I was first called—having gotten started on my way of restoring who he was before primal pain destroyed him. I say "destroyed," for when, on the first day of primal therapy, I spread out a chronological sequence of black-and-white photos of my life, my therapist looked at them, pointed across them until he reached one when I was thirteen and had felt the trapdoor closing in my head, and said to me: "The destruction of Vic." It was mind-blowing to me that just from pictures he could pick out when my destruction was complete. But, just as certainly as I know I am not the person I was before therapy, I know that I still have unresolved primal pain and must still live by the primal maxim. When I became a primal person, I set my feet on a path toward the restoration of childhood consciousness, and I still walk the path.

Another change that has meant a great deal to me has been the restoration of the ability to give and receive love. By love, I mean acceptance. To love someone is to accept that person totally as he is. To be loved is to be able to receive acceptance, that is, to be able to allow oneself to be enveloped without either losing oneself or backing away for fear of losing oneself.

That I can give and receive love has made it possible for me to have healthy relationships with my children. It has permitted me for the first time to love a woman and have fewer subconscious expectations of her to give me what my mother couldn't. I can now relate to authority figures without always attempting to make them into the nurturing father I never had. My life as a primal person has made it quite clear to me, however, that whether it be a new love or new confrontation with arbitrary authority, deeper aspects of primal pain or pains not previously primaled will be triggered. I know I will never evolve to the point where primaling will be unnecessary.

My sleep is much different. I used to wake up suddenly with my heart pounding and not know why. In my earlier dreams that I could remember, I would be terror-stricken. The symbolism in some of those dreams was for birth trauma. In others, I was fleeing some danger, my legs so heavy that finally I dragged them behind me as I clawed my way on the ground. No longer am I assailed in my sleep to that great extent by ascending primal pain symbolized in some story line.

Formerly, I was so tense that when I wore a short-sleeved shirt, I could see the sleeve vibrating as it lay against my upper left arm. Also, I had a hot spot in the middle of my left shoulder blade that seemed never to go away. That tension has dissipated.

When I started therapy, The Primal Institute recorded my voice. After I had been in therapy for some time, I heard the tape again. I was struck by how dead my voice was. It was a monotone that came from back in my throat. My voice, now, is alive. It is multi-toned and comes from the front of my mouth. Prior to therapy, I was dead inside and my voice showed it. Now I am alive inside and my voice shows that too.

How I play chess has changed dramatically. I used to play defense almost exclusively. When I saw an opportunity to take the offensive, I got so nervous that quite often I made disastrous mistakes. Also, I was so afraid of making a mistake that I couldn't make up my mind what move to make. I studied the same moves over and over, taking so much time my opponents reacted negatively in one way or another. Now I play offensively, enjoy the battle, analyze the board much more quickly and rarely make an obviously bad move. Much of my childhood was built around never making a mistake, for doing so inevitably brought the wrath of my parents. After primaling hundreds of times on that feeling, I have been freed from the paralysis that attends the fear of punishment for making a mistake.

A similar difference has occurred in my tennis. Instead of being able to find ways to win close matches, I found ways to lose them. More often than not, that way was to double fault on crucial points. Whether it was painting a window sash, sawing a piece of wood, or learning how to drive our stick-shift car, my father made me so tense that I couldn't perform properly. That tenseness carried over into tennis and was part of that feeling of being afraid to make a mistake. Before I had to give up tennis because of my shoulder and wrist, I could still double fault on a crucial point, but I was more likely to play up to my abilities and find ways to win.

With regard to my macrophotography, it was not a case of before and after so much as it was a matter of how the photography changed as I changed as a consequence of primaling. I began experimenting with macrophotography of wildflowers only months before entering primal therapy, so there is no long pre-primal history with which to compare results. As a consequence of primaling incrementally reducing self-awareness and increasing consciousness, what latent creative talents and beauty of person that lay hidden beneath a defensive self-awareness rose to the surface and were expressed on film. Even if the enthusiastic response to my slide shows weren't there, I am constantly astounded by the extraordinary creativeness and beauty that seems to flow through me and out onto a screen where others can appreciate it too. It is as if the consciousness who is me is linked with a universal consciousness, and I have nothing to do except to be a conduit. In the thirty-five years I've been doing macrophotography, one of the constants has been being surprised by joy. Truly, it has been, and is, a labor of love.

When I am the least unconscious, the experience of being connected is very strong. From a grain of sand or a no-see-um to the most distant galaxy, I feel a warm, vibrant, loving, familial relationship. It is a feeling that pervades the totality of my experience, which means that it is all-encompassing. And, since there is nothing but life everywhere, no one is left out—not that grain of sand, not a mountain, not a creek, a river, a lake, or an ocean, not a plant and not a creature, whether it creeps, crawls, oozes, swims, glides, flies, or walks upon two legs, four legs, six legs, eight legs, or dozens of legs.

Another way of saying it is that in consciousness I experience events, which are selves-in-relationship. In self-awareness, one experiences subjects and objects. Instead of experiencing pure interrelationships, one experiences one's own separateness.

I do have a problem, though, with fully connecting with most human beings. Since only a thimbleful of people have had any kind of an experience—a primal, a conversion, an enlightenment, or otherwise—through which they know that self-awareness or ego or the personality is controlled by primal pain or sin or desire or what-have-you, all others have no idea that, basically, they are unconscious or asleep or a pre-programmed robot. Other than other primal persons, I have found my deepest connections with those who have had experiences that have opened their eyes to the "true" nature of what is commonly referred to as self-awareness AND to the reality of other worlds in which the "true" nature of self-awareness is given a parallel but mutually exclusive expression.

All together, then, this is where I'm coming from as I write the history of the devolution of consciousness into unconscious self-awareness.

CHAPTER 2

THE PRIMAL LIFE

Most Everything You Need to Know About Living a Primal Life But Didn't Know Enough to Ask

In this chapter, I explore in a comprehensive but not exhaustive way all about primals and living a primal life.

Definition of a Primal

A primal is the experience of living—for the first time—painful conditions and events that were too traumatic to endure during birth, infancy, childhood and adolescence and so were repressed.

Another way of describing a primal is that it is a controlled nervous breakdown or psychotic break. What happens in a nervous breakdown is that a sufficient amount of primal pain breaks through the defense system that is unconscious self-awareness to cause the person to fall apart and not be able to function. It is not so severe as to cause self-awareness to lose touch with its own sense of reality. A psychotic break is much more severe in that an amount of primal pain has broken through so as to cause self-awareness to become delusional in a desperate attempt to maintain its integrity. In a primal, only so much primal pain is allowed through the defenses as a person can handle. It is in that sense that a primal is a controlled breakdown, nervous or psychotic. But, words or definitions or descriptions can at best only point toward what a primal is because a primal is beyond any conception of which unconscious self-awareness can think.

Behind describing a primal as having a controlled breakdown is the certainty that a suppressed consciousness-in-pain exerts a constant upward pressure to break through self-awareness so that primal pain can be resolved. This is both a bane and a blessing. It is a bane in that for one who knows nothing of what is happening when primal pain is breaking through, life involves a lot of suffering. It is a blessing for a primal person in that he knows what is happening and grasps the opportunity to primal the ascending pain and, thus, resolve it out of his system and, in the process, become less unconscious and less self-aware. This blessing is the organism's built-in drive for health and wholeness.

As in rocket launches, so with primals, there is a window of opportunity that is available through which to be successful when conditions are right. If there is either too little or too much ascending primal pain, one cannot primal. As one gains more access to one's pain, the window of opportunity can become like a large picture window, making it easy to become successful in getting into a primal.

The suppressed consciousness-in-pain is wise in his determination to resolve his primal pain. Normally, primal pain laid down in adolescence, which has a lower valence than primal pain laid down earlier in life, is allowed to rise first toward breaking through self-awareness. Later, as the person is able to resolve primal pain that occurred at earlier ages and that is of a higher valence, consciousness permits that pain to ascend. In time, if necessary, primal pains of the highest valence—those involving birth—are allowed to surface. In the case of birth trauma, it might take hundreds of primals to resolve the experience.

In my own case, I fell into a fairly common exception to the normal sequence. Persons who are cut off from their emotions to a large extent are likely to go right down to primal pain laid down in infancy. My very first primal was a baby primal. I made it a point not to seek for this early pain but to concentrate first on my teen years and then on earlier years, so that the normal sequence of feeling primal pain would be followed.

The suppressed consciousness-in-pain is also wise in that when there has been a particularly traumatic event, whether or not it involves being born, only a portion of the feeling-filled memory is permitted to be recalled at a time. An excellent example of this happened with my former wife, Lisa. When she was a child, she had a pet duck who greeted her at the front gate each day when she came home from school. One day, the duck was not there to greet her. When she was called in to dinner, she went into shock when she sat down and discovered that her pet was the main course. She remembered little else than this when she first primaled this experience. After, perhaps, ten primals, she could remember seeing the murder scene with its scattered feathers and splattered blood.

As will be covered elsewhere, the brain has three levels. At birth, only the deepest level is functioning fully. That level controls all the survival specializations such as breathing, digestion and the heart. Since that level is the only one mature enough to function, primal pain experienced by the baby is handled there. This means that primal pain laid down on that level can only be resolved when connections between that level and the feeling and thinking levels have been reopened.

A primal on the deepest level is a primal without words. Obviously, this is so because a baby has no words with which to think. In the primal, there is just the raw feeling and wailing. If it is a birth primal, even wailing is not possible and only constricted, wriggling-like movements are evident.

There are definite signs when a primal is going to descend to this lowest level. For me, by far, the most frightening sign that can occur to indicate that a huge, bottom-level primal is about to erupt suddenly is the feeling that I'm going to lose my mind and never get it back. Of course, that doesn't happen. If I can handle it, what happens is that I experience consciousness. If I can't handle it, the primal is aborted. An example of a bottom-level primal erupting this way follows in the section on ways to get into a primal.

Other signs that a primal I'm in is going to drop down to an infant level are the following:

> My knees draw up into a fetal position.
>
> My hands will come together at my chin.
>
> A single, painful feeling will start to repeat itself verbally until my mind goes blank and the words stop, but the feeling goes on.
>
> I get a unique sensation in the back of my throat that happens just before the baby cries start.

These signs might not all appear, nor in the order stated, but usually this has been so.

Regardless of what level I've primaled, there is always a double awareness. Losing my mind in a primal is not the same as, say, an epileptic fit in which the afflicted person has no memory of what has happened. In a primal, I am conscious of the fact that I am an adult experiencing a primal, and I am conscious of being at some earlier age in some degree of pain in a particular circumstance. This is important for me because it lets me know that at any time I can come out of the primal.

Because of the very nature of unconscious self-awareness as a defense system holding back primal pain, self-awareness is likely to dismiss primaling as something it doesn't want to get into. One argument it gives is that it can see no reason why anyone would want to dredge up the past. The past is dead and gone. Live in the present. What self-awareness does not know is that the past is not dead and gone. The unmet needs of childhood and the pain that accompanies that deprivation control every thought, every emotion, every sensation and every act of self-awareness. Self-awareness is directed by a past that lives in every cell and cries out for resolution. Primaling resolves that painful past, thus enabling a conscious person to truly live freely in the present.

Another argument unconscious self-awareness uses to reject primaling is its assertion that primaling is nothing more than wallowing in one's suffering. I can state the refutation of that assertion: Rather than wallowing in suffering, primaling is the ending of suffering. But, one has to experience a primal to really know that this is so. There is a world of difference between suffering and experiencing primal pain. Suffering is the state of being of unconscious self-awareness. Before a primal starts, I suffer with some feeling of fear, anger, or hurt. Once I drop into the primal pain, I know I am in excruciating pain but, wonder of wonders, I'm no longer suffering. In feeling my primal pain, I feel a great release from it and, consequently, end suffering to the extent I've felt my primal pain.

A third reason unconscious self-awareness disapproves of primaling is that it sees it as nothing more than blaming one's parents for one's problems instead of taking responsibility for oneself. Self-awareness sees nothing more in primaling than playing the role of being a victim and, hence, never picking oneself up and getting on with life. What self-awareness cannot know is that all its attempts at being responsible for itself get it nowhere because it has no experience that its attempts are lacking the knowledge that they are controlled by primal pain. By primaling, I take full responsibility for my life. When I primal, I allow to surface and be expressed toward my parents all the painful feelings caused by their lack of proper nurturance and all the longings I had for them to really love me and care for me. Yes, my parents were to blame for how neurotically self-aware I became, but by primaling my repressed feelings toward them I am becoming a more healthy, less unconscious person.

A fourth reason why primaling might be rejected by unconscious self-awareness is the affront caused by our claim that unless primal pain is resolved no real healing is taking place. We know for ourselves, though, that everything else we ever did to mitigate our suffering was just tinkering with the defense system of self-awareness. This included every kind of psychological therapy, religion and all Ways of Life.

Should one decide to enter primal therapy at The Primal Foundation, it is important to note what the main objective of one's therapist is. It is to help the patient learn what to do so that he can primal on his own without assistance. In a sense, the role of the therapist is to make himself unnecessary. Naturally, the amount of time required will vary with each patient.

Nevertheless, even after one has left formal therapy, it can be rewarding to use the buddy system to help get into primal feelings. The basic role of the buddy is to be a quiet but sympathetic listener. Often, all it takes to get into a primal is being able to tell your story to a friend who will really listen to you. The reason for that is easy to comprehend: It is what you wanted from your mommy or daddy and didn't get.

Sometimes a buddy should take a more active role. Simply reflecting back what the primaler has related shows a sympathetic understanding that can open the gates to primal pain. Or, if appropriate, a kindly embrace might be enough to trigger primal pain. In general, a buddy should not direct things, but rather flow with the primaler. That course prevents the buddy from the possibility of unwittingly imposing his own suppressed, unmet needs on the primaler.

There is an admonition for anyone who might want to begin primaling: It is a lifetime commitment. Be certain that becoming a primal person is what you really want for yourself. Becoming a primal person means the systematic dismantling of unconscious self-awareness, which is nothing more than a defense system holding back your primal pain. If you start and then quit, you could leave yourself in worse shape than before, because now your primal pain has greater access to awareness and will cause greater suffering. At the beginning of a primal life, things are going to get worse before they get better, and one needs to recognize this and prepare oneself to persevere through the rough times when primal feelings might be spontaneously erupting, seemingly forever.

As for living a primal life, there is just one simple maxim and one corollary to it. The maxim: "Go for what you want in life, and when primal feelings come up, primal them." The corollary: "Don't dump your primal feelings on others, as they have no place to go with their feelings as you do with yours." The maxim and its corollary have served me well through the years. The more faithful I've been to them, the less unconscious I've become.

Living by the maxim does not mean one goes about perpetually suffering or that one pokes about everywhere, searching for one's primal pain. A primal person allows himself to feel and enjoy good feelings as long as they will last. The maxim does mean, however, that each and every experience can become grist for the primal mill.

A Word of Caution in Following the Maxim

When I've wanted to determine just what I've really wanted in life, I've gone to a place inside of me where I cannot lie to myself. There I've asked myself two inseparable questions: What do I really want to do? and How can I be really good to myself, good in the long, not the short run? Sooner or later, the answers will come. The question now arises: Will following through bring harm to myself or to anyone else? If the answer is in the negative, I will go forward with the answer. I mention this because some persons are so damaged with primal pain that they will hear voices that will tell them to do things that are harmful to oneself or to others. In which case, action should go no further than expressing the desire to do the harmful act. Expressing the desire is to be done in such a way as to bring up the primal feeling that most certainly lies behind that desire and to primal that feeling, thus defusing the desire to do something harmful.

Five Ways of Getting Into a Primal

My Pitch Pine Primal

The first way is that it might happen spontaneously. The following is one I experienced while attending one of Tom Brown's survival classes. It happened in the morning of our last day of the class.

Each of us was to go our own way and spend some time alone in whatever way he chose. I wandered off into the forest, but not too far, as it was easy to get lost since, in no matter which direction one looked, it looked the same.

The forest, for the most part, is one of pitch pines that are so close to one another that most of them are less than one foot in diameter and do not reach their full diameter of from one to two feet. The morning was windy. The trees, for almost their full length, were swaying in the wind. I was as melancholy as the sigh of the wind through the upper branches. An inner voice said to place my hand on one of the trunks to sense the swaying movement. The voice continued that I should place my cheek against the trunk to sense the rough bark. Without expectation, I complied. Before I knew what was happening, I was filled with a peace that is beyond ordinary understanding. No sooner was my total being flooded with this incredible feeling of harmony than the floodgates burst to an equally incredible feeling of pain. Undammed, a Niagara of tears fell in a torrent. I convulsed in wracking sobs against the tree, holding on now with both arms. Inside me, back and forth, I swung between feeling the harmony with my mommy and daddy with which I was born and with the complete and total denial of that harmony that was the painful, desperate reality of my childhood.

The connection was unmistakable. My desire to find harmony with the natural world was a symbolic gesture to fulfill what can never be fulfilled: my childhood need for loving and accepting parents. My interest in harmonious living with the natural world continues, but it does so, as far as I can tell, minus any unconscious drive to satisfy a primal need for mommy and daddy.

My M.A.S.H. Primal

The second way is being in a present, painful experience. It can happen reading a book, seeing a movie or play or TV program, or listening to music or watching athletes perform, or in any real-life situation. The common factor in all of these situations is that something happens that makes you cry.

It must be remembered here that contrary to what self-awareness tells us, there is no such thing as crying out of happiness or joy or peace. Keeping that in mind, this next primal illustrates this point. It happened while I was watching an episode of M.A.S.H.

A cardinal is coming to visit the 4077th. Father Mulcahy is upset. He wants all of his flock to be angels, but they're only men and women in a just-behind-the-lines mobile surgical unit. Two buddies are in the hospital. One has only a broken arm, but the other is in critical condition and needs blood. The first one says they have the same type and offers his. When it is tested, it appears he has leukemia.

When Hawkeye has to tell him about the likelihood of leukemia, I start to break up and primal. Father Mulcahy has already been shaken up by the early arrival of the cardinal. It's late Saturday night. Father Mulcahy has not had time to prepare his sermon for the service the next day. He spends the whole night with the leukemia-stricken soldier. He forgets about the service. Everyone is waiting for him. Someone goes to the hospital and gets him. He is in his bathrobe.

Father Mulcahy begins an extemporaneous sermon, contrasting his own selfish desires with the unselfish desires of the leukemia-stricken soldier, who wants to stay and help his buddy. I break up even harder as Father Mulcahy is overcome himself as he delivers his sermon.

I'd seen this episode before but had forgotten what happens next, so it took me by surprise and smashed right through what was left of my defenses. Father Mulcahy then introduces the cardinal, a large man physically, who comes up to the pulpit and embraces Father Mulcahy, who is much smaller than the cardinal. The camera zooms in on the embrace—chest-high on the cardinal, the priest's face against the cardinal's chest. The pain of seeing the love I never got crushes any final resistance. I erupt into strangled cries. I fall back lengthwise on the couch. My knees come up into a fetal position. I feel the baby cries in the back of my throat. They erupt, accompanied by convulsive sobs. All I can see is the priest's head against the cardinal's chest and I know that's what I needed but never got from my father.

My First Primal

The third way is deliberately recreating in the imagination a scene from the past. When this is done, it is best to lie on one's back, arms extended down along one's sides, palms up. The idea is to be in a vulnerable position. It helps if there can be dim lighting. It also helps if one can feel that one will not be disturbed or will not disturb others who don't know what is going on.

The first example is my very first primal on about the fourth day of therapy at The Primal Institute in Los Angeles.

I lay on my back, head on my pillow, legs stretched out and my arms by my side, hands palm-up. I told my therapist about how I had left the apartment at school and left Greg crying alone in his crib and about how bad I still felt about doing that. He said, "Can you feel what Greg must have been going through?" I answered: "If I can feel that, I'll primal." As I said that, I flashed back to that Sunday morning in November of 1968 when I experienced that desolate loneliness that turned my life around. I sank back into those feelings while seeing Greg in his crib. I imagined and described to my therapist in terms of those feelings that that is how Greg must have felt—frightened, desolate and terribly alone. In the space of seconds, without willing them to do so, my knees came up to my chest in a fetal position. My hands came together in front of my mouth. It opened. My tongue protruded. All images left my mind. My eyes closed. I felt a warm, soft pressure on my belly that melted everything beneath it. Then I was aware of something issuing from my throat but had no conscious control over it: the cries of a tiny baby.

The primal lasted less than a minute. I was amazed at what had happened. During it, I was always aware that I was in the present. I was also aware I was reliving a deep pain as a baby but, surprisingly enough, it didn't hurt.

A second example occurred several months into therapy during group therapy. This primal ended a dry period in which I was having a problem getting into primals. Among other things, it illustrates that even though nothing seems to be happening on the surface, as long as one keeps trying, something goes on in the subconscious. A process has begun and continues whether or not one is conscious of it.

My Primal Scream Primal

It happened after my therapist had spent some time with me and had moved on to be with another patient. I was getting into a scene with my mother when I was sixteen and had decided to go to the movies with my friend, Roger. When I informed my mother of my plans, her instantaneous response was, "NO." I asked her why. She said she didn't have to have a reason. I stormed out of the house. I went to Roger's house, but my mother had already called his mother. Roger's mother then told me that she couldn't let Roger go with me. Defeated, I scuffed my way to a park near my house where I commiserated with myself until dusk. I went back home and sat dejected on one of the concrete-topped brick sides to the front entrance of our house.

I continued to get into that incident about going to the movies. I imagine my mother walking down the gangway toward me from the back of the house. Everything about her—her twisted face, her stiffened walk, her rigid arms—tells me how angry she is. I feel my resignation deepen. She spits out her question: "Did you go to the movies?" I answer as I did then: "No." With her face still twisted in anger, she tells me her monstrous lie: "You know your father and I love you and want the best for you." In contrast to the original incident in which I just sat there silently, knowing she didn't love me, as I lay there at The Primal Institute I let my resignation fall away. I take a deep breath and allow my original, gut feelings at long last to find expression in words. "You're lying. You've never loved me. You never wanted me. I can never please you. Everything I do is wrong. I'd do anything for you if only you'd really love me. I just want you to hold me close to you and to tell me everything's going to be all right. I need you. Please stop lying and love me."

Her face does not change. She turns and flounces back up the gangway. As she nears the rear of the house, I continue to allow my original feelings to surface for the first time. Through my tears I cry out: "Don't leave me. Don't turn your back on me." I stretch out my arms to her, beseeching her to come back, but to no avail.

All of a sudden, my mind is blank. I see only a deep black darkness with millions of pinpoint lights. I start to panic. I feel I'm losing my mind. A presence within me notes I am losing my mind, notes my rising panic and says, "Go for it." In the next instant, the top of my head blows off. I start to scream no ordinary scream. "I" am not screaming; there is only screaming. My total being is a scream. No conscious effort is being made. Nothing is held back.

In a moment it is over. I know I have experienced a major breakthrough. I feel tremendous relief. The experience was another startling confirmation of the primal process.

My Aborted Primal

The fourth way is also a deliberate recreation of the past in the imagination, but it is of something one is going through in the present. It just wasn't possible—for one reason or another—to primal the feeling at the time. In the example, I don't fully primal. In fact, I bail out of the primal because my fear level was too high. It illustrates in addition, then, that we have an ability to abort a primal if it gets to be too much.

I was in love with Ida, but she rejected me and broke off our relationship. I was devastated. I primaled many times about her.

In this primal, I was checking off each aspect of my personality I had offered to Ida, all of which she turned down. As I felt her rejection of each trait, I experienced a vast emptiness in its place. I disappeared in chunks with each rejection. As I reached the end of the list of my personality traits and sensed the end of me was coming near, I panicked at the prospect of being no more. I couldn't stay with what was happening, aborted the primal and came out of it.

My Birth Primal Dream

The fifth way is in a dream. It is to be remembered that in a dream it is primal feelings that give rise to both the story line of the dream as well as to the emotion in the dream. This is contrary to what seems to be the case, that the story line gives rise to the emotions experienced in the dream. What is significant about this primal-in-a-dream is that behind the story line I was in a birth primal.

I was dreaming I was inside some gigantic hollow cube in space. The cube was made up of smaller cubes, also hollow. I felt my brain whirling around. I was reeling. I spoke to Greg, and he said it was nothing. I looked up, and very high up on top of the whole cube a man was spread-eagled. I was overwhelmed. Then I was outside of the whole cube, and it was whirling and reeling in space. I felt I was going to primal.

The scene changed to a basement where the box was that I primal in, but the front was missing. It was dark. I felt myself entangled with some straps that I had trouble getting off. At the same time, there was something else that was weighing me down. I got free and went to leave the basement. At the door, I turned back and saw short lines of light scattered around the darkness. I went upstairs to a crowded kitchen. My wife and children were among those present. They were all busy. I told my wife she'd done something she shouldn't have: moved the box to the basement without telling me. I felt as if I were going to primal. I wanted to scream, but I couldn't even make a sound. I tried and some small sounds came out. I felt as if I were dangling in midair. I woke up feeling I had been able to do partially what I want to do fully: primal in my dreams.

Primal Connections

Like most everything in being a primal person, a primal connection has to be experienced to be understood. Possibly the best way to convey what they are all about is to express some of the exclamations that often accompany them. "Aha, now I know with every cell of my being why I am the way I am!" "Aha, now I understand why I act the way I do!" "Aha, now I know what it is I've been holding back against all these years!"

Although a primal connection bears a resemblance to an insight, it is only a superficial one. An insight is only an intellectual break-through; it does not also include the full, emotionally painful content of the remembered childhood situation. An insight leaves intact the primal pain that was suppressed initially. An insight, therefore, is actually an intellectual defense against primal pain because it further insulates the person from his primal pain. In contrast to a connection, which arises out of the whole brain, an insight arises out of the thinking brain alone and thus has no power to heal, but only to defend and to suppress intellectually.

Connections can be quite specific in nature. For example, I know from many primals that the reason I've gotten tense when I've been playing tennis and double faulted away a match is that my father was so hypercritical that he made me so tense and nervous that I couldn't perform in a relaxed manner. Connections can also be so general as to cover everything. For example, after one primal I had the experience that my whole personality—my entire self-awareness—was nothing but a defense system holding back all of my primal pain.

Connections are what happens when neural pathways are reopened among the sensing, emotional/sexual and thinking levels of the brain. As such, there is little to distinguish sometimes between a primal and a connection. Connections, though, might continue for some time after a primal, so it is convenient to distinguish one from the other.

The essence of primaling is the reestablishment of connections, which is another way of saying that the essence of primaling is the replacement of the categories of self-awareness with the categories of consciousness. In consciousness, there are neither the self-aware categories of "inner" or "outer" worlds nor the categories of physical, emotional, or mental. In consciousness, there is just experience, which is the sole component of reality. For purposes of discussion to understand connections, however, it is helpful to use the categories of self-awareness to grasp what happens when connections are made in a primal.

The inner aspect of a connection has three dimensions: the physical, the emotional and the mental. The physical component is the reconnection of the three levels of the brain. The emotional component is the reconnection between present emotions of anger, fear and pain with their original sources in childhood. The mental component is the reconnection between presently held ideas about religion, philosophy, politics, loved ones, or co-workers, for example, with specific primal pains for which these ideas are specific defenses.

The outer aspect of connections has three dimensions as well. The physical component is the replacement of a tri-level cosmos, which reflects a tri-level, truncated brain, with a cosmos of one level of reality. The emotional component of suffering with anger, fear and pain is replaced by an even-tempered joy in living. The mental component of a pain-suppressing intellect is replaced by an outlook on life that is not pain-driven but is spontaneous and experiences life as an integrated whole.

Emotional Signs of the Presence of Primal Pain

Experiencing an emotion, except under some circumstances, is a near-certain sign that primal pain is what is being felt. While it is possible to feel an emotion that is not related to primal pain, it is best to assume that all emotions are primal in origin. Doing so keeps one open for the possibility of having a primal.

The big three of emotions are anger, fear and pain. Anger's range is from mere annoyance to uncontrollable rage. Fear runs the gamut from mild anxiety to absolute terror. Pain's continuum is from a single tear to gut-wrenching sobs to a primal scream.

A special note needs to be made about anger. Anger, 100 percent of the time, is a cover-up for pain. Often the pain is suppressed so fast that one is only aware of being angry. It is much easier to go on the offensive and be angry rather than be vulnerable and feel pain. When I am angry with someone, I ask myself how that person has hurt me.

A note also about fear—fear arising from imminent danger might not be related to primal pain at all. On the other hand, if primal fears are there, they will accentuate present fear and cause an overreaction.

Pain, too, requires a special note. All pain is a sign that something is wrong, but what is wrong might not be primal in origin. Being burned or cut or injured in an accident are obvious examples.

One final note is in order. Emotions experienced in a dream are primal in origin. Emotions give rise to the story line of the dream and not the other way around.

Clues That Primal Pains Are Controlling the Present

Since there are an infinite number of facets in the personality of unconscious self-awareness, clues to the hidden presence of primal pain are equally as varied. Everyone is unique. The following list is therefore but a sampling of clues—or symptoms—of the presence of primal pain.

But first, I want to make note here that there are two other main schools of thought regarding how these clues are to be interpreted. These schools are opposed to each other and united in their opposition to a primal perspective.

The primal perspective is that since it is an all-encompassing experience of pain too traumatic to integrate that causes these clues or symptoms to appear, it is a faulty diagnosis that assesses either a mental/emotional cause to them or a physical one. The primal treatment is to look upon the clues as symptoms of underlying, suppressed, painful experiences and allow the clues to be pathways to primaling those experiences.

In contrast, the mental/emotional school treats the clues as being psychosomatic, that is, all the clues have a mental/emotional cause. As such, all the varied therapies that come from this school will boil down to insights. However, since insights leave intact primal pain, the therapies can only alleviate symptoms; they do not cure. If the treated person later finds himself in a situation of sufficient stress, his old symptoms will recur or new ones will form.

The other school treats the clues as being entirely of physical origin. In this school, mind and emotions are but an outgrowth of particular combinations of chemical secretions and electrical impulses. The therapy of choice, therefore, is the intake of more chemicals to redress the chemical imbalance that causes the clues or symptoms to appear. Again, it is symptoms that are dealt with, not real causes. If the chemical additives are stopped, the symptoms return.

All religions and all philosophies of life also leave primal pain untouched. They, too, relieve only symptoms. They do alleviate suffering through some form of analgesic, which is good, because if one doesn't know the primal way, it is better not to go through life suffering with one kind of symptom or other. The beauty of primaling is that it actually removes the cause of the symptoms with which we suffer and, thus, is truly curative. It restores consciousness or, to be more accurate, primaling makes one ever less unconscious.

A Sampling of Clues or Symptoms of Primal Pain

Feeling sad: a state of suffering that will result in depression if it does not give way to crying.

Being overweight: probably results from the defense of swallowing one's pain to keep it down.

Being resigned: a state of suffering in which one has given up hope of ever being loved.

Hoping: a state of suffering in which one struggles to be loved.

Struggling: a state of suffering in which one keeps trying to be loved or trying to make a love relationship or employee/boss relationship work, for example.

Feeling helpless: a state of suffering in which one knows one can do nothing to get the love one needs.

Having ulcers: probably results from not being able to stomach one's pain any longer.

Being constipated: probably results from continually being uptight about how to be or what to do to please in order to be loved.

Having a stiff neck: probably results from being stiff-necked about some situation in which one feels wronged or self-justified or self-righteous.

Being self-righteous: a defense under which precisely lies a specific primal pain.

Feeling frustrated: a state of suffering in which one feels that one could never do enough or be good enough to be loved.

Having headaches: probably results from trying in vain to intellectually figure out an emotion rather than feeling it.

Stuttering: probably results from having mixed emotions.

Having tics: probably results from the muscular release of an excessive amount of emotional tension.

Feeling lonely: a state of suffering in which one feels rejected by everyone.

Feeling suicidal: a state of suffering in which one feels so lonely and rejected that death would be a welcome release.

Intellectualizing: a defense that analyzes emotions and effectively suppresses primal pain.

Speaking in a monotone: being in so much pain from being squelched constantly one has lost any vibrancy at all.

Having insomnia or any other sleep disorder: probably results from primal pain arising with sufficient force to interfere with sleep.

Needing always to be right and wanting never to make a mistake: a state of suffering in which one was always being criticized no matter what one did or how well one performed.

Overreacting: a state of suffering in which the primal pain underlying a specific kind of situation magnifies one's emotions out of proportion.

Underreacting: a state of suffering in which the primal pain underlying a specific kind of situation is so great as to shut down one's emotions completely.

Drinking alcoholic beverages: Regardless of what kind of drinker one is, the effect of alcohol is that of a painkiller.

Smoking: Like alcohol, it is a painkiller.

Coffee: Likewise, it is a painkiller by making one hyper.

Taking "uppers": They make one hyper, releasing primal pain from which one must run.
Taking "downers": They make one lethargic, blocking the surge of primal pain so that one can slow down.
The choice of one's vocation: Behind that choice often is the perpetuation of childhood struggles.
Being in love romantically: Behind that choiceless choice is the continuation of one's struggle for love, for romantic love is not love at all but infantile need masked as love.
"Excessive" masturbation: a state of suffering in which one substitutes sensual gratification for mommy or daddy love.
Flashing: a state of suffering in which one is asking, "Please pay attention to me, Mommy."
Don Juanism: a state of suffering in which one searches in vain for the mother love he never got.
Nymphomania: a state of suffering in which one searches in vain for the daddy love she never got.
Cyclic, self-destructive patterns of behavior: a state of suffering in which the original prototypical struggles for love continue to be run off in symbolic form.
Diagnoses of schizophrenia, manic-depression, or paranoia: All these are merely descriptions of specific effects of great primal pain.
An ongoing need for any or all of antacids, laxatives, painkillers, or sleeping pills: All of these are drugs to relieve the symptoms of specific effects of primal pain.

Can anyone say he is free of any of the signs or clues or symptoms of primal pain? How does anyone know if primaling is right for him? For me, it was trying anything and everything to right what I knew was wrong with my life: I did not know how, either to give or to receive love. When I read Janov's *The Primal Scream,* I knew this man knew the truth about me. I went through formal primal therapy. It was exactly what I needed to begin the process of stopping suffering, of being able to love and be loved. So, inform yourself. You will, if you're sufficiently motivated. You'll go for it, if and when you have some experience that lets you know what unconscious self-awareness is all about.

I end this chapter with a word of caution. Your self-awareness is there for a purpose and that is to shield you from your primal pain. Do not attempt to remove your shield without full exploration of how you should go about doing so.

I'm also ending this chapter with a word of encouragement. Your unconscious self-awareness serves as the only guide you'll need to get back to your primal pain. Your thoughts and your emotions are your vehicles. What you need to get started safely is proper instruction—perhaps formal primal therapy—by someone who knows the way because he's been there many times over.

PART II

THE PRIMAL BASIS
FOR VARIOUS ATTRIBUTES
OF UNCONSCIOUS SELF-AWARENESS

CHAPTER 3

THE BASIC SPLIT: THE SUPPRESSION OF CONSCIOUSNESS BY UNCONSCIOUS SELF-AWARENESS

"[The] separation of oneself from one's needs and feelings
is an instinctive maneuver in order to shut off excessive pain.
We call it the *split*" (emphasis added)
—Arthur Janov in *The Primal Scream*

Since I maintain that the whole history of humankind has been one of the devolution of consciousness into unconscious self-awareness, I feel it necessary to go on at some length to describe how this devolution takes place in a child. Any number of researchers has studied this phenomenon, but none has put forth an adequate explanation of why or how it happens. The literature on this subject usually refers to the event as the basic split and mistakenly calls the result self-consciousness.

Some self-aware researchers have referred to a child's psyche as "cosmic anonymity." This point of view implies that the absence of self-awareness means oblivion or something like the state of nirvana. Others have used the words "infant-world-unity" to describe a child's psyche. This concept, too, implies an absence of any awareness of a self. My experience is that a pre-self-aware child's psyche is that of a self-in-relationship. Consciousness is selves-in-relationship, selves knowing themselves solely in terms of relationships.

For you to grasp what the basic split is all about, you must first be willing to assume that the self you bring to this study has two purposes. The first is that of preventing you from experiencing that the reason for the basic split is to protect you from experiencing the catastrophic primal pain of your childhood. The second—as contradictory as it might seem—is that of guiding you toward healing that split, of restoring consciousness.

The split probably begins with conception. Since modern humans certainly are unconscious, that is, we have a self-awareness that totally suppresses consciousness, the newly fertilized egg is already somewhat unconscious. The sperm and egg that united were initially damaged by the primal pain of both parents, and their parents before them, going back countless generations. The mother's diet, her level of stress, her ingestion of legal as well as illegal drugs and whether or not she really wants to make a home for her child all have a direct bearing on the status of the consciousness of the fetus.

Since the mother is unconscious, whether or not she's been drugged, the birth of her baby will not be completely natural. Whether she knows it or not, she might be holding back, causing her baby to be terrified and to have to fight for his life if he is to be born. Later, when the child's self is developing, the initial fight for survival might be triggered every time the self feels itself to be in a "tight spot."

In addition, since the mother is unconscious, she might have such fear about giving birth that she tightens rather than relaxes her cervix, thereby requiring drugs to kill the resulting pain. The painkillers might make the baby so drugged that later his developing self will always feel out of it when stress arises.

Because the delivery room staff, including the doctor, are also unconscious, the conditions the baby encounters on being born can also contribute to his terror and to his being traumatized. Air-conditioning, being held upside down and spanked, being removed from his mother, being given painful eye drops and a few days later being circumcised all make for trauma that can permanently skew the self, insuring an unbalanced personality, i.e., an unconscious self-awareness.

After birth, if the needs of the newborn baby and the growing child are not met, the basic split continues to widen, that is, the child's consciousness constantly devolves into unconscious self-awareness. Since, at birth, the only part of the brain that has matured is the part that governs sensations and the survival organs, a baby's first needs are to be held and to be caressed, to be fed, to feel safe and to be comfortable. When the emotional brain begins to mature at about six months, the baby's secondary needs are emotional. He needs to feel loved and to have the freedom to express his own feelings without the fear of having them squelched. Later, as the thinking part of the brain matures, his needs include an atmosphere conducive to learning and to being understood. Along the way, he needs to be allowed to be his own person and to develop at his own pace. He needs an environment that is stable, calm and predictable.

Since babies and young children are helpless and vulnerable, if their needs are not met, the pain is so great they must defend themselves from feeling the pain by becoming unconscious of it. This pain has come to be known as primal pain. The younger the infant or child, the more life-threatening is his primal pain. The child, therefore, automatically becomes unconsciously self-aware in the interests of survival.

The child survives by suppressing primal pain through a combination of defenses that are appropriate in each Stage of his maturation. If the child's needs continue to go unmet, he must choose to become more and more defended and unconscious of himself. Finally, if the situation does not change, there will come a time when he has to choose to become totally defended and totally unconscious, his pain being too great to carry on otherwise.

Defenses have a life of their own. When the entire defense system has reached a certain, critical level of development, the child has his first experience of being self-aware. It is the first experience of the self as being separate from the body and from the world. There is now a self in here and a world out there. The age at which this occurs varies with the amount of primal pain that must be suppressed and defended against. The greater the pain, the earlier it happens. Initially, the experience of being self-aware is intermittent, but sooner or later it becomes a constant of psychic experience. Even so, after self-awareness becomes a constant, it remains in the background of consciousness and only comes to the fore when primal pain necessitates a higher level of defense. Finally, the level of primal pain increases to the extent that self-awareness not only is a constant of psychic experience but takes over completely from consciousness.

The defenses a child needs to become unconscious of his primal pain are organized into a comprehensive system. Usually, this system has become completed by the age of six. A person's defense system is more commonly known as his personality or ego or the "I" of everyday experience or the self, rather than for what it is. This is so because the self is unconscious of itself as being a defense system suppressing a consciousness-in-pain because of needs going unmet. Further, it is one of the functions of the defense system to deny that a suppressed consciousness-in-pain even exists.

The complete suppression of the pain of unmet needs by the defense system constitutes the change from consciousness into unconscious self-awareness. This is the content of what is meant by the basic split. Once it has crystallized, the self feels its state of being to be the natural one and the only one possible.

After the split, the self does have awareness, but it is unconscious of its own nature and of its function as a defense system. It is but a puppet on a string, dancing to whatever discordant tune is played in the subconscious by his unmet, infantile needs, forever screaming for satisfaction.

Some persons are so well-defended they have no inkling of the split and for whom what is written here is nonsense. For others not so well-defended, there is a sense that something is wrong with their lives. It is those persons who will find in these pages something that speaks to them about what is wrong and what to do about it.

CHAPTER 4

THE LOCATION AND UPWARD MOVEMENT OF UNCONSCIOUS SELF-AWARENESS IN THE BODY

Ideally, at the beginning of each human life, the whole organism is fully conscious, as is each cell. If that is the case, the whole organism is the seat of consciousness. Such consciousness is diffused equally throughout the entire organism. Whether or not pure consciousness was ever a condition of the earliest true human beings probably never can be known. What is known is that the most ancient oral traditions and the oldest artifacts reveal that human beings were already self-aware. This means that primal pain had very early beginnings in human life, but its origins are lost in antiquity. These traditions also reveal that self-awareness had a specific location within the body.

One such oral tradition has to do with shamanism. In it, the skeleton is experienced as the location of self-awareness. In another, the lungs and breath are the seat of self-awareness. The use of red ocher on the body, dead or alive, or on artifacts suggests blood as being the source of self-awareness. It is natural that bone, breath and blood are the first locations of self-awareness in the body because, while they are not the whole organism as is the case for consciousness, they are spread out in the body. Subsequent seats of self-awareness will be much more localized.

As for establishing the internal basis for bone, breath and blood being seats of self-awareness, at this point I have not been able to make the connection for bone. The connection can be made, however, for breath and blood. At birth, just the sensing/survival brain, which mediates all the visceral, survival functions, is mature enough to process primal pain. Since regulating breathing and blood flow are two of its functions, it is clear why self-awareness would first make itself known there.

In what I judge to be later oral traditions, the seat of self-awareness is now low down in the viscera. Primal pain has increased to the extent of causing self-awareness to become more localized. The attributes of consciousness are still very much in evidence despite that self-awareness overlays consciousness to a greater extent. It is still the case that children are born highly conscious and, in spite of becoming self-aware, retain much of the attributes of consciousness throughout their adult lives.

From my experience in primaling away my primal pain and from my historical research, I make the generalization that the less primal pain there is, the more consciousness is diffused throughout the body. Also, in general, the more primal pain there is, the more self-awareness there is and the higher and more localized in the body it is.

As the child's needs continue to be unfulfilled, compounding the amount of primal pain that cannot be integrated, the sensation of where one's self is located in the body rises along the midline of the viscera. As it does so, the self becomes progressively more unconscious of what is going on below it. The balance between consciousness and an unconscious self-awareness is constantly shifting toward unconscious self-awareness.

In time, if needs continue to go unmet, the sense of the location of self-awareness will rise to the head. Since there is considerable difference in the amount of primal pain in families, there is wide variation when a child has his first experience of a self-awareness located there. This does not mean that from that point on that self-awareness is permanently locked into the head. Usually, there is a Stage in which there are periods of consciousness and then of self-awareness, but the periods of consciousness become ever fewer and shorter. In our society, by the age of six, a self-awareness located in the head has become a permanent sensation.

Because unconscious self-awareness is synonymous with defense system, it is also the case that by age six a child's defense system is permanently in place. Defense system also means the same thing as personality in this context, so it is also true that a child's personality is usually set by this time as well.

When someone in our society thinks back to when he had his first experience of self-awareness, he is mindful only incidentally that the sensation of self-awareness is located in his head. He assumes that this is where it always has been. There is good reason for this assumption. All previous experiences of self-awareness at lower levels have been suppressed due to rising levels of primal pain. The self, therefore, is unconscious of its own development.

From age six on, then, the person is just about totally unconscious. no longer present is the experience of the whole organism being conscious. Because of primal pain due to basic needs being unfulfilled, there has been a devolution from consciousness into unconscious self-awareness. The self—now located in the head—feels itself to be conscious, but it is an illusion. It is but a defense system covering up the pain of unmet infantile needs and is driven by that need to everlastingly seek its fulfillment symbolically in desires—symbolically because the person is now unconscious of why he thinks, acts and feels the way he does. And because those primal-pain-driven desires are insatiable, an unconscious self-awareness is condemned to a life of suffering, whether it knows this or not.

While it is true that a few fortunate persons have little primal pain and, therefore, suffer little, the well-defended person who apparently is not suffering might very well have a body that is being secretly ravished by the stress of primal pain.

It took thousands of generations for the sense of where self-awareness was located in the body to rise from low down in the gut up to the head. Also, in each successive generation, every child encapsulated the entire history of all of his ancestors. For example, in ancient Egypt during the period that mummification was practiced, self-awareness was felt in the heart. (It was the heart that was weighed in the balance, not the brain, to determine the ultimate fate of the deceased. The brain was discarded because they thought it was a useless part of the body.) At that time, each child had a self-awareness that was first located in the gut. In discrete stages, the sense of where self-awareness was located rose to the heart. There was no conscious memory of any of the previous, lower locations of self-awareness. When self-awareness had risen to the heart, it was assumed that that was where it had always been located.

Today, however, particularly in Western civilization, the load of primal pain is so great that children are born much less conscious, lose consciousness rapidly and surely by the age of six are unconscious with self-awareness located in the head. Ask anyone today where self-awareness is located and he will point to his head. Suggest that it might be located in his liver—some ancient peoples knew it to be located there—and the response will be: "You've got to be kidding. That's just a myth."

Generally speaking, there is a correspondence between a rise in the body of the location of self-awareness and a greater degree to which self-awareness is cut off from the body. The same correspondence takes place with the deities. Each rise in their location in the cosmos signifies the loss of a connection with the cosmos. When self-awareness has risen to the head and cut itself off from the body, the Supreme Deity has no connection to the cosmos; he is completely separate from it.

If it weren't for the traditions that reflected the sense of the location of self-awareness to be in bone, breath, or blood, or in the liver (as in Mesopotamia) or in the heart (as in Egypt), it is likely we would never know that self-awareness had locations other than the head. Not likely, that is, except for the discovery through primaling that beneath self-awareness is a consciousness-in-pain that is diffused throughout the organism.

CHAPTER 5

THE EXPERIENCE OF TIME AS CYCLICAL AND LINEAR AND OF SPACE AS INNER AND OUTER WORLDS

At the outset of this discussion on time and space, you must remember that there's no evidence to indicate that humans were ever in a state of pure consciousness. However, if there ever were pure consciousness, one aspect of it would be the presentness of who is. I say the "presentness of who is" rather than the "presentness of what is" because what I'm trying to convey is that in consciousness there is no such thing as a thing. In consciousness, every so-called thing is in reality a living being. To a pre-self-aware child, a stuffed teddy bear is, in reality, a close and personal friend. To Native Americans, the planet is the living manifestation of our Earth Mother. The sum total of every so-called thing—the cosmos—is a living being—consciousness.

Again I say the presentness of who is is a characteristic of pure consciousness because in consciousness there is no time; there is only the present moment. The presentness of who is, is easily observable in young children, in that they have little or no conception of how long an hour is, for example. Also, it seems to them that the days of childhood are repeatable forever. This discussion begins, then, with the assumption that children start out conscious but with some level of primal pain, and therefore have little or no conception of time.

At such time as the level of primal pain reaches a critical point in consciousness, unconscious self-awareness results. One modification that begins to take place in the ongoing devolution of consciousness into unconscious self-awareness is the change from the experience of the presentness of who is into the experience of time and space. The experience of time has two aspects: cyclical and linear.

The primary primal basis for self-awareness's experience of time in the external world as linear—meaning irreversible—is as follows. Self-awareness comes about because the child's needs are not being met and he is in too much pain to remain conscious. The child becomes what he has to become to preserve life itself. He becomes self-aware. This choice is irreversible for a child. It is irreversible because once the choice is made he becomes unconscious of the fact that he made the choice to become self-aware. It is irreversible because now so much primal pain has been laid down that the child cannot remain conscious and survive.

It is the child's not being able to go back to a conscious state—that what he has done is irreversible—that is the primary basis for experiencing external time as linear, that is, irreversible.

The primal basis for self-awareness's experience of time in the external world as cyclical is as follows. The child struggles to have his needs met symbolically, fails and then starts the struggle all over again. It isn't the struggle-fail-struggle cycle itself that provides the basis for cyclical time but that, in addition, the cycle returns to the initial starting point between child and parents. That starting point is at the onset of self-awareness when it was able to suppress what pain was there, producing a condition of starting afresh all over again. In the beginning, that cyclic return to the onset of self-awareness was unceasing. It is this never-ending internal cycle that is mirrored in the external world of self-awareness as cyclical time, unceasingly returning to the Golden Age. The Golden Age refers to the ideal persons and conditions that existed when the ordered cosmos was created from the watery deep or from whatever was the undifferentiated, initial matter of the pre-ordered cosmos. So, with the onset of self-awareness, there is the basis for linear time—due to the irreversibility of becoming self-aware—and of the experience of time as being cyclical—due to the endless struggle to satisfy suppressed, unmet, infantile needs symbolically, ever returning to the initial starting point.

At the onset of self-awareness, the experience of time is totally cyclical. While the basis for linear time is there, the experience of it comes later. As long as a child is able to forgive and to forget and to return to how things were at the onset of self-awareness, his experience of time will remain solely cyclical. But, once the amount of primal pain has jumped to a level where the child can no longer forgive and forget, he does not return to the initial starting point. Self-awareness has irreversibly jumped to a new level of unconsciousness that becomes the new starting point. Now cyclic time cannot return to the original starting point. It can only return to the new starting point.

Now there is the experience of time that has elapsed from the original starting point—to which it can never return—to the new starting point. That experience is the first one of irreversible linear time with its past, present and future. It is the change from unconscious self-awareness being primarily in the right lobe, emotional/sexual brain to the left lobe/thinking brain—due to a discrete increase in primal pain—that is ultimately responsible for the change from cyclical to linear time. A basic trait of the left lobe/thinking brain is that it reasons in a linear mode.

Now cyclical time takes place within the context of linear time. Initially, cyclical time transpired with the same events endlessly repeating themselves in a circle. Now events in cyclical time take place as if they were in a whirlpool, descending and circling around a linear center line that has a nonrepeatable beginning and will have a nonrepeatable ending.

In the fatalism of external cyclical time, there is both pessimism and optimism. In spite of life always getting worse, in spite of order constantly disintegrating into chaos, at least annually there will be a time of renewal. This is based on the internal, cyclical, primal experience of a child. Life always gets worse, primal pain always piles up, but full reconciliation with one's parents will again take place sometime.

By the time of the Indo-Europeans, the experience of linear time came to include successive Ages. In Hindu/Buddhist thought, a Yuga is an Age. The first Yuga is 4,000 years long, preceded and followed by interim periods of 400 years. The second Yuga is 3,000 years, preceded and followed by interim periods of 300 years. The third Yuga is 2,000 years, preceded and followed by interim periods of 200 years. The fourth Yuga is 1,000 years, preceded and followed by transition periods of 100 years. The total of 12,000 years makes up a Mahayuga, which is a complete cycle. At the end of the cycle, there is a Pralaya, which is the destruction of the cosmos. At the end of 1,000 cycles, there is a "great" destruction. And at the end of 2,560,000 Mahayugas, there is a final destruction. Thus, while time seems to be endlessly cyclical, nevertheless there is linear time consisting of some 30,720,000,000 years.

From one Yuga to the next, there is a progressive decline in life expectancy, in intelligence and indeed in all aspects of life. Each successive Age is more depraved than the last. With regard to the Buddhas, the first one lived 80,000 years, while Gautama Buddha, the seventh, lived only a hundred years.

Cyclical time was first measured by the monthly cycle of the moon and the yearly cycle of the sun. By the time of the Indo-Europeans, including the Hindu/Buddhists, cyclical time was measured in cycles inconceivably long. Linear time was measured along a line that was also incomprehensibly long: the time from one discontinuous Age to another. It is apparent that by the time of the Hindu/Buddhists that even in cyclical time periodic renewal was no longer possible.

Various peoples besides the Indo-Europeans have posited discontinuous Ages, the North American Hopi among them. This reflects a universal experience that the present condition of humanity was reached in discontinuous stages and not in an unbroken continuum of deterioration. The basis for this worldwide phenomenon is to be found in the experience of self-awareness. It develops in discontinuous stages. Primal pain has to build up to certain critical levels before the next layer of defense has to be laid down to suppress it, at which time in religious terms humanity is seen as having descended to a new low in depravity.

This whole concept of time—in which the rate at which the human condition declines accelerates from cycle to cycle—represents an accurate picture of what actually was happening. It was a religious expression of what I see from a primal perspective. The rate at which primal pain increases accelerates from generation to generation.

My experience as a primal person is that the process of restoring consciousness also occurs in discontinuous stages. Between primals it seems as if nothing is happening, especially if there is an extended "dry" period. But once the next primal happens, it becomes clear that subconsciously things had been building up and then releasing, recreating a new level of less unconsciousness, discrete from the old level.

When the child can no longer forgive and forget and realizes in his new self-aware status that, at least to some extent, his parents are not going to fulfill his needs, he jumps into linear time. In particular, it might be that the child realizes that he can't go back anymore to trusting his parents to be truthful. He senses that they could lie again to him in the future. Or, he knows that to avoid being battered in the future, he must become completely submissive now. What is being experienced here is the past, present and future of linear time.

The impossibility of returning to a Golden Age is the indication in the external world when the internal cycle of being able to return to the original condition of self-awareness is no longer possible. It is a sign that self-awareness has irreversibly jumped to a new level of unconsciousness. It is a sign that linear time had now become a part of the people's experience.

It took from a past too distant to contemplate, down through countless millennia to the 1st millennium BCE, for the dominant experience of time to change from cyclical to linear. Through the ages, primal pain and suffering increased in discrete stages. Over tens of thousands of years, due to these increases in pain and suffering, the stages of the change from cyclical to linear time were marked by a combination of discrete, simultaneous changes in self-awareness. First, incrementally, self-awareness had to sever its ties to the body with its cyclical rhythms because the body is where pain and suffering are experienced. And, second, incrementally, self-awareness was reaching new, less conscious and more chaotic cyclical starting points.

In the external world, this is evidenced by the decline in the importance of the stately, cyclical rhythms of the cosmos and the increase in the importance of measuring linear time with a clock. It is also evidenced by discrete jumps in the disintegration of the entire cosmos—humans included—back into the primordial chaos.

In the Middle East, by the 1st millennium BCE, a civilization's basic experience of time was linear rather than cyclical. Now, annual rites can only be reminders of, and commemorative of, an initial act of creation of an ordered cosmos. The initial act of the formation of the cosmos cannot be recreated. At this Stage for self-awareness, humanity had been created in an initial state of perfection, but it and all of creation from the very beginning have been in a steady decline toward chaos. Hope now lies in a regeneration that will take place at the end of linear time when chaos will be replaced with order. Of course, there were many people there whose experience of time was still cyclical, as was the case in all the noncivilized parts of the earth. It is just that it takes only a certain, critical number of people to change in order to alter the character of any society.

The rate at which the experience of time changed from cyclical to linear for our Middle East ancestors was determined by the rate of change they experienced from consciousness to unconscious self-awareness. The rate of change from consciousness to self-awareness and from cyclical to linear time is determined, first of all, by the phenomenon that each succeeding generation bears a heavier load of primal pain. This is evident because each new generation over the millennia has been less able to nurture its young. This whole treatise is a marshalling of the evidence to support that claim. What has happened from generation to generation as a consequence of a heavier burden of primal pain—and is continuing to happen—is that self-awareness is occurring earlier and earlier in children. In exceedingly ancient times, self-awareness probably occurred in late adolescence. The ratio of the aspects of consciousness over those of self-awareness was high. Now, in modern children, self-awareness can occur perhaps as early as age two and certainly by six years of age. In other words, the rate of change from consciousness to self-awareness has constantly accelerated from generation to generation. The first factor that determined the rate of change from the basic experience of time as cyclical to that of being linear is that of heavier total loads of primal pain.

The other factor that determined how fast consciousness changed into unconscious self-awareness and time changed from cyclical to linear was the incremental increase in the valence of specific primal pains, particularly those occurring at birth, which had never before been experienced. By valence is meant the degree of life or death threat in a given situation to a child. The greater the threat, the higher the valence.

As primal pain increased from generation to generation, making each less able to provide loving nurture, severe threats to life occurred ever earlier, eventually going back to birth itself. Primal pains laid down during this time to a completely vulnerable and helpless baby can be of extremely high valence. When primal pain levels were low, mothers gave birth naturally and easily. Any primal pains endured by the baby were low in valence, and continued to be low throughout childhood. When primal pain levels got much higher, mothers began to have difficulty giving birth. Primal pains suffered by the baby got to be catastrophic, and the valence remained high during childhood.

So, throughout human history the valence of primal pains increased, adding significantly to the total increase in the load borne by each generation. It is the combination of the ever-increasing valence of primal pains and the total load of primal pain that determines how fast self-awareness occurred and how fast time changed from cyclical to linear.

Just as the endless attempt by unconscious self-awareness to symbolically fulfill unmet, infantile need is the basis for cyclical time, and the formation of self-awareness itself is the basis for linear time, so the rate at which the change occurs from consciousness into self-awareness is the basis for the sense of how fast time passes in the cosmos. Millennia ago, when cyclical time was dominant, the moment-by-moment sense of change was almost imperceptible. The relative imperceptibleness of the passage of cyclical time was a reflection of how imperceptible were the changes over millennia of consciousness into self-awareness. The day, the month, the year, the equinoxes, the solstices, the appearance of comets, the conjunctions of the planets and the eclipses—in other words, the stately, bodily rhythms of nature—were the means to measure cyclical time. Such structures as buildings and megaliths assisted in those measurements.

As the rate of accumulation of primal pain increased, so did the speed of the transformation of consciousness into unconscious self-awareness. When once it might have taken tens of millennia for any significant change to take place, there came a time when, perhaps, it might take only a millennium. In time, as self-awareness came to dominate, even smother, all of consciousness, so linear time came to dominate, even smother, cyclical time. The moment-by-moment sense of time became quite perceptible. Linear time came to be measured by the abstract, mechanical workings of clocks, of which the second hand plainly shows how fast time is ticking away.

Cyclical time was slow. The sameness of life was characteristic of it. Linear time is now so inconceivably fast it is measured in the nanoseconds of Quantum Mechanics. The speed-of-light pace of the changeableness of life is characteristic of life today. It is indicative of how fast self-awareness must run to keep from being overtaken by an astronomical explosion of primal pain. The level of primal pain is now so high and pushes so hard to burst through self-awareness that self-awareness has to move fast to keep itself constantly diverted from having to face the imminence of its own disintegration. It is like being in a very leaky boat and having to bail furiously in order to keep afloat, not drown and be no more.

Whether in cyclical or linear time, change has nearly always been associated with the cosmos disintegrating back into the primordial chaos and with the re-creation of the cosmos. (An exception to this was in the 1800s when Darwinian evolution was misinterpreted and then matched with philosophical theories of change in which human progress was a given.) When pure cyclical time was the people's experience, the re-creation of the cosmos took place at least annually. When linear time became dominant, the re-creation was looked forward to as happening at the end of time.

Hope in the re-creation of the cosmos is mirrored by the childhood hope that if one can be better and do better, one's parents will fulfill one's needs. The hope, both internally and externally, suppresses the pain of suffering. If one abandons the hope-dope, pain arises. That is why, primally, hope for a better day as a way to live is seldom abandoned; the withdrawal symptoms are too severe.

After the Stage has been reached that re-creation cannot go back to the Golden Age, it is sensed that things are always getting worse. The primal basis for this has been outlined earlier. Suffice it to say that with each discrete rise in primal pain, there is an incremental change from consciousness into unconscious self-awareness. Deterioration in the quality of life becomes an experience of life that cannot be denied, except to further suppress the suffering due to primal pain.

The way in which change for the worse was taken into account when cyclical time was still the predominant experience was to posit discontinuous Ages that progressively got worse. Time inside an Age was cyclical but between Ages was linear. When linear time became the predominant experience, history was sensed to repeat itself in a cyclical fashion, but ever getting worse along a downward line of linear time.

When the dominant experience of time is cyclical, past, present and future are rolled up into one. In each present moment, the entire past and future are repeated. In the subordinate experience of time as linear, past, present and future are posited to a First Age, all previous Ages, the present Age, future Ages and the Final Age.

When linear time becomes the dominant experience of time, time stretches back into the past until one comes to the beginning of the first and only Age. The present is a fleeting experience, forever sliding into both the past and the future in which time ultimately will end. In the subordinate experience of time as cyclical, the self feels that it goes around in circles and that history does too.

Memory is a phenomenon present in the timelessness of consciousness as well as in the cyclical and linear time of self-awareness. The crucial difference is that in unconscious self-awareness the memory is trapped in the past, while in consciousness it is free to roam the past without being attached to it. Self-awareness is attached to the past because the suppressed, unmet, infantile needs of childhood subconsciously dominate every thought, word, emotion and deed of self-awareness. Insofar as one resolves one's primal pain connected to these unmet needs, one frees oneself from one's past even though the memory of it remains.

Timelessness or the presentness of who is, is the experience of consciousness. In consciousness, change is ceaseless; however, it neither goes in circles nor has either a beginning or an ending. It is change that moves either toward disintegration or toward integration.

Experiencing one's primal pain in primals restores one incrementally to a condition in which neither cyclical nor linear time exist. Since the effect of primaling is to remove from one's organism the reverberating cycle of struggling, failing and struggling again, the experience of time as cyclical occurs less and less. Also, since the effect of primaling is to reverse the effect of the formation of self-awareness in the first place, the experience of time as linear occurs less and less. What one is left with is the restoration of the experience of timelessness that is characteristic of young children.

Space

In consciousness there is a continuum of experience in whom the experiencer and the experienced are one and the same. There is no observer *in here* who observes an object *out there*. There is just pure seeing. "I" am "my" experiences. Since all of this is so, there is no experience of space.

A baby in a crib, reaching for the mobile suspended out of reach above his head, is instructive here. We watch the uncoordinated effort to grasp the mobile as if it were within reach. Our conclusions don't go beyond the point of stating that in time the baby's efforts will be more coordinated, and he will be able to stretch up and grasp the mobile. I said that it appears that the baby reaches for the mobile as if it were within reach, but that is precisely what the baby is experiencing. The baby is still in a conscious, pre-self-aware state of being, so, for the baby, he and the mobile are one and the same. They are part of each other. The baby fully expects to be able to grasp the mobile.

Earlier in this chapter and in previous chapters, I've fully described how, when and why unconscious self-awareness forms. When it does, there is now a self in here who experiences a world out there. No longer are the experiencer and the experienced one and the same. There is now an "I" in here that is distanced from what is out there. There is the experience of extension, of space. Therefore, it is the very formation of self-awareness that provides the basis for all forms of space.

Space has two extensions or planes: the horizontal and the vertical. These extensions are the experience of the everyday world out there. Ascending on the vertical plane one comes to the upperworld and descending on it one arrives at the underworld. When self-awareness is in its first two stages, space is experienced almost completely on a horizontal plane. In the third Stage of self-awareness, the tripartite self and cosmos come into being. To the horizontal plane of the cosmos are added an underworld and an upperworld. These planes of space are fully covered in chapters that include the tripartite self and cosmos and on the destination of the dead. By the 1st millennium BCE, primal pain had reached such a level that self-awareness felt that it had to get out of space and time if it were to eradicate its suffering. That effort is detailed in the fourth Stage of the development of self-awareness: transcendence.

Summary

In consciousness there is the self-in-relationship in the context of the ever-changing present moment and of being at the center of one's experience. I say "experience" rather than "space" because in consciousness there is no space in the way unconscious self-awareness locates itself.

When self-awareness first came about, one of the first effects upon it was to remove it from the flow of the ever-changing present moment. This precluded self-awareness from experiencing the past as continuously evolving into the present. Now the past was fixed, fixed because it stopped at the self, which was now removed from the flow. As primal pain levels have increased and the self has become ever more isolated and removed from the flow, the past has become ever more fixed. Now, without the consciousness of an ever-evolving past and without being at the center, the isolated self has just gotten lost in a trackless space with a meaningless present and an unchartable future.

CHAPTER 6

THE EXPERIENCE OF A SUPREME DEITY, OF THE FOUR MOTIFS OF RELIGION, OF THE CHAKRA SYSTEM, AND OF THE ROLES OF HOPE/STRUGGLE, FAILURE/ RESIGNATION AND ACTING IN/ACTING OUT

The Purpose of this Chapter

The first thing I intend to establish in this chapter is that unconscious self-awareness must experience life in dualistic terms, the most basic of which is self/other. I intend to show that it is part of the nature of self-awareness that it experiences itself as being in here and that the world is out there.

The second notion I intend to establish is that the world in here and the world out there mirror each other. I intend to demonstrate that, historically, once there was a self-awareness in here that experienced itself as being distinct from the body, there was a supreme deity out there who was distinct from the body of the cosmos.

The third proposition I intend to establish is that, historically, the four sequential motifs of religion historically mirror the child's same sequential motifs in his responses to primal pain. Those motifs are placation (Stage I), reimmersion (Stage II), power (Stage III) and transcendence (Stage IV). Also, I intend to show that the first three motifs of religion follow the sequence of the maturation of the three levels of the brain—the sensing/survival, the emotional/sexual and the thinking.

The fourth proposition to be founded is that the Chakra system of transcendence is representative of Stage IV religion. In connection with that, I will also compare it with the primal way toward consciousness.

To conclude the chapter, I'll discuss the roles of hope/struggle, of failure/ resignation and of acting in/acting out as they relate to the four motifs.

The Experience of Life in Dualities by Self-Awareness

In Part II, Chapter 3, I covered how a consciousness-in-pain must be suppressed in order for the organism to remain viable. I indicated that the organism's defense system to suppress primal pain has a life of its own and that my name for the defense system is unconscious self-awareness. I noted that the literature on this subject refers to this event as the basic split and calls the result "self-consciousness." In what follows, I'll show that it is in the very nature of self-awareness to experience life dualistically. It cannot help but experience itself as being in here while the world is out there.

From the instant moment of conception, the newly fertilized egg knows himself only in terms of relationships, beginning with his mother. The relationship is so interconnected that the relationship is that of but one life. In no way would the conscious fetus experience that he, as a separate individual, was in a relationship with another separate individual, i.e., his mother. However, to whatever extent the mother has primal pain is the extent to which the fetus is subject to it and is beginning to defend himself against it by withdrawing from the relationship. Tests show that even simple-celled creatures withdraw from pain.

After birth, and as the child's primal pain begins to build, the process of withdrawing from pain continues. This means that the child is in the process of continuing to cut his interconnections with his parents: the source of his pain.

The internal counterpoint to the cutting of external connections is the severance of interconnections among the sensing, emoting and thinking levels of the brain. At some point, so many of the interconnections are cut that the unity of the brain is destroyed, the oneness of psychic experience shattered.

The cutting of interconnections, both externally and internally, is the building of a defense system. A wall is going up much like the walled cities of old or like the gated communities of today that cut themselves off from the outside.

At some point, and it varies from child to child depending upon how deeply and rapidly the child accumulates primal pain, the cutting of interconnections and the building of the defensive wall reaches a critical point and the defensive system of the child becomes aware of itself. Again, it is much like a walled community taking on a life of its own, separate from the rest of the urban area around it.

Once there is the simultaneous split of unconscious self-awareness from consciousness and of the child from his mother, the oneness of life has been split into the duality of self and other. Once there is self-awareness with a life of its own, it experiences itself as being in here experiencing a world that is out there. It is, therefore, dualistic in its very nature.

Now, instead of a consciousness that knows himself only as a constellation of interconnections amidst a myriad of other constellations of interconnections, there is an isolated, dualistic self-awareness in here that gets evermore cut off from a world out there as primal pain increases. As I've stated in other chapters, the ever-increasing gap between the world in here and the world out there will take place in distinct stages rather than in a smooth continuum.

Increases in primal pain levels not only determine the stages of the gap in the dualism between in here and out there, they determine the dualistic nature of the world in here and the world out there. When self-awareness has formed and is in Stage I, survival is the motif both in here psychologically and out there in religion. When primal pain has caused self-awareness to jump to Stage II, reimmersion is the motif both in here psychologically and out there in religion. Again, when a sufficient increase in primal pain has made self-awareness jump to Stage III, power to satisfy wants and to overcome feelings of helplessness characterizes both the world in here and the world out there. Still later, in the 1st millennium BCE when primal pain has caused the paradigm change from Stages I-III to Stage IV, transcendence is the motif both in here psychologically and externally in religion or in some philosophy of life.

The dualism of self and body created by the formation of self-awareness deserves special attention. The evolution of this dualism is revealing of the devolution of consciousness into unconscious self-awareness.

Historically, self-awareness has experienced the self/body duality in one of three ways. One is that self-awareness is immortal and embedded in a mortal body. The second is that true self-awareness lies in some form of a supra-self-awareness that transcends ordinary self-awareness and the body. The third is that self-awareness is nothing more than a physical or material phenomenon that arises out of a combination of electrical discharges and chemical reactions in the brain.

The conception of self-awareness as being immortal and embodied came first, historically. This was so because an embodied immortal self is the first image self-awareness has of itself upon its crystallization out of a state of consciousness-in-pain. Put differently, the crystallization of self-awareness is the incremental severing of its ties to the body in order to defend itself against primal pain.

The means that self-awareness used historically to defend itself from primal pain were necessarily body-oriented because self-awareness was body-oriented. The means used were placation, reimmersion and power. Nevertheless, regardless of it never being without a body, self-awareness experienced itself as being immortal. In the outer world, the mirror image was of the duality of a Supreme Deity who coexisted with matter. This conception of the self and of the Supreme Deity went unchallenged until the advent of Buddhism and Christianity.

The second form of self-awareness came about in the 1st millennium BCE By then the level of primal pain had risen so high that none of the body-oriented means of placation, reimmersion and power sufficed to assuage the pain and suffering of self-awareness. Desperate measures were called for. The solution—for those fortunate enough to find it—was to rise above self-awareness into Buddha Consciousness or into the Mind of Christ or into the Pure Reason of Greek philosophy, all three of which are forms of what I have named the supra-self-awareness.

This way of coming to terms with the self/body duality by rising above self-awareness was to completely detach from self-awareness and the body. In

Buddhism, the self/body dualism was eliminated by positing that matter was an illusion of self-awareness and that the supra-self-awareness of Buddha Consciousness alone was real. Matter was a function of mind. In Christianity, the self/body duality was eliminated by positing that the body and matter were created by God, thus subordinating matter to be a function of Mind or of God. In Greek philosophy, the mind/matter duality was done away with by positing that every material object was but a manifestation of an ideal, subjective Mental form. Matter was a function of Mind. Mind, in the form of Pure Reason, was the ultimate reality.

The third conception of self-awareness as a phenomenon of electricity and chemistry had its beginnings when primal pain became so great that no Stage IV sacred or secular form of a detached supra-self-awareness was adequate to defend against primal pain, let alone any of the prior defenses of Stages I, II and III being adequate to do so. The conception of self-awareness arising out of a combination of electrical discharges and chemical reactions has come to its logical conclusion in our own day. The self/body duality has been eliminated by finding that the self or mind has no independent reality, but is simply a function of matter.

Another duality of self-awareness that illustrates the devolution of consciousness into self-awareness is that of the division between Sacred and Secular. It first came about in the 1st millennium BCE In the West, Greek philosophy was the first secular response to the failure of religion to assuage primal pain and the suffering that comes from it. Although Greek philosophy was secular, like the Stage IV religions of Buddhism and Christianity, it was a Way of Transcendence from self-awareness and the body. By our own day, a supra-self-awareness-oriented Secularism has evolved into a body-oriented Materialism. Hence, the Sacred/Secular dualism of the 1st millennium BCE has become the Spiritualism/Materialism duality of today.

Here are five ways the Spiritualism/Materialism duality manifests itself:

(1) In Spiritualism, the supra-self-awareness is given by the deities. In Materialism, self-awareness is an accident of matter.

(2) In Spiritualism, there are deities in the outer world, and in the innerworld there is Buddha or Christ Consciousness, for example. The deities and Buddha or Christ Consciousness have primacy over matter. In Materialism, there are no deities in the outer world and in the inner world self-awareness is a physical happening.

(3) Spiritualism as a defense against primal pain and suffering transcends self-awareness and the body. Materialism as a defense against primal pain and suffering manipulates body chemistry to restore that which self-awareness conceives as normalcy.

(4) In Spiritualism, an enlightenment or conversion experience is necessary to utilize transcendence as a means to rise above a suffering self-awareness.

In Materialism, an awakening is required to believe that the use of chemicals will cure the mental and emotional illnesses of self-awareness.

(5) In both Spiritualistic and Materialistic settings, in childhood the defenses of placation, reimmersion and power will run their courses. Those courses will be modified, however, by parents who will apply either Spiritualistic or Materialistic remedies to their children's symptoms of suffering.

In the field of psychiatry, the finding that the self is nothing but a physical phenomenon arising out of a combination of electrical discharges and chemical reactions has resulted in a pendulum swing away from therapies directed toward self-awareness to therapies directed toward the biology of the body. Mental and emotional illnesses are attributed to chemical imbalances, so the preferred method of treatment is to prescribe chemicals to redress the imbalances. In essence, all these chemicals are painkillers to counteract suffering due to huge amounts of primal pain that have altered body chemistry.

Even in the so-called healthy population, the symptoms of rising primal pain are everywhere and being treated chemically to reduce suffering. Television, newspaper, magazine, billboard and internet advertising is a clue as to how many millions of us are dependent on one kind of painkiller or another to get us through the day or night: alcohol, nicotine, caffeine, sleep inducers, tranquilizers, mood elevators, aspirin, ibuprofen, Advil, Tylenol and dozens of others constitute but a modest list of all we consume. We need chemicals for our bowels because we are "uptight." We need antacids because we can't "stomach" things anymore. We need hunger depressants because we can't stop "swallowing" our emotions down and then eating until we are unhealthily overweight. We need muscle relaxants because we are "ticked" off. We need analgesics for our brains because we try in vain to figure out our emotions intellectually until our heads ache with frustration. The dead end of consuming chemicals to end our suffering is fast upon us. Each new "medicine" sooner or later becomes ineffective in suppressing primal pain. Futilely, does a suffering self-awareness treat the symptoms of suffering while the real cause—primal pain—goes untreated because it is not known or acknowledged.

Here is an aside on the use of chemicals to assuage pain and suffering. The ancient shamans used chemical or herbal remedies, too, as part of their stock of cures, but their primary focus was on self-awareness as the cause of all ailments. Today the use of chemicals or herbs to redress chemical imbalances has all but pushed aside mental or emotional therapies, which have been ineffective to relieve self-awareness of suffering.

As a final word in this section on the dualistic nature of self-awareness, I want to say something about how the field of physics has become Materialistic. Today's physics reduces the cosmos to a set of equations or to a mathematical formula. It conceives of the cosmos as a great symmetry or as a great computation. To reduce the cosmos in this manner is to fall into the trap of Materialism. To reduce the cosmos to an illusion of self-awareness or to the creation of a Supreme God is to fall into the trap of Spiritualism: the other half of the dualism. To me, Kosmos is the name of the person who encompasses all there is. I am a micro-cosmos in Kosmos, much as a single cell is to the whole body or as a molecule of water is to the whole ocean. To me, Kosmos is a personal name I give to consciousness.

My experience of who Kosmos is goes back before all conceptions of the cosmos by self-awareness. It goes back before the Reductionism of modern physics. It goes back before the 1st millennium's Stage IV Spiritualism and Materialism. And it goes back before the Pantheism of Stages I-III. Kosmos is a living being. My experience isn't so much a writing off of God or the laws of physics as it is of relating to the earth, for example, as an organ in the living body of Kosmos. Humans are like the white cells in our own bodies, free to roam around and do what's necessary for health and wholeness. Unfortunately, most of us have turned cancerous, i.e., become unconscious and blindly harm each other and the earth organ in our care.

The World in Here and the World Out There of Self-Awareness Mirror Each Other

In Part II, Chapter 3, on the basic split, I established that at some point in a young child's life his defenses against primal pain crystallize to the extent that the defense system becomes self-aware. I went on to say that this first experience of self-awareness was episodic, that is, it was of brief duration and that consciousness returned for a time before self-awareness reasserted itself to defend against increased primal pain. Consciousness is cognizant of the onset of self-awareness, but is powerless to stop its growth because primal pain is pain too great to integrate. Consciousness, like Hal in the movie *2001* with the removal of his memory banks one by one, feels the incremental loss of himself. Consciousness also feels the incremental growth of self-awareness. I suggest that during this period before self-awareness took over completely there was an increasing sense of the existence of a Supreme Deity until, with a permanent self-awareness, there was a sense of the undeniability of the existence of a Supreme Deity.

Further, I went on to say that eventually self-awareness became a permanent experience but stayed in the background until some new trauma demanded it come forward and suppress consciousness of the pain. It is this early status of self-awareness in the inner world that I find mirrored in the status of the Supreme Deity in the external world as spoken of in the most ancient oral traditions. It is self-awareness's dualistic nature that is the basis for its inner experience of itself as being mind and having a body. It is also the basis for its external experience of a Supreme Deity and of a coexistent world of matter.

Here I will describe but one characteristic of the Supreme Deity in the earliest traditions that fully demonstrates that the inner and outer worlds of self-awareness mirror each other. (In Part III, Chapter 7, on the origins of the cosmos and the beginnings of humanity, I explore in full detail just how self-awareness and the Supreme Deity mirror each other.)

In what I believe to be the earliest oral traditions regarding the Supreme Deity, after the work of transforming the amorphous watery deep into the cosmos is complete, the Supreme Deity recedes into the farthest reaches of the cosmos. The oral traditions say that He only comes near when the people have so disobeyed his commandments that great chaos is the consequence. He then makes an appearance and does whatever He feels necessary to redress the situation.

This scenario is an exact mirror of what self-awareness must do in its earliest stages to restore order to a consciousness in chaos because of primal pain too traumatic to handle. In each Stage of religion, the same will be true: The Supreme Deity and the self will mirror each other, as will all the dualities of self-awareness. Ancient peoples, however, did not make the connection that their external religious ideas were projections of their internal state of being. It is my position, not theirs, that the inner state of being is responsible for external worldviews.

The Four Motifs of Placation, Reimmersion, Power and Transcendence Mirrored in Both Self-Awareness and Religion

The quintessential point I want to establish in this section is that internally it is the sequence of the maturation of the three levels of the brain and what they mediate in the body, together with the matching psychic defenses of self-awareness against primal pain, that externally creates religion and determines the historical sequence of the motifs of religion.

Since the earliest experiences of primal pain are locked away from self-awareness in the lowest level of the brain—the sensing/survival system—self-awareness can now only intellectualize in symbolic fashion the trauma of birth, for example. From being entangled with the umbilical cord, self-awareness might reason that life is but a series of restricting shackles. Hence, all theologies, philosophies *and* all the countless Ways of Life are but symbolic ideations of the deepest primal pain.

The first level of the brain to mature is the sensing/survival system which mediates the basic survival functions of the body. It gives rise to the first motif of self-awareness and of religion, which is to placate one's parents and one's deities in order to survive. The middle level of the brain—the emotional/sexual system—is next to mature and mediates, among other functions, the emotions and sex. This, in turn, gives rise to the second motif of self-awareness and of religion, which is reimmersion into the womb and into the Mother Goddess in order to get needs met. The top level of the brain—the thinking system—is the last to mature and is the ideational area of the brain. This, in turn, gives rise to the third motif of self-awareness and of religion: the use of power by the intellect to satisfy wants, which are none other than suppressed needs resurfacing as insatiable desires, and to compensate for feelings of helplessness in getting needs met.

Before self-awareness comes about, a child is using all three motifs. When self-awareness occurs, automatically he is in Stage I and mainly using placation to get his needs met. To a lesser extent, he is also finding ways to reimmerse and to use power. The same is true for religion during Stage I. In Stage II, both with a child and in religion, placation and power will play lesser roles than reimmersion. And, in Stage III, the use of power will dominate, while placation and reimmersion will be subordinate. By making these connections, it now becomes possible to examine the history of the motifs of religion and thereby deduce the history of the devolution of consciousness into unconscious self-awareness.

The connection between the nature of self-awareness as a defense system holding back primal pain and the use of religion as part of its defense system by self-awareness is demonstrated by the history of the four dominant motifs of religion. The dominant motif of the earliest religions was the placation of the Transformer Deities in order to secure what the people needed for survival. Historically, the second dominant motif of religion was the reimmersion into the Mother Goddess in order to overcome separation anxiety. The third dominant motif of religion was the co-opting of the power of a Warrior God in order to satisfy wants and to overcome feelings of helplessness. And, historically, the fourth dominant motif of religion was the transcendence of unconscious self-awareness in order to rise above all suffering.

The four motifs suggest a way of thinking about self-awareness as a defense system that is new to me. The new way is to see the defenses of self-awareness categorized under the headings of placation, reimmersion, power and transcendence.

Pain too traumatic to integrate is automatically suppressed, but suppression is not 100 percent effective. (Fortunately, it is not because, if it were, we wouldn't know buried primal pain was there.) Some primal pain leaks through and is experienced as physical, mental and emotional suffering. That is why subordinate defenses are employed to mitigate one's suffering. These subordinate defenses of placation, reimmersion, power and transcendence are what is mirrored in religions, philosophies and Ways of Life.

Dr. Janov's research has shown that prior to a sufficient maturation of the thinking brain, an infant's organism simply shuts down against primal pain too traumatic to handle. There is no corresponding response in religion because religion cannot come about until there is self-awareness. Dr. Janov's research also shows that after a sufficient maturation of the thinking brain, a child does begin to use the four motifs of defense—placation, reimmersion, power and transcendence—to hold back primal pain, although he does not group defenses according to this scheme. That scheme is my observation after researching Janov's books and correlating his clinical insights with the four stages of religion. Once primal pain has increased to such a level as to produce self-awareness, the four motifs of placation, reimmersion, power and transcendence are mirrored in religion.

Since the four motifs of religion match the four motifs of self-awareness, any date conjectured for the beginning of religion also indicates the beginning of self-awareness. The carbon-dating of artifacts that imply a religious usage provides an outside date for the onset of both self-awareness and of religion.

What is so amazing about the history of the evolution of religion is that it tells us when, in time, self-awareness must have already come about, when it jumped from its first focus on placation to its second focus on reimmersion, to its third focus on power and to its fourth focus on transcendence. The advent of reimmersion in Mother Goddess religion gives us the ending of Transformer Deity religion with its emphasis on placation. The beginning of Warrior God religion signals the fading of reimmersion in Mother Goddess religion and the onset of power in Warrior God religion. Similarly, the advent of the religions of transcendence, such as Buddhism and Christianity, indicate the abandonment of all three of the previous stages in religion and of self-awareness for those who had either an enlightenment or a conversion experience.

As far as the antecedents of Western civilization are concerned, it is possible to assign some approximate dates for the inward foci of self-awareness and the outward foci of religion. From some indeterminate time down to about 10,000 BCE, the emphasis is on placation in both self-awareness and religion. The period of 10,000 BCE to 3500 BCE is when reimmersion was the focus of self-awareness and religion. The ascendancy of power came about 3500 BCE and today is even more firmly entrenched. The 1st millennium BCE is the era when transcendence first became the focus of self-awareness, of religion and of philosophy. It, too, is even more in evidence today than it was then. Over the millennia, it was the increases in the valence of primal pains and the increases in the speed of their accumulation that determined when these overlapping periods had, or continue to have, their main emphasis.

Survival/Placation

In full consciousness, there is no necessity to be driven to survive. It is accepted that all of life continuously changes from one form into another. Killing to eat is simply the way things are. Every creature kills to eat—big ones eating smaller ones, but in the end the smallest of all eat the biggest of all. Our ancestors knew that animals and plants gave up their lives—as much as they were taken—so that our ancestors might live. They also knew that in death they were giving up their bodies that other creatures could live. In full consciousness, everyone provides for everyone else, so everyone is taken care of naturally. No placation is necessary to induce a creature to give what he is designed to provide for the whole.

All pain arouses the organism into a survival mode. If the pain can be integrated, it is dealt with and done with. If the pain is too traumatic to be integrated, it is suppressed and dealt with symbolically by the thinking part of the brain. Even though the specific incident or environment has been survived, the organism remains in a survival mode. Religion is the symbolic form in which an organism preoccupied with survival deals with life.

Since a child is absolutely dependent upon his parents for his survival and his parents are still trying subconsciously to get their own suppressed, unmet, infantile needs met, the child must placate them by giving them what they want in order for the child to have any hope that his own needs will be met. Hence, the child, in order to mitigate suffering due to his survival needs not being adequately met, placates his parents.

In all likelihood, the brains of the earliest self-aware adults were still mostly integrated among all three levels. This means that these adults probably had symbolic access to primal pain defended against on the lowest brain level, which mediates the vital organs of the body. This explains why the first motif of religion to be emphasized is survival and the means used to ensure it is placation of the deities.

If there ever were a time when humanity was without primal pain and was fully conscious, there would have been no such thing as placation. Children would have been properly nurtured by the cosmos. In a condition of full consciousness, children would have venerated their parents. Adults would have venerated the elders of their people, and their ancestors and indeed the whole of the rest of the living cosmos including plants, creatures, the land, the air, the water and all the sky beings. By veneration, I mean an attitude of loving respect for the wisdom and benevolence of the entire cosmos. Veneration is the entire web of interconnections with past generations and with all who is. The oral traditions of indigenous peoples preserve this very ancient state of being when humanity was the least unconscious.

After a number of years of primaling, I began to experience that same veneration, that same loving respect for the wisdom and benevolence of the entire cosmos. Primaling was returning consciousness to me, and in doing so it made me realize that the loving benevolence of an all-wise cosmos was working things out for me so that I could restore myself to consciousness.

With the onset of unconscious self-awareness in humanity, the self began to experience itself as being disembodied, at least to the extent of surviving the body's disintegration at death. Likewise, because of the dualistic nature of self-awareness, the selves of all the other beings of the cosmos and of the cosmos itself became disembodied as well. Consequently, the onset of self-awareness means that the veneration of deceased ancestors, plants and creatures starts becoming transformed into the placation of the desires of the ancestors who have taken up residence in some creature important to the survival of the people. The same transformation from veneration to placation takes place with the selves of the plants and creatures the people depend upon for food. Likewise, the sky beings, principally the sun and moon, must also now be placated to do their part for the people's survival.

Animism is the name most commonly given to the beliefs of people in this earliest Stage of religion. The focus of it is the placation of the selves of the slain food animals and plants to induce them to become reborn so that there will be a never-ending supply of food for the people. These beliefs mirror the necessity of a child to placate his parents to induce them to fulfill his needs.

Through thousands of years, the increases in primal pain caused discrete, incremental changes in the belief system surrounding placation. One change was in the nature of the animal or plant self to be placated. Apparently, at first, it was the selves of the slain animals or plants themselves who were placated. Then there came to be animal or plant Masters or Mistresses. In time, these became Gods and Goddesses.

These modifications reflected the increasing power children felt that their parents had over life or death. With each discrete increase in primal pain, children had less trust in their parents to fulfill need, less trust that their parents' power of life or death would be used for life rather than death. Similarly, adults felt it was more problematical whether or not the animals would continue to be willing to die so there would be food. There was increasing doubt that the power of life or death of the Supreme Deity would be used for life. The power struggle between children and parents was reflected in the power struggle between the people and their deities. In time, children felt parents had an absolute power over life or death, and this was also true for the deities. What is reflected in many oral traditions is the arbitrariness of the personalities of the deities. Unquestionably, this is a reflection of how arbitrary parents had become in the extension of loving nurturance to their children. Nevertheless, as long as a child has hope of being loved, he will continue to blame himself for his suffering. When hope runs out and resignation sets in, a child will blame either or both parents or he will make excuses for them as to why they are not being nurturing. The same holds true between a people and their Deities in all four of the motifs of the Stages in religion. I explore this mirror phenomenon more completely in Chapter Nine: The Destiny of the Dead in the context of Israel's troubled history.

The substance of placation for a child is the doing of whatever needs to be done in order to survive and the becoming of whomever he has to become to ensure survival. In essence, this means the sacrifice of who he is, that is, consciousness, in favor of unconscious self-awareness: the person he has to become in order to survive. It means total subservience. It means the total sacrifice of consciousness.

The substance of placation for the people of their deities eventually reaches the same situation. The people must do whatever the deities want and become whom they demand them to be in order to feel that the deities will take care of them.

One characteristic of the subordinate deities, whose job it is to take care of the day-to-day running of the cosmos, is that they become depleted, exhausted in their work. They must be replenished, lest the cosmos fall back into a state of initial chaos. The people must make sacrificial offerings to them in order to restore their strength. In the beginning, sacrificing plants and animals was sufficient to satisfy the deities. Eventually, when primal pain had risen high enough, human sacrifice was necessary to satisfy them.

This running down of the deities parallels what was happening between children and parents. Parents are driven by their suppressed, unmet, infantile needs. The natural burden of attempting to fulfill the needs of children comes dangerously close to exposing the parents' unmet needs. When this occurs, the threat is there of the chaos of parental rage descending upon the children. Children respond by sacrificing whatever they have to, including all of themselves, to restore their parents to strength to carry out their responsibilities as parents.

Sex/Reimmersion

Since no amount of the child's sacrifice of his consciousness is sufficient to placate his parents and, thus, get what he needs, his primal pain and suffering increase to the point where he actively seeks to escape his suffering. He does so by immersing himself in some activity in which he loses awareness of his suffering self. Symbolically, he seeks to reimmerse himself in the womb where his needs were met.

In all likelihood, in adults in the second Stage of self-awareness, even symbolic access to the lowest brain level was largely cut off. Now, while adults had only some indirect access to the lowest level of the brain, they still had much indirect access to the middle level, which mediates sex, among other functions as well. This explains why the second motif of religion is to lose awareness of the suffering self. The loss of the self in sexual orgasm is used to become reimmersed in the Mother Goddess in order to mitigate suffering due to needs not being met.

$$\frac{\textit{Needs/Wants}}{\textit{Helplessness}} \longrightarrow \textit{Power}$$

Eventually, the inability of either placation or reimmersion to get needs met or to escape from the pain of them not being met heightens a child's feelings of vulnerability and of helplessness. He knows he must do more if he is to remain viable. What he does is suppress his needs. He denies he has needs at all. But unfulfilled needs do not go away; they resurface in the thinking brain as insatiable wants or desires. We are wont to think of desires solely in terms of material objects, but desires are immaterial as well. Desires can be mental or emotional too. That desire itself is insatiable means that it inevitably leads to continued suffering. Now, to compensate for his vulnerability and helplessness, the child learns to accumulate and use power to overcome his feelings of helplessness and to get his desires satisfied.

What has happened in the brain as a whole at this point is that most of the connections between the emotional/sexual brain system and the thinking brain have been blocked. Self-awareness is now largely confined to the thinking brain and consists almost exclusively of thoughts. The child begins to use thought power to satisfy his wants or desires.

Primal pain determines the amount of blocking between the thinking brain and the emotional/sexual brain. In the most extreme cases, the person feels no emotions at all, even if he is, for example, angry. In everyone else, to whatever extent, painful emotions are not experienced but rationally suppressed.

This third Stage in self-awareness is also mirrored in religion in that the desires of the Supreme Deity are also insatiable. This aspect of self-awareness and of religion is seen clearly in Twin, the ancestral first King of the Indo-Europeans, who laid claim to all cattle. The desire of the Indo-Europeans to possess all cattle was insatiable. It is also obvious in Aztec religion in which the Supreme Deity demanded the sacrifice of ever more hundreds of victims.

In this third stage, the act of eating takes on a whole new meaning. While in consciousness there is simply the experience of vitality in eating, now the consuming of plants and animals is experienced as appropriating their powers. The appropriating of the powers of plants and animals by self-awareness is to overcome its sense of helplessness and powerlessness in getting its needs met. The progression is to ever greater sources of power to compensate for increasing feelings of powerlessness as primal pain levels go up. First the source is plants and animals, then humans and then, finally, to the deities themselves. Eat God and gain his power. Even in a religion of transcendence such as Christianity, we find the vestiges of Stage III power religion in the eating of the bread as the body of Jesus and the drinking of the wine as his blood.

Another way to understand this phenomenon of eating to gain power is that power is an addicting intoxicant. It gives one the feeling of being in control instead of feeling helpless. And, like any addicting drug, more and more of it is necessary to fend off feelings of being at the mercy of one's environment.

This third Stage in self-awareness is mirrored in religion's third Stage in its conception of the Supreme Deity as a Warrior God. The child's struggle for power over his own helplessness is mirrored by the accumulation and use of power in Warrior God religion. The cosmos is no longer felt as a loving nurturer but as an arbitrary power dispensing the needs of life willy-nilly. Warrior God religion is concerned with the accumulation and use of power to compensate for feelings of helplessness in a fickle world. In whatever form the repressed needs of the people resurfaced as desires, thought in the form of theologizing was used to rationalize the satisfaction of those desires by conceiving of a religion in which the satisfaction of those desires was ordained by their Warrior God: a god of power. From Europe to India, the Indo-European Gods and the Semitic Yahweh reflected this third Stage in self-awareness and religion. Representative of these Gods were Thor, Zeus, Mars, Jupiter, Baal, Ahura and Indra.

Of course there was conflict between peoples before the Indo-Europeans, but with them is when we can accurately say that modern warfare was born. The superior metals of their weapons and their horse-drawn war chariots swept away all enemies. In addition, they were so rabidly ferocious in battle that we get the word "berserk" to describe them. To win in hand-to-hand combat, they had to lose themselves in a mindless frenzy.

The duality of the self/other split of self-awareness helps to account for this behavior being possible. The ultimate root of warfare lies in infantile rage toward parents—the first others—who cannot meet their children's needs. Primal-pain-burdened parents cannot help but dehumanize their children. If the dehumanization has gone far enough, it is easy to dehumanize all outsiders as others and categorize them as nonhuman, thus making war legitimate. An indication of how far the dehumanization process has gone is the extent to which the other is dehumanized or demonized.

Down to this day, to a degree unimaginable thousands of years ago when Warrior God religion began, the use of power to satisfy insatiable desire grows at an alarming rate. Today, even religion itself—the basic purpose of which is to mitigate suffering—has largely lost its way by using power to satisfy its prodigious wants, both personally and institutionally. It is seen most clearly in organized religion's grasp for power for itself or in its unholy alliance with business or political organizations to further its own agenda of insatiable wants.

Transcendence

While the sequence of the first three stages of self-awareness and religion follow the stages of the maturation of the three levels of the brain, the fourth stage—transcendence—comes about because of the inability of the three motifs of placation, reimmersion and power to mitigate suffering adequately. Transcendence as the fourth Stage comes about because there are only three brain levels. There is no place to go except into transcendence from self-awareness, which in itself is inseparable from the three truncated levels of the brain. A child for whom nothing works to alleviate suffering eventually gets to the point where he feels he must transcend his suffering self insofar as it is possible for him to do so. From that point on, he seeks to perfect his transcendence so that he does not have to suffer at all.

In adults, in the fourth Stage of religion, neither placation of the deities nor reimmersion into the Goddess, nor co-opting the power of a Warrior God work any longer to alleviate suffering. Self-awareness is seen as being part of the problem of suffering and, as such, cannot be part of the solution to suffering. Therefore, adults who have gotten into this Stage transcend self-awareness and supplant it with some form of what I call a supra-self-awareness. In secular terms, it might be called Pure Mind or Pure Reason. In religion, two of the most prevalent forms it has taken are the Mind of Christ and Buddha Consciousness.

From a primal viewpoint, what causes the jump from Stage III of self-awareness and of religion to Stage IV is the severity of primal pain that is laid down in the sensing/survival brain before the emotional/sexual system and thinking brains have matured sufficiently to process pain. This is primal pain laid down before the infant is six months old. It is pain that is inaccessible to unconscious self-awareness, hence the suffering it causes is absolutely intractable. This is what actually causes self-awareness to realize that it is part of the problem and that it must be left behind for a higher state of being: a supra-self-awareness, Pure Reason, the Mind of Christ, or Buddha Consciousness.

All so-called higher states of being are states of transcendence of self-awareness. They are the ultimate defense against the unending upsurge of primal pain because they cut off all avenues back to primal pain. In contrast, the primal person opens these avenues in self-awareness so that he can feel his primal pain and thus end his suffering.

The Chakra System as Being Representative of Stage IV Religion

The origin of the Chakra system is lost in antiquity. The system as we know it today dates from the 1st millennium BCE It was then that religions of transcendence from self-awareness and the body came about, and that is precisely what the Chakra system is all about: transcendence.

While ancient itself, the Chakra system most likely is based on the still more ancient ascent of the shaman to the sky. In all likelihood, the seven-rung ladder of the shaman was reinterpreted into the seven vibratory centers of the body. (Shamanism receives full treatment in Chapter 10.) By the 1st millennium BCE, the highest rung on the shaman's ladder and the highest Chakra center represented that point at which the shaman or the yogic had completely transcended self-awareness and the body, had left suffering behind and had become ecstatically reunited with the Divine.

The whole Chakra system of seven vertically aligned centers reflects the total range of levels at which one might live. The three lowest levels are the ones on which all unenlightened persons live. Levels four through seven exhibit ever greater transcendence from self-awareness and the body until, at the highest level—the crown of the head—one has completely transcended self-awareness and has become reunited with the ALL. As such, the Chakra system is representative of Stage IV religion.

The Chakra System and the Primal Process

Although by the 1st millennium BCE, the sense of the location of self-awareness had risen to the head, in the Chakra system the focus of self-awareness was still no higher than Chakra #3, which was located at the level of the navel. Though self-awareness was located in the head, it had no connection with living at the Chakra levels located there.

My research indicates that by the 1st millennium BCE, primal pain had driven the sense of the location of self-awareness, in discrete stages, up to the head. Self-awareness had no knowledge that it was a defense system holding back gut-level primal pain that held self-awareness prisoner. In this sense, the Chakra system and a primal understanding of the nature and location of self-awareness are different yet correlated.

Since, in the Chakra system, the self is inextricably bound up with power, sex and survival, it takes an experience of enlightenment, in which one looks down upon the self and the body, to realize that the self and the body are part of the problem of suffering. In the experience of enlightenment, one realizes that one must transcend the self and the body if one is to end his suffering. In general, I have given the name supra-self-awareness to the "one" who has the enlightenment experience. In a Buddhist context, that "one" is Buddha Consciousness.

From the perspective of primal consciousness, an enlightenment experience is the unforgettable, momentary, total blocking of thoughts, emotions and sensations which are the elements of self-awareness. Taking the place of unconscious self-awareness is an even more unconscious supra-self-awareness who is totally transcended from self-awareness and the body. Transcendence is a layer of defense on top of what self-awareness can provide as a defense against primal pain.

The First Three Chakras and the First Three Stages of Self-Awareness

The Chakra system of vibratory centers in Far Eastern religions and for Hopi Native Americans reflects the biological sequence of the maturation of the three levels of the brain and of the nature and sequence of the locations of self-awareness in its upward movement in the body.

Regardless of whether or not the religion in which the Chakra system is embedded has posited a Paradisal period, the Chakra system assumes that everyone begins life at Chakra #1—survival. This center is located low down in the gut. In my experience, everyone begins life conscious. It is only when primal pain has become great enough that one becomes self-aware and centered around survival. It is hardly coincidental that Chakra One correlates with the first of the brain centers to mature. This center governs the vital organs of survival and correlates with why self-awareness, when it first comes about, senses its location to be low down in the viscera.

Chakra #2 is located a little higher in the gut and means living life centered on sexual gratification. It implies that at least one is living above the level of mere survival. Again, it is not by chance that this Chakra correlates with the second of the brain centers to mature: the emotional/sexual system, which mediates sex and the emotions. Consistent with a rise in primal pain, self-awareness rises to this location and is centered around the reimmersional aspects of sexual orgasm in which self-awareness is lost in the experience.

Chakra #3 is located about the level of the navel and centers on a life that is built around the use of power to satisfy desires. This is the highest level that an unenlightened person can live. I find it highly significant that this Chakra accurately duplicates the third Stage in the development of self-awareness. In this stage, self-awareness suppresses needs, only to have them resurface as desires. Just as the person living at the level of Chakra #3, self-awareness uses the thinking brain—the third and highest level of the brain to mature—to think of ways to use power to satisfy one's desires.

In the Chakra system, as long as one continues to live centered on survival, sex and power, one will inevitably continue to suffer in this life. Similarly, as long as self-awareness continues to placate to survive, to reimmerse to escape and to use power to satisfy desires, it will never extricate itself from suffering.

To conclude this section, I want to make clear that it is not the structure of the brain that is responsible for life being one of suffering on the levels of survival, sex and power. While that is the givenness of the Chakra system, it is primal pain that drives self-awareness to live on those levels. Consciousness is the givenness of life in which the three levels of the brain are not skewed by primal pain. But, again, whether or not humanity ever existed in a condition of pure consciousness will never be known.

Chakras Four Through Seven and the Fourth Stage of Religion: Transcendence

Chakras Four through Seven are the incremental stages the supra-self-awareness goes through to transcend ordinary self-awareness and thus achieve full release from a state of suffering.

The fourth Chakra is located in the heart. Living at that level enables one to be compassionate. Compassion is what results when one has transcended far enough from the human condition to recognize that everyone is caught up in a condition of desire, which is the cause of all suffering.

The fifth Chakra is located in the throat and is the Stage in which one seeks God. Seeking God represents a complete turning away from seeking the fulfillment of desires. It is a higher level of transcendence.

The sixth is located between the eyebrows and is the Stage when one has achieved wisdom. Wisdom is what results when one has transcended the thoughts of self-awareness and entered, for example, the Mind of Buddha.

The seventh Chakra is located at the crown of the head. To be there is to have transcended the illusion of self and body and become completely reunited with the ALL. All desire has dropped away and all suffering has ceased.

The Chakra system also recognizes that the process of transcendence is just that—a process in which one goes back and forth between a higher and a lower Chakra until, with faithful discipline, one does fully achieve living at the higher Chakra. For example, when enlightenment first takes place, there is an alternation between the supra-self-awareness being awake and living at the level of the heart Chakra or with self-awareness being awake and living at Chakras One, Two, or Three. At first, the supra-self-awareness will often fall asleep and then wake up to realize that self-awareness had taken over yet one more time. In time, the supra-self-awareness will stay awake continuously at the level of the heart Chakra. Then the process begins all over again between the fifth and fourth Chakras. And so on through the seventh Chakra.

The Primal Process and the Transformation of Unconscious Self-Awareness Into Consciousness

Fortunately, the same symptoms of primal-pain-driven desires that cause all of our suffering are also the avenues back to our primal pain. Even with an unconscious self-awareness located in the head, cut off in large part from the body, primal pain still has access to it. Even with a self-awareness located in large part in the thinking brain and cut off from the lower brain centers, there are still enough neural connections to give primal pain, disguised as suffering, entry into self-awareness. Therefore, primaling, when experienced properly, resolves primal pain and reduces suffering, thus incrementally eliminating unconscious self-awareness and restoring consciousness.

Since self-awareness is unconscious of itself as a defense system holding back what it can of ascending primal pain, an awakening is required to give one the experience of self-awareness for what it is, a defense system whose every thought, emotion and deed is directed by primal pain. My awakening came when I read *The Primal Scream* back in 1974. I was still reading the Introduction when I found myself exclaiming, "This man knows the truth about me." The man, of course, was Arthur Janov.

I've reflected much on that experience. First of all, it was unforgettable and forever changed my life. Once knowing self-awareness—that is, the Vic I knew of everyday experience was totally controlled by primal pain—there was no going back to living the way I had since closing off at age thirteen. Secondly, I know that what happened was a momentary reopening of the neural connections among the three levels of the brain, such that I had a fleeting experience of consciousness simultaneously with an experience of self-awareness. Originally, "I" sensed "I" was standing back from self-awareness. Having primaled hundreds of times, I now know that the "I" who was standing back was "my" first experience of "my" consciousness diffused throughout "my" body.

In the beginning of being a primal person, one is far more unconsciously self-aware than conscious. At some point, after who knows how many primals, one becomes less than more unconscious and knows it unmistakably. I knew it first as a coming together of my mind and my emotions and sensed it as being sanity. Later, I sensed consciousness as an all-knowing and all-wise presence diffused throughout me. Concurrently, there was the sense of a diminishing unconscious self-awareness that was descending in the body—just the reverse of what happens in childhood.

From the perspective of biology, primaling is a descent through the three brain levels, opening long-closed passageways. It is the "physical" component of the experience of consciousness.

A Comparison of the Movement Toward Enlightenment With the Movement Toward Consciousness

At the outset of this section, I want to clarify the relationship of religion, of unconscious self-awareness, of the supra-self-awareness and of Consciousness. First of all, in religion, when it moves from Stage III to Stage IV, it is still religion. But, secondly, either in religion or in some secular mode, it is the supra-self-awareness that begins the process of transcendence. The object is to leave self-awareness behind. And, thirdly, in a primal person, it is consciousness that resolves the primal pain that causes self-awareness to come about, thus dissolving self-awareness.

It will do well to clarify here some possible confusion between the sense of self-awareness being in the heart and the sense of the supra-self-awareness being at the heart Chakra. As I spelled out in Part II, Chapter 4, as primal pain built up through the millennia, the sense of the location of self-awareness made discrete jumps up the midline of the viscera. At some point in time, it did reach the heart. We are particularly aware of this in Egyptian history because, for however long a period it was, Egyptians felt self-awareness to be in the heart, which was weighed in the balance by the gods when one died. Supporting evidence also comes from their practice of mummification; the brains were removed because, as far as they knew, they served no purpose. In our day, because of vastly greater levels of primal pain, a self-awareness located in the heart ends within a few years of life. We know this because from a very early age we've experienced our self-awareness as being in the head. So as self-awareness rises in the body, it is incrementally detaching from the body, but always remains attached to it. So each step upward that self-awareness takes is one more step in the direction of suppressing primal pain, but it can never fully do so.

In contrast to self-awareness being in the heart, when the sense of the supra-self-awareness is at the heart Chakra, the supra-self-awareness is not only transcending the body, it is transcending self-awareness as well. It is because the supra-self-awareness is transcending both self and body that it can end its suffering. Self-awareness at any level within the body cannot be compassionate, but the supra-self-awareness can because it no longer has to live on the levels of survival, sex, or power.

The first comparison I want to make between the movement toward enlightenment and the movement toward consciousness has to do with comparing the initial experience of enlightenment with the initial experience of a primal knowledge of self-awareness. In the enlightenment experience, one knows that one's self-awareness is totally being controlled by the desires associated with Chakra levels One through Three. In a primal awakening, one experiences one's self-awareness as being totally controlled by suppressed primal needs, which have resurfaced as desires. Biologically, in the enlightenment experience, the thinking brain has been effectively cut off from the middle or emotional brain and from the lowest or sensing brain. The perceived result is that thought and emotion are stilled and what arises from that stillness is the supra-self-awareness.

What I've just described as taking place biologically needs further explanation because of a misconception by those who practice transcendence. They believe that it is "thought" that creates emotions. Therefore, they seek to quiet the mind in order to quiet the emotions and, thus, be able to transcend. Actually, it is the other way around: It is the emotions and sensations that cause thoughts. In the practice of transcendence through meditation, for example, focusing one's attention on one's breathing effectively quiets one's emotions which, in turn, quiets one's mind. In order for one to get into the detached state of a supra-self-awareness, the thinking brain must become completely insulated from the sources of primal pain in the middle and lowest brains.

In contrast, in a primal awakening, the neural connections among all three brain levels are reopened. What arises out of a brain connected on all three levels is the experience of consciousness: the psycho/physical state of a pre-self-aware child. Therefore, the difference between the supra-self-awareness and consciousness is that the former arises out of a disconnected brain and the latter out of a connected brain.

Next I will compare how the Chakra system in its movement toward full enlightenment treats self-awareness and how self-awareness is treated primally. By following the Chakra system, one incrementally transcends self-awareness in four discrete stages. These stages are the four higher Chakra levels. The flip side of a decrease in self-awareness is an increase in enlightenment.

In contrast, the primal path toward consciousness means going fully into self-awareness—its sensations, emotions and thoughts—in order to pass through self-awareness and experience the primal pain that self-awareness has been defending against. With the incremental resolution of primal pain, in discrete stages unconscious self-awareness decreases and consciousness increases.

The practitioners of enlightenment, transcendence and the Chakra system feel that they are on a path toward greater consciousness. From a primal perspective, that path is one toward ever greater unconsciousness. The systematic transcendence from self-awareness in the Chakra system is, in reality, the laying down of four more levels of suppression, thus resulting in greater unconsciousness. Another way to say this is that while all the Ways of Transcendence, by whatever names they are called, ascend through the body until it is left behind, the primal way is to descend through the body until it is purged as much as possible of primal pain.

The way of transcendence and the Chakra system assume that self-awareness and its attachment to desire is the starting point for each reincarnation of humans. Accordingly, from the Chakra perspective, transcendence is a description of the journey from an unconscious self-awareness to a conscious supra-self-awareness.

In contrast, the primal way says that we all begin life more or less conscious and that due to a critical level of primal pain we become an unconscious self-awareness. The primal way is a description of a journey from unconscious self-awareness back into consciousness. As noted above, one who is on the enlightenment path does not realize that that path is one toward ever greater unconsciousness because it is nothing more than laying down ever more effective defenses against primal pain.

The movement toward enlightenment and the movement toward primal consciousness can also be compared on the basis of what happens over time in the disciplines of each way. In the primal life, the one discipline is that when feelings come up as a consequence of living one's life, one is to primal those feelings and not suppress them. What results is that as life goes on and pain is primaled there is less pain to primal. One is simply more and more conscious or less and less unconscious and suffers less and less.

In contrast to the primal person having ever less necessity to primal because his pain is being resolved, the person who follows the enlightenment path can never stop practicing the disciplines of transcendence for, if he did, his suffering would return. Indeed, even with a committed devotion to enlightenment practices, if there is sufficient stress, the whole defense system can be overloaded and a mental/emotional breakdown occur.

The Roles of Hope/Struggle, of Failure/Resignation and of Acting Out/Acting In in the Four Motifs

As I've indicated in Part II, Chapter 4, Page 48, as far back as we can project in our history, humans have been self-aware. This means, to whatever extent in any particular time, parents are unable to nurture their children naturally. Parents, then, hold out the promise of fulfilling their children's needs if only their children do enough and are good enough. Because the parents subconsciously are still struggling to get their suppressed, unmet, infantile needs satisfied, what they require of their children is really the symbolic satisfaction of the parents' needs disguised as rules for their children's behavior.

This scenario sets up a cycle that starts out with the children being hopeful that if they struggle hard enough, their needs will be met; they will not suffer anymore. It is a vain hope. What the children are trying so hard to do and to be cannot satisfy their parents. No degree of performance, no degree of being perfect, can suffice to meet the suppressed, unmet, infantile needs of the parents. The children continue to suffer. At some point, the children realize that their efforts have failed, and they become resigned to their suffering. In time, the feeling of resignation runs its course. Something triggers renewed hope that they will be nurtured, and the cycle begins again. From hope and struggling-to-end suffering, to failure and resignation-to-suffering, so it goes, endlessly repeating itself.

This scenario also takes place between a people and their deities. The inner cycle of hope, struggle, failure *and* resignation is mirrored in the same outer cycle in religion. The cycle is repeated within each Stage of self-awareness and within each Stage of religion: Placation, Reimmersion, Power *and* Transcendence.

In the beginning of Stage I of self-awareness when placation of one's parents is the main motif to try and get needs met, it will take a long time for the period of the child's hope and struggle to be nurtured to end in failure. The period of his failure and resignation to suffering will be short. As primal pain increases, the period of time grows shorter in which he hopes his needs will be met and struggles to get them met. Also, the period of time increases in which he experiences failure and resignation to the reality that his needs are not being met. By the end of Stage I of self-awareness, the periods of time in which a child will hope and struggle will be quite short. The periods of failure and resignation will be long.

This cycle of hope/struggle and failure/resignation was true when self-awareness first came about in the distant past and is still true today. The difference is in how long a child might stay in Stage I. Because the first Stage of religion had placation as its main motif, it is my position that in that distant past children grew into adults staying in that first Stage of self-awareness: placation. Today, a child might pass into the fourth stage, the supra-self-awareness, before he is six years old. The difference is accounted for by an incredible increase in primal pain.

What was true for each person during Stage I of self-awareness ages ago was also true for the religion of any given people ages ago. At the beginning of Stage I religion—Placation—the periods of struggle to please the deities were long, while the periods of societal resignation to suffering were short. By the end of Stage I, the reverse was true.

This same sequence was followed in Stages II, III and IV of self-awareness and of religion. In Stage II, there were ever shorter periods of hope that the struggle to reimmerse was successful and suffering mitigated and ever longer periods of failure and resignation in which reimmersion was not successful and suffering was not mitigated. In Stage III, there were ever shorter periods of hope that the struggle to satisfy wants and to overcome feelings of helplessness through the use of power would be successful and ever longer periods in which the struggle was unsuccessful. The struggle inevitably ended in failure and resignation as wants are insatiable because of being driven by suppressed, unmet, infantile needs. In Stage IV, the hope is that the struggle to transcend self-awareness itself will succeed, thus ending suffering.

Today the majority of people are still in Stages I, II and III; they never do really find a way to make transcendence work in either a philosophy or a religion. Of those that do, only a small percentage grasp the fundamental importance of separating completely from self-awareness by means of a supra-self-awareness, and so most religious people still suffer with a Stage I, II, or III self-awareness.

Today there is one extremely significant sign that even those who practice transcendence are failing in their struggle to end suffering. That sign is Materialism. It comes about because of the failure of a Spiritualistic transcendence to assuage suffering. In historical sequence, Materialists most likely come from the ranks of Spiritualists. Materialism denies the existence of deities. It is an ever-growing movement, but it has not, as yet, taken over.

Also, what I see happening today in religion is a disillusionment with Stage IV transcendence and a return to Stage III with its use of power to satisfy insatiable wants and to overcome increasing feelings of helplessness. This phenomenon is most apparent in theocratic-minded persons who seek to use the coercive power of government to do what they feel helpless about, that is, preventing what in their view is the moral decaying of the nation.

Within each Stage of self-awareness and of religion, another way to describe the sequence of hope/struggle and failure/resignation other than as a cycle is as a pendulum swing from acting out to acting in. Hope and struggle is the acting-out phase. One actually tries to do something about the condition of suffering. Failure and resignation is the acting-in phase. One turns inward in a stoic attempt to mitigate the level of suffering.

The acting out/acting in pendulum swing not only applies to what happens within each stage, it also accurately depicts what happens when a paradigm jump is made from one Stage to the next. Stage I—Placation—is an act-out. Stage II—Reimmersion—is an act-in. Stage III—Power—is an act-out. And Stage IV—Transcendence—is an act-in.

Materialism might also turn out to be the fifth Stage in self-awareness and religion. If so, it would fit right in with the acting out/acting in pendulum swing from one Stage to the next. In contrast to the passive inwardness of transcendence, Materialism is active and outward in the sense that it is concerned with behavior modification and the use of chemicals to end suffering.

I have no information from the history of religion that indicates that within each Stage there is an acting-out/acting-in pendulum swing or a cyclic movement between hope/struggle and failure/resignation. I base it on my understanding that the devolution of consciousness into unconscious self-awareness proceeds unevenly and incrementally in discrete stages as increases in primal pain take place. Most certainly, I base it on my primal life, which is the evolution of consciousness out of unconscious self-awareness. I act out by going out into life for what I want. I act in when feelings come up as a consequence and I primal them. The process proceeds unevenly and incrementally in discrete stages as primal pain is resolved. What I have put forward in this section is a reasoned guess as to how, millennia ago, humans moved from Stage I to Stage IV in self-awareness and in religion.

The chart that follows helps to illustrate that through the ages in our devolution from consciousness into unconscious self-awareness we have swung back and forth between acting out and acting in, between gender orientation and between left- or right-brain dominance. The swings have taken thousands of years to occur. The chart shows that even in the reverse process of becoming less unconscious there is a swing between acting out and acting in.

Primaling as the means to regain consciousness began just over forty-five years ago. This means that the children of the first persons to become primal persons are now in their child-bearing years. These children are only the third generation of persons to experience the benefits of what primaling can offer. Is there time enough left for enough of humanity to become sufficiently conscious to avert destroying ourselves and our earth mother? (These last words were written December 16, 2004, twenty months after the United States invaded Iraq in a preventive war to gain control of Iraq's oil and to privatize its entire economy in the hands of U.S. and British corporations.)

The Pendulum Swings of Unconscious Self-Awareness Through the Millennia

Act Outs		Act Ins
Stage I—Placation	→	Stage II—Reimmersion
↙		
Stage III—Power	→	Stage IV—Transcendence

Act Outs		Act Ins
Stage I—Neutral	→	Stage II—Feminine
↙		
Stage III—Masculine	→	Stage IV—Neutral

Left Brain/Right Brain Dominance		Left Brain/Right Brain Dominance
Stage I—Neutral	→	Stage II—Right brain-emotional
↙		
Stage III—Left Brain-Intellectual	→	Stage IV—Neutral

The Primal Maxim

Acting Out		Acting In
Going for what I want in life	↔	Primaling the feelings that come up as a consequence of going for what I want

Insofar as I still have unresolved primal pain, the pendulum swings of unconscious self-awareness still apply.

If you have read this far and what I've said does not resonate with you, you might want to stop here. Everything that I say from here on is derived from what has preceded it.

PART III

HISTORY OF THE DEVOLUTION
OF ORIGINAL CONSCIOUSNESS
INTO UNCONSCIOUS SELF-AWARENESS
FROM THE ONSET OF SELF-AWARENESS
TO THE EARLY YEARS
OF THE 1ST MILLENNIUM A.D.

CHAPTER 7

RELIGIOUS BELIEFS REGARDING THE ORIGIN OF THE COSMOS, INCLUDING THE BEGINNINGS OF HUMANITY

Introduction

Since everything I write in this history is based on my experience as a primal person, since I did not begin life as a fully conscious person and since I am still controlled by whatever residue of primal pain I have, to some unknown extent everything I write is tainted with unconscious self-awareness. To start with then, because I cannot say there was ever a time when I was without primal pain, I cannot say that there was a time when humanity was not infected with primal pain and in a state of pure consciousness.

As far as I know, all adults, no matter where in the world, exhibit unconscious self-awareness and the symptoms of primal pain. So all children in the world, even those just conceived, have primal pain. As far as I can tell for today, there is no time before primal pain for anyone, but there is a time of consciousness in childhood prior to self-awareness.

Everyone has a memory of some event in which one was aware of one's self that was prior to all other self-aware events, but no conclusion can be drawn about whether or not that self-aware experience was the first one of being self-aware. It can only be said that in that event one was self-aware. At some point in life, without one remembering when, unconscious self-awareness became a permanent experience. Primal pain had risen to such a level as to require constant suppression. Once that has occurred, one can reason that there was a time when one was conscious and not self-aware, but—outside of a primal—one cannot experience what consciousness is like. The level of primal pain is too high in the suppressed consciousness-in-pain for self-awareness to handle it.

To repeat, the implication of all that I know regarding primal pain, consciousness and unconscious self-awareness for the tracing of human history is that as far back as there is any evidence of human beings beyond that having to do with survival, there is evidence of primal pain and of self-awareness. We can go on to make conjectures of what life was like back then, based upon what we know of pre-self-aware childhood, but the conjectures remain just that: conjectures. The earliest reasonable dates that can be assigned to the appearance of self-awareness have to do with tools and weapons, the treatment of the dead and the female figurines of the Paleolithic.

I do know in addition, though, that as an outgrowth of hundreds of primals that there have been profound changes in my life. With each primal, there has been an incremental decrease in unconscious self-awareness and an incremental increase in consciousness.

One of those changes that has a bearing on origins has been a dimming of the self-aware experience of the separation between an inner world and an outer world and a brightening of the conscious experience of one world. The self-aware experience of the duality of inner and outer worlds mirroring each other is being replaced by the conscious experience of one world. I am returning, however slowly and fitfully, to the state of being in my childhood when the attributes of consciousness were more pronounced than the characteristics of unconscious self-awareness.

Another of the changes that is taking place that has a bearing on beginnings is that my experience of cyclical and linear time is being replaced with the experience of an ever-changing present moment. This, too, is an indication of the greater consciousness of childlikeness. Young children, as everyone knows, have little conception of time. This means I am not caught up in the question of origins, as is self-awareness. Basically, what I experience is a labyrinth of interconnections that stretches out from me in all directions, of which there is no beginning nor ending.

A third change toward greater consciousness and childlikeness that continues to take place that has relevance here is that less and less is there the experience of any lifeless thing. Larger and larger is the experience that the entire cosmos, from the smallest to the largest, is a "who" rather than a thing. Once again, only a casual observance of young children makes obvious that what self-awareness calls a stuffed animal is for a child a close and personal friend. Life is everywhere in the greater consciousness of young children.

So, in consciousness, there is the presentness of the experience of life everywhere in one world that is constantly changing. This contrasts with unconscious self-awareness, which experiences the dualities of inner and outer, past and future and matter (things) and mind (life). Therefore, in consciousness, any tradition regarding the origin of the cosmos does not compute. While, in contrast, self-awareness cannot help but think in terms of origins.

Just as in childhood before unconscious self-awareness becomes a permanent experience, there are alternating periods of consciousness and of self-awareness, so in our very ancient history there must have been alternating periods of consciousness and of self-awareness in adults. It is reasonable to assume during this Stage when consciousness prevailed that the cosmos was alive and there were no deities. It is also reasonable to assume when self-awareness prevailed that it held conceptions of deities and of origins. Of that period we can know nothing for, as in childhood, once there is a permanent self-awareness it assumes that it has always been and interprets life accordingly. That is why the earliest traditions regarding the origin of the cosmos presuppose the existence of a Supreme Deity who always has been, who is a mirror of a self-awareness thought always to have been.

Comment is also necessary here on the source material for this chapter. The speed and depth at which primal pain has accumulated in the multitude of indigenous peoples around the world varies almost infinitely. The source material indicates that ancient traditions incorporate almost infinite variations of the basic theme of the devolution of consciousness into unconscious self-awareness. My purpose is to sort out the evolution of the main story line of the devolution of consciousness into unconscious self-awareness, and to look for its origin in the natural responses of the human organism to primal pain. Sorting out the main story line is complicated by the tendency of self-awareness to recast earlier traditions in its own likeness.

Oral Traditions

It is the oral traditions of tribal peoples that provide us with the earliest evidence that consciousness was beginning to devolve into unconscious self-awareness. Probably, oral traditions predate prehistorical artifacts by thousands of years. Oral traditions begin with a description of primordial events. These stories reveal that as far back as we can go humanity was already self-aware.

There is a close correspondence among all these traditions that is accounted for by the universal effects of primal pain upon people. The differences in the content of oral traditions are accounted for by geography, climate, flora and fauna and the level of primal pain.

Oral traditions cannot be expected to be logically consistent. Within a tribe, there will be persons in varying stages of unconscious self-awareness. Certainly, this would be so among the three or four generations alive during any given period. This accounts for the survival of earlier cosmologies, while newer ones are added to the repository of traditions. Earlier traditions might be retained whole or in part. Later conceptions of deities might be ascribed to earlier cosmologies, transforming them wholly or in part to reflect a later Stage in self-awareness. So oral traditions are filled with paradoxes. What holds the tribe together is an acceptance of each person's cosmological experience without regard for the inconsistencies among them.

Because oral traditions do not distinguish among earlier or later conceptions of deities, it is not possible to use them by themselves to trace the devolution of consciousness into unconscious self-awareness. For prehistory, I will use, in addition, the experiences of my childhood and of my primal living as an adult as a guide to select from the oral traditions what I feel to be the main stages in the devolution of consciousness into self-awareness.

Natural Religion

Introduction

The most basic division of religion in general, and specifically with regard to origins, is the split between Natur(e)—al Religion and Supra-natur(e)—al Religion. Natural Religion takes in the first three stages of religion, which are body-oriented and focused on the earth and sky. It includes ancestor worship, totemism and animism. The three stages are distinguished by the nature of the supreme deity: Transformer Deity, Mother Goddess and Warrior God. The second period—Supra-natural Religion, which we are still in—is oriented around transcendence and focused on heaven and hell. In this fourth Stage of religion, the supreme deity is a Creator/Father.

All through the three stages of Natural Religion and of fourth Stage Supra-natural Religion, the self and the supreme deity mirror each other. In Stage I, the self and the deity are co-existent respectively with the body and the cosmos. In Stage II, they are manifestations respectively of the body and the cosmos. In Stage III, they are alternate forms respectively of the body and of the cosmos. And in Stage IV, they are prior to and independent of the body and cosmos, respectively.

The First Stage: The Transformer Deity

The earliest accounts of the origin of the cosmos that lie behind Western civilization are not really of creation but of the transformation of a primordial or formless watery deep into the cosmos, however it is known by a particular people. Hence, the first Supreme Deity, rather than being a creator of matter, is a transformer of matter into the cosmos.

Concomitant with the transformation of the watery deep into the cosmos, one of two things happen. Either the Transformer Deity directly makes the earth, sun, moon, stars and all the other aspects of the cosmos and they come alive as subordinate deities, or he creates the subordinate deities whose manifestations are the earth, sun, moon, stars and other parts of the cosmos. This is the way all self-aware but still very conscious ancient peoples experienced the cosmos, especially the earth, moon and sun as being not just alive but alive as deities.

When the Supreme Deity formed humans, he gave them self-awareness according to these traditions. The outer world scenario of creation is a reflection of the inner experience of self-awareness that some force outside of itself caused it to come into being. Self-awareness is correct in positing an outside force. It cannot recognize, however, that the outside force is actually the inner force of an overload of primal pain that necessitates the formation of unconscious self-awareness to protect the viability of the organism. It cannot, because basic to self-awareness is the loss of all knowledge of primal pain as part of the protection it provides to the organism. From the moment of a permanent self-awareness, the memory of life before self-awareness is altered by self-awareness to protect the organism, not only from pain too traumatic to integrate but from any knowledge of it at all. Self-awareness now experiences itself as having been present since birth, which is the basis for saying that self-awareness goes back to creation.

There is, however, a paradoxical experience that is explored in Chapter 9: The Destiny of the Dead. Self-awareness, according to other facets of Stage I religion, is immortal. That is, just as the Supreme Deity and matter have always co-existed, so have self-awareness and the body. So, at death, self-awareness is reincarnated into another body, not necessarily a human one.

Likewise, there is a paradox regarding the status of the primordial, watery deep. On the one hand, it appears to be inert matter. On the other hand, it appears to be unmanifested deities whose manifestation is the cosmos.

As has been noted above, a widespread choice of the substance to be transformed into the cosmos is a formless watery deep. This choice is quite natural, as the earliest experience of a newly conceived human being is that of being immersed in water and, at the time of birth, emerging from a watery deep. In self-awareness, the original emergence of humans from the primordial water is a mirror of the amniotic fluid of the womb and of the baby's emergence from it.

In what I consider to be the oldest of the traditions regarding the origin of the cosmos, no thought is given as to the status of the water of the primordial, formless deep, whether it be calm or chaotic. This is so because up until a specific point in Stage III there is no cognizance of a sub-self-awareness. Until that point, creation is simply making manifest the unmanifested, the transformation of the formless into the formed, the natural fashioning of the entire cosmos, including self-aware humans, out of the primordial watery deep. In addition, since there was no cognizance of a sub-self-awareness, there would as yet be no conception of an underworld as part of the cosmos.

Neither was there any characterization of the deep being feminine, even though the womb was the metaphor for the deep. Stage I was, in large part, gender—neutral. In Stages II and III, the watery deep was a manifestation of the Goddess.

I call attention here to the absence of any statement in Stage I as to the status of the watery deep, because at a given point in Stage III it is considered to be in a state of chaos. The mirror image of this in self-awareness is the cognizance of a sub-self-awareness, which is always in a state of chaos because of primal pain. At this point, the level of primal pain has risen in the consciousness-in-pain to such an extent that now self-awareness knows of its existence symbolically as a sub-self-awareness.

All characteristics attributed to the Supreme Transformer Deity reflect the human condition, but one in particular mirrors early stages in the devolution of consciousness into unconscious self-awareness. That trait is one of generally being only remotely present and only intermittently coming near and interfering in the affairs of humans. In what I believe to be the oldest of the traditions regarding the origin of the cosmos, the Transformer Deity, after completing his work, disappears almost completely into the remote regions of the heavens. Or, he disappears even sooner if he has delegated the work to subordinate deities. The only time he makes an appearance is when either humans or the subordinate deities have disobeyed his commands to such an extent that he must do something about the ensuing chaos.

A good example of this pattern is the Eskimo god Sila. Sila, at one and the same time, is among the people and also incomprehensibly distant. When the people are living as they should and acting out of reverence, Sila does not communicate with humans and remains withdrawn into his own infinite remoteness. Sila only comes near when disobedience causes chaos.

Another example, this one from the Asiatic Yakut, illustrates the tacking on of newer traditions to existing ones. The older parts of it are from Stage I, while the newer are from Stage III. From Stage I, he is inactive, shines as the sun, does not answer prayer and only grudgingly mixes in human affairs when the situation is extraordinary. From Stage III comes his name: The Lord Father Chief of the World. That he speaks through the thunder places him with the Storm deities of Stage III.

The human condition that is the mirror for a Supreme Deity who is generally remote and occasionally near is of a person who has grown from childhood into adulthood with just enough primal pain to produce self-awareness, but one that is usually in the background and only comes to the foreground when a particularly painful situation requires self-awareness to take over. Depending on the level of primal pain, either consciousness is near and self-awareness remote, or the reverse.

As was mentioned above, the Supreme Deity came near when disobedience to his commands resulted in chaos. This reflects the child's blaming of himself for the painful chaos in his life. His parents cannot be at fault, for there is the natural expectation that they will meet his needs. If they don't, it must be because he is not measuring up to their natural expectations of him. He is being disobedient. This is the way that self-awareness protects the child from experiencing an onslaught of primal pain caused by needs not being met, and so great an onslaught that it cannot be integrated. Self-awareness blocks out the devastating realization from the child that his parents cannot meet his needs. It substitutes willful disobedience as the cause. This enables the child to hope that if he can be what his parents want him to be they will nurture him. This hope is also mirrored in the people's relationship with their Supreme Deity.

In all the ancient traditions, after the completion of the formation of the cosmos, a Golden Age follows. Words like harmony, balance and interrelatedness best describe the quality of life in it. Humans, accordingly, start out in an ideal state of self-awareness that is conditioned upon continued obedience to the Supreme Deity.

In every case in these traditions, the Golden Age comes to an end. It does so because of the persistent, willful disobedience of commands of the Supreme Deity. As a consequence, humans and human society begin to lose the qualities of harmony, balance and interrelatedness. The losses take place in distinct stages, whether fast or slow or great or small, in proportion to the ever-growing, incremental disobedience of humans to be and to do what the Supreme Deity demands of them.

Primally, at first, in the oneness of consciousness, a child is able to return to a condition of being totally conscious and of being totally open to his parents after each episode of primal pain. This period has no mirror reflection in religious tradition. It takes the formation of self-awareness, which assumes it has always been, to break up the oneness of consciousness into the mirror reflections of the self/other duality and of all other dualities that are characteristic of all religions.

At some point, primal pain becomes too great. The child cannot remain totally conscious and totally open to his parents. To suppress the consciousness of pain too traumatic to integrate, unconscious self-awareness necessarily forms—however translucent it might be in its initial state. To begin with, self-awareness is mostly successful in mitigating primal pain. It is this first Stage of self-awareness that is mirrored by the Golden Age, but mirrored in a distorted way. The nature of the distortion—the substitution of self-blame for parental neglect as the cause of suffering—has been discussed above.

That self-awareness is just mostly successful in suppressing primal pain is also mirrored in what happens in the Golden Age. The traditions tell us that some suffering—due to disobedience—started in the Golden Age. Primally, self-awareness was not meant to be a perfect defense against primal pain (see discussion in Part I, Chapter 2, on the organism's built-in drive for health and wholeness). Some of it does leak through and causes all the multitude of sufferings known to humans.

The Golden Age ends, we are told, because disobedience to the Supreme Deity has become so pervasive and so flagrant that he will tolerate it no longer. Humans must now accept a less-than-ideal existence. It ends the accessibility to humans of returning to an initial, ideal state of being. Primally, the accessibility of returning to a fully conscious state ended with the onset of a permanent self-awareness.

The ending of the Supreme Deity's tolerance of human disobedience signaled the end of the Golden Age. The ending of the ability of consciousness to tolerate primal pain had already been signaled by humans becoming more self-aware than conscious. The ending of the Golden Age is a distorted image of the suppression of a consciousness-in-pain by self-awareness. The loss of an ideal state of self-awareness and the subsequent loss of ideal qualities in discrete stages are mirrored by the loss of a mostly conscious state of being to one of being mostly self-aware and the subsequent loss of the qualities of consciousness in discrete stages.

Most Jews and Christians have never read any other scripture than the Bible. Hence, they are totally unaware of the exact parallel between the first few chapters of Genesis and the creation traditions of all other religions. What I point to here is the universal sameness of the Golden Age—by whatever name it is called—to the Garden of Eden. It is the universal sameness of the effects of primal pain that accounts for the parallels.

In the Garden, as in a Golden Age, life starts out ideally and idyllically for the first people. In the Garden, Adam and Eve are prohibited from eating the fruit of the tree of good and evil. In all traditions, there are either prohibitions or commandments to follow to please the Supreme Deity. Adam and Eve disobey, as do the ancestral first people of all other Golden Ages. In Genesis, as well as in all other accounts, the consequence of disobedience is a fall from grace, resulting in a tragic decline in the quality of life without any possibility of returning to the ideal state of being. In Genesis, it means expulsion from the Garden. In all other traditions, it means the end of the Golden Age.

Two Mesopotamian epics that probably were known by the Biblical writers further illustrate the primal dynamics of the child blaming his own disobedience for why his parents fail to nurture him. Both in the epics of Atrahasis and of Gilgamesh, it is human disobedience and rebellion against the deities that causes the deities to unleash floods as punishment for the people's waywardness.

The Second Stage: The Mother Goddess

The second Stage in the evolution of beliefs regarding the origin of the cosmos is one built up around the nature of the Mother Goddess. A case has been made, however, for a religion centering on her to be the oldest form of piety. In Europe and in the Near and Middle East regions, which are the source areas for Western civilization, archeological evidence points toward the worship of the Mother Goddess as being the oldest form of religion. The unearthing of female figurines, some dating back to 30,000-40,000 BCE, coupled with the absence of male figurines, strongly suggests that this is so. This view calls into question my placing the Stage of a Transformer Deity as being earlier.

In support of my view, there are a couple of points to keep in mind. The first is that when one form of religion is replacing another, the tendency is to treat the earlier form as being "primitive" or naïve. Actions are taken to obliterate any tangible reminders of the previous erroneous "myths" or "heretical" beliefs. Idols and sanctuaries are destroyed. Evidence of this tendency is well-documented when Warrior God religion was replacing the Mother Goddess, notably so in the Jewish scriptures, and again in the Christian era when temples of the Goddess were demolished.

This tendency to experience cosmic origins in accordance with the ascending religious perspective is a reflection of what happens primally with the evolution of unconscious self-awareness. Not only does self-awareness feel it goes all the way back to the beginning of life, it feels that, whatever the status of its ever-widening dualistic nature, that status goes back to the beginning as well. This aspect of self-awareness has been more fully discussed earlier.

The second point to remember is that the first three basic responses of a child to ongoing primal pain are mirrored in the first three stages in the evolution of religion. These responses are placation, reimmersion and power. Placation of parents is mirrored by the religious motif of placating or propitiation of the Transformer Deity. Reimmersion into the womb is reflected in the religious motif of reimmersion into the Mother Goddess. Domination of parents to get what one wants—needs having been suppressed—corresponds with the religious motif of equating the people's wants with the Warrior God's will for the people and the co-opting of God's power to satisfy those wants. The primal basis for these first three religious motifs has received fuller treatment in Part II, Chapter 6.

The direct relationship of a child's successive responses to primal pain with the first three religious motifs implies that, despite the archeological evidence, Mother Goddess replaced an earlier Supreme Transformer Deity. There is no question of the Warrior God replacing the Mother Goddess. While that process began in pre-history, it is amply documented after writing began in the middle of the 4th millennium BCE

In Mother Goddess religion, there are at least two complementary images regarding the origin of the cosmos. In the first, the Mother Goddess and the Cosmos are one and the same. Her body is the cosmos. In the second, the cosmos emerges from the Mother Goddess. There are artistic representations of her giving birth to the cosmos. The mirror image of these representations is, naturally, a human mother giving birth to her baby.

The first inference I make from this change from a Transformer Deity to the Mother Goddess is that she is always near. The Transformer Deity was remote unless disobedience-caused-chaos brought the Deity near.

Primally, this means that pain levels had risen to such an extent that now it was necessary for self-awareness to remain firmly in control. The viability of the organism required that the self give constant attention to the suppression of primal pain too great to be integrated.

In this stage, in addition to what he did in the first stage, the child suppresses his pain by seeking to lose self-awareness in an oceanic reimmersion into the womb. The child feels a compelling urge to be at one with his mother, or a desire to become reunited with her. Reimmersion into the womb and reimmersion into the Goddess mirror each other.

In another place I have discussed the inevitability of self-awareness to experience life in dualistic terms. The self/other duality, because it breaks the oneness of the interconnectedness of consciousness, results in the desolation of separation anxiety. Unconscious self-awareness attempts to end the anxiety of separation by the second motif in religion: reimmersion into the Goddess. Mother Goddess religion is an indication that due to primal pain the child has become so disconnected as to feel the desolation that separation from his mother means. Reimmersion into the Goddess is a symbolic and futile attempt on the adult level to get infantile needs met. It mirrors the child's futile desire to go back into the womb where his needs were met.

The Third Stage: The Warrior God

The Proto-Indo-Europeans are the first people to jump to Stage III. We know nothing of them directly. Their existence is inferred from linguistic studies of their descendants, the various Indo-European peoples. Our earliest knowledge of the descendants is when they begin to invade Europe, the Middle East and the Far East, starting perhaps as early as the 5th millennium BCE Their original homeland is in dispute, but the most likely place is an area northeast and north northwest of the Black Sea. They have already passed through Stages I and II, and the linguistic studies shed no light on these stages.

From my research on the Indo-Europeans, I have concluded that their creation beliefs can be divided into those that came about prior to their invasions of the Mother Goddess cultures and those that came about afterwards. In those that were prior, I found one major divergence and one common theme. The major divergence was whether or not the Supreme Deity had anything to do with the creation of the cosmos. The common theme was that humanity and the cosmos are alternate forms of each other.

In one creation tradition in which the Deity was not active, Man, the first priest; Twin, the first king; and Ox pre-exist. The tradition doesn't say why, but Man and Twin cooperate to create humanity and the cosmos. Toward that end, Man sacrifices Twin and Ox and from their parts fashions all the parts of the universe.

In a tradition that illustrates the common theme, the Supreme Deity dismembers the first Man and from his body parts creates the cosmos. But, it is equally true that humanity is formed from the parts of the cosmos. The body and the cosmos are alternate forms of each other. This tradition might very well be a sublimated carryover from Stage II, in which the Mother Goddess is alternately the Unmanifested and the Manifested.

Underlying all these traditions is a primal foundation. Because of an overwhelming amount of primal pain, it is necessary for consciousness to be sacrificed. In its place arises the dualism of self-awareness and the body. Self-awareness doesn't know why it and the body exist because suppression of the knowledge of a buried consciousness-in-pain is necessary to maintain the viability of the organism. The self-aware child knows he must continue to sacrifice himself to please his parents in the hope of being properly nurtured. It is this reality that is mirrored in the traditions outlined above.

When we are well into the third Stage of religion and the Indo-European invasions of Mother Goddess cultures are well-advanced, the original Indo-European ideas of creation are merged with those of the conquered Mother Goddess peoples of Stage II. Now we see a return to the concept of a watery deep from which the cosmos is formed. In Stage I, no mention is made of the status of the primordial watery deep; it is just formless. This is so because in that Stage self-awareness is so successful at maintaining order that it does not know of a chaotic sub-self-awareness, i.e., the consciousness-in-pain. Now, in Stage III, the status of the watery deep is a crucial element of the creation beliefs. The deep is now not only in a state of chaos, it is made to be identical with a demonized Mother Goddess in the form of a Serpent. And, now in Stage III, there is a return to a Transformer Deity who converts the watery deep into the cosmos. In this later period of Stage III, the Supreme God is not only the Transformer God, he is a Warrior God who is a deity of storms and of the mountains.

I find it not only fascinating, but corroborative of what modern cosmologists are saying about what the conditions were prior to the Big Bang. One view is that there was a "singularity." The other view is that there was a "superhot stew." These views correspond with my view of what Stage I and Stage III religion experienced as the condition of the watery deep from which emerged the cosmos. The singularity is the same as the calm, watery deep, while the superhot stew is the same as the chaotic, watery deep.

Before proceeding further with origins in Stage III, I want to point out something about our sources of knowledge of the Mother Goddess. It is unthinkable, during her long reign as the Supreme Deity, that even a part of her was characterized as a demon. It is my position that any source that portrays her as the personification of Evil or the Demonic is a reinterpretation of her by Indo-European cultures with a Warrior God religion that is in the process of taking over areas where she reigns. The name of the Supreme God of the Indo-Europeans was Light. Mother Goddess was both light and darkness, but both sides of her were recast into everything Evil and Demonic. The Indo-Europeans felt they had a God-given mandate to bring enlightenment to those peoples who still worshipped a Mother Goddess, whom the Indo-Europeans experienced as a demon.

The Indo-Europeans also felt that they had a God-given mandate for conquest. They believed that their Supreme Deity had provided cattle to them for their exclusive use. Therefore, if any people were found to have cattle, they must have stolen them from Indo-Europeans. By the time of the Indo-Europeans, the domestication of cattle was widespread, so it was easy for them to justify expansion through warfare to reclaim stolen cattle.

With regard to warfare, the Indo-Europeans are given credit for the first use of the horse-driven war chariot, a weapon that demoralized their enemies. The period of Indo-European expansion also saw the invention of metallurgy. Copper and brass weapons were used first, and then toward the end of the period iron was used.

In order to make more solid the connection between pre- and post-invasion creation stories in Stage III, additional background on the changing relationship of the Warrior God with the Mother Goddess is provided here. The place to start is during Stage II, when reimmersion is the main motif and placation and power play minor roles. During this stage, there was a subordinate God of the stormy skies who was also a Warrior god. Baal, for example, who is mentioned many times in the Jewish scriptures, is a Warrior God who is a consort of the Mother Goddess. The Mother Goddess having a Storm God as a consort is mirrored by a self-awareness that is predominantly located in the emotional/sexual brain, and subordinately located in the thinking brain.

This God of the stormy skies was manifested as a bull, whose bellowing was heard as thunder. To the invading Indo-Europeans, it was anathema that the Mother Goddess cultures had a bull god, let alone that he was subordinate to the Goddess. Remember, that for them they were the only people divinely ordained to own cattle. If other people had them, they must have stolen them. So one of the first things they did was to give the name of their own Supreme Warrior God to the subordinate Warrior God of Mother Goddess religion. Later on, they used the subordinate status of the Warrior God to the Mother Goddess as part of the rationale for demonizing her.

With regard to the beliefs of the Indo-Europeans about the Mother Goddess during their own passage through Stages I and II, nothing is known. To what degree they had a memory of their own past is problematical. It is certain that they would have considered their earlier beliefs to be primitive or naïve or misguided. What is known about their beliefs concerning the Goddess prior to their invasions of the Mother Goddess cultures is that she is relegated to the underworld.

A comparable situation occurred with the European invasions of the Americas. They were like their Indo-European ancestors in that they had no memory of the earlier stages of their beliefs. They just considered the Indians' beliefs to be primitive or reinterpreted them in terms of Catholic Christianity.

In addition, it is important to note the effect that cognizance of a sub-self-awareness during Stage III had on the attitude toward the Mother Goddess and toward everything feminine. In the early phases of Stage III, there had to be a place for goddesses of minor status because, up through Stage III, all three motifs of Natural Religion are always present. There must have been present a lesser role for reimmersion, regardless of whether or not it were into the Goddess. Whatever role she had, she was not involved with creation, nor was she demonized. Once there was cognizance of a suffering, chaotic sub-self-awareness brought on by a huge increase in primal pain and identified with the feminine, it was inevitable that creation traditions eventually include the demonization of the Mother Goddess in the form of a Serpent representing the primordial, watery deep.

What follows now is my judgment as to the chronology of the evolution of the relationship between the Indo-European Warrior God and the Goddess of the invaded cultures, resulting in her demonization and finally with her demise in Western culture.

In Phase One, the Mother Goddess marries the Warrior God. I believe the impetus for this comes from the Mother Goddess culture as an accommodation to the invading Indo-Europeans but before they have consolidated their power. An example of this is Hera marrying Zeus. Eventually, Hera becomes subordinate to Zeus. This accommodation represents an awareness by a Stage II self-awareness of the increasing role of the male-oriented thinking brain in self-awareness.

In Phase Two, the Mother Goddess is transformed into a male deity. An example is in Arabia where Ishtar becomes Athar. This is one of those occasions in which an older, more primitive belief is recast into beliefs of current understanding. The supreme deity cannot be a female; the deity must be male. The sex change is represented in self-awareness by the takeover of the left-lobe thinking brain from the right-lobe emotional/sexual brain and the cutting of connections between the two brains. (See Part III, Chapter 12, for a complete discussion of the assignment of gender to the two brains.)

In Phase Three, on the cosmic level, the Warrior God marries the Mother Goddess. On the human level, Indo-European kings married Hittite queens in order to legitimize their position as supreme rulers. The kings represented the Warrior God, while the queens represented the Mother Goddess. The marriage was an act showing that the Warrior God had replaced the Mother Goddess. The internal counterpoint to this marriage is an acknowledgement by self-awareness that emotions have a legitimate but lower place to thinking in self-awareness.

In Phase Four, the Mother Goddess becomes the Goddess of War and Love. After the Warrior God marries the Mother Goddess, it seems plausible that that is when she was made out to be a wife fit for the Warrior God: a partner in war and love. Each people had their own name for her. For the Mesopotamians, it was Ishtar. For the Syrians, Anat. For the Arabs, Atar. For the Greeks, Astarte. For the Egyptians, Isis. For self-awareness, the transformation of the Mother Goddess into the Goddess of Love and War represents the co-opting of the emotions in the pursuit of the satisfaction of insatiable wants.

Making her into a Goddess of Love and War was the work of the Indo-Europeans. It was the Indo-Europeans who invented war as we know it, who made it into the instrument to carry out the political ambition of conquest. Such a role for the Goddess did not come about until the Indo-Europeans.

Reference to the Goddess also as a Goddess of Love is a reinterpretation of her role. In Stage II, she is the Goddess of fertility and sex but not love. Love, meaning the romantic love with which we all are familiar, probably was only an aberration in Stage II. That romantic love in Stage III became so important and prevalent to warrant making the Goddess the Patroness of Love is testimony to a big jump in the level of primal pain wherever this occurred.

Romantic love is the reawakening of the agony and ecstasy of infantile feelings. The ecstasy is the feeling of openness, closeness and attachment one has with one's parents when one is first born, when the expectation is there that one's needs are going to be met. The agony is the feeling of pain when one's needs are not met and are not going to be met. As I've said over and over again, it is this pain that must be suppressed if the organism is to remain viable.

Romantic love is the past masquerading as the present. When one falls in love, one's defenses are let down, allowing the infantile feeling of need to arise, but directed toward the loved one rather than toward one's parent. Romantic love is best understood by the expressions, "I can't live without you" or "I'll die without you." Those statements are true, however, only for the past when one would die without being taken care of by a parent.

Romantic love is an excessively needy state born of an infant's life-or-death dependence upon his parents to fulfill his needs. Romantic love is the infant's state of being of absolute need surfacing into unconscious self-awareness, giving rise to the feeling of being in love.

In Phase Five, the Goddess is dethroned as wife of the Warrior God and his partner in love and war and demonized as Evil personified. It was the introduction of romantic love into the human condition in Phase Four that made the demonization of the Goddess inevitable.

From Europe to India, there are traditions of Storm or Mountain Gods overthrowing a demonized Goddess who is portrayed as a serpent or dragon and associated with darkness, evil and chaos. In India it was Indra defeating Danes. In Anatolia, it was the Storm God over Illuyankas. In Canaan, it was Baal over Lotan or Lawtan. In Israel, it was Yahweh over Leviathan. But perhaps the most oft-quoted tradition was that of Marduk over Tiamat, a story that came from Babylon. Prior to the territorial expansion of the Indo-Europeans, Marduk probably was a minor deity of the mountains in the Mother Goddess culture of Babylonia. The Indo-European invaders adopted him as their own and elevated him to be the supreme deity.

In the Indo-European revised tradition, Tiamat, the Mother Goddess, becomes the watery deep itself, which is personified as a dragon. She has now been demonized as a Serpent Goddess, which gives Marduk ample justification for killing her and then forming the cosmos from her body. In one version of the story, humanity is formed from the blood of an equally depraved deity.

The Marduk/Tiamat creation tradition marks the complete subjugation of the Mother Goddess cultures by the Indo-Europeans. It is evident by reason of the five phases of the relationship of the Warrior God to the Mother Goddess that the Indo-Europeans did not immediately force their religion upon the Mother Goddess cultures. What they did was to accelerate the pace of discrete jumps from Stage II to Stage III, an inevitable outcome even if the invasions had never occurred.

By whatever date is assigned by linguistic studies to the original creation tradition of Marduk and Tiamat, it is the earliest date in the Middle East for the demonization of the Mother Goddess: It signals that a big jump in primal pain has occurred. Women and the Goddess are no longer merely being blamed for suffering and chaos, but being demonized for it as well.

Since the womb is the metaphorical basis for the deep, the womb must have been demonized as well. With a demonized womb and humanity being born of the blood of a depraved deity—according to one version of the Marduk/Tiamat story—the basis is there for claiming that humanity has always been depraved. Obviously, this is a reflection of late Stage III thinking on the degree to which humanity has lost its initial goodness. In my words, it reflects to a high degree the devolution of original consciousness into unconscious self-awareness. This revelation of just how far humanity has fallen from a state of grace is adopted by Christianity in the concept of original sin.

With regard to a Golden Age in Stage III, perhaps there was one at such time as when humanity was formed from the blood of Marduk. Mostly likely there was no Golden Age in the later versions of Marduk's exploits when humanity was formed from the blood of a depraved deity.

Another way in which the Golden Age was treated by these origin traditions was to posit subsequent, successive, discontinuous Ages. The Golden Age took place in the first Age, never again to be repeated.

But, regardless of whether or not there was a Golden Age in Stage III, it is clear that in Warrior God religion there has been significant development in unconscious self-awareness and a corresponding loss of consciousness. Primal pain is greater and, consequently, suffering is much greater. Personal and communal life have deteriorated considerably.

Also during this period, there were invasions by other Warrior God peoples, the Semitic Israelites among them. We learn of their history mainly from the Jewish scriptures. In the 1st millennium BCE, both the history of the Israelites and the history of their scriptures reveal the devolution of consciousness/self-awareness from the Stage III Warrior God to the Stage IV monotheistic, Creator-Father God.

How the opening verses of Genesis were read at the beginning of the 1st millennium BCE and how they were read at the ending of it lays bare the transition from a Transformer Warrior God to a God who creates the cosmos out of nothing. Since, when first we meet the Israelites, Yahweh is a Warrior God, I believe that the opening verses were originally read: "When God began to create the heavens and the earth, the earth was without form and void, and darkness was upon the face of the deep; and the wind of God was moving over the face of the waters." This reading clearly reflects a Supreme Transformer Deity who co-exists with matter—the watery deep—and who transforms formless matter into the cosmos. How they were read at the end of that age I'll go into when I discuss Stage IV.

The picture that Genesis 1 gives us is that of a cosmos that exists in the midst of the watery deep. The firmament was like an inverted bowl that separated the watery deep above it from the waters that were below it, which were gathered into the oceans, lakes and rivers. The flat earth with Sheol below completed the shell that kept out the watery deep from filling the air space between the ground and the firmament. The entire picture is symbolic of the fertilized egg forming in the waters of the womb.

Genesis 1:28-30 and 2:19, 20 clearly place the Israelites in Stage III of religion. Genesis 1:28-30 instructs humanity to have dominion over nature and subdue it. Genesis 2:19, 20 instructs humanity to name all creatures. To name someone is to have power over that someone. Yahweh gives power to humanity. It should be noted that these instructions were given before the Fall of humanity from a state of initial grace. After the Fall, no human could be a good steward. These verses show that when they were written humans had already arrogated supremacy to themselves. Instead of being harmonizers, as was true in Stages I and II, they were exploiters.

Genesis also maintains the tradition of an initial Golden Age for humanity. It calls the location of it the Garden of Eden, which name has taken on the connotation of an earthly paradise, just as did the Golden Age in other traditions.

Humanity, according to Genesis, begins life in a state of innocence. As in all the earlier traditions, Genesis says that the continuation of the paradisal age depends upon the obedience of the first humans to God's commands. And, as the Biblical writers were all too aware, because of the depths to which humanity had fallen by their own day, it was not long before the first humans disobeyed God and brought down upon all future generations the dire consequences of their actions.

The historical setting of the writers of the Biblical story of the Fall provided the rationale for the selection of a serpent as the provocateur who tempted humans to disobey God. Canaan, the land coveted by the Israelites, was inhabited mostly by people whose supreme deity was the Mother Goddess. As the Indo-Europeans had done before them, the Israelites demonized her to justify the legitimacy of their territorial conquest. Hence, the selection of a snake as tempter was not simply because serpents were thought to be more subtle than any other creature

God had made, as Genesis 3:1 says. To the Israelites—worshippers of the male Warrior God Yahweh—the serpent represented Mother Goddess who was the ultimate cause of all the ills of humankind.

In Stage II, the Mother Goddess was looked to as a source of wisdom. She was a trustworthy guide for self-aware humans in determining what was good for them and what was not. The snake was a manifestation of the Goddess, so the snake as the Goddess was reverenced and looked to for wise advice.

The third chapter of Genesis completely recasts Mother Goddess and the snake: her manifestation. Here, she is not represented as being identical with the cosmos, as she was in Stage II, but as the chaotic, primordial deep from which the Warrior God Yahweh brought order. The Yahwehist revisionists cast her in the role of an antagonist whose aim is to reduce order into its original chaos. She has had nothing to do with the creation of human beings into an initial, ordered, natural state as she did in Stage II.

The natural state into which Genesis has humans created is a state prior to self-awareness. It is one in which there is neither good nor evil. In it, one simply acts artlessly, innocently, without guile and with childlikeness.

Genesis 3 now makes the Goddess to be the one ultimately responsible for the introduction of self-awareness into human life and for its consequence: chaos. Her wisdom is recast as a temptation to become self-aware. She is made to lie about what will happen when humans obtain the self-aware state of the knowledge of good and evil. Instead of telling the truth that self-awareness brings chaos, she lies and tells them it will make them like gods. It still takes disobedience to make one self-aware, but the blame is placed on the Goddess.

Genesis 3 also makes another veiled reference to the Goddess. The fig tree was another manifestation of her. When Adam and Eve had eaten the forbidden fruit and become self-aware, they made aprons of fig leaves to hide their nakedness, meaning that sexual behavior in Goddess-dominated-culture was depraved. The surface intent of this was to justify the new sexual mores in Warrior God society, but the actual intent was to be able to prove paternity as now property was to pass through the male rather than the female line.

Genesis 3 also highlights Stage III's Warrior God's contention that the Goddess and all women are to blame for all the suffering in life. The whole context of Stage III religion means that it was no accident that Eve is made the culprit who is responsible for the ending of the idyllic sojourn in the Garden by Adam and herself.

The invasion of North America by European nations, starting in the 16th century, is instructive of what happened during the centuries the Indo-Europeans and the Semites carried out their God-ordained, manifest destiny in the Near to Far East. When the European nations began their territorial expansion into North America, the level of consciousness/self-awareness of the indigenous tribes was incomparably higher than that of the invaders. In the 500 years of European occupation, there have been deliberate policies of genocide, of ethnic cleansing and of the destruction of the Indian way of life. These policies have been so effective that, while many Native Americans pride themselves on their heritage, only a handful continue to exhibit those characteristics of consciousness that defined their ancestors. The rest have devolved to Stage III, the level of the invaders and their descendants. Tribal life, as it once was, has been totally destroyed and, as a consequence, Native Americans exhibit, even to a higher degree than the general population, all the physical, mental and emotional illnesses of Stage III self-awareness.

In the Near to Far East, basically the same thing happened as did later in North America. When the Israelites invaded Canaan, we are told of the wholesale slaughter of entire populations and of the destruction of places of worship of the Goddess and of any representations of her. In addition, since Yahweh was not the only Warrior God, only the most powerful according to the Israelites, the same treatment was meted out to the followers of these deities. The Israelites' identification of what they coveted with the will of Yahweh, their Warrior God, is the perfect mirror of what I have described earlier that a child does in this Stage of the development of self-awareness. He convinces his parents that what he wants is what they want for him, and he uses every source of power at his disposal to dominate his parents to make sure he gets what he wants.

To sum up, this period and area of human history was one of ever-increasing chaos and suffering. We can sense the depth of it in the personal laments and confessions of sinfulness in the writings left behind by various rulers of the time. The prophets of Israel describe it in vivid detail.

Reflections on the Role of the Cognizance of a Sub-Self-Awareness on Creation Beliefs

It is the cognizance of a sub-self-awareness by self-awareness that is responsible for the shifts in the creation beliefs of the Indo-Europeans. Self-awareness considered the sub-self-awareness to be the dark, shadowy subconscious half of itself. In reality, remember as I've stated elsewhere, the sub-self-awareness is the suppressed consciousness-in-pain. What brings about the cognizance of the sub-self-awareness is a significant enough jump in the level of primal pain so that self-awareness now becomes aware that behind it is a chaotic, suffering, shadowy, dark side of itself. And, in keeping with its nature, self-awareness now posits its sub-self-awareness as having its beginning at the time of creation as well as its own beginnings.

It must be remembered also that self-awareness comes about as the organism's automatic response to intolerable primal pain in order to preserve the viability of the organism. Up until the middle of Stage III, self-awareness has been able to suppress all knowledge of the chaos and suffering that lies behind it and that has caused self-awareness to come into being. Now it can no longer do so.

Since our inner and outer worlds mirror each other, cognizance of a sub-self-awareness had an immediate effect on self-awareness's conception of the cosmos. Before that cognizance, the cosmos was two-tiered: this world and the upperworld. Afterwards, the cosmos was three-tiered, an underworld having been added. The underworld is not to be confused with the primordial, watery deep, which reappears in Indo-European creation beliefs after their invasions of the Mother Goddess cultures are underway. The underworld is the place of the dead and receives full treatment in Part III, Chapter 9. When cognizance of a sub-self-awareness came about in Stage III, there must have been some recognition that the underworld was part of the cosmos, but I find no mention of it in the creation beliefs. At that time, the underworld was simply a place of eternal suffering. Later on, it became associated with a demonized Goddess. Still later, the sub-self-awareness became associated with the feminine, mothers being blamed for the existence of all the chaos and suffering of self-awareness and of the sub-self-awareness.

That the chaotic, suffering sub-self-awareness is assumed to go back to birth, just as does self-awareness, and that chaos is now posited back to the primordial watery deep, suggests an escalation of chaos in the entire process of conception, gestation and birth. Because of a shift in the level of primal pain, even more so than ever before, the first experience of a newly fertilized egg is that of being in an environment of chaos. Women now have so much primal pain that is leaking through self-awareness that it causes much stress and suffering. Since primal pain is pervasive, even the amniotic fluid that surrounds the fetus is in a state of turmoil. This also is a mirror image of the turmoil of the primordial, watery deep.

That the Marduk/Tiamat battle ends in the death of Tiamat and from her body the cosmos is formed suggests that the birth of a baby is now a life-or-death struggle. Because of primal pain, something has gone so seriously wrong with women that giving birth is no longer something that happens naturally. Babies are now born out of chaos, and perhaps Tiamat's death is suggestive that many more women are dying in childbirth. Genesis 3:16, which was written during the Warrior God Stage of Judaism, says that as a consequence of disobedience women will have greatly multiplied pain in childbirth.

Reflections on the Role of Marduk/Tiamat on Creation Traditions

The life-and-death struggle of Marduk and Tiamat suggests several things with regard to big jumps in primal pain levels. The first has to do with dualities in general. Marduk and Tiamat reveal that all dualities have now become more pronounced.

Specifically, Marduk and Tiamat indicate a greater split in the Mind/Matter duality. Up until this time, all deities were equally and reciprocally manifestations of mind (self) and matter. Now in Stage III Indo-European religion, the storm/warrior/thunder/mountain/sky god begins his transmutation into a deity who completely transcends Matter and is pure Mind. (The transmutation ends in Stage IV, for example, with the Christian God becoming wholly other.) At the same time, Tiamat in particular and the Mother Goddess in general are more firmly tied down to Matter, not just to this world but emphatically to the primordial deep and to the underworld.

What happened in the cosmic big picture in the Mind/Matter duality was mirrored on the personal level with unconscious self-awareness and the body. The denial and suppression of need that is at the core of Stage III means that self-awareness is simultaneously withdrawing from the body and its emotions, pain in particular. But in Stage III, it never fully withdraws from the body. As long as self-awareness feels it is capable of solving the problem of suffering, it sees no need for self-awareness itself to be transcended and be replaced with a supra-self-awareness that is wholly other.

Marduk and Tiamat reveal further that unconscious self-awareness now withdraws its identification with the Goddess and places it with the Sky God of Indo-European religion. The body is now identified with the Goddess. The seed is now planted to mature later in the belief that Matter is feminine and Mind is masculine.

Another indication of a significant increase in primal pain is that Marduk and Tiamat now represent Good and Evil writ large. Unconscious self-awareness now recognizes that it has a sub-self-awareness that is demonic and dark in its nature. In reality, the suppressed side is none other than consciousness, chaotic with primal pain.

The struggle between Tiamat (representing Chaos and Evil) and Marduk (representing Order and Good) is a continuing one. They engage in a never-ending cosmic battle. Tiamat struggles to bring about Chaos and spread Evil, while Marduk fights to preserve Order and bring about Good. For the first time, with Tiamat as a flying dragon, we have Evil risen to cosmic proportions.

Two of the versions of the Marduk/Tiamat story of origins exhibit an increase in primal pain from the earlier to the later version. In the earlier version, it is from Marduk's blood and from dirt that humanity is created. In this version, humanity is deemed to be good. In the later version, humanity is created from the blood of a depraved deity and so is depraved from the outset. I believe the mirror image of this is that primal pain has risen to such an extent that even young children are now beginning to exhibit the neurotic effects of primal pain.

In addition, the Marduk/Tiamat story dramatizes the passing of a period in which women were the equal or the superior of men. Matriarchy and matrilineality give way to patriarchy and to patrilineality. Femaleness is denigrated. Women are subjugated and treated as property. It is a sign of a greater split between the male/female duality and a higher level of primal pain. Now a wife goes to live with her husband's family, rather than he going to live with hers. From being able to draw upon the power of her own mother and grandmother, she comes under the power of her mother-in-law.

Reflections on the Role of Chaos and Order on Creation Traditions

As in Stage I, so in Stage III, self-awareness recognizes that it represents order, but with a difference. In Stage I, self-awareness is so successful at maintaining order in its inner world that it posits order in its outer world. In Stage III when cognizance of a chaotic sub-self-awareness takes place, a number of things happen, one of which is the positing of an underworld. A second happening is the realization by self-awareness that it had to come about to create order out of an internal chaos in order to retain the viability of the organism. A third happening occurs in the character of creation: The primordial, watery deep is in a state of chaos. Creation is now the making of order out of disorder, of structure out of chaos, of harmony out of disharmony, just as self-awareness brings order out of the chaos of the sub-self-awareness. A fourth happening is the positing of the sub-self-awareness to be present at birth, and that is because self-awareness posits itself as coming into being at birth.

There is a point in Stage III when the Mother Goddess is demonized and relegated to the primordial deep, where she becomes synonymous with chaos. An old Egyptian tradition exemplifies a variation of her demonization. Maat, a female, venomous viper, symbolized the order of the cosmos. As long as the king lived, she maintained order, but when he died, she was likely to escape and then chaos would return. The viper Goddess had to be kept under control.

Unconscious self-awareness feels that the order of the cosmos is constantly being threatened by the primordial chaos in the person of the Goddess breaking through and shattering the cosmos. Primally, this makes sense. When self-awareness is threatened by an upsurge of primal pain that could overwhelm it, the sensation is that the threat comes from behind self-awareness in the sub-self-awareness. Self-awareness is unaware, however, that the source of the threat to its existence actually comes from a suppressed, primal-pain-laden consciousness that exerts pressure to break through self-awareness.

Deep primals confirm what unconscious self-awareness fears. In primals in which the final vestiges of self-awareness are about to be blown away, the experience is one of being terrified that one is losing one's mind and will never get it back. It is this threat of losing one's orderly mind due to exploding primal pain that is responsible for self-awareness's terror of an overwhelming chaos that will sweep it away and for its doing anything it can to hang on to itself. It is this threat that is primarily responsible for the mirror experience of self-awareness that chaos lies behind the cosmos.

Reflections on the Historical and Primal Bases for the Blaming of Mothers and of the Mother Goddess for All of Humanity's Suffering and for the Demonization of the Goddess

Up to this point, I've consistently stated that children always blame themselves for their suffering when their needs are not met. I've said that they must do so for, if parents are to blame, children are without hope that their needs will be met. I've also consistently maintained that throughout Stages I and II it was disobedience of the Supreme Deity that brought suffering upon the people and that they had only themselves to blame for it. Up until the later phases of Stage II, neither men nor women blamed the other for the suffering they endured in life. Therefore, some historical and primal explanations are necessary to account for the blaming of mothers, women in general, the feminine and the Mother Goddess for humanity's suffering and for the demonization of the Goddess. The explanations take note that this is the only time in the history of our ancestors that children and the people did not blame themselves for their suffering.

Historically, when our ancestors moved from Stage I to Stage II of religion and of unconscious self-awareness, a female deity was elevated to be the Mother Goddess. At the same time, Stage I's motif of placation was replaced by Stage II's motif of reimmersion. Mothers and the Mother Goddess were given the primary responsibility for nurture. In time, primal pain rose to such an extent that reimmersion into mother and into the Mother Goddess began to be ineffective to mitigate suffering due to needs not being met. Reimmersion became less and less able to suppress emotional pain laid down in the emotional/sexual brain.

It was that lack of effectiveness and ability of reimmersion to mitigate suffering and to suppress pain that brought about a Stage III degree of unconscious self-awareness. That higher degree of unconsciousness, located in the left-lobe thinking brain, found it necessary to cut itself off from the emotional/sexual brain. That was the physical counterpoint to blaming the emotions, mothers and the Mother Goddess for all of humanity's suffering and for demonizing her. Since mothers and the Mother Goddess were given the responsibility for nurture, they were held accountable for their failures and blamed for continued suffering. It was reimmersion into mother that brought about reimmersion into the Mother Goddess. The less reimmersion worked, therefore, the more mothers, women and the Mother Goddess became scapegoats.

As primal pain continued to increase, as reimmersion was less and less resorted to, the Mother Goddess began to fade away. As needs were more and more denied and the use of power to satisfy wants and to overcome feelings of helplessness increased, the Warrior God came more and more into focus. The Mother Goddess disappeared. With her gone, children and the people could only blame themselves for suffering, while they placed their hope in fathers, in the Warrior God and in the use of power to satisfy want and to compensate for feelings of helplessness.

At the point in Stage III when cognizance of a sub-self-awareness came about, it was recognized that both men and women had a dark side. In keeping with placing blame, however, men blamed the presence of their own dark side upon women. In men, their light side-self-awareness-was deemed to predominate over their dark side—the sub-self-awareness. In women, the dark side was deemed to predominate.

The light, self-awareness side of women was denigrated as well. The light side of a woman was seductive, drawing a man close. Then she would turn and tear him apart. The greater physical strength of men, plus a culture of male domination, allowed men to demonize both the light, tempting side and the dark, rejecting side of women. Women had no choice but to do likewise to themselves.

The ultimate basis for demonizing the Goddess—for characterizing her as a sexual temptress who will seduce you and then turn on you and rend you—is the child's experience of his mother's tenderly pulling him close and then angrily pushing him away. The reason a mother does this is because of her primal pain. She believes she draws her child to her out of love. Actually, it is because of her suppressed infantile need to be wanted. Once she begins to feel her child's need to be wanted, she gets opened up to her own unmet childhood need to be wanted, can't handle it and reacts angrily to her child just as her own mother did with her.

Although a comparable scenario can be pictured for fathers, it did not happen. One reason is that while girls always remained in the company of women, when boys reached the age when they were to become men, the men took over their training. Daughters grew up to emulate the pull-push characteristics of women with men and with their children. Sons grew up to squelch their feelings and to experience women as being two-sided.

The fierce warrior was lionized as the best model for a father. The fact that in order to be a successful warrior one had to become inured to pain, and so unable to feel a child's pain, was not demonized or looked upon as a source of suffering for children. Being impervious to pain was manly and good for boys.

Another reason the Mother Goddess was demonized while the Warrior God was raised on high is that women went along with their own subjugation and demonization. They, as well as their brothers, blamed their mothers for all the chaos and suffering in life. So, by late Stage III, in religion, in the social order and in the family, we have firmly in place a culture in which everything female is demonized, denigrated and damned by everything that is male.

Attribute Chart

Male	Female
Life	Death
Growth	Decay
Day	Night
Sun	Moon
Invisible	Visible
Sky (not always)	Earth
Moral	Immoral
Order	Disorder
Rational	Emotional
Good	Evil
Ruler	Ruled

Supra-natural Religion

Stage IV: The Transcendent Deity

At different times and in different places, from the Near East to the Far East in the 1st millennium BCE, the lid of the pressure cooker of primal pain blew off. A jump took place in the devolution of consciousness into unconscious self-awareness that was unlike any previous one. The evidence for this radical break with the past lies, for example, in the emergence of Christianity out of Judaism and of Buddhism out of Hinduism. In the jump from Stage III to Stage IV in religion, there was an epoch-breaking shift from Natural Religion to Supra-natural Religion. From the immanence of deities to the transcendence of deities. From the immanent state of self-awareness to the transcendent state of a supra-self-awareness. From a self-awareness that had faith in and relied upon its own ability to mitigate suffering to a Supra-self-awareness that experienced self-awareness as being inseparable from suffering and that practiced transcendence from self-awareness as the only way to become separate from suffering. There was a realization that the innocence of human nature in the Paradisal Period had devolved into a jaded unconscious self-awareness that was unaware of its condition unless it experienced conversion or enlightenment.

In the Near East in Christianity, the inability of self-awareness to save itself was experienced as the self being in a state of sinfulness from which it could not escape. Every thought, every word, every action and every emotion—in other words, the whole person—was permeated with sinfulness. The self, therefore, was powerless to do anything effective to end its state of sinfulness, to please God, and so to end suffering. In the Far East in Buddhism, there was the same experience of the self. The condition from which self-awareness could not extricate itself was a state of desire.

Although Christianity and Buddhism give different names—sinfulness or desire—to how the converted or enlightened Supra-self-awareness experiences unconscious self-awareness, they mean the same thing. It is a state of being in which a lust for power and insatiable, infinite wants have taken control of self-awareness.

This new view of the self as being powerless to save itself means that by the 1st millennium BCE neither placation nor reimmersion nor power remained effective in mitigating suffering. Christianity and Buddhism reveal a radical new solution to the problem of suffering of which self-awareness is a prisoner. Their answer is that at the same time one must systematically and incrementally transcend the state of sinfulness or desire and embrace the characteristics of the Mind of Christ or of the Mind of Buddha. One does so by practicing the presence of Christ or of Buddha. That is, one seeks from moment to moment to have one's awareness include either Christ or Buddha looking down upon one with perfect love. Insofar as one is successful in maintaining an awareness of the perfect love, one is enabled to act as one who is free from the bondage to sinfulness or desire. The goal is never to be without the presence of Christ or Buddha in one's life and thus be free of suffering, which is the consequence of sinfulness or desire. This experience is that in which one feels one is incrementally transcending the body-bound chaos of self-awareness and being taken over by the mind-bound orderliness of the Mind of Christ or of the Mind of Buddha.

The process of the transcending of self-awareness into either the Mind of Christ or of Buddha, however, has proven to be an exceedingly difficult one. Very few have even had the kind of conversion or enlightenment experience that would let one know that one's unconscious self-awareness is totally unable to save itself from a condition of sinfulness or desire. Of those that have, many have been fooled into thinking that they had achieved the goal after just one such experience and aborted the gestation of their newly formed Mind of Christ as soon as it was conceived. Many others have wearied of the task and abandoned the effort someplace along the way toward full Christlikeness or Buddhalikeness. Accordingly, even among those who call themselves Christians or Buddhists, suffering has continued and is an even greater burden today than it was 2,000 years ago.

Up to this point in discussing the radical shift from the Third to the Fourth Stage in religion, I've covered the problem of suffering for unconscious self-awareness and the religious solution to the problem. Now I turn to the equally revolutionary concepts of the nature of the Supreme Deity, of the origin of the cosmos and of the nature of self-awareness.

In Stages I and III, there was a Supreme Transformer Deity (as Mind) who coexisted with Matter (the watery deep). There was equilibrium in the Mind/

Matter duality. This was mirrored in the experience of self-awareness (mind) which felt that it had always co-existed with the body (matter). In the second Stage, both the co-existence and the equilibrium of the Mind/Matter duality were maintained in the Mother Goddess who was both Mind and Matter. This, too, was mirrored in the experience of self-awareness as being both mind and body—equally.

Stage IV breaks the pattern of equal co-existence in the Mind/Matter duality. In the Far East, in Buddhism, Mind is all that exists. Matter is an illusion, a delusion of self-awareness. In the Near East, in a later phase of Judaism and in Christianity, God as Mind exists prior to Matter and creates Matter ex nihilo, that is, out of nothing. Recall that I believe that when Genesis 1:1, 2 was first written it was intended to be read: "When God began to create the heavens and the earth, the earth was without form and void, and darkness was upon the face of the deep; and the wind of God was moving over the face of the waters." This reading reflects the earlier view of the equal coexistence of Mind and Matter.

The Jewish and Christian view is expressed in the alternative way in which scholars say Genesis 1:1 may be read. The Revised Standard Version translates it: "In the beginning God created the heavens and the earth." This means that there was an actual beginning to matter. God created the formless, watery deep and from it fashioned the cosmos. Late Judaism and Christianity accordingly reflect the next stage in the devolution of consciousness into unconscious self-awareness: the split between Mind and Matter and between self and body.

As I've fully discussed in other chapters, unconscious self-awareness, by its very nature, is dualistic. It is impossible for it to have any conceptions that are not dualistic. It does seek oneness, but it achieves it by denying one side or the other of its dualistic nature. Hence, from its first formation millennia ago, it has always thought of itself as being immortal. That is, it has always distinguished itself from the body, which is mortal. Self-awareness has always said to itself, "I am not the body." (Except in the modern period when the mind/matter duality is also solved by self-awareness saying that the mind or self is a function of matter or of the body.) The statement "I am not the body," however, did not mean that self-awareness had no ties to the body. It did have ties (see Chapter 9, The Destiny of the Dead). What was new in the radical shift in the 1st millennium BCE was self-awareness saying, "I am not the body *and* I have no ties to the body." This conception of itself mirrored the new and radical conception of God as existing entirely apart from matter and creating it ex nihilo.

These new conceptions of self-awareness of itself and of the Supreme Deity have a foundation in what happens in humans when the level of primal pain jumps to a particular, critical level. These conceptions reveal that by the 1st millennium BCE primal pain had become so severe that nothing in any of the earlier religions was sufficient to end suffering. Neither placation nor reimmersion nor power worked anymore, either in religion or for children.

Children had reached the point where they could not remain connected to their parents because of the amount of primal pain they were causing. Parents were now so damaged by primal pain and, therefore, so incapable of meeting their children's needs that children, in desperation, began to build walls around themselves. Then nothing the parents could do would be felt. The feeling is: "Nothing works. I have to shut off to all pain." It is in the process of building this wall that one can actually observe oneself being hurt and yet not feel a thing.

It takes time, however, to construct an impenetrable wall. Children will continue to feel the pain of unmet needs and have to learn through experience how to perfect their defensive wall. If successful, even the cognizance of pain will be suppressed. The attempt to build this wall is truly a desperate one because it is exceedingly difficult to cut off all pain and experience complete surcease from suffering. Very, very few children or adults ever reach this point. Even those practicing some method of transcending self-awareness fall short of their goal.

This portion of the discussion of the primal foundation for what took place in religion in the 1st millennium BCE brings me back to Christianity and to Buddhism. Respectively, these religions were outgrowths of Judaism and Hinduism because neither of them was working effectively to end suffering. Also, Christianity and Buddhism were the natural religious extension an adult would make from children building a wall around themselves. The incremental achievement of attaining the Mind of either Christ or of Buddha is the use of religion to build a wall to separate oneself from a self-awareness that cannot save itself. It is nothing other than taking to the adult, religious level the child's feeling of "Nothing works. I have to cut myself off from myself completely."

To make the connection more secure of the primal foundation for the religious goal of Christlikeness or Buddhalikeness, I'll compare being in a state of primal pain with the conception of being either in a state of sinfulness or of desire. Primal pain is something that affects the entire organism. Primal pain is suppressed into the subconscious as are the unmet infantile needs that give rise to the pain. The pain and unmet needs unendingly drive every thought, every word, every emotion and every deed to satisfy those needs, which have resurfaced as wants. It is in the futile attempt to satisfy those insatiable wants that gives rise to all of our suffering. The Christian conception of sinfulness and the Buddhist conception of desire in the inner world are parallels of the primal foundation in the inner world that it is our vain attempts to use power to fulfill wants that cause all suffering.

The parallel does not extend to what is achieved by primaling one's pain with what is achieved by attaining the Mind of Christ or the Buddha Mind. They incrementally insulate one from self-awareness. That is, they perfect one's defenses against one's primal pain. Primaling goes into the wants of self-awareness and then through them to the pain of the unmet infantile needs below them. By incrementally feeling that pain and releasing it from the organism, primaling restores the consciousness of childhood. In other words, religion aids in the devolution of consciousness into unconscious self-awareness, while primaling aids in the reversing of unconscious self-awareness into consciousness.

In Judaism in the latter part of the 1st millennium BCE and in Christianity, the twin aspects of God as being the only God—monotheism—and his creating the cosmos ex nihilo have their foundation, as well, in self-awareness's reaction to a certain critical level of primal pain. In its previous Stage (Stage III), self-awareness still feels itself to be body-bound. Its defenses to end suffering, therefore, are mainly physical ones. In Stage IV, self-awareness feels it can no longer remain bound to the body, which is the source of its suffering, and crosses over a line to where its defenses are mainly mental ones. It is a deliberate effort on the part of self-awareness to complete the process of severing itself from the body in order to experience surcease from suffering.

Unconscious self-awareness will claim that it is immortal, but that claim is more a statement of a goal rather than a status achieved. Insofar as connections to the body are intact, self-awareness will continue to experience the signs of mortality: pain, suffering and chaos. However, insofar as it is successful in disconnecting itself from the body, it will experience itself as a free-floating self who can't be hurt and who can look down with equanimity upon its old suffering self.

It is the free-floating aspect that gives rise to self-awareness's conception of a wholly other, monotheistic God. By divesting itself of all connections, self-awareness is now in splendid isolation. It is alone and master of itself. It is this experience of itself that gives rise to the mirror experience of the one God creating the cosmos out of nothing.

Summary

In this chapter on what religious beliefs regarding the origin of the cosmos reveal about the devolution of consciousness into self-awareness, I've dealt extensively with the epoch-making shifts that took place over the millennia in both the outer and inner worlds. My goal was to reveal the connection between these religious ideas and the stages in the development of unconscious self-awareness.

"Okay. But so what? What does all of this have to do with me?" you might be asking. "So what that the first self-aware humans thought of God as coexisting with matter and now God is thought of as existing prior to and creating matter. So what that as a pre-self-aware child I did not have an inner world separate from an outer world, that I had but little conception of time and that I experienced my stuffed animals as alive and as my friends." What this all has to do with you and with me is that it shows that the history of our conception of the world out there mirrors our hidden history of being ever more isolated in here from our real selves, from all others and from what is really an alive universe. Whether it be the ancient history of our past as humans or the ancient history of yours or my childhood, the relevance of them for the present is there for those who have the ears to hear and the eyes to see.

CHAPTER 8

RELIGIOUS RITUALS SUSTAINING THE COSMOS

In the previous chapter, I indicated that I felt the earliest traditions of the origin of the cosmos posited a calm, formless, watery deep as a given. Because the watery deep was calm, I suggested that self-awareness as a defense system in the first stage of its development was able to suppress any knowledge of the chaotic subconsciousness-in-pain that lay below it.

All of the rituals of which I have knowledge presuppose a chaotic, formless, watery deep. This suggests that in Stage III later traditions have either adapted earlier rituals to be in accordance with current understandings or supplanted earlier ones. This also suggests that a chaotic watery deep means that self-awareness is aware that underneath it is a chaotic sub-self-awareness.

The rituals reveal that the cosmos is always in a state of disintegration, however slowly or speedily, toward a return to chaos. There was a very genuine fear that if the rituals were not performed or not performed correctly that indeed total, original chaos would return, engulfing everything and everyone.

The basis for this religious conception is to be found in the marvelous way in which the human organism is always moving toward resolving primal pain. I've discussed this elsewhere, but it bears repeating here. Primal pain is always exerting upward pressure to break through unconscious self-awareness to be experienced in a primal and, thus, be resolved out of the organism, returning the organism to consciousness. Self-awareness, as a defense system holding back upsurging primal pain, is never perfect. This permits some pain to leak through, which is then experienced as some form of suffering. For the primal person, this suffering is the avenue back to the primal pain behind it, and so to restored consciousness. For nonprimal self-awareness, however, this suffering, as its gets worse, threatens to overwhelm self-awareness and engulf it in a state of chaos in which the self is lost completely. Self-awareness, then, as the mirror image of the cosmos, is always disintegrating toward chaos.

The pressure cooker provides a good analogy for the dynamics of what the organism does with primal pain and why self-awareness has a continuing fear of chaos and of nonbeing. Just as the air pressure in a pressure cooker continues to rise, so primal pain continues to exert ever greater upward pressure, threatening to blow off the lid of self-awareness, causing an explosion of pent-up primal pain that disintegrates self-awareness into nonbeing.

Also, just as in a pressure cooker, some steam is allowed to escape, so a varying amount of primal pain rises into self-awareness. This causes self-awareness to be in a state of constantly adjusting the screws of repression to keep itself from exploding into nothingness.

The analogy also serves as a mirror for what happens on the cosmic level. Initial chaos continues to exert ever greater pressure on the order of the cosmos, threatening to blow it away, enabling the primordial chaos to reestablish itself. So, just as the sole function of self-awareness in the inner world is to maintain its own stability to preserve order, so the sole function of the structure of life in the outer world, with the cooperation of the deities, is to maintain its own stability to preserve the cosmos and everything in it from disintegrating into chaos.

What we find, in fact, in ancient societies is that all of daily life throughout the whole year is a ritual observance of what is required by the Supreme Transformer Deity to maintain order in the cosmos. There is a divinely ordered way to do everything. The correct way of doing things is initiated by subordinate deities and carried out for the first time by mythical ancestors or heroes. From then on, the correct ways were passed on from generation to generation by means of oral traditions. Writing was invented about 3500 BCE At first, writing was used to record things like the amounts of stored grain. By 2000 BCE though, the preserved writings of royalty reveal the deplorable state into which humanity has fallen. Some of them are quite moving lamentations on the human condition.

Another way of saying that all of daily life is a ritual observance is that there is no separation between religion and life. Likewise, there is no separation between unconscious self-awareness and the suppression of primal pain. The main function of self-awareness is to preserve the viability of the organism from the chaos of an overwhelming amount of primal pain. The main function of religion is to preserve the viability of the ordered cosmos from an overwhelming amount of primordial chaos. As an example, in Egypt the pharaoh was the incarnation of order, so his day-by-day ritualistic observance of the proper way life was to be lived was his main function.

Another example comes from the Indo-Europeans. The priest's responsibility was the maintenance of the cosmos, which required technically perfect ritual sacrifice. If the rituals were flawed, the cosmos was in danger of disintegrating into original chaos.

Whether it be the Egyptians or the Indo-Europeans or wherever this type of ritual took place, it reflects what must have been true for children. They had to be technically perfect in performing what their parents demanded of them or risk having their worlds fall apart because of parental wrath. And, just as it was true that the cosmos and the lives of children kept falling apart, so it was true that the performance of the rituals and childhood behavior was never enough nor was it good enough.

These ancient ways worked well to preserve order. Unconscious self-awareness still retained much of the characteristics of consciousness. While self-awareness, by its very nature, could not be totally interconnected with the cosmos; nevertheless, the ancient ways showed a profound respect for the welfare of all creatures and for the deities of whom all aspects of the cosmos were their manifestations.

Yet, there was always the threat of a return to chaos. As I've stated earlier, the blame for suffering and chaos was placed upon the people's neglect of proper ritual observance. It was their disobedience that brought calamity upon themselves. In addition, disobedience could include the breaking of a taboo or the entering into a forbidden zone. Also, in later times when primal pain had risen to such an extent as to preclude a satisfactory self-awareness from being formed, some persons were dominated by the darker side of a sub-self-awareness. They were thought to have practiced black magic, bringing suffering into the community.

The annual return to the beginning of the Golden Age in the New Year rituals is made possible by the people's acknowledging their disobedience, by their accepting blame for the ensuing chaos, and by their placating and replenishing their deities through sacrifices. This is mirrored by the self-aware child. His periodic return to the more or less satisfactory status existing after the onset of self-awareness is made possible by his acknowledgement of his disobedience, of his acceptance of blame for his own chaos and his placation of his parents through the sacrifice of some portion of himself.

Every ancient people experienced their particular location as being at the center of the cosmos. The night sky circling overhead gave visual evidence of this. Some oral traditions made reference to the polar axis and to the location of the people on that axis. In the northern hemisphere, the North Star's alignment with the polar axis was a powerful influence on the experience of being at the center of the cosmos. But regardless of where on the planet a people is located, their line of longitude is always in the same plane as the polar axis, giving rise to the experience of being at the center. This is mirrored by the experience of self-awareness, of being centered.

Self-awareness feels itself to be at the center when it is perfectly ordered. Indeed, as I've stated elsewhere, the sense of where the self is located in the body is always along the midline of the body, whether it be low down in the gut, in the heart, between the eyes, or on the top of the head.

The center is where order is experienced. Hence, all the rituals that bring order out of chaos center the self and consecrate the specific location of the people as the center of the cosmos.

What the self feels internally and what it sees happening externally due to the subconscious effects of primal pain is that it is being pulled off-center in a thousand different directions. The chaos of being pulled apart into nonbeing that self-awareness experiences is in reality a chaotic consciousness-in-pain who is diffused throughout the organism and who is threatened with nonbeing because the pain of unfulfilled needs is intolerable. It is interesting to note that while unconscious self-awareness considers itself to be immortal, when there is sufficient stress, it always panics at the thought of nonbeing.

In consciousness, order is not centered, as in unconscious self-awareness, but is diffused equally throughout the whole person. It is only because of primal pain that order is centered in self-awareness and why self-awareness fears disorder and nonbeing.

The self's fear of disintegration into nonbeing is mirrored in its fear of the disintegration of the subordinate deities into nonbeing, whose manifestations, in total, make up the cosmos. The people's disobedience to proper ritual observance causes both the internal and external disintegration into chaotic nonbeing.

There are two main types of periodic ceremonies. The first is the annual expulsion of demons, diseases and sinfulness. The second is the New Year rites that recreate the cosmos.

Demons, diseases and sinfulness had to be expelled. They were not going to leave of their own accord. The basis for this lies in the fact that primal pain remains in the system until it is expelled through a primal. And, although it is not apparent to self-awareness, the debilitating effects of primal pain on the organism are responsible for what self-awareness calls demons, diseases and sinfulness.

While the rituals of expulsion have nothing to do with the rituals that sustain the universe, they are part of the same process to restore conditions as they were at the beginning of the Golden Age—at least during the earliest stage of these rituals. At such time as it was recognized that self-awareness could not get back to the way it was at the beginning of the Golden Age, current rituals could only restore it or the cosmos to the way things were at the beginning of the current Age. Any ceremony having to do with the initial creation of the cosmos became merely commemorative.

In this regard, what I have found is that the human and cosmic conditions worsened for an indeterminate length of time from cycle to cycle, without getting so bad as to make it impossible to get back to the beginning of the Golden Age. Then, at some point, the level of primal pain reached a certain critical point at which it became impossible to return to the way things were at the beginning of self-awareness. Some degree of the characteristics of consciousness were lost permanently. This was then mirrored in the outer world: The Golden Age and the initial creation were relegated to mythical or dream time.

I want to emphasize that the rituals of expulsion of demons, diseases and sinfulness are not simply rites of purification. Participation in these rituals incorporated the added dimension of a rebirth, a new creation. As such, they have a symbolic resemblance to primals. In primals I have always felt that I was reborn: I was a new creation.

Some historians of this period have claimed that these two types of periodic ceremonies abolished space and time, in that they represented a return to the initial transformation of chaos into order. My experience tells me that this is not possible—except in a primal. Unconscious self-awareness forms because consciousness is in such pain as to be in a life-or-death situation. Therefore, self-awareness cannot return to that original condition. As long as a child can forgive and forget, he can get back to the way things were when self-awareness formed, but he can't go beyond that into consciousness. So, in the outer world, what actually happens in the rituals is the abolishment of suffering and chaos, which is the equivalent of forgetting and forgiving. Space and time come into existence with the transformation of chaos into order and remain in existence within the context of cycles and irreversibility.

Crucial to self-awareness as part of its defense holding back primal pain is the element of hopefulness that the struggle to get one's needs met will be successful. As long as hope can be maintained that the struggle will be successful, primal pain can be kept at bay. As a primal person, one learns as quickly as one can how to set aside hope and struggle so that one's primal pain can be felt and resolved.

Hope and struggle, therefore, play a large part in these periodic ceremonies. Basic to them is the hope that this time I and the community will be and do better, thus ensuring that the deities will take good care of us.

When cyclical time was dominant, hope for a new creation was always centered on a return to the Golden Age. When linear time became dominant, hope for a new creation was placed at the end of time. The transferring of the hope from the beginning of time to the end of time took place incrementally as primal pain increased in discrete stages.

The final point to be made in this general discussion of the rituals has to do with sacrifices made to the subordinate deities whose physical manifestations comprise the cosmos. In the course of their duties to sustain the cosmos, including providing for the needs of humans, the deities got rundown. They, too, feared disintegration into chaos. In the course of their duties to sustain the cosmos, humans had to see to it that the deities were replenished. It was a reciprocal arrangement.

The basis for this pact with the deities is to be found in the relationship children have with their parents. Just as the deities have needs and fear chaos, so do human parents. In their case, the needs are that their own unmet, suppressed, infantile needs masquerade as insatiable wants or desires. Their children are consequently put in the position of denying or sacrificing their own needs in order to attempt to satisfy the needs of their parents to stave off the parents' fear of chaos.

When children have to deny their own needs, they are really sacrificing themselves in the interest of survival. Incrementally, as primal pain increases, a child must eventually give up all of himself if he has any hope at all that his parents might fulfill his need. An ancient example of this is to be found in present-day Turkey. The New Year festival is one in which the struggle between the Storm God and the Dragon is reenacted. Since time is basically cyclical, the defeat of chaos (which the Dragon represents) must be accomplished annually. In each annual ritual, a human helps but dies in the end. Humans, then, are partners with the gods in maintaining order, but the price is death. This death is a mirror of the death of consciousness in order for the child to survive. The child has to deny himself and become what his parents want him to be in order to be able to carry on. Finally, he goes beyond even that and realizes that nothing he can do can satisfy his parents' infantile need; he is not either their mother or father—the only ones who could have satisfied those needs but did not.

Likewise in the cosmos, over millennia the deities constantly demanded more in the way of sacrificial offerings, the extent of their demands mirroring the extent of the demands of parents upon their children. At first, the ritual sacrifice of plants was enough to placate the deities. Later, it became necessary to sacrifice animals and then ever-greater numbers of animals. This corresponded to the ever-greater sacrifice of themselves that children had to make to placate their parents. Finally, it became necessary to sacrifice humans and, in some cultures, it took the sacrifice of hundreds of humans to placate the deities. Certainly, by this time, children had to give up all of themselves to satisfy their parents. By the 1st millennium BCE, for children, even the sacrifice of themselves was not sufficient to placate their parents, so high had primal pain levels risen. This was reflected in Christianity. According to the Christian Bible, humanity had become so depraved it could not save itself. God had to become the sacrifice in Christ to become placated.

"Okay, but so what? What does all of this have to do with me," you might be asking. Well, if your defenses are in good order, perhaps it doesn't have much to do with you; and that is not a bad thing. But, if your defenses are such that you do sense an underlying chaos, the relevance for you of the history of rituals to sustain the cosmos is obvious.

CHAPTER 9

THE DESTINY OF THE DEAD

The Purpose of This Chapter

What I intend to lay out for you is how religious conceptions of the destiny of the dead reveal how self-awareness has become increasingly unconscious through the millennia. The symptoms of it are seen in the destinies themselves, in the ever-heavier burden of suffering of unconscious self-awareness and in the necessity of self-awareness to cut itself off a little more from the body with each jump in primal pain.

Introduction

At the outset of this discussion on the destiny of the dead, I want to refer again to certain characteristics of consciousness. These will provide a basis for how consciousness experiences death and from what point self-awareness departs in its beliefs regarding the destiny of the dead.

First of all, in consciousness, the tri-level brain is fully integrated. There is complete and open communication among the sensing/survival, the emotional/sexual and the thinking levels, such that there is the experience of but one level. The experience, also, is one in which there is no boundary between an inner world and an outer world. There is the experience of one world, of one consciousness who stretches out in all directions, interconnected, interrelated and integrated with all who is—meaning an all-encompassing consciousness. This means there is no experience of space.

Secondly, in this one world of consciousness, there is no experience of time, neither cyclical nor linear, which is subdivided into past, present and future. There is the experience of the ever-changing, but ever-integrated presentness of the totality of all who is.

In addition, in this one world of consciousness, one knows oneself only in terms of relationships. There is no experience of a separate self, separate from other separate selves or of a self that is experienced distinct from the whole of all who is. The experience of knowing oneself only in terms of relationships ultimately goes back to conception. The fertilized egg knows himself only in relationship to his mother. The umbilical cord fully demonstrates that one cannot tell where the mother ends and the baby begins or vice versa.

Each of us, then, is a unique set of interrelationships who comes into being within the totality of all interrelationships and who goes out of being within that same totality. Life, then, is a particular combination of interrelationships who comes into being and death, then, is the disintegration of a particular combination of interrelationships. In other words, the totality of interrelationships—consciousness—remains a constant but is ever-changing as the countless number of combinations of interrelationships who make up consciousness disintegrate and reintegrate into new, living beings.

Finally, for consciousness, death is real. It is total. There is nothing left over that survives the death of the body. In consciousness, death is accepted as part of the very nature of all who is. Consequently, death is neither fought against nor denied; it is neither hung onto desperately nor thrown away carelessly; it is neither to be lamented nor sought after, unless as the only way out from unbearable pain. Death simply is a fact of life.

Because, in consciousness, interrelationships are everything, it is reasonable to assume that prior to the historical appearance of self-awareness there was veneration of parents, grandparents, elders and ancestors. The accumulated wisdom of living and deceased generations was respected, used and passed on with accretions from the present generation. In the traditions of Native Americans, we can see the vestiges of this intergenerational connectedness.

For all of the period of prehistory, that is, prior to the 4th millennium BCE, only educated guesses can be made about the significance of any artifacts discovered or archeological remains uncovered. The presence of figurines or of phallic symbols do not, of themselves, suggest that self-awareness has taken place. The presence of useful articles in graves does suggest that self-awareness has taken place and that there is belief in an afterlife. Likewise does placing the body in a fetal position or facing it toward the East. Similarly does the presence of shells shaped like a vagina suggest rebirth.

One ancient practice that has produced a number of theories has to do with the treatment of the skulls of the deceased. All of the theories I've read about suggest some form of religion, which, in turn, implies some stage of self-awareness. My guess is that the practice of the decapitation of the dead had to do with veneration and not with anything to do with religious beliefs regarding the immortality of self-awareness. I believe that preserving the skull in a special place was a means to keep fresh the memory of the deceased. In some cases, the forehead was painted red, and the face filled out with clay. To me, this is far more consistent with a simple remembrance of the dead and a veneration of them for their wisdom, rather than some religious cult of the dead. The practice is consistent with consciousness, but not with self-awareness.

Also, whatever use was made of the decapitated skulls, in no way was self-awareness experienced as being in the head. During this stage in our development, if people were conscious, that sense would be diffused equally throughout the organism. Even if they were self-aware, the sense of where it would be located was low down in the gut. It won't be until the 1st millennium BCE that we can establish that the sense of the location of self-awareness was in the head.

At some point during the Paleolithic, the level of primal pain rose to the extent that it became necessary for our ancestors to jump from a state of consciousness to one of self-awareness in order to survive. Perhaps this explains why our Neanderthal cousins did not survive; they were not able to suppress primal pain. Their pain became unmanageable and death was the only way out.

The leap from consciousness to self-awareness represented a shift to the Nth degree in how our ancestors felt about themselves. It wasn't, however, as if the characteristics of consciousness were completely lost at once and replaced at once by those of self-awareness. Each incremental increase in primal pain resulted in a greater takeover of consciousness by self-awareness that was reflected in, among the whole range of characteristics, self-awareness's notions of its own post-mortem destiny. An analogy will help to visualize what began to happen.

In the analogy, imagine a glass of clear, pure water. It represents a conscious child. Now, picture an eyedropper filled with ink above the glass. The dropper represents parents who are so filled with primal pain they cannot fulfill their child's needs. The ink represents primal pain. As the child's needs are not met, the ink of primal pain drips into the child. The ink diffuses throughout the water, and, at first, no change in the color of the water can be detected. But, at some point, a change in color can be seen. That is the point at which self-awareness has occurred. All of the characteristics of consciousness have now been colored by primal pain and self-awareness, but not obliterated; the water is still very clear. As the child's needs continue to go unmet, the ink of primal pain continues to obliterate more and more of consciousness. The water of consciousness is constantly getting darker. In discrete steps, the characteristics of consciousness are being replaced with those of self-awareness. When the child grows up, the ink of primal pain in his life is darker than in his parents, so when he has children, primal pain and self-awareness build up even faster in them. And so on through one millennium after another until, in our own day, there is precious little of consciousness remaining.

The Destiny in Stage I

I move on, then, to an exposition of the destiny of the dead in Stage I of self-awareness and religion. Upon the death of the body, self-awareness fully expects to be reincarnated in a new body. As to why "reincarnation" rather than some other destiny, certain characteristics of the first stage in the formation of self-awareness are determinative of the earliest conceptions of the destiny of the dead. (For a full explanation of the formation of self-awareness, refer back to Part II: The Primal Basis for Various Attributes of Self-Awareness.) These characteristics appear simultaneously along with their religious counterparts. Therefore, the order in which I explore them is not an indication either of their chronological appearance or of their importance.

When self-awareness becomes a permanent psychic experience, it loses any knowledge of the consciousness-in-pain from which it has crystallized. This is so because the very purpose of self-awareness as a defense system is to shield the organism from being conscious of pain too traumatic for the viability of the organism. The result is that self-awareness experiences itself as always having been the psychic experience of the organism. It is in a state of denial.

Another characteristic of this initial stage in the evolution of self-awareness is that the sense of the location of self-awareness is low down in the gut. There is good reason why this is so. The first of the three brain centers to mature is the sensing brain, which monitors all the visceral survival functions of the organism. These are located in the gut. Also, it is in this area of the brain where primal pain is first laid down and defended against. It is natural then that the first preoccupation of self-awareness is with survival, even though it takes a sufficient maturation of the emoting and thinking brain centers as well to allow self-awareness to take place.

A third characteristic of self-awareness is that it experiences life in dualistic terms. This is an inevitable consequence of the severing of connections among the three levels of the brain—in order to suppress primal pain—and of its counterpart, the severing of connections to parents in order to defend against pain. The jump from a conscious state to the state of unconscious self-awareness as the necessary outcome of suppressing pain, therefore, produces a condition in which self-awareness experiences itself as a being separate from everything else. The dualism is expressed in any number of ways: self and other, self and body, mind and matter, inner world of the self and outer world of the other and time and space, for example.

The dualism of self and body leads to the observation by self-awareness in Stage I that, while it has close ties to the body and is never without a body, the body deteriorates with age while self-awareness itself remains the same. The sense of the location of self-awareness in Stage I is low down in the gut, which is evidence that it feels close to the body even though separate from it. By way of comparison, when Stage IV of self-awareness comes about, it feels itself to be located in the head with only tenuous connections to the body.

The dualism of inner and outer worlds is evidence that self-awareness now conceives of itself as a being separate from all others. This sense of separateness lends itself to how self-awareness conceives of its destiny upon the death of the body.

A fourth characteristic of self-awareness is the replacement of the ever-changing present moment of consciousness by a sense of time, which is broken down into cyclical time and linear time, which is broken down further into past, present and future. In Stage I of self-awareness, the preponderate sense of time is cyclical. In the child's relationship with his parents, the child is able to forgive his parents for not meeting his needs in the past, is able to forget past hurts and is able to return to a condition of trust that they will meet his needs in the future. His relationship with them is predominantly cyclical. Likewise, societal relations with the deities is mainly cyclical. The cycles of the moon and sun deities and of the earth deity are basic to the self's experience of life. That life basically is cyclical is quite determinative of the destiny of the dead in Stage I. However, there are some traditions in which reincarnation is into something quite permanent like a rock. This suggests a conception of time more linear in nature.

The combined effect of all these characteristics of self-awareness lead it to conceive of itself as being immortal, but never without a mortal body. The mirror image of this inner world is an outer world of immortal deities who are never without a primordial, watery deep/cosmos. A further effect is that being immortal in a context of cyclical time means that the self is reincarnated every time the body dies—eternally. Finally, the effect is to produce in the external world the religious conception that the ultimate source of self-awareness's experience of its own immortality is the Transformer Deity. Self-awareness is the immortal breath of the Transformer Deity that animates the mortal body, as the breath of the Deity animates the cosmos.

In a somewhat paradoxical sense, the immortality of the deities refers not to a disembodied Spirit but to the permanence of their manifestations, such as the sun, moon, stars, or mountains. When humans long for the immortality of the deities, their reference point is the "bodies" of the deities, it being a given that the self—whether it be human or divine—is not subject to death. Immortality for humans is having a body that is not subject to decay.

Reincarnation is to be thought of as being on a horizontal plane, due to the dualism of inner and outer space. It does appear, in this stage of religion, that there is a two-tiered cosmos: the deities on a higher level and the universe on a lower one. The image is much more of the deities and the universe existing side by side. Both are very intimately connected, and attention is focused on the cosmos as the physical manifestation of the deities. The reflection of the outer world in the inner world of self-awareness is one that suggests, likewise, that the self is intimately connected to the body and attention is focused on it. The suggestion is there that the self is on a higher level than the body, but they act more as if they existed side by side.

Oral traditions reveal much regarding reincarnation. In every case, oral traditions of a Golden Age speak of it as having ended in a past so distant that people of the present time cannot count the intervening generations. No one in his present reincarnation has any direct experience of what life was like in the Golden Age. The traditions also contrast the ideal state of being of the people in the Golden Age with the incremental decline of that ideal state of being during all of the successive Ages down to the present.

With regard to time, the traditions reveal that between successive Ages the sense of time was linear. It is evident from other parts of the traditions that within an Age time was sensed as cyclical. The implication of this dual sense of time for the religious life of the people is that rites of renewal can only get the people back to the state they were in at the beginning of the current Age. The people cannot get back to the more ideal states of previous Ages.

With regard to the destiny of the dead, I conclude that these traditions imply that successive reincarnations are to lives of ever-greater pain and suffering. With each new loss of a portion of the ideal state of being that was characteristic of the Golden Age, there is a new, less ideal set point for the next reincarnation.

These religious, oral traditions mirror what a child experiences when he is born into a familial environment of primal pain. Things will never be as good as they were, and he will have to endure an ever-growing burden of pain and suffering. And, with each incremental increase in primal pain, there is a discrete jump in the loss of the characteristics of consciousness and a corresponding jump in the attributes of an unconscious self-awareness.

In the beginning of Stage I of self-awareness and of religion, there is a neutral attitude toward reincarnation. I surmise that by the end of the stage the attitude toward it might have turned somewhat negative. By that time, placation was not sufficient to mitigate all suffering. In discrete steps, life became successively filled with more suffering. Reincarnation was then into a new life that began with more suffering than did the previous reincarnation.

This indicates that linear time was becoming a bigger part of the experience of self-awareness. The emergence of reimmersion as the focal point of religion signaled the failure of placation to suppress pain and the need for something to fill the breech in the defense system of self-awareness.

At this point I want to clarify the distinction between death and the disintegration of the order of the cosmos back into the disorder of the nothingness of the original primordial state. The distinction is that while there is no fear of death, there is a fear that the ordered cosmos could disintegrate into disordered nothingness.

There is no fear of death because self-awareness experiences itself as being immortal and believes totally that when the present body dies, it will be reincarnated into a new body. There is a fear, however, that if the deities—whose manifestations are the cosmos—are not properly placated, neither the deities nor the cosmos will survive. The deities become depleted in trying to fulfill their duties to maintain the cosmos. Their needs are placated through ritual sacrifice, thus insuring that the cosmos will survive. (See Part III, Chapter 8, on rituals to maintain the cosmos for a complete exposition on this subject.) Placation of the deities, therefore, is necessary for reincarnation to continue.

There is a primal foundation as to why self-awareness does not have a fear of death but does have a fear of the disintegration of the cosmos back into its primordial state of unmanifested nothingness. The formation of self-awareness includes the beginnings of all dualities, which includes that of an immortal self and a mortal body. This duality represents, among other things, a specific defense against the actual threat of death for the infant due to needs not being met. This accounts for why there is no fear of death. Since the formation of self-awareness as a defense system only suppresses, but does not do away with, the pain of needs not being met, the upward pressure of primal pain to become conscious continually threatens self-awareness with disintegration. It is this threat that is mirrored in self-awareness's conception of the cosmos as being continually threatened with disintegration back into the primordial nothingness.

In Stage I of self-awareness there is yet no experience of an underworld to which go either all the dead or only those who are depraved. Also, in this stage, the primordial watery deep is pictured as calm. Together, these two religious conceptions indicate that self-awareness is still successful in defending the organism from any knowledge that underneath self-awareness is a chaotic consciousness-in-pain.

In addition, in Stage I the Transformer Deity is so remote that there is no conception of a heaven as a destination of the dead. With neither an upper nor a lower world, immortality and cyclical time, the destiny of the dead is reincarnation.

The Destiny in Stage II

In Stage II of self-awareness and of religion, the destiny of the dead is still reincarnation, but now it happens within the setting of Mother Goddess religion. No longer does it take place within the context of survival/placation. Now it takes place within the context of the sexual/reimmersion religion of Mother Goddess.

In the new context it is still true that self-awareness has no clue that it is an unconscious defense system shielding the organism from intolerable pain. It still feels it has always been the psychic experience of the organism.

The sense of the location of self-awareness is still low down in the gut, but it is higher up than in Stage I. Again, there is logic as to why. The second of the brain centers to mature is the emotional/sexual. It is in this area of the brain where pain is next laid down and defended against. It is natural that self-awareness's next preoccupation is with the emotions and particularly with the role of sex in Goddess religion.

This sense of the location of self-awareness still being in the gut indicates that the self still has close ties to the body and feels that it is never without a body. The body will die and decay, but the self will always be born again in a new one. Reincarnation is its destiny.

The sense of time in Stage II remains mainly cyclical. That, too, continues to support the belief in reincarnation.

In Stage II, the sense of dualism is strengthened. The alternate forms of the Goddess as Mind and as Matter contributes to the self's sense of personhood as mind and matter, which, in turn, lends itself to reincarnation as a destiny.

As in Stage I, all of these characteristics of self-awareness continue to give it the experience of being immortal. The self is like the Goddess, eternally being experienced as both Spirit and Matter in a side-by-side manner, rather than in a two-tiered cosmos.

Archeologists have uncovered womb-shaped mounds with vulva-like entrances. These structures suggest a prone Goddess. It suggests that Mother Goddess in her manifestation as Earth Mother was lying down, enabling all creatures to live upon her and to suckle from her. Further, there are signs that the mounds were used for worship and for burials. Eternally reentering the womb and reemerging from the womb characterized reincarnation.

The attitude toward reincarnation at the beginning of Stage II went back to neutral as reimmersion into the Goddess filled the gap and was effective in mitigating suffering. As the levels of primal pain increased through the millennia, thus rendering reimmersion ever less effective as a supplement to placation to suppress pain, the same story happened in Stage II as did in Stage I. Reincarnation was into a new life ever-filled with greater suffering. Linear time increased in importance. A negative attitude toward reincarnation returned. The emergence of domination or the use of power to satisfy wants and desires as the centerpiece of religion in the next stage indicated the inability of both placation and reimmersion to mitigate pain and the need to repair the defenses of self-awareness.

There are Sumerian and Akkadian traditions of Innana/Ishtar descending into the underworld—the permanent abode of the dead—to wrest control of it from Ereshkigol, her sister. Since it is my belief that cognizance of a sub-self-awareness and its mirror, the underworld, did not come about until the middle of Stage III, I consider these particular traditions regarding Innana/Ishtar to be Stage III reworkings of Mother Goddess Stage II religion.

The Destiny in Stage III

The epoch-destroying jump from the Mother Goddess religion of Stage II to the Warrior God religion of Stage III signals that the tremendous build-up of primal pain during Stage II has exploded, causing a major shift from consciousness to unconscious self-awareness. With regard to the destiny of the dead, it meant the radical shift from the endless cycle of reincarnation to a final end in the abode of a destination.

While the dominant characteristic of Stage I religion is placation and of Stage II is reimmersion, in Stage III it is power. And, while all three brain levels must be operative for self-awareness to occur, Stage I is centered in the lowest center—the sensing/survival brain; Stage II in the middle center—the emotional/sexual brain; and Stage III is centered in the highest center—the thinking brain. As I've continuously pointed out, there is a direct correspondence between the chronology of the maturation of the brain centers and the chronology of the main themes of the stages in religion. In Stage III the emphasis on power in self-awareness and in religion has a direct bearing on the nature of the afterlife in the destination of the dead.

With the jump from self-awareness being located in the sensing/survival brain to the emotional/sexual brain, access to survival needs is cut off. With the jump from self-awareness being located in the emotional/sexual brain to the thinking brain, access to emotional needs is cut off as well. All basic, infantile need is now effectively suppressed, but it doesn't go away. It stays in the organism, ever-striving for fulfillment. The upward pressure of need now resurfaces in self-awareness in the form of insatiable wants or desires.

The self, now located in the thinking brain, becomes the thinking self. As such, it conceives of every possible means to satisfy its desires. What characterizes the means used is power. The child will use every means of power at his disposal to dominate his parents to get what he wants. He grows up into an adult who endlessly attempts to satisfy insatiable desires, insatiable because they are endlessly driven by the underlying, unmet infantile needs. He continues to use every means of power at his disposal to dominate his situation to get what he wants, including religious rationale. More on this later.

It is this mind-set of always having unmet wants or desires that causes self-awareness to conceive of the afterlife in terms of an absence of want. After exploring some of the other radical changes from Stage II to Stage III, I will come back to the particulars of the absence of want in the destination of the dead.

The radical shift from reincarnation to a destination for the dead signaled the experience of time from being basically cyclical to being mostly linear. During Stages I and II, reincarnation, periodic renewal (cyclical time) and successive Ages (linear time) have as their basis the situation of a child who is ever less able to forgive and to forget and to begin fresh again with his parents. Once there is a destination for the dead, no periodic renewal and only the present Age, there is the underlying basis of a child who has reached a point where he feels that things just get worse, that they never get better and that he can no longer forgive or forget at all. He must shut out all pain. No beginning fresh again at any point means, for the individual, the end of cyclical time and the almost total emphasis upon linear time that is characteristic of Stage III in self-awareness and religion. There is still cyclical time. The annual sacrificial rites to recreate the cosmos from Twin and Ox are cyclical in nature.

The last era-ending change is in the concept of space. When Stage III of religion opens, the concept of space is almost entirely horizontal. By the end of Stage III, space has a vertical dimension that includes an underworld and an upperworld or heaven.

There are five phases in the concept of space in Stage III for the destination of the dead. Each successive destination denotes a discrete jump in the level of primal pain in the general population. In order of their appearance, they are:

(1) Everyone goes to a far-distant horizontal destination.
(2) Everyone goes to the sky.
(3) Everyone goes to the underworld.
(4) The diseased and aged go to the underworld, while those who have died in battle—heroes—go to the upperworld.
(5) All the evil go to the underworld, while all the good go to the upperworld.

In Stage III, regardless of the destination, it is a physical (a material) place. It isn't until Stage IV when there is a total break between a supra-self-awareness and the body that both the underworld and upperworld destinations take on a totally spiritual character. I'll go into detail about each of these destinations in turn.

At this point it is necessary to pause and say something about what it is after death that goes on to a destination of the dead. It is important to note that up through the end of Stage III religion the self still feels ties with the body; there is as yet no experience of a supra-self-awareness transcending self-awareness and the body. Next, it is obvious that all of the destinations of the dead are conceived in terms of ordinary physical reality. In addition, the self's new experience of linear time predominating over cyclical time and of the extension of space to immeasurably far distances has a direct bearing on self-awareness's conception of its life after death. What it comes down to is that self-awareness believes that it will be provided with a physical body fit for the next life.

There are two reasons why the first destination of the dead is on a horizontal rather than on a vertical plane. The first is that up to this point the self has been completely successful in preventing any awareness that underneath it is a chaotic, suffering sub-self-awareness. The second is that the self has not yet experienced so much primal pain as to cut itself off from the body to the extent that it feels itself to be elevated above the body. When that does happen, the destination shifts to the sky.

Sometime during Stage III, the total load and valence of primal pain increased to the extent that self-awareness became cognizant of what it termed its inner double. Because the inner and outer worlds always mirror each other, self-awareness now experiences an underworld aspect of the cosmos. At this point all the dead go to the underworld.

There are six cardinal directions to space: four horizontal and two vertical directions. In phases four and five of the destinations of the dead, there is a division between those who are consigned to eternal suffering in the underworld and those who find an end to their suffering in the upperworld.

Phase One: All the Dead Go to a Far-distant Horizontal Destination

As I've stated earlier, what characterizes the destination of the dead on a horizontal level is the absence of want. This means that for a period of time the denial or suppression of need was successful in mitigating suffering. At the very least, one could look forward to an afterlife free of unfulfilled want; suffering would end with death.

The Happy Hunting Ground is the name some North American Native Americans gave to this horizontal destination of the dead. That they felt it necessary to label it as the "happy" hunting ground leads me to believe that they considered it to be a land of inexhaustible plenty in contrast to this life in which scarcity during the winter months meant being something less than happy.

Directly opposite to the North American Indian's positive view of the absence of want is the negative view of the Proto-Indo-Europeans. For them, the afterlife was one without cares, tears, cold, snow, labor and darkness. The quality of life in the realm of the dead was marked by the absence of the physical changes that plague this life: disease, infirmity and death.

In Proto-Indo-European society, the king is responsible for the welfare of the people. It is significant then that the dead are ferried across a body of water to the land of the dead by Twin—the primordial first king—in the guise of an old man. Ultimately, he leads the dead to a place where their complete welfare is taken care of, a place where, at last, the suffering that inevitably accompanies insatiable wants will end. In other traditions, it is the shaman who is the ferryman who conducts the dead over the waters that separate this life from the afterlife.

Phase Two: All the Dead Go to the Sky

The shift from a horizontal to an upward destination for the dead indicates a discrete jump in the level of primal pain in the general population. It indicates that self-awareness has now been forced to begin to elevate itself above the body. The increase in primal pain has meant that the self has had to cut itself off from the body to a greater extent in order to handle the increase in pain. Up to this point in the mind/body dualism, there has been equality. Now the balance shifts in favor of mind *over* body.

A destination in the sky also indicates a loss of hope in a final resting place that will be free of suffering. In Stage III of religion, the subordinate deities suffer when they are not properly ritually sustained by the people. So being with the deities means that suffering continues insofar as the people do not correctly carry out their ritual obligations.

There are many ways in which the dead can ascend to the sky. Among them are ropes, ladders, arrows, birds, or the rainbow. All of these means suggest that as yet there is no underworld as part of a worldview and to which all the dead go.

Phase Three: All the Dead Go to an Underworld

It is the positing of an underworld presided over by a subordinate deity that gives the certainty that by that time self-awareness was now cognizant of a suffering sub-self-awareness. Historically, the most common way that unconscious self-awareness has spoken of its suffering sub-self-awareness has been to call it a double. At one and the same time, the double is the underside of self-awareness and has a location beneath it. For self-awareness, when it first became cognizant of an underworld, it was a given that the Supreme Deity had created Hades as an underworld to the cosmos and created a suffering sub-self-awareness as an underworld to self-awareness. (The sub-self-awareness is in reality the unknown, suppressed consciousness-in-pain.) Self-awareness was not cognizant of the reality that it was a discrete, monumental increase in primal pain that caused self-awareness to be aware of a suffering sub-self-awareness. Self-awareness, therefore, did not realize that its conception of an underworld was a projected mirror of its own inner state. Three thousand or more years had to elapse before the knowledge of primal pain would make clear how and why our inner and outer worlds mirror each other.

To explain further, the basis for the 180-degree reversal in direction for the destination of the dead has to do with the drive of the organism to resolve primal pain and return to a state of consciousness. Primal pain is always exerting upward pressure on self-awareness—to break through it, become conscious, become resolved and thus restore the organism to a state of consciousness. At this point in our history, primal pain had risen to such a level that its upward pressure had made the self cognizant of something beneath it that threatens to break through and engulf self-awareness in unimaginable suffering.

Since the inner and outer worlds always continue to mirror each other, for the first time the cosmos includes an underworld. Now, self-awareness feels that at death it will fall into and become engulfed in an underworld abyss of eternal suffering. The suffering will be eternal because in the inner world the upward pressure of primal pain never ceases.

The shift from phase two to phase three confirms that suffering does not end, even with death. If anything at all characterizes the descent of the dead to an underworld, it is that life there is dark, shadowy and filled with suffering. Whatever depth of dark suffering is perceived in the sub-self-awareness is mirrored in life in the underworld.

In stark contrast to the lack of a fear of death in Stages I and II and in phases one and two of Stage III, now there is anticipation of suffering for eternity in the underworld. The fear of death is the mirror of the self's fear of being overwhelmed by a suffering sub-self-awareness.

Paradoxically, the sub-self-awareness is also associated with the primordial deep. Oral traditions tell self-awareness that people, as well as the whole cosmos, were formed out of the formless primordial substance, whether water or something else. Besides the sub-self-awareness being a place of untold suffering and a mirror for the underworld, it is also the mirror for the chaotic, primordial deep from which an ordered self-awareness emerged. In other words, self-awareness brought order out of a chaotic sub-self-awareness. Consequently, the sub-self-awareness creates not only a fear of death and going to the underworld, but a fear of total annihilation as well in the primordial chaos.

Phase Four: The Diseased and Aged Go to the Underworld, While Those Who Have Died in Battle—Heroes—Go to the Upperworld

In Stages I and II, there was an ever-declining hope that reincarnation brought about an end to suffering and a fresh start without suffering. In Stage III, phases one and two, there was a renewed hope in an afterlife in a far-distant place, either horizontally or in the sky, free of suffering from unfulfilled want. In phase three, that hope was again abandoned, everyone going to the underworld and continuing to suffer. In phase four, hope for an end to suffering in the afterlife was reborn, but it was available now only to the warrior and priestly classes who went to the upperworld. Commoners—the third class in Indo-European society, the food producers, those who died of disease and old age—had no hope and upon death continued to suffer in the underworld from unfulfilled want.

In Part II, Chapter 5, I fully explored the cycle of hope, abandoning hope and regaining hope in the context of the basis for cyclical time, but there I used the cycle of struggle to get needs met, failing to do so and abandoning the struggle and then renewing the struggle. Struggle and hope are intimately related in that it is hope that one's needs will be met that drives one to continue the struggle to get them met. By Stage III, however, needs have been suppressed and the struggle is to satisfy insatiable wants, which are the surface manifestations of unmet need.

What is apparent in this stage of Indo-European religion is that it will take heroic efforts in this life to earn a place in the upperworld in the afterlife where one is free from suffering, free from the bondage of everlastingly having to struggle to get wants satisfied. It will take more power than what is ordinarily available to the commoner to end suffering. It takes the ultimate use of power in war to overcome the demon Mother Goddess whose followers have stolen cattle belonging to the Indo-Europeans. Recall that it is only the Indo-Europeans to whom the

Supreme Deity has given cattle. If any other people have them, they must have stolen them.

In war or dying in battle, the warrior accumulates the fame that does not decay. It is this fame that qualifies him for a place in the upperworld. Since this fame is thought not to decay as does everything else in the world, it represents to the warrior an ultimate hope that his struggle to end suffering will be successful. It is this hope that makes him a "berserker" and sustains him in battle.

This Indo-European conception of an immutable fame might be the forerunner of the New Testament injunction to store up treasures in heaven where they neither rust nor decay. The New Testament, though, transformed the very material treasure of accumulating cattle into the nonmaterial one of spiritual deeds.

The specific primal mirror for this attitude in Indo-European religion is what parents communicate to their children. They lead a child to hope that if he performs heroically enough to be and do what his parents want, the parents will love him. It is the child's experience that no matter how hard he tries, it is never enough, it is never good enough. Just as the hope that he will be loved if he is heroic enough sustains the child, so the warrior is sustained by the hope that he will go to the upperworld if he is heroic enough.

Also in phase four, with a fame that does not decay, we have evidence that self-awareness has cut itself off from the body even more. It suggests a self-awareness that has been forced by an increased level of primal pain to elevate itself higher in the body just as the Supreme Deity continues to elevate himself higher in the sky.

It is perhaps at this time in Indo-European religion that the figure of Kolyo is introduced as the person who conducts the deceased to their appointed destination, either up or down. The front side of Kolyo, who is female, is beautiful and vibrant with health. Her backside is horrific with snakes, worms and the stink of decay. The symbolism suggests that deceased heroes see her front side only as she conducts them to the upperworld. Likewise, it suggests that the deceased, both old and diseased, see her backside only as she conducts them to a life of eternal suffering. Kolyo will undergo reinterpretation when the final development of the destination of the dead takes place for Stage III religion.

That now some people, heroes who have died in battle, go to an upperworld and all the rest go to an underworld reveals a greater degree of unconscious self-awareness. Self-awareness has had to cut itself off from primal pain to the extent that the bonds that formerly bound all the members of the society together in reciprocal equilibrium have been severed. Prior to this distinction between the favored few and the unfortunate many, there was only societal "salvation."

When there was just societal salvation, interrelationships were more intact. A child's extended family was intimately involved with caring for him. His primal pain came as much from aunts and uncles and grandparents as it did from his parents. Hence, the stages of placation, reimmersion and power that the child went through took place within his extended family. The lives of all members of the group were bound up together. There must have been a uniformity of experience, such that all children turned out with much the same character to their self-awareness. This meant, in turn, that in religion, salvation—however it might be defined—was of the whole group. All members suffered the same fate. There was no such thing as individual salvation.

As primal pain increased through the millennia, causing the self to withdraw ever more surely from the extended family, the interrelationships that bound a society together were ever more surely being weakened and broken. Parents ever more surely became solely responsible for the care of their children. The child's response of placation, reimmersion and power became ever more directed at his parents alone. As a consequence, religion became ever less a societal experience and ever more an individual experience.

There is now individual salvation. In this division into the saved and the unsaved, we see the beginnings of individualism and what that means for the breakdown in the cohesiveness of society. Here lie the beginnings of the strong, i.e., male warriors, arrogating to themselves all the perks of society. Remember that it is dominance and the use of power to get what one wants that characterizes self-awareness and religion in Stage III. It is the initial move in the subjugation of women and the change from matriarchy and matrilineality to patriarchy and patrimony.

That the backside of Kolyo and the underworld are synonymous with rotten decay reveals that now there is a sub-self-awareness so filled with suffering from the pain of unmet, infantile need that the sub-self-awareness is sensed as being rotten with decay. The sub-self-awareness is now something truly to fear and to be defended against. Self-awareness does so by cutting itself off from it as much as possible.

Phase Five: The Evil Go to the Underworld. The Good Go to the Upperworld

The final development in Stage III of beliefs regarding the nature of the destination of the dead is now based on ethical or moral behavior. The good go up and the evil go down.

In one Indo-European tradition, Mithra, the Sun, is the Savior of the moral person. Apparently, the moral deceased must first spend three days in Hell before Mithra rescues him and conducts him to Heaven. Perhaps an examination of the deceased goes on in Hell to determine whether or not the deceased's life warrants a permanent abode in Heaven. There is also a deity of Hell who presides over the immoral who must suffer and be punished eternally.

The most significant development in Stage III is the demonization of Kolyo, of the Mother Goddess and of the deity of the underworld. Closely associated is the reinterpretation of the serpent who stole the first cattle and took them to a cave in primordial time. The serpent who did so was recast as the Mother Goddess, and for this she is demonized. In this last reinterpretation of the destiny of the dead in Stage III, Kolyo is in reality the demon Mother Goddess who conducts the deceased to the underworld. The deity of the underworld now is seen as the demon Mother Goddess. The epic of Gilgamesh is a good example of Warrior God religion recasting women and the Goddess as demonic: creatures who will seduce you and then tear you apart. (See Part III, Chapter 7, for a full description of the transformation of Mother Goddess into a demon.)

The experience of underworld demons such as Kolyo is the clue that unconscious self-awareness now feels its sub-self-awareness or double to be demonic. When self-awareness has sunk so low as to feel its double is evil, the mirror image of it has to be an underworld presided over by the Evil One, by whatever name he or she is called. Just as the mirror image of self-awareness is the Supreme Deity, so the mirror image of the demonic sub-self-awareness is the subordinate Evil Deity. (This is the basis for whom Christians called Satan or the Devil.)

That the evil person upon death goes to the underworld and that the good person upon death goes to the upperworld indicates that primal pain has increased to the point where parents are judging their children to be evil or good. Earlier, when the old and diseased went to the underworld and the warriors went to the upperworld, there was no judgment that the old and diseased were evil. The accumulation of fame by the warriors was not a judgment of goodness in the sense that a lack of fame was a sign of being evil.

Stage III: Judaism and Early Christianity

It is an oversimplification to use the word "Israel" to cover the various national identities of the people of Yahweh, but it will serve well enough for my purposes here. As far as a time frame is relevant for the nation of Israel, I have chosen the anointing of Saul as king, circa 1,000 BCE, as the beginning of the nation-state.

As far as I can determine, the most common understanding of the destiny of the dead down to the second century BCE was that everyone upon death went to Sheol. It was an underground abode and was a place of eternal suffering. The Jewish scriptures offer a number of explanations as to why the people and the nation suffered so much from foreign invasions and why Sheol was the destination of the dead. The one that appears to have carried the most weight was the one offered by the prophets. They claimed that the reason the people and the nation suffered so much was because of disobedience of the Law.

For the purpose of emphasis, I repeat the substance of the primal rationale for the positing of Sheol that is under the heading Phase Three: All the Dead Go to an Underworld. Essentially, it is the sensing of a suffering sub-self-awareness that is present, even in the best of times. Concomitantly, children are feeling that they must perform in order to have any hope of getting what they really need: being lovingly nurtured. The time comes when children realize that no matter how much they do to satisfy their parents, it is never enough. No matter how good they are, they are never good enough to please their parents. Children, then, resign themselves to a permanent condition of suffering. It is this condition that is mirrored in the external world of everyone going to Sheol upon death.

This explanation for the people's and the nation's suffering because of disobedience of the Law was accepted by the people and the nation down to the beginning of the second century BCE. In the year 198 BCE, Syria gained control of Palestine. In the year 175 BCE, Antiochus Epiphanes became the ruler of Syria. He was enamored with Greek culture and forced it upon his entire kingdom. Understandably, this was resisted by the Israelites. Reaction by Syria caused widespread destruction in Israel, including of the Temple itself.

This destruction and repression caused a crisis in how the people and Israel interpreted their history because the people were making an extra effort to follow the Law. Since, clearly they were Yahweh's chosen people, they could expect that if they were obedient, Yahweh would protect them. But, instead of being protected for following the Law, they suffered continuous invasions. There was ample justification for the fear of the nation collapsing under the pressure to change. The crisis was solved by a line of reasoning that has come to be called Apocalypticism. The word means an unveiling or a revealing of the secret knowledge of what Yahweh was doing. The core of this knowledge was that, for some unknown reason, Yahweh had allowed evil forces to take control of the world. Soon, however, the Son of Man would come and overturn all of the evil forces in order to establish God's Kingdom on earth. Israel would be given a fresh start in Yahweh's Kingdom. Soon meant imminent.

When the Son of Man came, there would be a day of judgment. Those judged to be unrighteous were to be sentenced to Sheol as were those who had died and lived an unrighteous life. The dead who had led righteous lives were to be resurrected with bodies fit for the new Kingdom, as well as those who were alive and righteous on that day. This scenario fits into the general character of Stage III in which in the final destination of the dead there would be an absence of want. However, this represents a unique change from the general pattern of the destiny of the dead in Stage III in that for Israel there were no Phases Four and Five. It fits also because of a reliance, not on personal power to overcome a sense of helplessness, but on Yahweh's power to do so. Naturally, there is an internal apocalyptic primal mirror for this external world of apocalypticism.

The mirror of the conviction that the end is near for Israel is that of a child who feels that he cannot hold out much longer to be loved. His hope is faltering. He has struggled to the extreme to do what his parents want him to do and to be whom they want him to be. He is close to admitting failure and giving in to resignation. He still desperately clings to the hope that his parents will see his dire plight and love him before his hope runs out and resignation sets in. Because parents unconsciously are trying to get their children to meet the parents' unmet infantile need, parents inevitably fall short in meeting their children's need for unconditional love. Apocalypticism is an excellent example of how the hope/ struggle <-> failure/resignation inner need for parental love is mirrored in the outer world in the need for God's love.

There is a difference between the hope/struggle <-> failure/resignation cycles in childhood and as an apocalyptic adult. In childhood, the cycle repeats itself endlessly. In apocalyptic adulthood, the attempt is made to arrest the cycle in the hope/struggle episode. The goal is to avoid failing and falling into resignation. The hope is maintained by saying as often as necessary, "Yahweh will intervene very soon."

There is also a primal mirror for the apocalyptic conviction that Satan is currently in control of the world. It reflects a time or times when children are making every effort to be obedient, but their parents are treating them worse than ever. Children don't know why this is so. Yet, children will come up with any and all reasons to excuse their parents. Why? Because to lose all hope in your parents ever really nurturing you is to wish you were dead. Three common excuses are: My parents love me the only way they can; my parents are doing the best they can; my parents will soon come through; just you wait and see. Whether it be as a child bewildered because his parents are withholding love or as an apocalyptic Israelite bewildered because Yahweh is withholding protection, it is a great mystery for which there is no satisfactory answer.

The interchangeability of the language of a supreme deity and parents reflects the mirror image of the words used—

"Children repent of your disobedience, for then you will experience my love for you."

"Confess that you are totally to blame for your situation."

The same mirror effect applies to what children of a people of God might reply.

"Yes, I can really feel it; this time they (or God) will surely turn soon and love me."

"I do repent; the day my dream comes true is close."

After some 170 years had elapsed since the beginning of the apocalyptic movement had begun in Israel, the intervention of Yahweh was still delayed for reasons unknown. Rome was the latest of the occupying powers controlling the strategic Palestinian trade route. Yet, the apocalyptic movement was still widespread and strong. It was at that time that John the Baptizer and Jesus of Nazareth, both fully imbued with an apocalyptic message, began their prophetic ministries.

The Gospels' accounts of the temptations of Jesus at the beginning of his ministry showed how he was fully into the power motif of Stage III. The accounts show how he changed the reliance on personal power to overcome a feeling of helplessness to a reliance on Yahweh's power to do so. His rejection of turning stones into bread, his refusal to test Yahweh by throwing himself off the top of the Temple and his repudiation of being ruler of all the kingdoms on earth indicate that he was fully conscious of the corruption of power for personal use. Let power be in the hands of Yahweh alone.

From a background steeped in the best traditions of Judaism, Jesus preached a gospel of repentance now. Now, because the coming of the Son of Man with power was imminent, bringing in Yahweh's good kingdom on earth, Jesus told his disciples that some of them would be alive when it happened, so near was the long-awaited vindication of the righteous upholders of Yahweh's Law.

In the coming of Yahweh's Kingdom on earth there would be an end to suffering. The healing ministry of Jesus was the sign of that. Because there was to be a general resurrection of the dead, the death and resurrection of Jesus was the surest sign that the kingdom was already beginning.

The repentance of which Jesus preached included the experience that the whole of one's being was in a state of sinfulness. One had to turn away 180° from that state of being. The Greek word for repentance means to make an about face. To repent meant to abandon a self that cannot save itself from that condition of sinfulness.

The difference between the exhortations of Jesus to repent and parental exhortations to their children to admit of their disobedience is that God delivers on his promise to end suffering, while parents cannot deliver. As such then, Christianity is the perfection of the secondary defenses against primal pain. The two secondary defenses primarily involved are placation and power. Repentance of one's sinfulness is mirrored in placation whether it be of parents of God.

The imminent return of the Son of Man with power is mirrored in the secondary defense of accumulating power to compensate for helplessness in getting one's needs met. The difference between a person's use of power to overcome helplessness and the Son of Man's use of power to overcome helplessness is that God is not corrupted by power, as are humans.

When Jesus spoke of the coming of the Son of Man with power, he was talking about the overthrow of all temporal kingdoms and the institution of God's good kingdom on earth. Pilate confused Jesus with Barabbas who was an insurrectionist determined to overthrow Rome and restore Israel to political independence. Pilate represented a corrupted use of power.

In summary of the ministry of Jesus Christ (the Messiah), I conclude that it falls within the parameters of Stage III's insatiable want and a compulsion for power. That is, what Jesus preached concerning the coming Kingdom was that in it there was an end to suffering caused by insatiable wants. In keeping within Stage III, Jesus foresaw in the coming kingdom an absence of want. His entire ministry of healing, his death and his resurrection demonstrated the power of Yahweh to overcome one's sense of helplessness in saving one's self from the death-causing power of Satan.

The apostle Paul was the most influential of the leaders of early Christianity. Proof of that lies in the decision of church leaders several hundreds of years later to include his writings in the Canon.

Paul was an apocalyptic, Pharisaic Jew. He believed that the end was imminent and that Yahweh would soon establish his kingdom on earth. He believed in a general resurrection. The unrighteous were sent to Sheol; the righteous would take their place in the new Kingdom of Yahweh on earth. Paul's beliefs regarding the destiny of the dead changed after he had his conversion experience.

Prior to his conversion, Paul, as did all other peoples who were in at least Phase Three of Stage III, made the connection between a suffering, sub-self-awareness and an underground place where everyone went after death to continue suffering for eternity. After his conversion, Paul changed his beliefs about the destiny of the dead. Paul now felt that his innermost subconscious self was a Child of God. He now saw that his surface self was a sinful self; it was a Child of Satan. These changes resulted in a drastic revision Paul made in his beliefs regarding Sheol and the destiny of the unrighteous.

Since Paul now felt that his subconscious self was a Child of God, he lost the psychological foundation for the positing of a place like Sheol in the outer world. Consequently, there was no destination for the unrighteous upon death; they were simply no more. This is supported by the fact that in all the letters that are fully attributable to Paul, there is no mention of Sheol.

The 180° change in Paul's conception of himself as a consequence of his conversion has a primal mirror. When a person has a primal, awakening experience, he now knows that his subconscious self is not just a suffering self, he is the primal-pain-laden child who had to be suppressed in order to survive. He now knows that every thought, every emotion and every deed of his surface self is unconsciously controlled by his buried, primal-pain-laden self.

In summary of the ministry of Paul, I conclude that it was his conversion experience that changed him from an apocalyptic Pharisee Jew into a Jewish apocalyptic follower of Jesus. Everything that Paul did or taught should be interpreted in the light of the imminent return of Jesus the Christ to set up Yahweh's good kingdom on earth. It seems apparent that Christianity began as an apocalyptic religious faith and remained so at least through the first century CE.

The Destiny in Stage IV

The radical shift from the Warrior God religion of Stage III to the Stage IV religion of transcendence signaled the most profound jump ever in the devolution of consciousness into unconscious self-awareness. What took place was the leap from the body oriented defenses of self-awareness to the mind-oriented defenses of a supra-self-awareness. Self-awareness is embodied, and the defenses of placation, reimmersion and power exhibit that embodiment. By a supra-self-awareness, I mean a transcendent psychic rising above of self-awareness.

By the middle of the first millennium BCE, in the Far East, suffering had increased to such an extent that no effort that an embodied self-awareness could make sufficiently mitigated suffering. No combination of placation, reimmersion and power sufficed any longer to end suffering. If suffering were to end, the body, the emotions and the thoughts of self-awareness had to be transcended.

The basic cause of this situation was hundreds of years of wave-upon-wave of Indo-European invasions of peoples from Western Europe all the way to India. As time passed, these continuous wars caused a massive breakdown in family life, which, in turn, led to a degree of primal pain that unconscious self-awareness could not handle.

It will never be known when the first humans oscillated between consciousness and Stage I of unconscious self-awareness or when humans became permanently, unconsciously self-aware. Stage I is characterized by placation of parents and of the Gods. Nor will it ever be known when humans devolved into Stage II's level of unconscious self-awareness and its defenses of reimmersion symbolically into the womb and into Mother Goddess. With more accuracy, it can be determined when humans devolved further into Stage III's depth of unconscious self-awareness. This is the Stage in which one feels helpless in getting one's needs met as a child and denies them, only to have them resurface as insatiable wants. This is the Stage in which one also has a compulsion for power to satisfy those insatiable wants and to compensate for those feelings of helplessness in getting needs met. As a child, the power of one's parents is coopted to satisfy those insatiable wants and to overcome those feelings of helplessness. As a religious adult, the power of the Gods is coopted to do just that.

We do know when the first major jump took place from Stage III to the Transcendence of Stage IV. Buddha was an historical person who lived about mid sixth century BCE. He founded the Transcendent religion that bears his name: Buddhism. We do know when the second religious jump took place to the Transcendence of Stage IV. From the Gospel of John, which was written late in the first century CE, we can determine that the power motif of the apocalyptic religion of Jesus and of Paul had morphed into the Transcendent motif of Stage IV.

From the Stage III Religion of Hinduism to the Stage IV Religion of Buddhism

In the Far East, the Transcendent supra-self-awareness took shape within the context of Hinduism/Buddhism. Buddhism arose as a response to the ineffectiveness of Hinduism to end suffering. Although the use of power dominates

Stage III religion, it was loss of hope in the ritual placation of the deities to get needs met that gave rise to Buddhism. Buddhism, however, was not the reformation of Hinduism; it was the complete rejection of it.

Initially, it was the Buddhists who first realized that everyone was so caught up in a state of desire that no one qualified for the upperworld where suffering would end. Most crucially for Stage IV religion, they also knew that self-awareness could not save itself at all. Neither placation nor reimmersion nor power, no matter how diligently they were pursued, ended suffering. Their experience was that self-awareness itself was part of the problem of suffering and therefore could not be a part of the solution to suffering. Desire and self-awareness were part of the same cloth and could not be rent apart. Buddhism's solution to the problem of suffering was to transcend self-awareness. Only by so doing could one escape from suffering.

To put it as succinctly as possible, the goal of Buddhism is to achieve Buddha Consciousness. What this means is what I call a supra-self-awareness. Buddha Consciousness or a supra-self-awareness is that one within us who does the transcending of ordinary self-awareness.

The rising above or transcendence of self-awareness is a process of becoming. Although within Buddhism it is claimed that it is possible to attain total Buddha Consciousness in an instant, that occurrence is exceedingly rare.

The process begins with at least a minimal awakening to the Four Holy Truths. The first is that suffering is part of the nature of self-awareness. The second is that desire is the cause of suffering. The third is that cessation of desire is the answer. And the fourth is that the path the Buddha took is the way to transcend desire.

The path has three aspects to it: morality, meditation and wisdom. Simply put, to be moral means not to injure living beings, not to steal, not to be sexually immoral, not to lie and not to use alcohol or drugs. In meditation one cultivates the right attitudes of the Eightfold path, which is broken down into right understanding, right thought, right speech, right bodily action, right livelihood, right moral effort, right mindfulness and right concentration. Meditation, among other ways to move toward Buddha Consciousness, provides an attitude within which to carry out the disciplines of morality. Wisdom is actually what following the moral precepts and Eightfold Path lead to and is another way of expressing Buddha Consciousness.

An essential part of the Buddha's experience was that self-awareness was not immortal. For him, self-awareness or the ego-self was wholly of the ever changing impermanence of the world of appearances. It came into being at birth and disintegrated at death. Equally essential was his experience that the supra-self arising in him was absolutely still and totally transcendent of self-awareness and existed in an eternal realm. Ordinary self-awareness is not immortal, but Buddha Consciousness is.

This brings me now to the destiny of the dead in Stage IV religion in the Far East, specifically in India. India had been invaded by the Indo-Europeans and consequently was introduced to Warrior God religion. In it, as we have seen, reincarnation in Mother Goddess religion was replaced with a destination for the dead. By the end of Stage III, the ideas in place about the destination for the dead consisted of a worldly heaven for the righteous and a worldly underworld for the evil. Those who responded to the suffering of this life morally went up and those who responded immorally went down.

In the Upanishads—Hindu writings brought together from about 600 BCE to 300 BCE—reincarnation is enunciated for the very first time. Of course, this is a reaction to current feelings about the condition of humanity and its ultimate fate. Reincarnation also undergoes significant changes to reflect current religious understandings.

In Stages I and II, reincarnation was a neutral concept. No moral judgments were implied. Everyone was reincarnated into lives of ever-increasing suffering due to ever-higher levels of primal pain. In Stage IV, moral judgments applied because by this time it was already felt that some deserved Heaven while most deserved Hell. Through its experience of an ever more transcendent Buddha Consciousness, Buddhism introduced the possibility of an end to reincarnation for those who dedicated themselves to the path of achieving Buddha Consciousness. Those who remained unawakened and attached to their self-awareness had bad Karma and were reincarnated into ever-grosser life forms. Those who followed the Buddhist way toward full enlightenment were reincarnated to ever-finer life forms. Once full Buddha Consciousness was achieved, the cycle of karmic suffering was broken and nirvana attained. Full union with the eternal Universal Self was accomplished.

In Buddhism, the concept of a destination for the dead of Stage III is retained. What changes is that instead of the destination being to some material, worldly upperworld in the sky it is to a transcendent, otherworldly upperworld. This tells us that due to a tremendous increase in primal pain in the 1st millennium BCE, if one is going to escape from a life of suffering, one must transcend from self-awareness. The new self that arises is what I have named the supra-self-awareness. Whether through religious or secular means, few achieve it to any degree. The vast majority of people in the Far East go through the motions of their religions without ever having an experience in which they have stood back and seen self-awareness for what it is in their cultures: a state of being—driven by desire to satisfy insatiable wants—that can only continue suffering.

The process of being on the path toward Buddha Consciousness has parallels with being a primal person. For the devout Buddhist, reincarnation is to ever-purer lives. For the primal person, each primal results in a life that is more conscious and less self-aware. The two paths, however, lead in opposite directions. The religious path of transcendence leads to another more perfect defense against primal pain. It is another layer of defense. The primal path leads to the removal of pain and thus to a process of stripping away defenses because they are no longer needed.

From the Stage III Religion of Jesus to the Stage IV Religion About Jesus

I turn now to the Middle East and to what Christianity started becoming during the balance of the first century CE after Paul's ministry. By the end of the first century of the Common Era, the Son of Man had not returned in power and in glory, ushering in the Kingdom of God on earth. There was an extreme loss of hope in the followers of Jesus that the Kingdom of God on earth was going to come at all. In these early followers of Jesus there arose a resignation so deep that it transformed Christianity from the power motif of Stage III to the transcendent motif of Stage IV. Hope/struggle <-> failure/resignation as a sequence common to all Stages is now carried on within the content of Stage IV Transcendent Christianity.

In primal terms, primal pain had increased in children to the point where no defense composed of any combination of placation, reimmersion and power sufficed to end suffering. Unconscious self-awareness had to be transcended into an unconscious, supra-self awareness to preserve the viability of the child. It was this situation that was mirrored in these truly desperate, late first century CE Christians that resulted in the new paradigm of a Transcendent Savior.

Two books included in the New Testament canon shed light on the path Christianity took during the second half of the first century CE. They are: The Apocalypse (Revelation) of John and the Gospel of John.

There is much scholarly speculation about when the Revelation of John was written. Dates as early as 64 CE and as late as 115 CE have been proposed. I find that there is a compelling reason for choosing the earlier date. It is evident from the book of Acts and from Paul's letters that there were vibrant and widespread apocalyptic gatherings of the followers of Jesus throughout cities around the Mediterranean and farther to the east. It is reasonable, then, to assign the Apocalypse of John to the 64 CE date. It would have been written at the height of the apocalyptic movement. The author continues the apocalyptic message of Jesus and of Paul that the end is near, so be prepared for it. In Primal terms, Revelation's Jesus is the culmination of Stage III's unconscious self-awareness with its emphasis on power. The religion of Jesus was the final act of hope for Stage III Christians.

I think it is correct to assign the Gospel of John to the end of the first century CE. The book's author completely strips Jesus of his apocalyptic message. His major emphasis is demonstrating that Jesus is, in fact, the Son of God and is One with the Father. His concern is the credentials of Jesus. In contrast to the Jesus of the Synoptic Gospels who shunned giving signs, John's Jesus is almost continuously giving signs that he is who he says he is: the Son of God who is One with His Father. His goal is to prove that Jesus is Transcendent so that one can be confident in placing his faith in Jesus and be rewarded with eternal life in a Transcendent Heaven. As a corollary to this goal, he warns his readers that if they reject this offer of salvation, upon death they will be punished eternally in a Transcendent Hell. In Primal terms, this gospel portrays Jesus as belonging to the Transcendence of Stage IV.

Summary

I began by outlining some of the characteristics of consciousness as a starting point from which to examine the first three stages of self-awareness and the evolution of its religious conceptions of death. I dealt with the specific problem of what to make of the decapitated skulls found in Paleolithic caves.

When self-awareness first occurred in history, initiating Stage I in religion, I noted a number of characteristics of self-awareness that had a direct bearing on how it conceived of itself and of death. There was no knowledge of a suppressed consciousness in pain. There was a specific location for self-awareness in the gut. There was the dualism of self and other. There was a sense of time, both cyclical and linear. There was a belief in its own immortality. And there was belief in reincarnation as its eternal destiny. I indicated that throughout Stage I, in discrete steps, reincarnation was to lives of increased suffering and pain.

Next, I pointed out that the survival/placation motif of Stage I no longer was effective in mitigating pain, which ushered in the sex/reimmersion motif of Mother Goddess religion. Continued to be explored was reincarnation as the destiny of the dead, but now it was to be reconceived within the Goddess and to be reborn to a new life.

The appearance of Warrior God religion was the signal that Stage III religion had begun with its motif of power. It meant the end of reincarnation and the beginning of there being an ultimate destination for the dead that was characterized by an absence of want and by an end to suffering. I posited that there were five phases to the destination of the dead, of which only the first two were free of suffering. I noted that in the third phase cognizance of a sub self awareness brought on the experience of an underworld. When phases four and five came about, I pointed out that they were very early indications of the idea of individualism as opposed to communalism because now, for the first time, there was individual salvation for the favored few. The plight of most people was to continue a life of suffering in the underworld.

I introduced the special case of apocalyptic Judaism within Stage III. It kept the concept of Sheol as a destination for those who were evil. It reintroduced the concept of the horizontal destination of Phase One, but the Kingdom of Yahweh on earth was reserved only for those who repented and were faithful to the Law.

I followed this with the apocalypticism of the Jesus of the synoptic Gospels who kept Sheol for the unrepentant and kept the Kingdom of Yahweh on earth for those who repented and lived lives relieving the sufferings of others. In keeping with apocalyptic Jesus, Paul, too, envisioned a Kingdom of God on earth for the faithful in Christ. Paul differed from the synoptic Jesus in that Paul no longer believed in the existence of Sheol; the dead simply were no more.

In my discussion of the fourth stage of religion—transcendence—I laid a foundation for determining that there had been a catastrophic increase in primal pain by the 1st millennium BCE It resulted in a shift that posited the necessity of a total break with self-awareness. That total break resulted in a hope for an afterlife in a transcendent Heaven, free from all suffering.

Buddha and the Jesus of the Gospel of John represent the fourth Stage in religions of Transcendence. Stage IV Buddhism and Christianity, by transcending unconscious self-awareness into an unconscious supra-self-awareness, perfect the defenses against primal pain, thus ending suffering. Primaling, in contrast, breaks through self-awareness to where primal pain can be experienced, thus eliminating the very cause of suffering and allowing original consciousness to return to the person.

As a further note on the destiny of the dead, it cannot be emphasized enough that Christianity as a Stage IV religion of Transcendence is a religion about Jesus and is not the religion of Jesus. His apocalyptical Jewish religion fits squarely into Stage III, as does Paul's, with its emphasis on the "warrior" aspects of God as much as on his Fatherly aspects. Jesus, as did Paul, proclaimed the horizontalness of a Kingdom of God on earth. That was the religion of Jesus and of Paul. By the end of the first century CE, Christians were beginning to proclaim the verticalness of a Kingdom of God in Heaven. That was a religion about Jesus. For Jesus and for Paul, the destiny of the faithful was the resurrection of a mortal body as an immortal body. For those living at the end time, in the blink of an eye, their mortality would be put on immortality. The apocalypticists, filled with a profound resignation, found, at hand, a ready-made solution for their problem: Greek philosophy. It had already been taken over by Transcendence. The body and everything about it must be transcended. One must be aware of one's self as an immortal soul housed in a physical body. Similarly, God is immortal and transcends the physical universe. Resurrection morphed from that of the total person (body and soul) to that of the flesh alone because the soul was already immortal. Thus, by leaving behind apocalypticism—the religion of Jesus—and by accommodating itself to Greek philosophy, Stage IV Transcendent Christianity became the religion about Jesus. Christianity, now stripped of an apocalyptic threat to Rome and imbued with a Greek philosophical worldview, in time, (313 CE) became the official religion of the Roman Empire. Seventeen hundred years later, Christians are still faced with the problem of deciding between the religion of Jesus and the religion about Jesus.

Not everyone, in fact, relatively few people are able or willing to commit themselves to follow their religion's discipline for transcending Stage I's Placation, Stage II's Reimmersion and Stage III's Wants and Power of unconscious self-awareness. The extremely high degree of primal pain that has infected us all for 2000 years is more than a match for most people to transcend into the state of a complete supra-self-awareness in which there is no more suffering. When a Christian person realizes that, despite his every effort, his child of Satan is very much in control, it might make him wonder when, and if, his suffering will end. It is this state of mind that periodically brings on apocalyptic movements.

There is a primal mirror for the condition as well. This same extremely high level of primal pain means that a primal person has an equally difficult time successfully dismantling his defense system of unconscious self-awareness, primaling and living without suffering. When having a much needed primal eludes someone, it might make that someone wonder when, and if, his suffering is going to end. It might make him forget that primaling is a life-long process and make him wish for a cataclysmic primal that will apocalyptically end all further need for them.

"Okay, but so what? What does all of this have to do with me?" you might be asking. Whether or not you are wondering about the relevance of what the evolution of religious ideas about death has upon your life, keep in mind that what I am interested in is building an historical foundation that will result in your drawing the conclusion that, yes, I in particular, and we humans as a group, are unconscious and headed for chaos. This is an invitation to examine your own beliefs about what you feel your ultimate destiny is and to compare it to what I suggest is the destiny to which consciousness points.

CHAPTER 10

SHAMANISM

The Purpose of This Chapter

I intend to demonstrate that shamanism is at the very core of religion and that the history of shamanism clearly reveals the devolution of consciousness into unconscious self-awareness. Further, I intend to point out that the history of shamanism follows the same sequence as does a child's reactions to primal pain. And I intend to show that every step of the shamanic journey replicates, in symbolic fashion, every step of a primal experience.

Who and What Are Shamans?

Shamans. Who are they and what do they do? A shaman is a person who has received a special gift that enables him—or her—to undertake a perilous journey on behalf of his community into the unseen half of reality in order to secure some benefit for his people and to return safely with it.

Unlike one definition of the shaman that restricts his activities to healing, mine is broad enough to encompass other roles such as carrying propitiatory offerings to specific deities or escorting the deceased to the domain of the dead. Another definition emphasizes one component of the journey—ecstasy—as being the central element of the journey. The shaman's experience of ecstasy, however, is a by-product of his success in the journey, but not the purpose of it, which is to return with some boon for his people.

The Parallel Between a Primal Person and a Shaman

A primal person is one who has learned how to undertake the perilous journey into his subconscious in order to secure the benefit of the release of primal pain. This benefit is the incremental transmutation of self-awareness back into consciousness, and to return safely with a state of being altered toward greater consciousness. It isn't necessary here to expand upon this statement of who a primal person is because, in Part I, I have thoroughly explored the whole range of the primal experience.

Dating the Various Shamanic Traditions

The main problem I face in relating shamanism to the history of the devolution of consciousness into unconscious self-awareness is that self-awareness always assumes that its understanding of itself is the way psychic behavior has always been as far back as humans have existed. Consequently, all the research that's been done on shamanism in the last three hundred years has been through the eyes of an unconscious self-awareness. To complicate matters further, the shamans who have been studied during this period also reflect their own current status of unconscious self-awareness.

My task has been to sort all this out and place the information available on shamanism into the chronological stages of religion: survival/placation, sex/reimmersion, power/domination and transcendence/transformation. Researchers of the past three hundred years have paid lip service to the evolution of religious ideas, but their picture of shamanism has been a static rather than a dynamic one. Thus, they give the impression that their descriptions of the phenomenon are the way shamanism has always been. I use the word "shaman" to cover an experience that has as many equivalents as there are traditional peoples and covers thousands of years in which the nature of the experience changed as primal pain increased from generation to generation.

The four dominant themes of religion provide the structure as to where in history to place what information we do have on shamanism, and to infer what shamans have done in each of the stages of religion. Remember, self-awareness is a compound of defenses holding back primal pain in order to keep suffering at a minimum. Those defenses are placation, reimmersion, power and transcendence. Remember, in the first stage of religion, as in the first stage of self-awareness—its mirror—placation is the first of the four defenses to be emphasized. In the second stage, reimmersion. In the third, power and, in the fourth, transcendence. In each stage of both religion and self-awareness, the problem is how to survive without suffering. Each stage of religion and of self-awareness comes about because the previous one has failed.

The work of the shaman with regard to the destiny of the dead provides another clue as to dating the tradition that deals with it. Since reincarnation is the destiny in the first two stages of religion, I conclude that shamans had no duties with regard to the dead. It isn't until Stage III that there is a destination for the dead, so any shamanic tradition that involves the dead being escorted to their destination must be assigned no earlier than Stage III religion.

The destination of the dead to an underworld provides still another clue to dating a particular shamanic tradition. An underworld does not become a part of religious thought until the latter part of Stage III. Prior to an underworld in Stage III, the dead went to some far-off horizontal destination.

The degree to which a shaman works with individual problems and for the community as a whole further enables one to date a tradition. The earlier the stage, the fewer individual problems there will be and the greater will be the attention given to communal survival. The earlier the stage, the healthier people will be because of lower levels of primal pain.

Whenever placation involves the sacrifice of domesticated animals, that gives an outside date to the tradition. Likewise for when metals are mentioned. It doesn't necessarily mean that the whole tradition can be dated no earlier than domestication or smelting. Usually there is an amalgam of traditions, older ones being dropped only when a major shift toward unconscious self-awareness has occurred.

It is having access to his primal pain, which has been symbolized within the context of his people's worldview, that produces a shaman and his ideation of his experiences. The specific content of his ideation is what dates his time in history. For example in Stage I, the extent of the unpredictableness of his deities is a mirror of how unpredictable were his own parents in meeting his needs. Again, in Stage III, whatever ideation he has of the demons of the underworld is symbolic of the level of suppressed primal pain in his subconscious. In general, if his ideation has mainly to do with placation, he is in the first stage of self-awareness and of religion. If his ideation is primarily sexual, he is in the second stage of self-awareness and of religion. And if his ideation centers around the mastery of power, he is in Stage III of self-awareness and of religion.

Shamans as Forerunners of Change

There is a dynamic tension between the inherited worldview of the shaman and the worldview of his own experience. He is born into a given worldview but, since his primal pain is either greater than that of the general population or his defenses are weaker, his greater devolution into unconscious self-awareness results in modifications that he contributes to his people's ever-changing worldview. The modifications come from what he experiences on his journeys. For example, he might bring back either a song or a dance or a ritual that will not only aid his people but alter their worldview.

Since a shamanic journey is a symbolic primal, what happens to the shaman on his journey has a primal foundation. Primaling is the act of the organism altering its own past states of consciousness/self-awareness, thereby changing the present as well as the future. Primaling resolves past primal-pain-saturated states, thus severing the organism's attachment to the past. The result is an organism in which the balance is tipped evermore toward consciousness. The organism is evermore free to create a conscious universe, rather than the universe it has to in order to suppress the pain that causes its unconsciousness.

Every time I primal there is a new creation. The old universe is demolished and a new, more conscious one is created. This primal experience is symbolized in the shaman's journey when he returns with something new for his people.

The Primal Basis for the Shamanic Notion of Illness

Earlier, I've written extensively on repressed primal pain being the cause of all forms of the suffering of self-awareness. Here, I will but note that for the shaman the cause of suffering is in self-awareness, not in the body. His understanding is in direct contrast to most of modern medicine, which subscribes to a biological basis for both physical and mental illnesses. It must be said, though, that there are current moves toward a greater understanding of mind and body affecting each other.

The primal basis for suffering does not recognize this mind-body duality. In childhood consciousness, there is no distinction between mind and body, inanimate and animate, or any other duality; there is just experience. Hence, when a child experiences pain because his needs are not met, his organism as a whole is affected.

When the pain reaches a certain, critical level, self-awareness occurs. Because the unmet need continues to strive for fulfillment, it drives self-awareness to try to fulfill the unmet need. That self-awareness can only try to satisfy the insatiable wants into which the needs have been transformed is the cause of all human suffering. The shaman looks to the right place to get at the cause of suffering, but what he sees is the energy of repressed pain symbolized as malevolent spirits or demons.

The Primal Basis for the Shaman's Diagnostic Abilities

Most often, shamans are chosen from adolescent boys or girls who exhibit what we call extreme neurosis or even psychosis. For the ancients, such behavior indicated that these children had an access to the unseen world that was not available to anyone else. From a primal standpoint, anyone who exhibits neurotic or psychotic behavior is one who has easy access to his unseen, subconscious world of primal pain because his pain is erupting all over the place.

At first, of course, the neophyte shaman was confused, even frightened, by his access to the unseen world. Under the guidance of an elder shaman, the neophyte learned how to interpret his experiences so that he could visit the unseen world and obtain cures for his patients. In addition, as part of his training, the neophyte acquired "helpers" to assist him in his work or on his journeys. They might be animals or birds or even insects. In Stage III, most likely they are demons he has mastered.

The neophyte primal person's experience is parallel to the neophyte shaman's. When a primal person's self-awareness is threatened with disintegration, he knows that what is happening is not the onset of psychosis but the eruption of primal pain into awareness. At first, this is frightening. With the guidance of a therapist or a buddy-helper in the shamanic sense—the primal person learns how to allow self-awareness to disintegrate, which permits him to descend into the subconscious to experience a portion of his primal pain. In time, the neophyte primal person learns to primal on his own.

Concomitant with this self-knowledge is an understanding of the very nature of self-awareness, of how it forms in the first place and what it is designed to do: suppress awareness of unbearable primal pain. Since only the content of self-awareness is different from person to person, a primal person can see into the pain in anyone's life. The shaman, too, sees the form and destiny of the self, but it is within a religious worldview that is symbolic of the reality of primal pain.

The Primal Basis for the Universality of Shamanism

Shamanism is a universal phenomenon because primal pain is present worldwide. Also, shamanism is the same worldwide because the effects of primal pain on consciousness and self-awareness are the same everywhere. The differences between cultures regarding shamanism are accounted for by the level of primal pain in each culture at any given period in its history and in its environmental setting. Regardless of the symbolism of the verbal trappings of any people's worldview, the nature of the shamanic journey is the same.

Joseph Campbell's *The Hero With a Thousand Faces* wonderfully illustrates the parallels in shamanism worldwide. For most purposes, his heroes are shamans. His heroes go through the same call, the same initiation, the same journey, achieve the same goals and go through the same return with a gift for the benefit of the people that shamans go through. Shamanism is basically related to the Stage of religion of a people and only incidentally to their environmental setting.

Religion, Shamanism, Paradise and the Fall

A shamanic experience, although there was no name for it when it first happened, marks the beginning of religion. The shaman was the first of his people to become self-aware, and with self-awareness comes external religion as its mirror. This person was the first of his people to experience primal pain symbolically. Shamanism is, therefore, the heart and soul of all religion. Even Jesus Christ can be interpreted as the Shaman who brings that role to its ultimate fulfillment in his work upon the cross, in his descent into Hell, in his ascension, in his resurrection and in his return with the gift of salvation and life.

The centrality of shamanism to the formation of religion is made clear in the crucial role of shamans during the Paradisal Period. The first ancestor way back in the dawn of time might be considered to be the first Great Shaman. It is he who would have received and passed on to his people the initial ways in which the people were to live to honor their creator. It is the shaman to whom was given the songs, dances and rituals that defined the ceremonial life of the people. It is the shaman to whom the first instructions were given on how to perform the sacrifices that would satisfy the deities whose needs were as real as were the people's.

Without exception, a Fall has always occurred to end the Paradisal Period. After the Fall, becoming a shaman was to become as all people were before the Fall. Then, everyone could fly. Now, only shamans can. Then, everyone was able to communicate with the spirits. Now, only shamans can do so. Then, humans, plants, creatures and even what we call inert today talked with each other. Now, only shamans do that.

The very existence of shamanism universally is testimony to the devolution of consciousness into unconscious self-awareness. Each separate people recognizes that in the distant past everyone was much healthier and in the Paradisal Period not only had no illnesses but their bodies did not die and decay. The increasing importance of the role of the shaman as healer is evidence of the weakening of the immune system because of the stress primal pain places upon it.

The primal basis for a shaman being able to return to the way people were during the Paradisal Period is that he has learned how to suppress his primal pain to the extent of ending all the suffering that came about because of the Fall. This is symbolic of what primaling accomplishes, which is the restoration of consciousness before the formation of self-awareness.

The Call

The shamanic experience begins with a "call." The shaman feels himself to be chosen by the deities for this special role in the community. The call might come to either an adolescent boy or girl. The call might come in a vision or a dream. The chosen one might be called while in a feverish sickness. Perhaps the one like this who is best known to North Americans is Black Elk from *Black Elk Speaks*. Irrespective of the details of the call, what is believed to be happening is the bestowing of a gift, a sensitivity to the unseen world that, with training, can be utilized for the benefit of the community.

In primal terms, what is happening is that a young person, either because he has great primal pain or is poorly defended or both, is vulnerable and open to his pain. His visions or dreams are symbolic ideations of the energy and content of his primal pain. The visions and dreams are accurate symbolic representations of primal pain in the context of any given worldview or religious stage. Thus, the young person has gained the knowledge of the dynamics of self-awareness and can use that knowledge for the benefit of his people.

Shamans, then, are persons who have an access to the unseen world that all others do not. They are those who are able to penetrate the self of ordinary reality and enter an extraordinary reality. The nature of that journey into the other reality will be determined by the stage of their self-awareness and its mirror, their religious Stage.

Shaman's Training

The most important aspect of a shaman's training is his experience of the interconnectedness of his self-awareness with his own body and with the spirits, deities and demons who inhabit all of reality. In every stage of self-awareness and of religion, the shaman knows that it is when the self has lost its center, become unbalanced, or is not in harmony with the spirit world that illness, misfortune and suffering occur. It is the expertise he develops regarding his own suffering that enables him to diagnose and treat the sufferings of others.

Almost equal in importance for the neophyte's training is the teaching provided by his peers, which commonly includes deceased shamans. If that is the case, the tradition must come from Stage III religion or later, as reincarnation precludes that happening in Stages I or II. The job of the master shaman is to teach the neophyte how to navigate in the spirit world. The master shaman doesn't have to teach the neophyte how to enter it; he is already open to it because of his visions and dreams.

The training a young shaman receives will be commensurate with the current stage of self-awareness. For example, in Stage I there will be a low level of illness and a high level of communal concern with survival. Hence, his training will emphasize the correct way to carry propitiatory sacrifices to the deities. In Stage III, for another example, the main emphasis of the training will be on mastering the use of power to influence and control, for a variety of purposes, the demons of the underworld and spirits and deities of the upperworld. Stage III, you recall, is the stage in which power is used to gain whatever it is the community desires to satisfy symbolically unmet needs for which desires have been substituted.

The training a shaman receives from the elder shamans is commensurate, symbolically, with what happens in formal primal therapy. The job of the primal therapist is to guide his patient into making connections between his current suffering and the pain of his suppressed, unmet adolescent, childhood and infantile needs. That experience, basically, is a primal. It might involve gentle crying or gut-wrenching sobs or a soundless, terrifying struggle to be born. In effect, the therapist works himself out of a job in the same way a senior shaman does with his trainee.

A Comparison of Primals With Trances

Primals—and their counterpart, trances—occur on three levels. The top level does not involve the loss of self-awareness. The two lower levels do.

A top-level trance involves primal pain in the emotional/sexual and thinking brains that was laid down *after* self-awareness formed. In trance, the shaman is diverted from his pain through singing, dancing, chanting, dreaming, drumming and sex. To a casual observer, it might appear that the shaman has lost self-awareness, but he has only been temporarily diverted from his pain. Up until there was an experience of a sub-self-awareness in the latter phases of Stage III, a top-level trance was the only one possible.

While in shamanism the aforementioned trance-inducers resulted in the suppression of primal pain in order to get into a trance, in primaling they are used to open one up to one's pain. For instance, I have sung a song my mother used to sing to me in order to get into a primal scene with her in which I plead with her to love me the way she loved my younger brother. Another instance is my dreams. They have often been the entry into a primal. On occasion, I have primaled on a dream while still sleeping and experiencing the dream.

A middle-level trance involves primal pain in the emotional/sexual and thinking brains laid down *before* self-awareness occurred. A middle-level trance does involve the loss of self-awareness, but, since the thinking brain is involved, the descent to that level does not cause one to feel as if one is going to lose one's self forever. Likewise with a middle-level primal, since the thinking brain is involved, there is no panic that one is going to lose one's mind.

A bottom-level trance involves primal pain that is laid down solely in the sensing/survival brain, as the emotional/sexual and thinking brains have not matured enough to assist in primal pain containment. That maturation takes place at about six months of age. In both the shaman's trance and a person's primal on this level, there is the undeniable experience that one is losing oneself. Breaking through to this level can cause extreme panic. I'll leave the rest of the discussion of the primal basis for this bottom-level trance until I cover the latter phases of Stage III of shamanism.

The Shaman's Ascent and Descent

As with all other aspects of the devolution of consciousness into self-awareness, the character of the shaman's ascent and/or descent is determined by the stage of self-awareness and of religion in which he lives and by where he lives. The presence of an ocean, for example, probably dictates that there is a descent, regardless of whether or not an underworld is part of the shaman's worldview. Unfortunately, so little information is available on shamanism in the first two stages of religion that only guesses can be made about the shaman's ascents or descents during those periods.

Without exception, traditional peoples, no matter where they live, feel themselves to be on the central axis of the earth. They feel themselves to be at the center of the universe. One has only to look at a globe of the earth to realize that no matter where one places one's finger, it is on a longitude that connects the poles. Traditional peoples observed the nighttime sky from dusk until dawn and marked the circular motion of the stars and planets. Of course, the closer to the poles, the more pronounced was the circular motion. In the northern latitudes, the polar star was the center about whom all the stars circled.

Being on the axis of the earth set the stage for the shaman's descent and ascent along the axis. The central axis could be a mountain, a building, the center pole of a tent, or the World Tree. The most ancient cities of China, Mesopotamia, Egypt, Central America and elsewhere were built around sanctuaries, that is, they were centered around a sacred space. This space was the center of the world where communication between the upperworld, this world and the underworld could take place. Irrespective of how the center is conceived, it is along that line that the breakthrough is achieved to the lower and upper worlds. Details specific to each stage and corresponding primal bases will be covered in the sections devoted to each of the three stages.

The Primal Basis for Shamanic Flight and Ecstasy

Flying is a theme common to all stages of shamanism because suppression of all sources of suffering and pain is necessary to give the self the experience of free-floating above the body. The more successful he is in suppressing his pain, the higher he will experience flight and the more complete will be his ecstasy. A modern name given to the experience is astral travel. The same can be achieved through all forms of meditation because they involve the suppression of the sources of pain: the body, the emotions and the mind or ego self.

In Stages I, II and early Stage III in which there is no underworld, the shaman achieves ecstasy upon entering the unseen world, having diverted his self-awareness from surface distractions. In that phase of Stage III when an underworld becomes a part of his worldview, a shaman must first descend and master the demons of the underworld. When he has done so, then he can ascend ecstatically to the upperworld.

The Primal Basis of the Return of the Shaman to Ordinary Reality

The experience of a shaman upon return to everyday self-awareness is that he has been somewhere else, that he has been to a place of extraordinary reality. On all trance levels, he has flown to the farthest reaches of his world. On the bottom level, he has journeyed into and out of a terrifying underworld.

When a primal person comes out of a primal, his experience is the same, but it is shorn of the religious symbolism that surrounds the shamanic journey. Even after a primal centered in the emotional/sexual brain, one knows that one has been back into one's childhood, feeling what one could not feel at the time because it was too traumatic to handle. The feeling of having been somewhere else after a sensing/survival brain primal is infinitely more pronounced. It has been a descent not only into pre-self-awareness—the middle level—but into the pain of experiences that could be managed only by the sensing/survival brain, the only part of the brain mature enough to process the pain. The primal person has been somewhere else too. He's been as far away as his own birth.

The Shaman's Use of Crystals

The use of crystals by shamans is universal. For the Hopi, the crystal objectified the center that controlled the shaman's eyes. When he looked through the crystal at his patient's psyche, his own center made contact with his patient's center. Thus, he could see in what way his patient was off-center. For the Mexican Huicols, their wise ones, who were more than fifty years old when they died, were reincarnated as crystals five years after their deaths. Neophyte shamans were apprenticed to these wise reincarnations. The shamans became channels for the wisdom of these ancient ones.

The universality of crystals can be accounted for by the clarity of insight and vision that occurs when ordinary self-awareness is out of the picture, that is, when all thoughts and emotions are effectively suppressed. When the shaman suppresses thought and emotion by means of his religious symbolism, he can look down on self-awareness and see it for what it is: a prisoner of demons. The shamans didn't really need crystals to do this, but they were a handy, power-invested tool for diagnosis.

I have experienced something very similar to what a shaman does when he gazes into his crystal. For over thirty years I have created fine art, abstract, macro photography. Early on, I discovered that the condition necessary to produce a winner was to let my mind go blank. When I did so, all that was left were lines, shapes, textures, colors and movement. It was pure seeing. There was no "I" in here looking at an object out there. The experience was much like a baby taking in the world visually without having any words to think about and to name the shapes in the experience. Another way of describing the experience of this way of seeing is that whatever is on the other side of the lens loses its objective reality.

Many revelations have come to me through the years because of preparing myself to let my mind go blank when my eye goes to the viewfinder. Two of them are relevant to shamanism. The first is that when I project the slides onto a screen, I see myself on the screen—not just my surface self, but who I am in my subconscious as well. The lens is my crystal that reveals me to myself. And, when others permit themselves to stare blankly at the projected abstract images, they gain insight into their deeper selves too.

The other relevant revelation is parallel to the Huicol shaman's experience. Since "I" am out of the picture—or totally into it—when the shutter is released, I feel that I do not create the images. In retrospect, I feel as I experience the projected images that I am only a conduit for the overwhelming beauty of consciousness, much as the Huicol shaman is a conduit for the wisdom of the ancient ones reincarnated into crystals.

Degradation of Shamanism

The degradation of shamanism refers first of all to the inevitable decline in shamanic powers after the Fall. During the Paradisal Period, shamans flew bodily on their journeys. After the Fall, the details of shamanic flight were determined by the particular stage of religion and of self-awareness they were in.

Degradation refers, secondly, to the shortcuts to trance that inferior shamans took in order to achieve the trance state of being. Drugs were the main artificial means used. The use of psychotropic plant derivatives was dangerous. Even for tribal peoples, they could cause fearful hallucinations. From a primal standpoint, the drugs blasted away the shaman's self-awareness. He was confronted directly with his underlying primal pain, but it was symbolized in images representing the demonic beings of the underworld. Things like clothes, drums, poles, singing and dancing were not considered to be artificial but part of the instructions given to achieve the trance.

Shamanism in Stage I of Religion

General Consideration

The best evidence of shamanism in Stage I is that which is pictured on the walls of the Lascaux and Trois Fréres caves. I will devote a separate section to them in this chapter. As for the statements that follow here, they are conjectures based on the nature of the first Stage in self-awareness and of its mirror: Stage I religion.

With regard to time, the ever-changing presentness of who it is that characterizes consciousness has been replaced with cyclical and linear time. Probably, linear time is restricted to the certainty that never will it be possible to get back to the Paradisal Period. All other experience of time will be cyclical. However, the experience of time will be close to that of consciousness, in that the words to express time most likely are something like "now" and "not now."

With regard to space, the absence of an experience of space in consciousness has been replaced with the experience of an "I" in here who experiences a world out there. This gives rise to the experience of extension or of space. However, the experience of space will be close to that of consciousness in that the words to express space are something like "here" and "not here."

In this Stage, space will encompass one external world. There is an experience of up and down, but it will be felt as up or down in the here-and-now.

The universe the shaman lives in is a personal one. Just as he experiences himself as being coexistent with his body, so that is true of all reality. Whether one is referring to a creature, a plant, a stone, a mountain, a river, or the sun, all have a self that is coexistent with his bodily manifestation. The shaman, as did all the people, communicates directly with all these other selves. And all of them had the same range of personality traits that characterized humans.

In this Stage, the work of the shaman will not include escorting the deceased to a final destination. That will not happen until Stage III. Reincarnation in this Stage precludes such a thing happening. Remember that in this Stage the self is never without a body.

Also in this Stage, since there is yet no awareness of a sub-self-awareness, it is not possible for the shaman's work to include journeying to an underworld. The conception of an underworld as the mirror of awareness of a sub-self-awareness must await Stage III.

In this Stage, generally speaking, people are going to be quite healthy, as the level of primal pain is quite low. When the shaman treats someone who is ill, he will use his crystal to see into his patient's gut, for that is where in this Stage the self will be located.

For the most part, the shaman's work will be concentrated on communal rather than individual concerns. This is a reflection of the high level in Stage I of the interconnectedness of all who is. The self still knows himself more in terms of relationships than an as individual.

The Role of Placation

Elsewhere I've discussed the "whys" and "wherefores" of the chronology of the major motifs of the first three Stages of self-awareness and of religion: placation, reimmersion and power. Here, I'll confine myself to exploring two characteristics of primal-pain-laden parents who are mirrored in the deities that have a bearing on the theme of placation in Stage I. These are capriciousness and getting rundown in the effort to properly nurture.

Parents are capricious in the care of their children because the children's needs can trigger, without warning, the parents' suppressed, unmet, infantile needs. This results in the parents becoming angry and withdrawing their nurturance from their children. The deities, since they have the same personalities as do humans, act the same way towards humans, of whom they are to take care. So the shaman, who is more familiar with this than anyone else because of his having to endure much capricious neglect, becomes the expert at placating the deities to secure favorable treatment from them.

Capriciousness can take the form of natural calamities, of injuries and of the scarcity of game. It is perhaps the latter of these about which we know the most. During the Paleolithic, it is evident that there were deities who were the Animal Master or the Mistress of Animals who had to be placated to make sure the hunted animals continued to be willing to give up their bodies so that the people could eat and survive. While in a trance, the shaman flew to the Master or Mistress, carrying with him appropriate sacrifices, to intercede on behalf of the people. If he were successful, he returned with instructions, songs, dances and rituals that, if properly carried out, would placate the Master or Mistress and thus secure survival.

In this Stage there was no fear of death because when the body died the self was always reincarnated. There was a fear, however, of a return to the nothingness of pre-creation. All the subordinate deities—whose manifestations were all the parts of the cosmos—together with the people were instructed by the Supreme Deity to maintain the orderliness of the cosmos so that it did not disintegrate into the disorder of pre-creation. The subordinate deities became exhausted in their work to sustain order and needed regular offerings from the people to become restored and able to continue their work.

When disorder appeared in the cosmos, it was because the people had neglected to offer proper sacrifices to the deities to sustain them. The people were at fault for the disorder—such as a natural calamity—that threatened their well-being. The shaman's role was to go into a trance, fly to the deities, discover how the people had failed, secure a remedy and return with new instructions on what to do to make sure order was restored.

Sacrifice and propitiation to sustain the subordinate deities has its mirror in the relationship of children and primal-pain-burdened parents. The parents have unfulfilled, infantile needs. Without realizing what they're doing, parents require their children to fulfill parental needs. Children learn through trial and error what they must do—what they must sacrifice of themselves—to satisfy their parents so that they will think of their children as being good children and deserving of order, stability and nurturance.

One example of the role of placation will suffice to show its role in Stage I. For the Iglulik Eskimos, animals have souls that must be placated because their bodies have been taken for food, clothing and shelter. If the animal souls are not pacified, they might become vengeful. This belief is the counterpoint of children realizing that if they do not placate their parents, their parents might become angry and take out their own vengeance upon them.

The Cave Paintings of Lascaux and Trois Fréres

The paintings in the caves at Lascaux and Trois Fréres are the only hard evidence we have of the nature of shamanism in Stage I. Even here, the interpretation we place upon these images is conjectural. My own interpretation is based upon my conclusions as to the nature of self-awareness and of religion in Stage I.

My interpretation is also based on my understanding that for traditional peoples there is no such thing as "art for art's sake." No matter what is created by traditional peoples, whether it be a dwelling, a weapon, a utensil, jewelry, or a painting, the creation is a living manifestation of some person, some creature, or some deity. Further, that living manifestation is inextricably connected to some aspect of the life of the people. It isn't until some point in Stage IV of self-awareness that art as a symbol or as a representational image comes into being.

My abstract photography has given me an experience of the images as being a living manifestation of who I am at the deepest level. When I project the images onto a screen, I feel that they are a living manifestation of myself. The consensus of those who have experienced these images is that yes, they are truly alive and speak to the person who is experiencing them. The photography has enabled me to experience the cave paintings of Lascaux and Trois Fréres as they were intended to be experienced: alive persons and creatures communicating directly with the experiencer.

Since the paintings in both caves were done long before the advent of Mother Goddess religion, the main theme of both is placation for survival. The difficult passageways into the caves and the domed areas of the paintings might very well symbolize the vagina and the uterus, however. In which case, the shaman's or shamaness's relationship was with an Animal Mistress, not the Mother Goddess.

In the Lascaux cave, the shaman is endeavoring to ensure a renewable supply of bison. In Trois Fréres, besides bison, the hunted animals are stag, horse and lion. In keeping with Stage I religion, the shaman might be offering the bison as a food offering to replenish a deity who has become depleted from his cooperative work with THE PEOPLE in maintaining the orderliness of the cosmos.

There are any number of possible interpretations of the bison in Lascaux. He could be the primordial animal who is the tribal ancestor. He could be the Animal Master. He could also be a manifestation of the Supreme Deity. Regardless of the interpretation, what is happening is a mirror for what children must do: placate their parents so that they will continue to be nurtured. In addition, the bison could be a helping spirit to assist the shaman on his journey. Or he could even be the means of transportation for the shaman in the Trois Fréres rendition.

In Lascaux, the means of flight are obvious. The shaman has been transmuted into a bird, and his bird wand is by his outstretched bird-foot-like hand. He could even be born of a bird-woman. The transmutation into a bird is achieved in the trance state in which, because of being cut off from all sources of primal pain, the self feels itself to be floating freely and can go anywhere.

In Trois Fréres, the means of flight is a bow. Perhaps the shaman is the arrow who is launched up to a heavenly realm. Traditionally, the bow has also been a means of calling spirits who fly to the shaman. The means depicted in Trois Fréres to achieve a state of trance is the transmutation of the shaman into a bison through the medium of dance.

Finally, with regard to the erect penis of the shaman in Lascaux and what appears to be a huge penis on the bison, many conjectures can be made. One possibility is that the bison mates with the Animal Mistress and out of that union is the birth of the first shaman. Another possibility is that it equates the loss of self that occurs in both sexual ecstasy and in the shamanic trance. Notwithstanding all probable explanations, my feeling is that the erect penises have to do with the second main theme of self-awareness and religion: sex/reimmersion. All three themes are present in Stage I, but sex/reimmersion is a secondary theme of lesser importance to survival/placation. Hence, my interpretation of the significance of the erect penises is that they signify the ecstasy that occurs when all sources of primal pain have been cut off and entry into a trance happens.

Shamanism in Stage II of Religion

General Consideration

There is a paucity of information about shamanism in Stage II of religion, which centers around Mother Goddess. The probable cause is the negative spin that Stage III religion placed upon Stage II. The male God-of-Power replaced the Goddess and put her down as being the cause of Evil. She was either subjugated or reinterpreted or vilified or suppressed or subjected to any combination of strategies to depose her.

Secondly, the minor role of reimmersion in Stage I as a journey into the extraordinary world that lay behind the self, in Stage II became the main focus of Mother Goddess religion and of all the mystic and Gnostic movements that came later. Reimmersion came to the fore because placation failed to secure from the deities the nurturance necessary to satisfy the people's needs. In pain and in despair, the people sought reimmersion into the womb of the Goddess where all needs would be met and there would be surcease from pain. Placation is still necessary (Stage I), and Power (Stage III) still plays a minor role in alleviating pain. Survival is the key in all three Stages. Self-awareness does what it has to do in order to survive.

What happens in reimmersion is the diversion of self-awareness from itself. The self seeks diversion from itself in order to feel no pain. The role of the shaman is to lead the people into a state of reimmersion into the Goddess or into possession by her, which means the same thing.

Since demons do not come about until Stage III, there is no fear that an evil spirit will snatch away one's self. In Stage III, one of the skills a shaman must master is how to gain control of contrary or Evil spirits.

Sexual Orgasm as a Metaphor for Reimmersion

As can be seen from the Lascaux cave painting, sex played a role in Stage I shamanism. I have concluded that sex played a major role whenever the call, initiation and instruction of the neophyte shaman featured sex. I have assigned those traditions that featured sex to Stage II.

A common occurrence in stage II is for the prospective shaman to receive his call while dreaming. In the dream, the dreamer has sex with a spirit woman who calls him to be a shaman. Another likely scenario is for a spirit woman to appear to someone on his sickbed. She calls him to be a shaman and that she will be his wife. If he refuses, she says she will kill him.

A fantasy I had when I was nine years old and sick with a life-threatening kidney infection illustrates in part the universality of this kind of experience. At the time, I was confined to my bed for a period of six weeks. I became bored. Idly, without having any reproductive knowledge, I began to play with my penis. I rubbed it against my thigh. At first it was just pleasurable. Then the sensations escalated to such a high point at the moment of orgasm that I had to let go as if I were holding onto an electrical rod and lightning had struck it.

At this same time, I had some big-little books, among which was one entitled *Buck Rogers in the 25th Century.* The antagonist in the story was the Dragon Lady. I fantasized that she had captured me and had me tied nude to a table. She wanted me to do something. I refused. She began to rub my penis against my thigh and, without letup, kept asking if now I would do her bidding. I refused and continued to refuse. When the sensation in my penis reached orgasm, I couldn't stand to refuse her anymore and gave in, saying, "Yes, yes, I'll do anything you want me to." Just like the shaman's sexual experience, so my sexual fantasy is an outworking of primal pain. My crying out at the moment of orgasm really means, "Yes, yes, Mommy, I'll do anything you want me to, only please, please love me." If I had been a member of a traditional society, my fantasy would have been interpreted as a call to become a shaman.

In the Buryat tradition, after the call, a shaman ancestor takes the soul of the candidate to the sky to instruct him and where the candidate will have sex with the nine wives of Tekla, god of dance, fecundity and wealth. When his instruction is finished, he meets his celestial wife-to-be and has sex with her. A tree, who is his celestial wife, is planted in his yard. A cord connects this tree with the candidate's tree in the courtyard.

In this Stage, it is common during a shamanic journey that the shaman will have sex with beautiful spirit women or a Goddess. In the Teleut tradition, it is likely that the shaman has sex with the Mother Goddess.

Sickness and Natural Calamities

Sickness, any form of a personal problem, or natural calamity is due primarily to an individual or the community as a whole being less than fully reimmersed in the Goddess or possessed by her. Secondarily, these misfortunes came about because of the failure to fulfill ritual obligations to the Goddess. Nature-ally, the Goddess is upset if the people are not fully reimmersed in her or are forgetful of their obligations to her. Her being upset is manifested in such things as drought or pestilence. The shaman—most likely a shamaness—leads the people into an acceptable relationship with the Goddess to restore personal closeness with her.

It is not in the Goddess's nature to be demonic. That does not come about until Stage III, when she is reinterpreted in order to make way for a male Warrior God. Therefore, the shamaness in Stage II does not appease malevolent spirits.

Means Other Than Sex for Reimmersion

Music, exhaustive dancing, drumming, singing and drugs were all used to initiate a loss of self-awareness. Those means to facilitate reimmersion or possession were not restricted to Stage II, but were used primarily for that purpose.

Shamanism in Stage III of Religion

General Consideration

The accumulation and use of power is the essence of shamanism in Stage III. In Stage I of self-awareness, of religion and of shamanism, placation was the primary way in which primal pain was managed. In Stage II, it was reimmersion. What gives rise to Stage III is a jump in the level of primal pain to the extent that now neither placation nor reimmersion are adequate to the task of suppressing primal pain. What became necessary was the denial or the suppression of infantile need itself in order to gain surcease from suffering engendered by the primal pain of needs not being met. The unmet, infantile need does not go away, however; it resurfaces as insatiable wants or desires. Concurrently, there is a feeling of helplessness in getting needs met. The feeling of helplessness is compensated for by a compulsion to accumulate and use power. It is at this point that the amassing and use of power comes into the picture. A child will use every means available to himself to use power to dominate his parents to get what he wants. The mirror of this is the nature of religion and of shamanism in Stage III.

The use of power in a futile effort to satisfy insatiable desires and to compensate for feelings of helplessness is a universal phenomenon. My focus here is on the specifics of the use of power in Europe, the Middle East and the Far East as the Warrior God religion of the Indo-Europeans conquered the peoples of Mother Goddess religion.

By far, most of what has been written about shamanism comes from late Stage III. The main source has been 19th and early 20th century, late Third Stage shamans who were interviewed by researchers whose self-awareness was at least late Third Stage. This presents great difficulties in determining what shamanism was like when Stage III first came about with the Proto-Indo-Europeans and the Indo-Europeans sometime in the 5th or 4th millennium BCE

The criterion, other than that of power, for placing what the researchers described into Stage III is what the information obtained from the shamans revealed about changes in the experience of space and time. With regard to space, the here and not-here experience of it changed to include a linear conception. Within Stage III, the changes in the linear idea of space provides a framework upon which to date the evolution of shamanism. The earliest linear conception of space was horizontal. In a far-distant place now there was a destination where all the dead went. In Chapter 9, The Destiny of the Dead, I indicated that Twin, the primordial first king, escorted the dead to their final abode. Twin might also have been considered to be the first shaman, but I have no evidence for that.

With regard to time, since the shamans now described a final destination for the dead, rather than reincarnation, it is an indication that linear time has now replaced cyclical time as the primary experience of time. When cyclical time predominates, reincarnation is likely to be the sole destiny of the dead. (See Part II, Chapter 5, for the primal foundation of space and time.)

The First Shaman in Stage III

Every shamanic culture has a tradition regarding the origin of its shamans and/or shamanesses. In one such tradition, the eagle is the father of the first shaman. In that culture, the eagle also represents the supreme deity.

In a Siberian Yakut tradition, the first shaman had immense power. He had such pride in his power that he refused to acknowledge the supreme deity of the Yakut. The shaman's body was made of snakes, which suggests that the source of his power was the Mother Goddess, one of whose manifestations is a reptile. Since in Stage III the Warrior God is replacing Mother Goddess, it makes sense that in response to the first shaman's arrogance the supreme deity attempted to kill the shaman by burning him. Out of the flames though, a toad emerged who became the source of the demons who supplied the Yakut with their shamans and shamanesses.

This oral tradition of the Yakut implies that everyone who acquires shamanic powers is the tool of a demonic Mother Goddess. My guess is that there is one tradition for shamanesses who consort with demons and another for shamans whose source is their supreme deity.

The preceding is borne out in a Germanic tradition. Shamanesses used a form of magic that could cause death, misfortune, or sickness. Shamans did not because to do so brought shame. This tradition reflects the efforts of a Warrior God society to demonize everything female.

The Neophyte Shaman's Call to Power

In the introduction to this chapter, I noted the primal basis for sickness as being the means by which an adolescent is called to become a shaman. By Stage III, phase three, the summons is specifically a call to power, power over demons who possess chaos-creating power and who exist in a free and untamed state. This is the mirror of a state of ego breakdown and of primal pain erupting uncontrollably.

Whoever is communicating the call to the neophyte reminds him that if he doesn't accept the call, he will die. From a primal point of view, the call is consciousness's way of leading a person to his pain in a gradual way. If a person refuses the call, he makes a frontal assault on his defenses that threatens to overwhelm self-awareness and cast the person into a psychosis that might become suicidal. The threat to the neophyte that he will die if he doesn't accept the call is based on the common knowledge that if you fight against your demons, you only increase their strength to the point of being destroyed by them.

My call to the ministry came at a time when I was a freshman in college and failing in chemistry and trigonometry. My self-awareness was in crisis, but I didn't know it. My self-awareness was threatened with failure due to unrecognized feelings of "I can't do it, Daddy (Mommy); I can't be what (who) you want me to be." More precisely, my call was to preach against false religion. It was to preach the truth. In actuality, it was a plea of "Please listen to me, Daddy (Mommy)." If I hadn't responded to the call, I would have been forced to confront the looming crisis of the viability of my self-awareness. I might have had a nervous breakdown or even have become so despondent as to commit suicide. Answering my call fended off my demons by acting out symbolically my infantile need to be listened to and to be myself.

The neophyte, by answering his call, exhibits a willingness to confront physical death in this world and psychic death in the underworld. For this experience he, or she, has the help of a master shaman or mistress shamaness to negotiate his perilous journey. Care must be taken that the demons do not take up permanent residence in the neophyte for, if they do, instead of gaining power he becomes ensnared in their power.

In Stage II, possession by the Goddess of one's self was sought after. Increasingly, however, in Stage III as loss of soul is associated with a demonized Goddess, loss of soul must be guarded against. Demon possession is to have lost one's soul. The master shaman helps the neophyte to gain spirit allies to navigate through the underworld.

One image of the neophyte's travail is that he must cross over a sword bridge, which symbolizes how difficult it is to keep from losing one's self in the underworld phase of his journey. The bridge is a reminder that narrow is the way to power and few there be who find it. It is likewise true in primaling. Some pseudo-primal therapists have opened up some of their patients to primal pain in the sensing/survival brain who weren't prepared for it and which caused them to become psychotic. In shamanic terms, they lost their souls.

As I have noted elsewhere, the transition from Stage II to Stage III religion involved the put-down of the Goddess. That same pattern is true in the experiences of the neophyte shaman. In Stage II, sexual intercourse with a spirit woman, Goddess, or celestial wife was a central part in his initiation. In Stage III, however, the celestial wife is a temptation to resist if he is to receive his powers. She offers him food and sex, which will make him forget that he is making the journey to receive his shamanic powers. In the Teleut (Asian) tradition, she resides in the seventh heaven, but he goes on to the fourteenth, the highest.

The offering of food to the neophyte shaman or of food and sex by a celestial spirit woman seeking to be his wife probably reflects what was happening as well in society in Stage III. To compensate for the disparity in physical strength between men and women, to an extent not seen before, women began to use sex as a means of power to get whatever they wanted from men.

The Underworld

It is universally true that there is no experience of an underworld until Stage III of self-awareness and of religion. A three-tiered cosmos consisting of an underworld, this world and an upperworld cannot come into being until there is a three-tiered psyche consisting of a sub-self-awareness, the body and self-awareness. Such a psyche does not come into personal experience until the power-dominated third stage of self-awareness. From a primal point of view, the sub-self-awareness is in reality the suppressed consciousness-in-pain.

As I've stated elsewhere, every place on the earth is on a longitude that connects the poles. At the very least, this gives rise to the experience of being at the center of the cosmos. By the third phase of Stage III, when an underworld is known, the center has become extended into being the central axis. At its lower end is the underworld, its middle is the land and seas and at the top is the upperworld. The axis passes through a hole, and it is through this hole that passage is made from one world to the others.

The World Tree is another manifestation of the three-tiered cosmos. Its roots are in the underworld, the trunk is this world and the top branches are the upperworld. This Tree is the means of descent and ascent in the cosmos.

There is a primal basis for a three-tiered self-awareness and its mirror, a three-tiered cosmos. In the first place, it is total primal pain that necessitates the formation of self-awareness to shield the child from intolerable primal pain. Absent any miraculous return to consciousness, the child's parents will continue to be unable to meet their child's needs. Consequently, primal pain will continue to pile up in the suppressed consciousness. In time, sufficient primal pain will accumulate to the extent that its upward pressure will cause self-awareness to become aware of a sub-self-awareness, a darker side of itself. The mirror of this is a dark, shadowy underworld of suffering. I say "suffering" because the upward pressure of primal pain translates into suffering for self-awareness.

But it isn't just the accumulation of primal pain to a critical point that produces the sensation of a sub-self-awareness. All along there has been an unfelt subconscious, due as well to the necessity of increasingly suppressing need itself. What characterizes Stage III as much as anything else is the complete denial of need. Up to this point, relatively speaking, need has been on the surface of self-awareness. Now need and pain together push upward, seeking expression and give rise to the experience of a sub-self-awareness.

At the same time, to mitigate suffering, self-awareness separates itself further from the body and its emotions, but not so far as to sever all connections. That occurs in Stage IV. Self-awareness elevates itself in stages all throughout its history, but in Stage III it is still body-oriented. There is, however, an increased importance given to the sky deities that reflects back upon how self-awareness conceives of itself.

The entrance to the underworld is often a small hole, as pictured in the hole through which the central axis goes. Or it might be some other narrow passageway. It might be through doors that open and close quickly. The paths leading to the underworld are difficult and filled with peril. From a primal point of view, the shaman encounters all sorts of primal-pain-created demons when he attempts to enter the underworld. The journey is an attack of self-awareness upon itself as a defense system. This attack enables the full energy of repressed primal pain to be released and experienced symbolically as demonic chaos.

In any event, when the shaman attempts to go into a trance, he is faced with what Janov calls the "window of opportunity" in primaling. The window is open to get into a primal when either there is an increase in feeling of pain to the point of eruption into tears or sobbing, for example, or when too much erupting pain has subsided to the point where one can handle it and go through the window of opportunity.

It is necessary to discuss the sequence in which primal pain was laid down historically in all three brain levels to understand the history of the shaman's experience of the underworld. Approximately 7,000 years ago when a sub-self-awareness was first experienced, primal pain laid down in the emotional/sexual and thinking brains was the bulk of primal pain. In general, parents were still successful enough in meeting their children's needs that primal pain laid down in the sensing/survival brain was significantly lower than pain on the other levels. So, when cognizance of a sub-self-awareness and an underworld first occurred, conceptions of them were driven by primal pain that was laid down after six months of age in the emotional/sexual and thinking brains. In turn, this meant that when the shaman descended to the underworld he was able or not able to speak in his trance. That depended upon his age at the time of the painful primal events that were symbolized during his shamanic journey.

The nature of the shaman's descent to the underworld in the earlier conceptions of it is revealed by what happens in a primal in the emotional/sexual and thinking brains on events that took place after six months of age, but before self-awareness took place. In the primal, there is a loss of self-awareness; one is really back into a period when consciousness was still able to hang on despite whatever primal pain was there. Yet there is no panic at losing one's mind because the thinking brain is still there in the primal experience.

As time went on and parents were increasingly unable to meet the needs of their infants under six months of age—at which time neither the emotional/sexual nor the thinking brain functions were sufficiently mature enough to help in pain management—primal pain had to be handled by the sensing/survival brain. It is there that the earliest primal pains are laid down, including birth trauma, which increased as women became ever more loaded with primal pain.

So, at this point, pain laid down in the sensing/survival brain began to dominate conceptions of the sub-self-awareness and the underworld. The energy behind the upward pressure of infantile needs to be satisfied and the pain of their not being met became such that that energy was experienced as one of being threatened by demons, both in the psyche and in the underworld. Now, in this latest conception of the underworld in Stage III, when the shaman descended to the underworld, he descended past primal pain laid down in the emotional/sexual brain to primal pain laid down in the sensing/survival brain. Now he not only lost self-awareness, he lost the cognitive functions of the thinking brain. It is the loss of the ability to think that gave rise to the feeling of losing one's mind that, in turn, gave rise to the various experiences of death, dismembership and resurrection characteristic of the latest of Stage III conceptions of the underworld.

The shaman's descent to a demonized underworld in the latest Stage III conception of the underworld is revealed by what happens in a primal taking place in the sensing/survival brain. One can go directly from everyday self-awareness to this deepest level of a primal or descend through primal pain in the emotional/sexual brain before experiencing a primal in the sensing/survival brain. My aborted primal on Ida illustrates what can happen when the descent goes from the thinking brain directly to the sensing/survival brain. My front-porch primal illustrates the descent first through primal pain in the emotional/sexual brain. (See Part I, Chapter 2, for the exposition of these primals.) In any case, it is the descent through the thinking and emotional/sexual brains that gives rise to the feeling that one is losing one's mind or what is symbolized in the shaman's dismemberment.

There is one very certain way of determining through observation alone whether a shaman is in the earliest conceptions or the latest conception of the underworld. A shaman sometimes speaks in strange voices that appear not to be his own. If the shaman talks at all, he is in a symbolized primal in the emotional/sexual and thinking brains in his underworld trance. If he were in a symbolized primal in the sensing/survival brain or in the early stages of the emotional/sexual and thinking brains, he could make any kind of vocalization, but he couldn't talk.

During Stage III, the conception of the underworld becomes thoroughly demonic in nature. This reflects the experience of a demonic sub-self-awareness dominated by primal pain in the sensing/survival brain that threatens to erupt and take possession of self-awareness. Now, diseases of all kinds—physical, emotional and mental—are the physical manifestations of disease spirits, whose home is in the underworld. All spirits, regardless of their home, have manifestations in the physical world.

The degree of terror associated with a descent into the underworld is directly proportional to the terror associated with a threatened eruption of one's demonic sub-self-awareness. That degree of terror increases with every increase in the amount of primal pain suppressed into the subconscious.

One of the most graphic representations of what happens in a shamanic trance is that of a skeleton. The shaman might wear a costume on which is depicted the whole skeletal framework. Carved or sculptured figures might expose either half or the whole of a skeleton. The figure might brandish a knife, indicating that the shaman's flesh was cut off. According to shamans from hunting and herding cultures, bone symbolized the source of life. To be reduced to a skeleton was to die and to be reborn, for, on his journey, the shaman's bones were reclothed with a body fit for astral travel.

All over the world there are carved, sculpted, or cast figures that show a neophyte shaman being devoured by an animal such as a bear, a tiger, or a jaguar. What is most significant is that the neophyte clings to the devouring animal with what appears to be affection. It is clear that he has conquered his fear and willingly submits to the loss of himself. Where large bodies of water are at hand, it is common for the neophyte to be eaten by a sea monster. The scriptural books of Ezekiel (bones) and Jonah (whale) suggest a relationship to shamanism.

Both the representations of a skeleton and the shaman-eating carnivore in shamanism have a parallel in primaling. Regardless of whether a primal in the sensing/survival brain happens precipitously from the thinking brain or descends more slowly through the emotional/sexual brain, there is the experience of losing one's mind. It is clear from this comparison that a shamanic trance is a symbolic primal. Further, just as the shaman knows that by submitting willingly to being devoured he will not be possessed by demons, so the primal person knows that by giving himself up to losing his mind, instead of being blown away, he will experience a portion of his consciousness-in-pain.

Undoubtedly, it is from the dismemberment, death and resuscitation sequence of the shamanic experience in Stage III religion that all subsequent death and resurrection themes arise in religion. There is an exact parallel to this in primaling. Many times, when I have come out of a primal, the primary feeling is that I have been reborn. A little bit of the old, unconscious, self-aware Vic has died and a new, less unconscious Vic has been resurrected.

Put another way, the realm of death to which the shaman descends is the death of the ego. At that point, he has broken through ego defenses and encountered primal pain, which is symbolized in demonic forces. Just as the elder shamans teach the neophyte to accept rather than fight the demons, so a primal therapist assists his patient to accept his primal pain rather than fight it. Again, as the neophyte learns to assimilate the demons, he can ascend via the World Tree or Cosmic Bird, for example, realize a solar identity and return to the middle world of human affairs. Likewise, the primal person partially cleanses his subconscious of primal pain and incrementally transforms his unconscious self-awareness back into consciousness and returns to his life a changed person.

Here, I want to call special attention to one aspect of the shaman's descent into the underworld: the mastery over fire. However it is experienced and described, the encounter in the underworld with the demons is one in which the heat of a consuming fire is endured. It is a purifying fire that enables the shaman to identify himself with the Sun. To become one with the Sun is to achieve an awakening as to the nature of the self that one can never forget. The change in awareness is irreversible.

As to be expected, there is a primal explanation for the shamanic experience. Core body temperature is affected by primal pain. It takes energy to suppress primal pain. Janov's studies show, I believe, that primaling, by reducing the amount of suppressed primal pain, allows one's organism to run cooler.

Janov's studies also show that when a primal in the sensing/survival brain is on the verge of breaking through, unconscious self-awareness fights to head it off, which raises core body temperature. This is the basis for the shamanic symbolism of fire and its mastery as one of the components of a shamanic journey into the underworld.

As to the irreversibility of awakening that is central to the shamanic experience of the nature of the self, the same is true for the primal person. Once one has made the connection between present suffering and primal pain, that is, has experienced that unconscious self-awareness is nothing more than a defense system holding back primal pain, one can never forget that every thought, every word, every emotion and every act is driven and controlled by buried primal pain. A primal person can never go back to living as if self-awareness were consciousness.

Various shamanic traditions indicate that not all shamans made the descent to the underworld. For some, I'm sure the descent was too threatening. In primal terms, they had too much primal pain and too fragile defenses to be able to handle going forward to meet their demons.

With the Asiatic Altaic people, there was a gender-driven separation between those who went to the underworld and those who didn't. In their culture, shamanesses went only to the underworld and their color was black. Some of the shamans were white and went only to the upperworld. The rest of the shamans were both black and white. They went both to the lower and upper worlds.

This scenario confirms that in Stage III, regardless of where in the world it takes place and when it does, femaleness is put down as being demonic. The color chosen for shamanesses is significant as well. The underworld is a black place. It also confirms that some shamans do not have the power to descend to the underworld and survive. The gender-driven separation of roles is a sure sign that the tradition comes from the last Stage III conception of the underworld.

The Attainment of Power

Although shamanic traditions relate that power is given to the neophyte when he ascends from the underworld to the upperworld, it is his successful mastery of the power beings of the underworld that constitutes his attainment of power. It most often happens in the midst of a personal crisis, for it is then that the self breaks and the power beings attempt to possess the neophyte. It is the elder shamans who teach the neophyte how to master the spirits.

Primally, what is happening to the neophyte is that he has poor defenses, and great primal pain is erupting, causing neurotic, if not psychotic, reactions. In primal therapy, a therapist guides the patient on how to experience the erupting pain, rather than symbolizing it as is done in shamanism.

The power beings who began as the antagonists of the neophyte now become his helpers, his spirit allies. Now they are at his service in his shamanic work.

His first work is that of healing himself of all the suffering caused by the demonic beings of the underworld. Once he has accepted those who were terrifying to himself, he becomes very sensitive to how they cause imbalance and disharmony and lead to every form of suffering. He is now in a position to be able to see which demons are tormenting his patients and to exorcise those demons. From a primal perspective, he understands the dynamics of the upward pressure of primal pain to gain access to awareness symbolized as demonic beings.

A second aspect of his work is guiding the dead to their ultimate destination. In Stage III, there are five distinct periods to this work, which reflect four discrete jumps in the level of primal pain generally. In the first period, the destination of the dead is to some far-distant place in this world. In the second one, everyone goes to an upperworld. In the third period, everyone winds up suffering in the underworld. In the fourth, the diseased and aged go to the underworld, while the heroes who have died in battle go to the upperworld. In the last period, the evil go to an underworld that is now the realm of just female deities, while the good go to the upperworld, the realm of male deities.

By way of illustration of the shaman's work in the latter periods of the destination of the dead, the Maso people of China relate that the shaman first has to escort the deceased past the demons who block the bridge to hell. The demons are there because of the sins of the deceased. Then the shaman escorts the deceased through hell and from there up to the realm of the deities. One must literally go through hell to get to heaven.

In the Indo-European tradition, a question arises as to who does the escorting of the deceased. In Part III, Chapter 9, I noted that Twin (or Kolyo) escorted the deceased to their destination. Is it possible that each was also considered as a shaman or shamaness?

A third aspect of the shaman's work has to do with war. He uses the power he has taken over from the power beings to achieve victory over non-Indo-European people who have cattle. Since the deities have given cattle exclusively to the Indo-Europeans, these other peoples must have stolen them. In the last period of Stage III, it is a demonized Goddess of the underworld who first stole cattle from the Indo-Europeans.

In general, throughout Stage III, the basic use of power is to satisfy wants and to overcome helplessness. As is apparent from their theology, the sky deities are co-opted to get them to use their power to assist the people in getting their wants satisfied and to get them to empower the people. This, as we know, is the mirror for what happens in the third Stage of self-awareness. In Stage I, the main focus is on placation of parents. In Stage II, it is the desire to lose one's self-awareness in some form of oceanic experience. And in Stage III, when needs are suppressed and resurface as wants, the main focus is for a child to use every means of power to get his parents to satisfy his insatiable wants and to overcome his feelings of helplessness.

The problem for the people is whether the shaman will use his powers for the good of his people or whether he will divert them for his personal use. The ordeals that a neophyte goes through tend to weed out the unworthy who would use power for evil, yet there are some who do. This same situation confronts every primal person. A primal knowledge of the workings of self-awareness enables one to be able to push someone's buttons to manipulate his behavior. For myself, the use of that power for anything but my own growth toward lesser unconsciousness is unthinkable.

The Ascent to the Upperworld

After his journey to the underworld where he has been tested and come through successfully, the shaman ascends to the upperworld. There are shamans who never journeyed to the underworld but who just ascended. Their powers were limited because of not being so arduously tested.

There were any number of means of ascent: fire, smoke, rope, vines, sunbeams, or a chain of arrows. Four of the main ways were by a rainbow bridge, a drum, a ladder and the World Tree. The rainbow, being a natural phenomenon, was an obvious choice as a means to ascend. The various shadings of the colors of the rainbow might have given rise to the positing of the number of the levels of heaven in any given cosmology. Drums decorated with rainbows are associated with the ascent of the shaman. The drum might also be experienced as a stag, a bird, or a horse. The hypnotic beat of the drum assisted the shaman in his ascent. A ladder, usually of seven steps, was common as the means to climb to the upperworld. A likely reason for seven steps was a heaven of seven levels made up of the moon, the sun and the five planets visible to the naked eye.

The World or Cosmic Tree was perhaps the last of the means conceived to ascend to the upperworld. Its imagery of a tri-level cosmos with roots in the underworld, trunk in this middle world and branches in the upperworld requires for its possibility a tri-level psyche, consisting of a sub-self-awareness, a body and self-awareness. The tri-level psyche did not come about until well into the third stage of self-awareness and religion, at which time it would tend to obliterate all earlier imagery.

There is a great deal of tradition that has grown up around the World Tree that has nothing to do with the shaman's ascent. The Tree means perpetual regeneration. All of life springs from the primeval waters beneath it. It should be noted though that the underworld to which the shaman descends is not the primordial deep from which the cosmos is ordered. Sometimes the cosmic pillar stands for the Cosmic Tree. In this imagery, the shaman makes propitiatory sacrifices to the deities. Sacrifice indicates the carryover from Stage I of the necessity of propitiation of the deities for survival.

Behind the imagery of the shaman's ascent is flight, the feeling one gets when one has suppressed sensations, emotions and thought from all three levels of the brain. Self-awareness, when it has suppressed all avenues of pain, feels itself to be free-floating. It permits, as I've said elsewhere, astral travel.

Ecstasy

Besides the feeling of free-floating when suppression of sensations, emotions and thought is complete, there is the feeling of ecstasy. The complete absence of pain is ecstasy. To feel is to suffer. Not to feel is to be ecstatic. Rapture is a word that also captures the nature of the experience. In a primal, the release of pain gives rise to the feeling of goodness or ecstasy or rapture in proportion to the amount of pain released. In contrast to shamanism in which suppression of primal pain gives rise to ecstasy, in primaling it is the release of primal pain that produces ecstasy.

As I indicated in the very beginning of this chapter, while ecstasy is a big part of the shamanic experience, it is not the goal of the shamanic journey. It is, rather, a result of the shaman's total success in mastering the demons that confronted him in the underworld and the attainment of power over them. Consequently, all other members of his people can experience only relative peace. They do their best to avoid demons and make offerings to the deities, but they cannot achieve ecstasy.

In Stage II of religion, in which there was no underworld, reimmersion into the Goddess was ecstatic. In that stage, it was not necessary to do battle with demons first in order to achieve union with the Goddess. It was only with a huge increase in primal pain, giving rise to a chaotic sub-self-awareness, that conquering demons became necessary to achieve ecstasy.

The Social Function of Shamanism

Throughout the millennia of Stage III religion there is an incremental decline in the scope and importance of the shaman's functions to the community and a corresponding increase in the scope and importance of his services to individuals. The underlying foundation for this change is the incremental cutting of the connections between self-awareness and the total organism because of ever higher levels of primal pain. Yet, during the whole period of Stage III religion, there are important communal aspects to the shaman's work. (See Part III, Chapter 8, on rituals to sustain the cosmos in which shamans must have played a major role.)

Shamans, no doubt, played a major communal role in Indo-European society. Prior to warriors going into battle, shamans probably were the ones who led the frenzied dances that transformed ordinary men into ferocious beasts of prey. "Berserker" was the word that described them—for obvious reasons.

The Seven-Rung Ladder and the Seven Chakras

As a final point in Stage III shamanism, I suggest that there is some correlation between the shaman's seven-rung ladder to the sky and the seven chakras leading to reunion with the One. First of all, the shaman must descend to the underworld, which is characterized by the suffering endured on chakra levels one through three: survival, sex and power. Whether it be the first three rungs on the ladder or the first three chakras, this is where all persons are when they begin their journey out of suffering and into ecstasy. Whether it is in meditation or shamanism, these lower levels are experienced as being inhabited by terrifying demons.

I cannot make a correlation between the top four rungs of the ladder and the four upper chakras, except for the top one, which is some form of union with the divine. Here, the same goal is reached; only the description of the experience is different. Perhaps both traditions are based on something I suggested earlier: the seven wandering stars being the seven levels of the journey.

Shamanism in Stage IV Religion

General Consideration

As I've stated elsewhere, the leap from Stage III to Stage IV religion represents a monumental jump in the amount and valence of suppressed primal pain. Up to this point, self-awareness has deemed itself capable of mitigating its own suffering. It has maintained some ties to the body. It has been able to hold on to the unity of its world—the underworld and upperworld being extensions of this world. But no longer. Self-awareness now sees itself as inseparable from a state of suffering, whether caused by desire or sinfulness. It severs its last connections to the body. It posits this world as being physical and the underworld and upperworld as being spiritual.

In Stage IV religion, we witness the total separation of God from the cosmos. God exists prior to the cosmos and creates it out of nothing. In the mirror image from which this conception of God comes, self-awareness experiences itself as being totally separate from the body. It is housed within the body and when it contemplates itself it has the shape of the body that contains it.

In Stage III, self-awareness still had ties to the body. The shift to self-awareness having no ties to the body in Stage IV had a profound effect on conceptions of the nature of the body with which the shaman flew. In Stage III, when a demon snatched a soul and took it to the underworld, that soul took on the same physical body it would have had if it were deceased. Remember, in Stage III, the underworld as well as the upperworld are as physical as this world. In Stage IV, when a demon snatched a soul and took it to the underworld, that soul now took on the same spiritual body it would have had if it were deceased. In Stage IV, both the underworld and upperworld have left behind the physical and are now conceived in nonmaterial, spiritual terms.

In Stage III, when the shaman journeyed to the underworld to retrieve a soul, he traveled with a physical body. In Stage IV, he did it with a spiritual body.

Two Worlds

In all of the so-called civilized world, I doubt that shamanism exists untouched by the Stage IV religion of transcendence. For example, some present-day North American shamans experience this world as only an apparent reality or as an illusion. The real world exists behind the world of appearances, and it is out of the unseen real world from which the world of appearances comes. Or, this world is an illusion, as is self-awareness itself, the real world and the real self being behind what is illusory. These concepts show the influence of a Far Eastern, Fourth Stage religion of transcendence. I don't know how far these shamans go with transcendence, but experiencing this world and self-awareness as illusory is definitely part of the whole picture of mitigating suffering through transcendence. By detaching one's self from the world of the differentiated many and entering the world of the undifferentiated One, surcease from suffering is achieved.

There is a primal basis for the experience of two worlds, albeit the shamanic one is symbolic. In a primal, there is a double awareness. In it, I am aware that I am an adult in a primal. At the same time, I am aware that I am at some point in the past as the child or infant I was then and experiencing some specific pain that has been repressed. It is this suppressed consciousness-in-pain that the shaman experiences and symbolizes that is the content of his real world behind his world of appearances.

In Stage IV religion and shamanism, unity of the two worlds is achieved by either denying the reality of the material world or by making matter a function of mind. Eastern religion does the former, while Christianity does the latter in that God creates the material world by his Word.

Asceticism, Heat and Creation

In Stage III, it was the shaman's struggles with demons that produced enough heat to be a purifying fire. In Stage IV, asceticism also produced tremendous heat—enough to create the cosmos.

Asceticism is a Stage IV phenomenon. It is part of the denial of the body in order to escape suffering. Asceticism is also an effort to transcend self-awareness. Asceticism creates heat because it is a direct attack on the whole defense system holding back primal pain. The more successful ascetic practices are, the more opportunity there is for primal pain to rise to the surface, which makes the heart race and body temperature rise.

The shamanic sensation of creating the cosmos is a parallel to my own experience. With each primal, I feel the old me and his world demolished. With each primal, I feel a new me and a whole new world created. This happens because the inner and outer worlds mirror each other. A new beginning inside means a new beginning outside. What also happens is that over time as primaling restores consciousness, the inner and outer worlds merge into one conscious world.

Christ and Buddha as Shamans

My study of both shamanism and religion bears out that those who formulated the traditions about Christ and Buddha were quite familiar with the central role of shamanism to religion. Their purpose was to show that the role of the shaman culminated in Christ or in Buddha. In the Christian tradition, Christ became the required shaman. In the Buddhist tradition, Buddha showed the way for everyone to become his own shaman.

With regard to the identification of Christ with shamanism, I mention some of the traditions grown up around his death that confirm the identification. The cross was the World Tree at the center of the world on which Christ descended to the underworld and ascended to the upperworld. The descent and the ascent are purely shamanic in nature. Being buried in a cave also symbolizes the descent. His being pierced with a sword is symbolic of the shaman being dismembered. His bodily resurrection and bodily ascension go all the way back to what every person could do in the paradisal time and what only authentic shamans could do after the "Fall." Although the seven last words of Christ on the cross are not found in any one of the gospels, that the final editors of the New Testament chose to make the number of final sayings seven is to make reference to the seven-rung ladder of the shaman.

The identification of Buddha with shamanism is equally as clear. In the moments before Buddha's enlightenment, he contends with Mara, the God of Death. Mara fails; Buddha becomes enlightened and the cycle of life, death and rebirth is broken. Buddha then ascends to the seventh cosmic level. His descent and ascent is on a stairway that is the axis mundi: the center of the universe.

In Indo-European rituals reenacting the creation of the universe from Ox, a shaman probably carried the bull sacrifice to the upperworld. In Buddhist theology, Buddha is the final bull sacrifice, ending the illusion that the universe is real. He ends the need for any further sacrifice. He is pictured as rising into the air, cutting his body in pieces, letting them fall to the ground and putting them back together. The dismemberment of the Buddha is an exact parallel of what happens to a shaman on his journey. In his work, the Buddha demonstrates that everyone can become like him: achieve enlightenment without recourse to a shaman.

Summary

Basically, what I've done in this chapter is examine the broad range of shamanic traditions and place them within the natural chronology of the stages of a child's responses to primal pain. This exercise demonstrated that throughout the millennia consciousness declined and unconscious self-awareness increased in that those called to be shamans were increasingly neurotic, if not psychotic. Equally basic, I've shown that there is not a single aspect of shamanism that does not have a foundation in a primal experience. This endeavor, therefore, demonstrated that the history of the shamanic trance, far from being a unique phenomenon, is the mirror image of the stages in a primal. Finally, I've shown that in Stage IV religion, the role of the shaman ends because the function of the shaman reaches its fulfillment in figures like Christ or Buddha.

Once more you might ask, "What has the history of shamanism got to do with me?" Once again, recall that my basic purpose is awakening you to the realization that so-called self-consciousness is really asleep and controlled by primal pain, that is, that self-awareness is really in a state of unconsciousness. By elucidating the history of shamanism, I sought to have you make the parallel connection between your own journey and the journey of the shaman.

CHAPTER 11

ZARATHUSTRA, ZOROASTER AND ZOROASTRIANISM

Because of the radical shift from Stage III to Stage IV religion in the 1st millennium BCE, special note is taken of the religious reformer Zarathustra. He is usually known as Zoroaster, the Greek form of his name. While some scholars doubt his historicity, most scholars place him from the 10th to the 6th centuries BCE in Persia, present-day Iran. Persia at this time was controlled by the Indo-Europeans who were in Stage III religion.

There are problems to overcome in determining just what Zarathustra's teachings were. Even historians doing primary research have major disagreements about core elements of Zarathustra's theology. In my judgment the contradictory interpretations of Zarathustra can be partially accounted for by whether an historian has remained essentially in Stage III or has moved into Stage IV. Probably, it is that we know more about what the historian thought about Zarathustra than what Zarathustra thought. The first problem is that, in the time frame and place assigned to him, writing itself was absent. The second is that for centuries after him writing was forbidden. It wasn't until the 5th century A.D. when the oral traditions were written down. None of that work is extant.

The earliest extant manuscripts date from the 14th century A.D. Avesta is the name given to the sacred literature of Zoroastrianism and comprises a number of separate books. One section of it, the Gathas, is credited to Zarathustra. Even so, one cannot be certain that what is contained in the Gathas accurately reflects Zarathustra's teachings. On the other hand, one cannot say that the other sections of the Avesta do not contain authentic reflections of his theology. I will take the position that any teaching that reflects Stage III is most likely an accurate portrayal of Zarathustra's thinking, and any statement that reflects Stage IV might or might not be attributable to him.

The traditions that grew up about Zarathustra's birth and life either pre-figure Stage IV religion or were revisions of earlier accounts in order to make Zarathustra's conception, temptations and life appear to be the model for the traditions that grew up around the conception, temptations and life of Stage IV Christianity's Jesus. According to tradition, Zarathustra's guardian angel entered an haoma plant that was eaten by a priest as he was offering a divine sacrifice. (The haoma plant was associated with the bull god and probably had mind-altering properties.) At the same time, a ray of heaven's glory entered a young noblewoman. The priest married the woman. The indwelling angel in the priest and the indwelling ray in the woman comingled in the sexual consummation of the marriage, thus conceiving Zarathustra. This tradition definitely reflects Stage IV religion in that humanity by this time has become so debased as to be incapable of saving itself from a condition of suffering; it takes the interference of the divine into the human condition in order to effect salvation. It is an indicator of how far consciousness has devolved into unconscious self-awareness that it cannot save itself from suffering. In all likelihood, this tradition originated long after Zarathustra's death by followers who sought to make parallels with the traditions growing up about the conception of Jesus.

Likewise, as with Jesus, when Zarathustra received his call to preach repentance for the Kingdom of Heaven was at hand, he withdrew from society to live in a mountain wilderness, eating cheese and plants. As with Jesus, Zarathustra was tempted unsuccessfully by the Devil. Also, as with Jesus, he was pierced by a sword. In contrast to Jesus' merely being pierced by a sword during his crucifixion, Zarathustra's wound was filled with molten lead.

On the one hand, it is easy to believe that Zoroastrian writers subsequent to Jesus used the gospels as a source for manufacturing an earlier tradition about Zarathustra. On the other hand, it is my conclusion that the gospel writers were quite familiar with earlier religious traditions having to do with shamans, saviors and their death and resurrection, for example, and quite deliberately sought to cast Jesus in the role of the final fulfillment of all religious traditions. Christians have a tendency to think of their religion as happening in a vacuum or "out of the blue," but it is plain to see that nothing takes place except in a historical context.

In the context of the parameters of time assigned to Zarathustra, I believe that Persian religion was evolving from Stage III to Stage IV. From the theological positions that I feel can be traced directly to Zarathustra, I conclude that he had one foot in Stage III and the other in Stage IV.

What places him in Stage IV is his claim in the Gathas that Ahura Mazda created the cosmos from his thought, that is, out of nothing. Creation ex nihilo is definitely a Stage IV phenomenon.

Concluding that Zarathustra believed in creation ex nihilo is strengthened by something else that almost certainly can be credited to him: his abhorrence of the traditional sacrifices to the deities. One of these sacrifices reenacted the creation of the cosmos as it had been done for thousands of years in Indo-European religion. Tradition held that Man (the first priest) sacrificed Twin (the first king) and Ox and from their parts fashioned the cosmos and humanity. The reciprocal metamorphosis of Twin and Ox with the cosmos and of humanity was a continuous process. At least annually, the sacrifice of an ox to the deities was ritually carried out to ensure the stability of the cosmos and humanity's place in it.

Since Zarathustra believed in creation ex nihilo, he was shocked at these rituals. He rebelled against the priestly sacrifices and announced to the world Ahura Mazda, the God who created the cosmos by his thought alone.

While that much seems clear, it isn't clear whether Zarathustra was a monotheist, a dualist, or a polytheist. The sources present a number of possibilities:

1. He was a strict monotheist—all other deities were but manifestations of Ahura Mazda or were illusions or were popular superstitions.
2. He was a polytheist, but Ahura Mazda was Supreme among many deities.
3. He was dualist in that Ahriman, representing Evil, was the other half of a Good/Evil cosmic dualism.
4. Ahriman was the creation of a polytheistic people.

I leave the question open, with the understanding that Ahura Mazda could create ex nihilo and still be either the only God or a Supreme God among many or one-half of a dualism with Ahriman.

Regardless of whether Zarathustra was a monotheist, a dualist, or a polytheist, he departs from the dualism of Mind and Matter that is characteristic of Stages I, II and III. By positing a creation of the cosmos ex nihilo, that is, out of nothing, he makes Matter a function of Mind, which is a characteristic of Stage IV religion. Buddha, his contemporary, thought that matter was an illusion. This is a different way in which the old dualism of Mind and Matter can be eliminated. Christianity would also solve the Mind/Matter dualism by reading Genesis 1:1 so that God created the cosmos out of nothing.

The jump from the dualism of Mind and Matter to the monism of Matter-is-a-function-of-Mind signals another jump in the devolution of consciousness into unconscious self-awareness. In order for self-awareness to conceive of a God creating matter out of his own thought, it must first have severed all ties to the body. Through the millennia, self-awareness had incrementally distanced itself from the body in order to defend itself from experiencing ever-increasing levels of primal pain. In Christianity, in Buddhism and in Zoroastrianism, the 1st millennium BCE witnesses the final break between self-awareness and the body, thus ending a dualism that was present from the initial formation of self-awareness in humanity. To mirror how self-awareness was now in splendid isolation from the body, self-awareness posited Ahura Mazda in splendid isolation from the cosmos. Since unconscious self-awareness has no real knowledge of how and why it exists, it cannot make the connection that its outer world is but a projection of, and a mirror of, itself.

Whether Zarathustra was a monotheist or a dualist does make a difference as to how he might have accounted for Evil in the ultimate sense in the person of

Ahriman. By the time of Zarathustra, the concept of Hades as a place of suffering for the dead had evolved into the concept of Hell where all the Evil were sent upon death. Hades reflected a sub-self-awareness that was in a state of suffering. Hell reflected a sub-self-awareness that had degenerated into an evil side of self-awareness. Zoroastrinianism makes Hell the abode of Ahriman who represented Evil raised to the same cosmic level of Ahura Mazda, who represented Good. But, were both Ahura Mazda and Ahriman part of the givenness of what is (dualism) or was Ahriman a creation of Ahura Mazda (monotheism)? The answer is not clear. What is clear is that for Zarathustra the dualism of Good and Evil is raised to cosmic proportions. In the dualistic interpretation of Zoroastrinianism, Ahriman is responsible for the creation of Hell; Ahura Mazda has had nothing to do with that.

The problem with claiming that Zarathustra believed that Ahura Mazda alone was God and was the Ultimate Good is that of accounting for Ahriman as the Ultimate Evil. Since unconscious self-awareness is dualistic by nature, it always fails to account adequately for Evil when it posits a monotheistic God of Good.

It is splitting hairs to say, as do some Zoroastrian and Christian theologians, that God created Satan who subsequently fell from grace by his own free will and that God, therefore, is not responsible for Evil. Since God created the Angel Satan with the capacity for Evil, one must compartmentalize one's mind to say that God is not ultimately responsible for Evil. To say that God is responsible for creating the capacity to become Evil but is not responsible if that capacity for Evil is exercised shows to what extremes unconscious self-awareness must go to overthrow its innate sense of dualism to achieve oneness.

The relationship of Ahura Mazda and Ahriman mirrors the dualistic internal conflict between self-awareness, which sees itself as good, and the sub-self-awareness, which self-awareness senses as being an evil underside of itself. Self-awareness has the same problem here that it has in the outer world for accounting for the presence of evil. Just as self-awareness fails in the outer world to account for evil, so in the inner world self-awareness cannot help but fail to account adequately for the presence of evil.

I think it is more likely that Zarathustra was a dualist with respect to Ahura Mazda and Ahriman, that is, that both were part of the givenness of what is. Partially, I base this on how crucial it was for Zarathustra that humans had free will to choose between Ahura Mazda and Ahriman. Dualism and free will are of Stage III, and together they represent that humans could still decide their own fate. Also, I base Zarathustra's dualism on the interpretation that, even after Ahriman is defeated at the end, he remains in charge of Hell and of all those who are condemned to spend eternity there.

Without a knowledge of primal pain, unconscious self-awareness labels the sub-self-awareness as evil and its counterpoint in the outer world as Evil writ large, by whatever name it is called. While consciousness does not deal in dualisms such as good and evil, it does have a point of view on the subconscious which is none other than a repressed consciousness-in-pain. The immediate cause of the subconscious is primal pain which, in turn, is caused by the lack of proper nurturance. Since, for consciousness, the only time is the present moment, the question of the ultimate origin of primal pain is no question at all. Primal pain is here and now, period. In other words, there is no place in consciousness for attempting to deal with the origin of primal pain, let alone the origins of the cosmos.

It is also appropriate to note here that just as primal pain is a fact of life, so is the built-in drive for restoring consciousness. Primal pain is always pushing upward, seeking to be resolved in primals and, thus, bringing back a state of consciousness.

In the Middle East in the 1st millennium BCE, Zarathustra is the last of the Stage III prophets outside of Judaism to showcase just how far consciousness had devolved into unconscious self-awareness. His concept of Hell fits perfectly into the fifth phase of Stage III's destination of the dead. Humanity is divided into the Good and the Evil. The Good go to the House of Song, while the Evil go to the House of Evil. The choices one has made during life determine to which House one goes. His concept of Ahriman as the Devil or as Satan in charge of Hell is a further development of such figures as Kolyo who escorted the Evil ones to Hell. (See Chapter 9 on the destination of the dead.)

The above conceptions came about because of increases in primal pain. The increase in primal pain to a sufficient level brought about the cognizance of a suffering sub-self-awareness. This, in turn, is responsible for self-awareness conceiving of an underworld in the macrocosm where all dead people go to suffer eternally. Then, when primal pain had again risen to a high enough level, the sub-self-awareness was deemed to be evil, so low had humanity sunk. As the mirror to this, Hades became Hell, the place where the Evil ones were punished.

Essential to Zarathustra's theology is that humans, just like Ahura Mazda, have free will to choose the Good. Here, too, Zarathustra is the last of the prophets outside of Judaism who still felt that humans had the ability to save themselves from a condition of suffering. Buddha, his contemporary in India, had already come to the conclusion that unconscious self-awareness could no longer save itself and must be transcended. Self-awareness was inextricably mired in a state of insatiable desire. It is this distinction between Zarathustra and Buddha that places Zarathustra in Stage III and Buddha in Stage IV.

With regard to time, however, Zarathustra's other foot is in Stage IV. In Stage IV, linear time now takes precedence over cyclical time. Zarathustra recognizes Ahura Mazda, who created time with creation and ends time with the renovation of the world at the end of an irreversible future.

While linear time is easily associated with Zarathustra, the 12,000-year length of linear time in his theology is not. According to Zoroastrian tradition, there are four 3,000-year periods. Within those periods, Ahura Mazda and Ahriman carry on a cosmic struggle for supremacy. There are varying interpretations of what takes place in each of the first three periods. All interpretations agree that by the end of the fourth period Ahura Mazda has defeated Ahriman. By winning the 4th epoch, Ahura Mazda secures the final triumph of Good over Evil. At that time, the faithful dead will be physically resurrected and live forever in a world free from decay and death. The evil will spend eternity in an outer darkness. There is a contradictory tradition that bespeaks Stage IV's monotheism. When those who have been sent to Hell have been purified, they will go to the House of Song, and Ahriman and Hell will be no more.

It was Zarathustra's birth that ushered in the final epoch. So, we are now approximately some 2,500 years into the final epoch. Even as I write, Ahura Mazda and Ahriman, unseen and unheard but not unknown, are engaged in the final, titanic struggle for supremacy. But, fear not, we are taught; the outcome is clear. Good will triumph over Evil. What calls into question crediting this whole idea of epochs to Zarathustra is the much earlier Hindu tradition of cycles totaling billions of years.

The cosmic battleground between Ahriman and Ahura Mazda is a mirror of what must have been happening in Zarathustra. In him, a battle was raging between the evil powers of darkness of his sub-self-awareness and the good powers of light of his self-awareness. Here, again, theology mirrors psychology. His theology is telling us to what extremes primal pain levels have risen in the suppressed consciousness-in-pain.

The eschatological battle in which Ahura Mazda defeats Ahriman represents the hope that is part of the nature of self-awareness. Every child hopes that if he makes the right choices, that is, does what Mommy and Daddy want, that he will be loved, that things will turn out right in the end. Hope, as always, is a defense against feeling the full impact of not being properly loved.

Hope, too, has a fall-back position if love and proper nurturance is not the outcome. In that case, the hope is that at least justice will be done. Since there is no justice in this life—the evil prosper and the good often do not—justice is hoped for, if not in the future, then in the hereafter.

In conclusion, Zarathustra was a reformer who retained some of the crucial elements of Stage III, among them being free will, the ability to save one's self and the dualism of Good and Evil. He was a reformer who moved partially into Stage IV, in that he eliminated the dualism of Mind and Matter, making Matter a function of Mind. I think the reason Zoroastrianism did not take hold as did Buddhism and Christianity was that humanity had already lost faith in its ability to save itself from a condition of terrible suffering and needed religions of Transcendence, such as Christianity and Buddhism, to do so.

Zarathustra. So what. "What possible bearing on my life can he have?" you might ask. Here is one example of his bearing on us today. He felt that Evil in the person of Ahriman was real. Today, even from a secular point of view that does not include the concept of evil, we struggle to understand the basis for the enormity of the crimes we commit against one another. My position is that the exceedingly high valence of the primal pain endured in the suppressed consciousness-in-pain is easily capable of erupting into unconscious self-awareness, driving some of us to unthinkable brutality. Zarathustra posited a cosmic battle between Good and Evil in the outer world to account for extreme suffering which then, as now, is mirrored by extreme suffering in our inner worlds.

CHAPTER 12

FROM THE CONSCIOUSNESS OF SELVES-IN-RELATIONSHIP TO THE DUALISM OF COMMUNALISM AND INDIVIDUALISM

What I intend to show in this chapter is the incremental degradation of the conscious state of selves-in-relationship into the evermore unconscious self-aware state of the dualism of communalism and individualism. As I have shown in Part II, Chapter 6, self-awareness cannot help but think in terms of dualities. As I have also shown in that same chapter, the ultimate cause of self-awareness and its increasing unconsciousness is the evermore increasing levels of primal pain.

In our past, if there ever were a time of pure consciousness, the relationship of each person to the community mirrored how the cells of our bodies relate to our bodies as a whole. That relationship is such that each cell acts for the benefit of the whole body; the whole body acts for the benefit of each cell. No cell is spending time trying to secure individual rights. The body is not spending time trying to secure communal rights. In consciousness, such concepts as individual or communal rights are nonsense. There are just selves-in-relationship.

With Native Americans, I have participated in prayer circles that emulate the cell/body relationship. We stood in as large a circle as needed and held hands with the person on either side of us. Each of us prayed for the whole group and for others whom we felt needed intercession. We did not pray for ourselves; others were praying for us. Those who felt a special need to be prayed for formed a circle in the center of the larger circle. Such ancient traditions are reminders of how things were when all of humanity was still in the dawning of self-awareness.

Historically, the formation of self-awareness means that the duality of individualism and of communalism begins. There is now a self-in-here that has begun to cut itself off from the world-out-there in order to defend itself against primal pain. At the outset of the formation of self-awareness, both the individual and the community exhibit high degrees of consciousness and low degrees of unconsciousness. This means that there is still more of the experience of being a self-in-relationship and much less of the individual and the community as being over and against each other.

As primal pain increases, the self-in-here must increasingly cut itself off from the world-out-there. Over time, this means that the individual and the community will exhibit less and less of consciousness and more and more of unconsciousness. It means that, over time, there will be less and less of the experience of being a self-in-relationship and more and more of the experience of the individual and the community as being in a state of tension.

Put another way, as consciousness loses out to self-awareness, communalism is less and less able to meet the real needs of individuals, and individualism is less and less motivated to meet the real needs of the community. Communalism will become more and more greedy for power to impose an arbitrary order upon individuals. Individualism will become more and more greedy for license to indulge its insatiable hunger for sex, money, possessions and power. Communalism will further divide itself into classes, and individualism will further concentrate its energies into achieving class interests.

In the brain there is a mirror image of what is happening externally in the movement from being a self-in-relationship to being an individual separate from the community. The movement is from more to fewer open connections among the sensing/survival brain, the emotional/sexual brain and the thinking brain. It is from sensations, emotions and thoughts being more to less integrated. It is from self-awareness being primarily in the sensing/survival brain to being in the emotional/sexual brain to being in the thinking brain.

Up through Stage II, the internal connections and integration of the three levels of the brain are such that significant ties remain between emotion and thought and between communalism and individualism. It isn't until Stage III, when needs and the physical and emotional pain associated with unmet needs—all social in nature—are denied, that the connections between emotion and thought and between communalism and individualism are broken to their furthermost extent. Taking over to an ever-increasing extent is an intellectualistic individualism and an individualistic intellectualism.

Communalism and Individualism in Stage I

Despite the existence of the dualism of individualism and communalism at the outset of Stage I, there was present a high degree of the characteristics of the pre-self-aware state of selves-in-relationship. Self-awareness and the community-out-there were but little cut off from each other. Connections between them were largely intact. Self-awareness willingly acted for the benefit of the whole community, and the community saw to it that everyone's needs were met. In the dualism, the balance was overwhelmingly on the side of a communalism for the good of everyone over an individualism centered on wealth and power.

One reason Stage I starts out highly communalistic is that in that stage our survival needs are mainly physical ones, and they are chiefly social in nature. An infant or small child cannot survive without parents and the larger community.

Another reason Stage I is principally communalistic is that until the end of Stage I the largest component of self-awareness is the survival or sensing brain. During that time, it is only to a lesser extent that self-awareness is composed of the emotional/sexual and thinking brains. Further, since the sensing brain mediates the physical, survival needs which, as I've said, are the most social of our needs, self-awareness in Stage I is in great measure communalistic and only slightly individualistic.

Customs, Taboos and Tension Between the Individual and Community

It seems reasonable to assume that the development of social customs began before the appearance of self-awareness. Customs are the way a people act as a whole. They enhance the communal welfare of the family, clan and tribe. They include those remedies that might be necessary to mend a rent in the social fabric when some anti-communalistic behavior has caused a tear. However, when religion became the ground upon which ancient custom was founded and ancient custom became the will of the gods, this development presupposed that humans had lost their original consciousness. It meant that, to the people, following the customs would maintain or restore the god-given conditions that existed during the long-gone Paradisal Time.

Taboos, on the other hand, were the earliest evidence of prohibited behavior. They were the initial form of Thou Shalt Nots. They were restrictions on behavior that were deemed to be detrimental to communal welfare. Their presence assumed that some individuals were so individualistic as to be capable of anti-social actions that must be curbed.

Thus, with taboos, we see the birth of the tension between the individual and the community. Probably little coercion was needed to motivate conformity to the taboos. The threat of banishment was enough to restore order. In those days, it was a reality that the community was necessary for individual survival.

Commune-ism

For traditional peoples there is no such thing as ownership of real estate, as we know it today. It was inconceivable that anyone could own air or water or land. There were loose boundaries that each people stayed within for hunting and foraging. The land was occupied in common.

In like manner, food was shared. No one went hungry. If one person starved, the whole community starved.

Moieties

In consciousness, the interdependence of everyone is the experience of everyone. One knows oneself only in relationships. Each contributes to the whole according to his ability and receives from the whole according to his need. It is only when self-awareness has arisen that the natural acts of giving and receiving are transformed into the creating and discharging of debt obligations. Even so, in traditional societies, which have a low degree of unconsciousness, debt obligations are rooted in the naturalness of the mutual interdependence of everyone.

Moiety is the name given to complex social arrangements regulating the carrying out of debt obligations. There might be any number of dualities of groupings that seek to preserve the harmony of interrelationships through the creation and discharge of debt obligations. A moiety is a custom that reflects that self-awareness has not developed to the extent of blotting out interdependence. It is a custom that can extend through the generations, further bonding the people.

Even in this early stage, self-awareness can be tempted to elevate itself above others. It can seek prestige from making great gifts and having great debt obligations owed to it. In consciousness, this does not happen. No one seeks prestige for carrying out what he can do for the community.

In these moiety gift exchanges, there is a brake upon any tendency of self-awareness to gouge or to shortchange, for to do so is to become a moral outcast. It is a case of seller beware. In contrast, in modern society it is a case of buyer beware because an isolated, independent, unconscious self-awareness feels no reason to have to establish and maintain communal relationships.

Veneration, Placation and Totemism

Long before the appearance of self-awareness, there was the veneration of elders. They were the repository for the accumulated knowledge and wisdom of the people. It was they to whom the people looked for guidance in every aspect of life. Veneration preserved and emphasized the interconnectedness of the generations. Once self-awareness occurred, placation of the elders and ancestors began to replace veneration. The intergenerational bonds remained strong, however.

Related to the communal aspects of veneration and placation is totemism. Totemism is the use of a particular animal species to represent the kinship of humans and animals and kinship relations between clans and within clans. Insofar as the totem animal might be a reincarnated ancestor it, too, might be venerated or placated.

Marriage

In Stage I, there was still so little unconsciousness that to a large extent lives were centered around the establishment and maintenance of interconnections among tribal members and with the ancestors. One's sense of self came from experiencing one's relationships with everyone else. Hence, it was the stability of the family that was of the greatest importance. One was born into a family and stayed in that family until death. One was nurtured throughout life, not only by one's immediate family, but by the whole tribe, so close were interrelationships. Most marriages were probably arranged to enhance the interconnections between families, clans *and* tribes. These customs made sure that the individual was never unsupported.

In Stage I, in a very small way, romantic love might have been a factor complicating marriage arrangements. As far as I can tell, judging from much later periods, romantic love was looked upon as a sickness that ought not to be the basis for marriage. Romantic love created instability and so was to be avoided.

Salvation

In Stage I, the primary motif of placation was directed toward communal rather than individual salvation. (See Part III, Chapter 9, for a complete exposition on salvation.) This emphasis on communal salvation evidenced that the communalism/individualism dualism was heavily weighted toward communalism.

Communalism and Individualism in Stage II

The Emotional/Sexual Brain

In Stage II, the largest component of self-awareness had shifted from the sensing/survival brain to the emotional/sexual brain. Present to a lesser extent were the sensing/survival brain and the thinking brain. While there was some movement from communalism toward individualism, the emotional/sexual brain kept communalism in the forefront. This was so because emotional needs are the next most social in nature to the survival needs.

In Stage II, communalism, for the most part, was for the good of everyone. This was so because there was as yet no class structure, as happened in Stage III to transform communalism into a parochial class interest. In Stage II, "the good of everyone" extended to the environment because all of what is now called inert matter was the tangible manifestation of the Mother Goddess.

In this stage, it seems likely that some form of ostracism was practiced to keep individuals who had the most primal pain from acting as independent selves and fracturing the unity of the community. Even more so than in Stage I, those persons had their self-awareness located primarily in the thinking brain. With this one exception, everyone else had his self-awareness located primarily in the communalistic emotional/sexual brain.

Reimmersion

Reimmersion as the dominant motif of Stage II blocked the physical, emotional and mental pain associated with needs going unmet. Since the emotional/sexual brain blocks, but does not actually deny, needs, self-awareness remained largely communalistic during Stage II.

Nevertheless, reimmersion further isolated the self-in-here from the community-out-there. This was so because reimmersion blocks the emotions, which are social in nature. The act of reimmersion is to cut self-awareness off from the outside world, which further increased the gap between communalism and individualism.

Property

In Stage II, property was owned by the political/religious infrastructure of Mother Goddess religion. Economies were communal in nature and were managed by the priestesses of the goddess temples. By the end of Stage II in the Middle East, we are well into the historical period. The earliest writings reflect the communal aspect of the ownership of property.

Communalism and Individualism in Stage III

Review of Relevant Background Information

In Part II, Chapter 6, I detailed the jump from Stage II to Stage III with regard to self-awareness and religion. I explained how the jump was based on a certain, critical increase in the level of primal pain. I repeat that information here because of its bearing on the dualism of communalism and individualism in Stage III.

By the end of Stage II, the failure of the main motif of reimmersion to get needs met or to escape from the pain of them not being met creates a crisis for the child. His needs are not being met, and he is helpless to do anything about it. Consequently, he has to deny his needs if he is to remain viable. Unfulfilled needs, however, do not go away, but resurface as insatiable wants or desires. To compensate for his feelings of helplessness, he is compelled to accumulate power to overcome his feelings of helplessness and to get his wants satisfied.

In Stage I, the sensing/survival brain with its main motif of placation is dominant. The emotional/sexual brain with its motif of reimmersion and the thinking brain with its motif of power are subordinate. In Stage II, the emotional/

sexual brain with its motif of reimmersion is dominant. The sensing/survival brain with its motif of placation and the thinking brain with its motif of power are subordinate. Now, in Stage III, the thinking brain with its motif of satisfying insatiable wants and the use of power to overcome feelings of helplessness predominate. The motifs of reimmersion of the emotional/sexual brain and placation of the sensing/survival brain play supporting roles.

In Stage II, the level of primal pain is such that there are still open pathways between the emotional/sexual brain and the thinking brain. Self-awareness is located primarily in the emotional/sexual brain. Since the emotional/sexual brain and the emotions are social in nature and the thinking brain and thoughts are private in nature, in Stage II one is mainly communalistic and secondarily individualist. In other words, in Stage II when one's thinking and emotional/sexual brains are quite open to each other, one is able to feel one's own pain and suffering. This enables one to be empathetic to the pain and suffering of others. This is one reason why someone in Stage II is more communalistic than individualistic.

In Stage III, the dominant thinking brain is no longer connected to real needs but to the denied real needs resurfacing as insatiable wants. Now, commensurate with his level of primal pain, the child must disconnect his thinking brain from his emotional/sexual brain and from emotions too traumatic to handle. Then he must concentrate his efforts on satisfying his insatiable compulsion for power to stave off feelings of helplessness and to satisfy insatiable wants. What I've done here is to establish the foundation for a Stage III level of communalism and individualism. In other words, in Stage III when one's thinking and emotional/sexual brains are far more cut off from each other, one is far less able to feel one's own pain and suffering. This precludes one from being empathetic to the pain and suffering of others. This is one reason why in Stage III we are more individualistic than communalistic.

The story of Marduk and Tiamot, deities of Babylon (described elsewhere in Part III, Chapter 7), is instructive here. Marduk was a Warrior God who was subordinate to Tiamot, the Mother Goddess, during Stage II. Tiamot was the mirror of a self-awareness located primarily in the emotional/sexual brain, which was dominant in Stage II. Marduk was the mirror of a self-awareness located in the thinking brain, which was subordinate in Stage II. The victory of Marduk over Tiamot was an indication that Stage III had arrived, with the individualistic thinking brain taking over from the emotional/sexual brain.

The Main Consequence of a Stage III Level of Unconscious Self-Awareness on Communalism and Individualism

My main point is that the historical onset of Stage III in unconscious self-awareness inevitably led to the full-blown development of society into classes.

Because of the nature of self-awareness itself, there would have been some small, incremental development of classes in Stages I and II. In Stage I, some small portion of self-awareness would have been located in the individualistic thinking brain. In Stage I, there would have been some denial of needs, some resurfacing of it as insatiable wants and some feelings of helplessness in getting those needs met. In Stage I, there would have been some accumulation and use of power to satisfy wants and to compensate for helplessness. Therefore, in Stage I there would have been a germinal concept of individual or private property within a general environment of communal or public property. Therefore, there would have been some disparity in even the small amounts of private property accumulated. Therefore, in Stage I in unconscious self-awareness, the seed is planted for the eventual division of society into classes. In Stage II, all of these conditions became worse because of a significant jump in the general level of primal pain in people.

All of these conditions immeasurably worsened when another big jump in primal pain brought on Stage III. Now, self-awareness is located primarily in the individualistic thinking brain. There is a great denial of needs, great insatiable wants and great feelings of helplessness in getting those needs met. There is a great compulsion to accumulate and use power to satisfy those great insatiable wants and to compensate for those great feelings of helplessness. Therefore, with the onset of Stage III there is a general environment of individual or private property, while the priority of communal or public property fades in comparison.

In Stage III, in unconscious self-awareness and in society the scene is set for the full development of society into classes. As the process unfolds of accumulating and using ever greater amounts of power to satisfy ever greater degrees of insatiable wants and to compensate for ever greater feelings of helplessness, ever greater disparities occur between the few at the top, who amass great wealth and power, and the masses at the bottom, dependent on the few for the meager satisfaction of basic necessities. In short, in Stage III in unconscious self-awareness all those conditions that led to individualism and to the accumulation of private property, led to the vertical stratification of society into classes.

Finally, in the process, the creation of classes leads to a parochial interest in the good of one's class and away from a universal interest in the good of the whole community. However, the top class must see to it that enough wealth trickles down to the lowest class in order to prevent revolution. Also, the lowest class must see to it that the top class is taken care of or the lowest class gets nothing.

By the time Stage III first came about, selves-in-relationship had devolved so far as to exhibit a dualism of communalism and individualism in which society is clearly divided into classes. Our ancestors—the Indo-Europeans who are the antecedents of Western civilization—were divided into classes. At the top were the priests. Then came the warriors. Next were the farmers/herders. At the bottom were the various Stage II, conquered Mother Goddess peoples.

Earlier I mentioned that the Indo-Europeans believed that their Warrior God had given to them alone the right to own cattle. If any other people had cattle they, therefore, had to have stolen them. This was all the pretext the Indo-Europeans needed to justify their conquests. Probably they were the first economic imperialists of Stage III, unconscious self-awareness. Monopolize the cattle market and dominate the world. In the 19th century in this country, it was monopolize cotton and dominate the world. In the 20th and 21st centuries in this country, it is monopolize oil and dominate the world. Economic imperialism is a predictable outcome ultimately based on a greed and a lust for power that comes about when infantile needs are not met.

Besides the division of society into classes based on wants and power, blame placed on the Mother Goddess, on mothers and on everything deemed to be feminine for continued suffering resulted in a class difference between men and women. In Stage II, as long as the dominant motif of reimmersion sufficed to mitigate suffering, supported by the subordinate motifs of placation and power, the cause of suffering was a nonissue. By the end of Stage II, full-out blame for unabated suffering was placed on the Goddess and on mothers. In addition, all the traits of the emotional/sexual brain and of the right lobe that were called upon in the failed motif of reimmersion were blamed for that failure and labeled as feminine. Blame for suffering was no longer genderless.

Both boys and girls blamed their mothers for continued suffering, and both men and women blamed the Mother Goddess for continued suffering. The case can be made for the blaming of mothers for the continuation of suffering. First of all, in bygone days, breast feeding often lasted until the child was two years old or even older. Up to this point, mothers probably had exclusive care of the child. In the second place, mothers usually were the main nurturers until both boys and girls reached puberty. It appears that primal pain levels had reached the point where mothers—fathers, too, for that matter—could no longer provide proper nurturance. Since mothers and the Goddess were the primary caregivers, it was easy to blame everything feminine for the continuation of suffering. Blaming mothers and the Mother Goddess for suffering meant a change from a female-oriented to a male-oriented society with everything feminine subjugated.

It meant a change in which women became a subjugated class. In this change can be found the double standard in sex to which men and women are held. (This is discussed fully elsewhere in this chapter.) It meant a change in that women could not only not own property, they became property to be bought and sold. (An example of this is described later in this chapter.) Women as property represented an overlap between economic and gender class structures.

The blaming of mothers and the Mother Goddess exclusively for continued suffering came to an end when the Mother Goddess was no longer around to blame. At least since her demise and the failure of Warrior God religion to assuage suffering, men have come in for their share of the blame for continued suffering.

Over the roughly 4,000-year period of the destruction of Stage II, Mother Goddess cultures and the consolidation of Stage III Warrior God cultures, more and more children suffered at the hands of parents who had a Stage III level of primal pain and individualism. In contrast to Stage II in which children came into adulthood being more communalistic than individualistic, in Stage III the reverse was true.

By the 20th century in the United States, the failure of male-dominated Stage III level of unconscious self-awareness to mitigate suffering had gone so far as to mean a significant weakening of gender class structure. In the 20th century in the United States, women had acquired the right to own property, gained the right to vote, experienced less job discrimination and obtained more sexual equality. This is happening, I believe, because men can no longer make women into a scapegoat for suffering.

Other Related Consequences for Communalism and Individualism As a Result of the Devolvement into a Stage III Level of Unconscious Self-Awareness

One of these related consequences was that class loyalty and social cohesion were greatly diminished. In and of itself, the division of society into classes meant the end of a communalism directed toward the good of the entire society. When class stratification was coupled with patrilineal succession in Stage III, the movement from communalism to individualism was greatly accelerated. In matrilineal Stage II, when children belonged to the mother's family, regardless of who the fathers were, the communalism inherent in matriarchy was maintained. Now, in Stage III, society became fragmented due to the substitution of individual wants for communal needs, the institution of private property and the onset of a patrilineality.

Another related consequence was the formation of the nation-states. Stage III produced the most unconscious and, therefore, the most power-hungry of virulent individualists. We know of these individualists as a succession of generals who were able to impose their will on everyone within range of their imperialistic power. They formed nation-states in which the rich and powerful, elite ruling class was allowed to take over and get what they wanted. In order to justify this, the interests of the ruling class were equated with the national interests. The nation-state, as much as classes, signaled the decline of a communalism emphasizing the good of everyone into a communalism emphasizing parochial class interests.

Historically, up through Stage II in the struggle between society and the individual, the whole community subjugated a selfish individualism that put its own interest above the interests of the whole community. Put differently, the struggle was between an interdependent community and an independent self. By Stage III, there is the beginning of a struggle by a highly selfish, individualistic, rich and powerful elite ruling class to use the nation-state to subjugate the community-at-large in the national interest, i.e., the interest of the ruling class. Throughout Stage III, one movement is toward an individualism freeing itself from communal restraints on personal aggrandizement at the expense of the general population. At the same time, there is a struggle between a communalism emanating from the lower classes who seek a more equitable distribution of total wealth and power and a communalism issuing from the upper class who seeks to consolidate and to expand their lion's share of total wealth and power. This creates an even greater disparity between the "haves" and the "have-nots."

In Stage III, there is also a struggle between an individual and the class to which he belongs. In the rich and powerful, elite ruling upper class, the struggle is to restrain individuals or entities with an uncontrollable greed or lust for power that threaten the security of the overall interests of the class. In the middle and lower classes, the struggle is among those whose sense of communalism is more for the common good, those who are more for class good and those whose interests reflect the interests of the upper class. This last group consists of those who have been successfully indoctrinated by the upper class.

In Stage III, because of the compulsion to accumulate and use power, another related consequence for communalism and individualism was the development of laws from customs. Customs are positive in nature and reflect commonly accepted ways of doing things. Laws are negative in nature, prohibiting certain kinds of behavior and threatening punishment as a deterrent to engaging in the prohibited behavior. This development of laws from customs paralleled the development of the nation-state from clan and tribe. This development is also a symptom of, among other things, an unconscious self-awareness that cares little for the common good and cares much for perpetuating, in the law, class interests.

Men: Left-Brainers; Women: Right-Brainers

An exceedingly significant related consequence of the onset of a Stage III level of unconscious self-awareness was the difference between men and women in the primary location of self-awareness in the total brain. It was the blame placed on the Goddess, on mothers and on what were now deemed to be feminine qualities for the failure of Stage II's main motif of reimmersion to mitigate suffering that caused this difference in the location of self-awareness, as well as in class differences.

In Stage III, a male-dominated, Warrior God class society forced women's self-awareness to stay much as it was during Stage II. That is, even though women had jumped to Stage III, a significant part of their self-awareness was to remain in the emotional/sexual brain and in the right lobe of the total brain. On the other hand, the self-awareness of men severed more connections to the emotional/sexual brain and between the right and left lobes. Their self-awareness was now primarily located in the left lobe, thinking brain.

In Stage III then, one of the major differences between men and women is that women, generally speaking, are going to be more emotional than men, and men are going to be more intellectual than women. At one end of the scale, some men will hardly feel anything at all. They will have no clue at all as to the suppressed emotions that are directing their lives. At the other end, some women will be so driven by their emotions that they will have little understanding of them. In consciousness, one knows what one feels and feels what one knows.

Another major difference is that women are going to retain more of the right-lobe traits of wholeness, spontaneity and synthesis that are associated with the reimmersion motif of Stage II. While women will have some of the left-lobe traits of sequence, analysis and abstraction, men will be defined by these characteristics, which come from the left lobe. In Stage III, women became right-brainers, while men became left-brainers.

To better understand what is going on here with these major differences, I repeat information about Stage II.

It is because the entire emotional/sexual brain matures before the thinking brain and because the right lobe (with its traits of wholeness, simultaneity and synthesis) matures before the left lobe that reimmersion becomes the motif of Stage II self-awareness and of religion.

During Stage II in both unconscious self-awareness and in religion, there is no gender distinction assigned to the right-lobe traits of wholeness, simultaneity and synthesis. In a state of suffering, both boys and girls used these traits to seek reimmersion into mother where needs were met and when there was no suffering. Both men and women used these traits to seek reimmersion into the Mother Goddess to mitigate a state of suffering. The phenomenon of Stage II Mother Goddess religion arises precisely because of the suffering child's desire to become reimmersed into his mother where needs were met.

Now, in Stage III, with a self-awareness more evenly balanced between the emotional/sexual brain and the thinking brain, women did not deny childhood needs as much as did men. This meant that women did not have as high a degree of insatiable wants as did men. It also meant that women's wants were different from men's. Since women traditionally retained more connections with the emotional/sexual brain, which is communalistic in nature, their wants tended to be social in nature. Since men now came from the individualistic thinking brain, their wants tended to be individualistic.

With self-awareness emphasized in different areas of the brain, women and men used different tools of power to satisfy their wants. With a significant portion of self-awareness in the emotional/sexual brain, women used emotion and sex to get what they wanted. Remember that the emotional brain also mediates sex. With a self-awareness located primarily in the thinking brain, men used intellect to get what they wanted. Plus, men used their greater physical strength to insure that they got what they wanted.

With Stage III, because women's psyches now stemmed primarily from the right-lobe, emotional/sexual brain and men's psyches arose primarily from the left-lobe, thinking brain, women suffered more than men did. A left-brained, male-dominated, Stage III, power-oriented culture insisted that women were right-brained and emotional/sexual brained by nature. Girls and women were taught to stay with their emotions and to cry when they were hurt and suffered. This denied women the opportunity of becoming better defended against suffering by becoming left-brained and thinking-brain-dominated. Since male-dominated, Stage III culture also insisted that for a boy or a man to cry was to be effeminate, they were taught to stifle their emotions and hold back their tears and so suffer less. Boys and men were allowed to move into a more defended state of being. But, since women were able to maintain more connections between the two lobes and between the emotional/sexual and thinking brains, they became less unconscious than men. They were closer to their pain.

That women suffer more also makes them more communalistic. Crying tends to bond people. That men suffer less makes them more individualistic. A stiff upper lip tends to isolate people. Yet, men will bond emotionally within male-only groupings. The bonding must be kept within the group, however, lest anyone accuse them of being homosexual or feminine.

Another aspect of the phenomenon of women being made to be right-lobe, emotional/sexual-brain-oriented, while men were allowed to be left-lobe, thinking-brain-oriented, is that women were far more likely to be cooperative, while men were far more likely to be competitive. Women sought each other out emotionally, while men sought intellectual exclusiveness. Each avoided what the other sought.

In summary, what happened in the jump from Stage II to Stage III with regard to distinctions between men and women is that women alone were associated with the characteristics of the whole emotional/sexual brain and the right-lobe traits of wholeness, spontaneity and synthesis. These traits are necessary to Stage II's motif of reimmersion into mother and into the Goddess. Men alone were associated with the characteristics of the whole thinking brain and the left-lobe traits of sequence, analysis and abstraction. These traits are necessary to Stage III's co-opting of power to satisfy wants and to compensate for feelings of helplessness. This is true for unconscious self-awareness itself and for the mirror images of a Mother Goddess or a Warrior God.

In conclusion, thinking brain characteristics are not masculine in nature; they are human traits divorced from emotional/sexual brain traits. Likewise, emotional/sexual brain characteristics are not feminine in nature; they are human traits divorced from thinking brain traits.

Similarly, in conclusion, left-lobe traits are not masculine in nature nor are right-lobe traits feminine in nature; they are human traits divorced from each other. Neither the left-lobe traits of analysis, sequence and abstraction nor the right-lobe traits of wholeness, spontaneity and synthesis are either masculine or feminine; they are just genderless traits of what the two lobes do. My source for this discussion on the traits of the left and right lobes of the brain is *The Alphabet Versus the Goddess* by Leonard Shlain. See also *The Biology of Love* by Arthur Janov.

Finally, I say again that reimmersion is not just a woman thing; it is a genderless defense of unconscious self-awareness against primal pain. The use of power is not just a man thing; it, too, is a genderless defense of unconscious self-awareness against primal pain.

What the Destination of the Dead Reveals About Communalism and Individualism

Another related consequence of the devolvement into a Stage III level of unconscious self-awareness was what the various destinations of the dead in Stage III revealed about communalism and individualism. In Stage III, I discovered five phases in the destination of the dead. The first three revealed that throughout those phases everyone went either horizontally or up or down to a final resting place. There was only communal salvation. In phases four and five, there was only individual salvation. In four, the diseased and aged went down, while war heroes went up. In five, the evil went down, while the good went up. At some point, therefore, in Stage III, individual salvation replaced communal salvation.

The Bearing That the Indo-European and Semite Invasions of Mother Goddess Cultures Had on the Dualism of Communalism and Individualism

My review of the historical antecedents to Western civilization leads me to conclude that the first people to make the jump to Stage III were the Indo-Europeans. There are at least a dozen distinct groupings of Indo-Europeans. Their location stretches from the Atlantic Ocean to the Bay of Bengal. It is through linguistic studies that we know that they are all related. We first come to know them perhaps around 3500 BCE when they—as Warrior God, Stage III peoples—began a several-millennia-long series of invasions of Stage II, Mother Goddess cultures. Even the linguistic studies shed no light on when the Indo-Europeans made the jump from Stage II to Stage III.

We first come to know the Semites through the Jewish Scriptures and what Christians call the Old Testament. While Abraham's date might be as early as 2000 BCE, we come to know the Israelites as such beginning about 1200 BCE with their invasions of what they called "The Promised Land." This area was bounded on the east by a north-south line between the Sea of Galilee and the Dead Sea and on the west by the Mediterranean Sea.

What we have in our historical background, therefore, is the accelerated devolvement of Stage II, Mother Goddess peoples into Stage III, Warrior God peoples and the continuous devolvement of the Indo-Europeans and Israelites. Stage III itself had a profound effect on the dualism of communalism and individualism, as did the clash between the various Mother Goddess cultures with the Israelite culture and the various Indo-European cultures.

Firstly, with regard to the Israelites, four of the Ten Commandments reveal the Stage III status of their culture. The first commandment is to "have no other gods before me." In early Israelite history, this did not mean monotheism. The existence of other gods was acknowledged. It did mean that Yahweh, the Warrior God of the Israelites, was predominant and all other gods were relegated to a subordinate position. The mirror image of this was a self-awareness that now put itself first and relegated all others to a subordinate position. In later Israelite history when there was monotheism, Yahweh and the self were in isolation. All ties to other gods or to other selves were severed. And, while all traditional peoples considered themselves to be *the* human beings, in Israel the sense of being a chosen people was extremely intense. The first commandment, then, indicated a huge jump toward an in-group kind of communalism that separated the Israelites from all other peoples.

The commandments not to commit adultery, not to steal and not to covet anything that was your neighbor's affirmed that now individualism and private property had taken precedence over communalism and communal property. These commandments sanctified private property and were indicative of a Stage III level of unconscious self-awareness.

The commandment not to commit adultery is instructional in that it did not preclude married men from having sexual intercourse with women other than a married woman. The intent of the commandment was to make sure that a wife's husband was the father of all her children, since private property was to pass through his line. This commandment was further evidence of a Stage III level of society.

Secondly, with regard to the Indo-European invasions of the various Mother Goddess cultures, I will center my attention on the Middle East and the Mediterranean area, as it was there that the foundations of Western civilization were laid.

Culture shock. That's the most accurate way I can describe what began to happen around 5500 years ago, when the various Stage III Warrior God peoples began to invade the various Stage II Mother Goddess cultures. To set that degree of shock in perspective, look no further back than to when England, France and Spain invaded the Americas. To the Europeans, the Native Americans were either sub-human, primitive, or child-like. To the Native Americans, the Europeans were like gods. A terrible shock came to the Native Americans when they understood, too late, that their entire way of life was going to be destroyed. Over a period of several thousand years, that is exactly what happened to the way of life of the Mother Goddess cultures. In Part III, Chapter 7, I've described the various phases of the changing relationship of the Warrior God to the Mother Goddess. That changing relationship also serves to show the destruction of the way of life of Mother Goddess culture.

With regard to what long-term effect these invasions had on Western civilization, what I find to be most illuminating is how the issues of sexual relations and property, both private and communal, would be intertwined and debated. What follows next is a brief description of the clash between the lesser unconscious state of the Stage II, Mother Goddess peoples and the greater unconscious state of the invading Stage III, Warrior God peoples.

How long before the Indo-Europeans and the Semites had devolved from Stage II to Stage III and had begun their invasions of the Mother Goddess cultures is not known. Consequently, it can't be known whether or not they were shocked at the sexual behavior of Mother Goddess cultures, or whether or not the memory of what they had gone through themselves was still fresh. Regardless of this, they considered the sexual behavior of Mother Goddess peoples to be immoral, especially with regard to women. It was anathema to them that a married woman had the freedom to have more than one sexual partner. For if she did, one could not be certain who the fathers of her children were. To preserve patriarchy, the invaders restricted a wife's sexual behavior to her husband.

In matriarchal Stage II, most property was probably owned communally and administered through the temples of the Goddess. Most likely, only personal items were owned individually. Whatever individual private property passed from one generation to the next one passed through the female line. With regard to sexual relations, men and women were essentially treated equally because it didn't make any difference who the father of a child was; the child belonged to the mother's family.

As I've noted previously, in patriarchal Stage III we find the beginnings of the concept of private property, and it was to pass from one generation to the next through the male line. This was protected by limiting a wife to sexual intercourse with no one but her husband.

In this devolvement of communal property into private property, women not only could not own property, they became the private property of men. I believe this came about because the Mother Goddess, women and what were termed feminine traits were blamed for the failure of reimmersion to continue to mitigate suffering. (I fully explore this subject in Part III, Chapter 6.)

In the Jewish/Christian/Muslim book of Genesis, there is a familiar story of how, in patriarchal Stage III, daughters were private property and sold to their husbands. Jacob fell in love with Rachel and agreed to work for his father-in-law for seven years for her hand in marriage. When the seven years were up, Rachel's father said that Jacob couldn't have her yet. Rachel was the younger of two daughters, and the elder had to be married first. Jacob then could take Leah, the older of the daughters, as his wife, but he would have to work seven more years for Rachel. It is usually not mentioned that this is an example of women becoming private property in Stage III.

In fact, the whole concept of marriage changed in the jump from Stage II communalism to Stage III individualism. Prior to Stage III, there was every conceivable form of marriage or even no marriage at all. Communal sex went along with communal property. What was sought in a woman or wife was fertility. A young woman having a child before marriage, if there were some form of marriage, was proof that she was fertile and, therefore, marriageable.

In Stage III, it was virginity that was sought in a bride for a monogamous marriage, monogamous, that is, for her. Since Stage III was patriarchal, it wouldn't do to marry a women who had children, unless she were the widow of one's brother.

What I've had to guard against in writing of this period is not viewing it from the point of view of the victors who always get to write the history of any period. To say that the people of the Mother Goddess cultures had freedom of choice with regard to sex and that their choices were immoral is to judge them from the perspective of the greater unconscious state of the independent self of the Warrior God Indo-European peoples or from our own day. To say that the communal ownership of property stifles an individual's motivation to produce is again to judge people in Stage II—who still have access to their needs—from the perspective of modern people in Stage III who are driven to satisfy individual, insatiable wants. Regardless, what went on in Mother Goddess cultures was shocking to Warrior God cultures.

Equally so, the behavior of the conquering Indo-Europeans and Semites was shocking to Mother Goddess cultures. To their mindset of emphasizing acting as a community as a whole, acting as an independent self, as did the Indo-Europeans, was unthinkably destructive of the community. As deeply as they might have felt about experiencing the disintegration of their way of life, ever-increasing levels of primal pain made it inevitable that Stage II would be engulfed by Stage III. In the dualism of communalism and individualism, Stage II's less unconscious priority of communalism was taken over by Stage III's more unconscious priority of individualism.

So, does this discussion of the devolution of selves-in-relationship into individualism have any bearing on our lives today? You bet it does. Doesn't an individualistic greed and lust for power explain most of what is behind the policies of the rich and powerful, elite ruling class? And, for the rest of each one of us, is it not true that we have insatiable wants and a compulsion for power to overcome our sense of helplessness?

PART IV

HISTORY OF THE DEVOLUTION OF ORIGINAL CONSCIOUSNESS INTO UNCONSCIOUS SELF-AWARENESS FROM COLUMBUS TO THE PRESENT DAY IN THE UNITED STATES

CHAPTER 13

COLUMBUS, COLONIALISM, THE FOUNDING FATHERS AND THE U.S. CONSTITUTION

Introduction

Everything that has transpired since the 1st millennium BCE is but a footnote to it. Even the appearance in the 1st millennium BCE of religions of transcendence such as Buddhism and Christianity have had no effect on this devolvement. Their abandonment of unconscious self-awareness in favor of a supra-self-awareness in the form of Buddha Consciousness and the Mind of Christ left unconscious self-awareness to continue to devolve with every increase in primal pain.

My goal in writing this history, as you know, is to help you understand our human experience from a primal perspective. Toward that end a study of the colonial and constitutional periods will facilitate that understanding because we still live under an 18th century view of government. I'll begin with Columbus, then describe conditions in the English colonies and cover our Founding Fathers as they crafted our Constitution.

Columbus

What cannot be ignored without arriving at a fatally flawed understanding of history, and particularly of the history of the Americas since 1492, is that ever since the ancient Indo-Europeans first devolved to the Stage III level of unconscious self-awareness, insatiable wants and a compulsion for power have dominated our behavior. To simply characterize the late 1400s, the 1500s and the 1600s as the Age of Exploration, as did the history books of my education up through high school, is to gloss over the "shock and awe" tactics, the terrorism and the incredible atrocities perpetrated by these euphemistically named explorers. Or, if a single sentence mentioning genocide is buried in a paragraph extolling at length the virtues of these men, it trivializes the enormity of their unconsciousness. In other words, we were indoctrinated with a romanticized version of admirals, generals, navies and armies from a European society obsessed with greed and power.

From the very beginning of the European military incursions into the Americas, greed was the wind that filled the sails of their ships. Whether it were Central or South or North America, massacre in the name of the Stage III Christian Warrior God was the self-justified means to satisfy a lust for gold or land.

Columbus wanted gold: gold for himself and for Spain to finance its imperialism. The Turks blocked the usual routes to the Far East. Knowing the earth was round, he concluded he could sail west and get there. He never did. He landed on Hispaniola, what is present-day Haiti and the Dominican Republic. Between his own journals and the books of a priest by the name of Las Casas who took part in the conquest of Cuba, the immensity of the crimes against the islands' inhabitants is detailed. A later report of 1650 indicates that none of the original inhabitants of Hispaniola or their descendents had survived the onslaught.

Columbus was not the only Spanish conquistador to exploit, to subjugate, to enslave and to decimate the native peoples of the Americas. Cortez did it to the Aztecs of Mexico, as did Pizarro to the Incas of Peru.

Colonial North America

In 1588 the English navy defeated the Spanish Armada. Now it was the turn of the English to do to the native peoples of North America what Columbus, Cortez and Pizarro had done in Central and South America. English sea power provided cover for the greed for new land and for people to exploit.

Regardless of what conditions in England made the euphemistically called settlers leave England for America, they were an invading army. The land was not vacant, but that did not prevent them from justifying taking the land for themselves. The governor of the Massachusetts Bay Company reasoned it this way. Indian land was legally a "vacuum." The Indians had not "subdued" the land, so the Indians had only a "natural" right to it, which carried no legal standing. They did not have the "civil" right to it that would have had legal standing.

The Christian invaders also appealed to their *Bible* for justification of their "settlements" on Indian lands. Psalms 2 was quoted. In it the Lord makes the nations "unto the ends of the earth" an inheritance for his people. The Lord says that his people shall "break them with a rod of iron [a rifle?] and dash them in pieces [with a rifle butt] like a potter's vessel."

Romans 13 was also quoted. The authority to which Christians were to be obediently subject was the Roman government, which was the servant of God. But now it was the "colonists" who were the authority, the servants and the ministers of God, and it was the Indians who must be subject to the God-instituted authority of God's people who were the inheritors of all nations.

Christian theologians also provided another justification for the extermination of Indians. Even though the Indians had had no opportunity to hear the word of God, they were condemned to Hell because Jesus said such things as, except through him no person could come to the Father. Cotton Mather, a Puritan theologian, put it this way after a particularly monstrous massacre of a Pequot village. "It was supposed that no less than 600 Pequot souls were brought down to hell that day."

Not all the Christian leaders saw what they were doing in such self-righteous terms. Roger Williams, a clergyman and founder of the Rhode Island colony, thought that the "most high Eternal will destroy . . ." what Williams described as "a depraved appetite after great vanities . . . ." Williams' words are just another way of describing what I call the insatiable greed and the lust for power of unconscious self-awareness. (See *A People's History of the United States* by Howard Zinn, pp. 12-17, for the source of this discussion.)

Nearly 400 years later, Indians, particularly Reservation Indians, are treated as an underclass. When we refer to them as second-class citizens, we are affirming that we live in a class society, without realizing that we are doing so. Their class struggles for what belongs to them by treaties continue to this day.

Even if it is difficult for Americans to see that we have always had a class society, if one thinks back to when we did have black slaves, that conclusion is inescapable. Slavery obviously represents a class society.

As early as 1619 the first black slaves were brought to North America. They were needed to work the plantations. Indians could not be forced to do it. White, indentured men could leave when they had fulfilled their contracts. Other white men were skilled in a profession and did not have to labor in the fields. Black slaves were necessary if the landowners were to acquire the big profits possible from their land. In the beginning it was the lucrative tobacco trade that provided the means to satisfy insatiable wants. Later, cotton was the means.

Just how profitable could slave labor be? James Madison, one of our Founding Fathers, said that for an investment of only twelve or thirteen dollars a year on one of his slaves he could make $257. That's a profit of around 2000 percent.

Well over 300 years later, blacks are still considered to be second-class citizens by many white citizens. Prejudice and discrimination against them remain entrenched in such institutions as the Republican Party. Senator Trent Lott's recent statement lauding racist Strom Thurmond's bid for the presidency in 1948 demonstrates that, regardless of denials, we have a class society.

For a vivid description of white class structure and conflict in colonial America, see Chapter 3 of Howard Zinn's *A People's History of the United States, 1492-Present.* As an example, Zinn notes that John Locke—whom historians consider to be the philosophical father of the Founding Fathers—wrote the constitutions for the Carolinas. His ideas were feudal in nature. He set up a feudal, aristocratic, oligarchic class society. In it, eight barons owned 40 percent of the land. It is apparent from the records of the time that a small class of merchants and a landed aristocracy ruled over the vast majority of the people who lived miserably poor lives. These poor included black slaves, indentured white servants and subsistence farmers.

Conditions for the indentured white servants were almost as bad as they were for black slaves. They could be bought and sold as slaves were. Beatings, rape and suicide were common. There were many rebellions against the ruling class, but none had any lasting benefits for these people.

Bacon's Rebellion in 1696 was notable. White frontiersmen, joined by slaves and servants, rebelled. Each group had different motives. Slaves wanted freedom. Servants wanted humane treatment during the period of their contracts. The frontiersmen wanted a reluctant ruling class, safe behind the buffer the frontier people provided, to make war on the Indians. The constant pressure of more poor, free whites for Indian land meant the constant threat of Indian reprisals. Uniting all the factions in the rebellion was "leveling"—the equalization of wealth. From 1620 to 1776, leveling was behind the innumerable struggles of poor whites against the rich ruling class.

At other times, the ruling class fomented war on the Indians in order to divert class conflict away from themselves. Frontier people would then be fighting Indians instead of rebelling against the ruling class.

The overall goal of the ruling class was to keep slaves, Indians and poor whites from combining forces. To keep blacks from aligning themselves with Indians, blacks could not go into Indian territory and treaties with the Indians required the return of runaway slaves. To keep poor whites who had completed their indentures from combining with blacks, they were given muskets, corn and cash. By law, blacks were forbidden from bearing arms. Racism was blatantly practiced to keep poor whites, blacks and Indians divided so that they would not combine against the ruling class. Also, the ruling class gave small rewards to a white middle class of independent farmers and city artisans to induce them to unite with the ruling class against poor whites, blacks and Indians.

In colonial North America, besides indentured or free poor whites, blacks—slaves or free—and all Indians, there was a fourth group that comprised 50 percent of the population who were subjugated and oppressed: women. It is easy to forget this because the history books we were usually exposed to ignored them, except for the wives of the ruling elite class. Since women had no part in public life and were confined to their homes, the problems they faced were endured in private.

As I indicated in the previous chapter, the second-class status of women began some 5,000 years ago when the Indo-Europeans jumped from a Stage II to a Stage III level of unconscious self-awareness. When Stage III brought in the primacy of private property, it made women into private property as well.

The immediate backdrop for how women were treated in the English colonies was how they were considered in England. The marriage of a woman was compared to a stream emptying into a river. The stream loses its name. The woman loses her name. Her "stream" is lost. She now has a superior, a master.

In the colonies she could be beaten, but not to the point of permanent injury or death. She could not own property, even personal property. Her husband was entitled to any wages she might earn. To have a child out of marriage was a crime.

In confirmation of my experience that a compulsion for power underlies Stage III, *The Spectator*, a well-known periodical in England and America, expressed a man's perspective on women. "Nothing is more gratifying to the mind of man than power or dominion . . ." over his ". . . family as a patriarchal sovereignty in which I am myself both king and priest."

A "pocket" book entitled *Advice to a Daughter* that circulated widely in the colonies in the 1700s confirms my experience that in Stage III, while women are forced to stay with more open connections between the thinking and emotional/sexual brains, men severed most of those connections and became more intellectual. In that book it says that men have a larger share of reason. It says that women are softer, which meant that they were more open to their emotions.

In 1619, ninety women, by their own choice, were brought from England to Jamestown to be sold as wives. The price was the cost of their transportation. They had no choice of a husband.

Any number of teenaged girls and women came over as indentured servants. Their lot was scarcely better than that of a black slave. Low wages, poor food, lack of privacy, makeshift beds, exhaustive work, whippings and sexual abuse characterized their treatment. For black, slave women, the situation was even worse, especially for sexual abuse. (See Zinn, Chapter 6, for a fuller exploration of the class status of women.)

The Declaration of Independence and the Revolutionary War

Class conflict had been at the heart of the whole 150 years of the colonial experience. It was clearly in evidence in the events leading up to the Declaration of Independence in 1776. There were many conflicts between the poor and the rich. Some of these conflicts were not just riots against oppressive governments but were, as Zinn says, "long lasting social movements, highly organized, involving the creation of counter governments."

In the 1700s there were many kinds of oppressive policies that provoked the poor, lower class against both the upper class, pro-British elite and the upper class, pro-colony elite. There were the Tenant uprisings of the 1740s, '50s and

'60s. There was the Stamp Act of 1765 imposed by England to pay for the French war. The Stamp Act triggered the Boston riots of 1767. There was the Regulator movement, beginning in 1766, of farmers who were overburdened with taxes and debts. The Boston Massacre of 1770 was a consequence of British soldiers taking jobs away from colonials. Impressment of colonials and the quartering of British troops were also part of the reason for anger against England. The Boston Tea Party of 1773 was still another example of resistance to England. What the pro-colony, political leaders were successful in doing was to divert attention away from their own greed and power and focus the people's grievances on England. By recognizing lower-class grievances, the upper class was able to mobilize enough of the lower class to support the upper-class goal of a revolt against England.

The upper class used a clever device to mobilize lower class support for the Revolution. They clothed their class goals in the language of liberty and equality. They spoke of "our" liberty, "our" property and "our" country. In the new country, the ruling elite neither ended slavery nor inequality.

Behind all the patriotic rhetoric of Patrick Henry and Thomas Paine for separation from England was the anticipation by the upper class that in the new nation "they could take over land, profits and political power" from the supporters of the British Empire, "hold back potential rebellions and create a consensus of popular support" for themselves as rulers. Henry and Paine eloquently diverted the lower classes from their just grievances against the upper class by stating that England was the common enemy of all classes. They were successful in fabricating the misleading idea that the Revolutionary War was fought on behalf of a one-minded people. It was a fabrication because after the war the ruling class was not about to do any kind of "leveling" to relieve the grinding poverty of the poor. So concludes Zinn. I believe the basic reason why Henry, Paine and the ruling class could gain the support of at least a sufficient number of the middle and lower classes to revolt against England is that all classes have in common a Stage III level of unconscious self-awareness. That is, to varying degrees everyone is in a condition of insatiable wants and a compulsion for power.

By 1774 the ruling class set in motion the final act that would result in the Revolution. They set up the Continental Congress, which was an illegal act. In 1775 after the Minutemen had fought British troops, the Congress opted for independence. A committee was set up to write a Declaration of Independence, but it was Jefferson who wrote it. It was adopted on July 2, 1776, and proclaimed on July 4, 1776.

The philosophical basis of the Declaration of Independence that is expressed in the second paragraph comes right out of 17th and 18th century British philosophy and economic theory. From Jeremy Bentham (1748-1832) came the idea that Happiness was the ultimate goal of humans and could be realized through a government based on reason and law. He saw humans in a natural state as primarily avoiding pain and seeking pleasure. This was an accurate set of assumptions about humans, but it isn't our natural state. Primal pain is the reason we are the way we are. Because of primal pain, we avoid the pain of needs going unmet and seek the pleasure of satisfying insatiable wants to whatever extent we can. From Thomas Hobbes (1588-1679) came the substance of what the Declaration of Independence means when it claims that "all men are created equal." That clause means that each and every man has the equal right to make a free gift of his natural right of self-preservation to a central government. The clause certainly did not mean for Jefferson or the other Founding Fathers that anyone from the lower classes was the equal of anyone of the ruling elite class. Nor did it apply to women, slaves, or Indians. From the English philosopher John Locke (1632-1704) came the arguments against absolute monarchy and the divine right of kings. Locke said that citizens have a duty to obey their ruler, but if the ruler's commands do not deserve obedience, then resistance is justified. Then it is the people who agree to unite to form a supreme government that deserves obedience.

There was a hidden agenda behind the ringing words of the Declaration of Independence. The hidden agenda was that the elite ruling class needed the support of a sufficient number of middle- and lower-class colonists to defeat England. The ringing words were to garner that support but without arousing those lower classes to fight against the entrenched wealth and power of the elite ruling class. That entrenchment had been going on for 150 years. Zinn notes that 69 percent of the signers of the Declaration of Independence held colonial office under England. It wasn't enough that they had immense wealth and power; they had to have it all for themselves.

Another part of the hidden agenda of the Declaration had to do with slavery. Jefferson's initial composition included an accusation that the King had been part of the slave trade and that he had resisted attempts to stop it. The support of the colonies in which slavery was needed for the economy was crucial, so the inclusion of slavery as a grievance against the King was dropped. So much for the unalienable rights of life, liberty and the pursuit of happiness. Slaves didn't count.

Class privileges were also in evidence just as soon as the Declaration of Independence was proclaimed. Zinn notes that in Boston four days after the reading of the Declaration the townsmen were ordered to show up for a military draft. The rich could avoid it by paying for someone else to take their places. The poor had no choice but to serve.

So, it was the poor who made up most of the colonial armies. It was they who fought and suffered. Conditions for them were terrible, causing any number of treasonous actions on their part. It was these poor men who were specifically excluded from voting because they were propertyless who fought the war on behalf of a propertied upper class.

During the war, it was the poor who suffered most. There were shortages of food. Robert Morris, one of the Founding Fathers, was even accused of withholding food from the market. Inflation was high. There were riots and insurrections. There were threats of slave revolts. One estimate judged that 10 percent of the population owned 60 percent of the new nation's wealth and owned as slaves one-seventh of the population. In some states some small concessions were made to maintain order and to stay in power.

The states drew up new constitutions after 1776. Maryland's is an example of how a rich and powerful, elite ruling class keeps power for itself. To run for governor, one had to own 5,000 pounds and, for senator, 1,000 pounds. So 90 percent of the people were excluded from office, but this created a serious problem of keeping the public in line. In general, in the new state constitutions, concessions to mollify the people were minimal. Property qualifications in some states were lowered. In Massachusetts, they were raised.

By no means was there a united people behind the war. In the South, the lower classes saw that, win or lose against the British, they would continue to be exploited by the political elite. In the deep South, many were Loyalists. In one instance, about a hundred of them were massacred. The general in charge was pleased with the effect it had on others who wanted no part in the war.

The Continental Congress governed the states during and after the war. It was dominated by the rich and powerful. The recent debacle between American Airlines management and their labor force is illustrative of how nothing has really changed with regard to class struggle. The airline's management had wrung extensive wage and benefit concessions from the union by claiming that bankruptcy was unavoidable otherwise. Without disclosing it to the unions, management was offering very generous wage and benefit increases to company officers if they would stay on at least to the end of reorganization.

Now back to the Continental Congress. It voted to give army officers half-pay for life if they stuck out the war to the end. In the meantime, soldiers weren't getting paid or getting paid in worthless scrip, and were suffering and dying while watching the rich and powerful of the Continental Congress enrich themselves.

With a final victory at Yorktown, Virginia, in 1781, the war was over. Without the aid of a large French army and a French naval blockade, perhaps the final outcome would have been defeat.

After the war, the enormous wealth of the Loyalists was confiscated by the rich and powerful American ruling elite, creating the richest ruling class ever to that date. Some land tenants were made into landowners. For many of the lower classes, the successful conclusion of the war meant only that they had exchanged one master for another: the British for the American elite.

By 1787 conditions throughout the nation caused widespread despair. The majority lived at a subsistence level. Most people lived on farms as poor freeholders, tenants and indentured hands. They were burdened with high rents, ruinous taxes and blood-sucking interest rates of 20 percent to 40 percent. Future harvests had to be mortgaged. When the debt-ridden person couldn't pay, he was jailed or sold out to service or sent to a poorhouse. No property was exempt from seizure. It was common for seizures to take place right before a harvest. In the cities there were many young beggars in the streets. Newspapers, which were owned by the creditor class, complained about them. A jail in Massachusetts in 1786 confined eighty-eight people, of which eighty-four were there because of nonpayment of debts or taxes.

By 1787 one-third of the white, male population was disenfranchised because of property qualifications, which were also so high that only a few could qualify for office. To be a candidate for the New Jersey Legislature, one had to be worth about $140,000. To qualify to run for the South Carolina Senate, one had to be worth about $1,000,000. In 1787 the French chargé d'affaires wrote to his foreign minister to the effect that there was a class of men in America who feared the efforts of the people to despoil them of their possessions. This class wanted a stronger government that would execute the laws for the exact payment of debts in order to establish good credit for America abroad.

In that same year in Massachusetts, a revolt by debt-ridden farmers began. It was known as Shay's Rebellion. Shay had fought in the war, been wounded and was now one of those debt-ridden farmhands. The rebellion continued throughout the bitter winter of 1786-87. Finally, an army, raised and paid for by Boston merchants, defeated the rebels. The general in charge urged mercy for the rebels. Samuel Adams, one of our Founding Fathers, said: "In monarchy the crime of treason may admit of being pardoned or lightly punished, but the man who dares rebel against the laws of a republic ought to suffer death." In the eyes of the oppressed, however, it matters not whether the oppressor wears a British or an American wig. Several of the condemned were executed. Some were pardoned. Within just three months the Constitutional Convention of 1787 was in session to create a strong central government that would protect the economic interests of the rich and powerful, elite ruling class against the economic interests of the poor.

The Founding Fathers and the Constitutional Convention of 1787

While I have stated it in various other places, the primal foundation for the philosophical, political, economical and psychological worldview of our Founding Fathers needs to be remembered here. In Stage III of the devolution of consciousness into unconscious self-awareness, despite every effort on his part, the child is unsuccessful in getting his parents to fulfill his needs. He feels helpless. The pain of not having his needs met is too great for him to integrate. Consequently, he suppresses his needs in order to remain viable. His needs do not go away, however, but resurface as insatiable wants. Now the child is driven to accumulate and use power to overcome his feelings of helplessness and to try to satisfy his insatiable wants. Because in Stage III the child has had to sever connections with the communalistic, emotional/sexual brain in order to suppress his needs, his self-awareness is now located primarily in the individualistic thinking brain. This means that his use of power to try to satisfy insatiable wants leads to the concept of private property.

In the minds of our Founding Fathers, who had no knowledge of primal pain, it was the natural state of humankind to be acquisitive of private property and to use power to get it. In their minds, it was also the natural state of humankind to form nation-states and governments to regulate the use of private property. John Locke was the one to whom the Founding Fathers mostly looked for the formulation of their own ideas. In 1689, Locke wrote his *Two Treatises of Government*. In the second, he said that the "great and chief end . . . of Men's uniting into Commonwealth, and putting themselves under Government is the Preservation of their Property" (*Democracy for the Few* by Parenti, p. 5). Therefore, the overall goal of the Founding Fathers was to create a Constitution for the new nation that would properly regulate the use of private property.

Also in the minds of our Founding Fathers was the observation that everyone was different with regard to his faculties. By "faculties" they meant what today we call "abilities." It is the difference in "faculties" that leads to variations in the amount of private property that men will acquire. In their minds, therefore, the difference in faculties inevitably leads to classes, which are natural to humankind. For them, the basic distinction between classes was the degree of wealth: the rich and the poor.

From the English economist Adam Smith (1723-1790) in his book *The Wealth of Nations*, our Founding Fathers found the confirmation of their views about the relationship between the rich and poor classes. Smith wrote that the "necessity of civil government grows up with the acquisition of valuable property." He followed that with the statement that until there is "property there can be no government, the very end of which is to secure wealth and to defend the rich from the poor" (Parenti, p. 5). Therefore, the overall goal of the Founding Fathers was not only to create a Constitution for the new nation that would properly regulate the use of private property, but to protect their immense wealth from the poor.

The Founding Fathers not only thought that humankind was acquisitive by nature, but also that it was predaciously self-interested. They came to this conclusion by their study of history, particularly of democratic societies in which there was direct majority rule. Without exception, they saw these societies as degenerating into the rule of a "rich demagogue who has patronized the mob" or into an aristocracy of "the original leaders of the democratic elements" (*The*

American Political Tradition by Hofstadter, pp. 15-16). John Adams believed that if we did create a democracy, property would be voted out of the hands of the aristocrats into the hands of new aristocrats who would act just as severely and sternly as the old ones.

The Founding Fathers also found support for their view of humankind as being predaciously self-interested in the philosophy of Thomas Hobbes who thought that in a state of nature life was "solitary, poor, nasty, brutish and short." On the other hand, Hobbes did not deny that humankind could act benevolently, have good will and be charitable—all based on reason.

Even though the Founding Fathers included themselves as having a predacious self-interest, nevertheless they considered themselves to be men of virtue, character and principle. Very likely they were influenced by a misrepresentation of the views of John Calvin, who was the main Protestant theologian behind Puritanism. Calvin did mean that God did reward the righteous. Calvin did not mean that if one were prosperous that it meant that one was righteous. I believe that what the Founding Fathers meant was that since it was the regulation of property that brought governments into existence and they had the most property that they were the best qualified to formulate the Constitution for the new nation. John Jay made it plain when he said that those "who own the country ought to govern it."

The Founding Fathers were right that humans are predaciously self-interested. They were wrong in thinking that that is the way we are by nature. We are this way because of primal pain. And, it is a matter of degree, both of primal pain and of a predacious self-interest. There can be less pain and fewer insatiable wants. There can be more pain and more of a predacious, insatiable greed and lust for power. There can be much capacity for love, compassion, sharing and other conscious attributes, or there can be much loss of them.

So that there be no doubt about what our Founding Fathers thought and what they sought to achieve in the Convention of 1787 in the formulation of a new Constitution, I include a section of direct quotes from them.

James Madison

He was thirty-six years old in 1787 and became our fourth president.

The definition of factions: "a number of citizens, whether amounting to a majority or minority of the whole, who are united and activated by some common impulse of passion, or of interest, adverse to the rights of other citizens, or to the permanent and aggregate interests of the community."

What a majority faction wants: "a rage for paper money, for an abolition of debts, for an equal distribution of property, or for any other improper or wicked project . . ."

". . . the most common and durable source of faction has been the various and unequal distribution of property. Those who hold and those who are without property have ever formed distinct interests in society." ". . . the first object of government [is] the protection of different and unequal faculties of acquiring property."

"To secure the public good and private rights against the danger of such a faction and at the same time preserve the spirit and form of popular government is then the great object to which our inquiries are directed."

The government must be designed "to protect the minority of the opulent from the majority."

Men of property possessed "the most attractive merit and had the most diffusive and established character."

On Gouveneur Morris: "He was forever inculcating the utter depravity of men and the necessity of opposing one vice and interest to another vice and interest."

"It was politic as well as just that the interests and rights of every class should be duly represented and understood in the public councils."

Alexander Hamilton

He was thirty-two years old in 1787 and was Secretary of the Treasury (1789-1797).

On Shay's Rebellion: The new government should be able "to repress domestic faction and insurrection." "The tempestuous situation from which Massachusetts has scarcely emerged evinces dangers of this kind are not merely speculative."

"All communities divide themselves into the few and the many. The first are the rich and the well-born, the other the mass of the people . . . The people are turbulent and changing; they seldom judge or determine right."

A permanent check over the populace should be exercised by "the rich and well-born."

John Jay

He was forty-two years old in 1787 and became the first Chief Justice in 1789.

"The people who own the country ought to govern it."

John Adams

He was fifty-two years old in 1787 and became our second president in 1797.

There could be "no free government without a democratical branch in the Constitution."

Roger Sherman

He was sixty-seven years old in 1787 and a Convention delegate from Connecticut. "The people should have as little to do as may be about the Government."

Elbridge Gerry

He was forty-three years old in 1787 and became Vice President in 1813. Democracy was "the worst of all political evils."

Gouveneur Morris

He was thirty-seven years old in 1787 and a delegate to the Convention from Pennsylvania.

"Wealth tends to corrupt the mind and to nourish its love of power and to stimulate it to oppression. History proves this to be the spirit of the opulent."

On why the House of Representatives should not be popularly elected: "The time is not distant when the Country will abound with mechanics and manufacturers who will receive their bread from their employers. Will such men be the secure and faithful Guardians of liberty? [liberty = private property] . . . Children do not vote. Why? Because they [lack] prudence, because they have no will of their own. The ignorant and dependent can be as little trusted with the public interest."

Because of what we were not taught in school and because of a national tendency toward being self-congratulatory and because we have raised the Founding Fathers to the level of sainthood, it is important to know what they meant by "liberty." Their meaning of liberty was at the very core of what they sought to accomplish in the Convention.

For our Founding Fathers, liberty is what comes about when government protects private property so that men are protected as they use their natural faculties in the acquisition and use of private property. Liberty means the freedom to invest, to speculate, to trade and to accumulate wealth without encroachment by either a sovereign or by the propertyless masses. Liberty is freedom from fiscal uncertainty, from irregularities in the currency, from trade wars among the states, from foreign tariffs, from attacks on the creditor class or on property and from insurrection.

Liberty is a social condition that is threatened by democracy. Democracy, which is unrestrained government by the masses, brings about the redistribution of private property. Hence, democracy destroys the essence of liberty itself.

Liberty did not mean freedom for the masses to acquire vacant land. Squatters had no right to unused land. But a dozen or so of the delegates to the Convention were land speculators, and they did have the prior right to unused land.

Liberty did not have the meaning for our Founding Fathers of granting freedom to either slaves or to indentured servants. Neither did it involve such crucial liberties as are contained in the Bill of Rights. The Bill of Rights was added to the Constitution after it was adopted. As a condition of adopting the Constitution, the States insisted on the addition of these first ten amendments. The motivation for doing so was not a love for these democratic rights, but a fear of rebellions if such rights were not safeguarded. The motivation was sober judgment. The agreement to add the Bill of Rights was evidence that we do have a class society with class struggle as well as class privilege.

Previously, I outlined the Founding Fathers' philosophy of government. It arose because of the necessity to regulate private property. They made a number of deductions from that philosophy that guided them in their deliberations in the Convention.

Firstly, government is ultimately based on the consent of the people in whom power finally rests. The problem, however, is that the people are not capable of governing themselves. Most men do not own property, and that means they lack what has come to be called "the necessary stake in society" in order to be good citizens. There was a sizable number of farmers who owned small farms. It was these men the Founding Fathers had in mind when they spoke of the consent of the people.

Secondly, since government is based on property, those who have the most property should be able to exercise the most power in government. Since the Founding Fathers assumed that those who have the most property are the most capable of governing themselves, they should have the most control.

Thirdly, since government is to be fair, every class should have a say in it. Madison said that it was "politic as well as just that the interest and rights of every *class* should be duly represented and understood in the public councils." I've italicized "class" in the quote to emphasize that a class society is the natural outcome of Stage III unconscious self-awareness.

And fourthly, since governments come into being to regulate private property, they assumed that politics and economics are inseparable. Our Founding Fathers were well aware of the connection between political form and economic self-interest and between political form and class. They saw that connection as being crucial for themselves as well as being crucial for the well-being of everyone else. They interpreted the well-being of everyone else as being coincidental with their own. They were guided by the desire to construct a government that allowed for an unspoken alliance between the rich and powerful and the government for the benefit, primarily, of the rich and powerful. Their desire was to consolidate the class structure that existed during the whole colonial period and during the period of the Articles of Confederation. They expected that their class would occupy almost all of the elected and appointed positions in the new government. John Locke, who was their mentor, provided a model: the Constitutions he wrote for the Carolinas in the 1660s. The model was an oligarchic class society. It's been said that, regardless of the form of government, the rich and powerful are the ones who rule.

The overall goal of the Founding Fathers was to create a natural government that would prevent the poor from plundering the rich and to prevent the rich from plundering each other. By a "natural" government, they meant one that was derived from their understanding of men as they existed in their original condition. The Founding Fathers were well aware of the "natural" writings of Isaac Newton, Thomas Hobbes, Jeremy Bentham, John Locke and Adam Smith, to name the most important. Madison put it this way: A "natural" government is one in which "its several constituent parts may, by their mutual relations, be the means of keeping each other in their proper places." Interests, factions, classes and the branches of government would balance each other out. That natural government they were seeking would be strong enough to control the people because they could not govern themselves and at the same time control itself from any excesses.

But were the Founding Fathers really interested in a true balance? I don't think so. The balance they sought was to keep things as they were: the unequal balance among the various classes at that time. They certainly did not want a balance between slaves and slave owners, between those with property and those without, between the indigenous Native Americans and the European immigrants and their descendants and between men and women. Neither slaves nor indentured servants, nor propertyless white males, nor women, nor Indians were among those who conceived the Constitution. Naturally, there were no factions present—as they used the term—to cause the Convention to degenerate into a "dark and degraded" picture of the "infirmities and depravities of the human character" (quotes around words used by Madison in the Federalist #37). The only faction present in the Convention was that of the rich and powerful, elite ruling class of the day. And, despite their avowed intent of playing off one faction against another in a government of separation of powers and of a federalist system of only delegated powers to the central government, they put together a Constitution that protected and abetted their own faction's predacious self-interest.

Their overall strategy was twofold: to create a federal system of which there would be a strong central government and within the strong central government a separation of powers. Consistent with that strategy was to make the nation as large as possible to hamper any majority faction from gaining power. Madison, in the Federalist #10, said the citizens who shared a common majority interest "must be rendered by their number and local situation, unable to concert and carry out their schemes of oppression." That same strategy to hamper factions included maintaining the then-current state structure to insulate geographical areas.

Additionally, the strategy to accomplish the goal stated above was to create a representative government that would prevent factions from succeeding in getting paper money or abolishing debts or making an equal division of property. Hamilton said that merchants were the natural representatives of their employees. He thought that landholders, merchants and men of the learned professions were the ones to hold public office.

The Constitution

Since the Convention was made up solely of white propertied males and their primary concern was the protection of all of their forms of property, in short order they approved a number of shelters. The land speculators among the delegates got what they wanted: Congress to regulate the "unoccupied" Western lands. Speculators in Confederate securities got what they wanted: the new government to honor the greatly depreciated securities at face value. Merchants and creditors got what they wanted: the States could not issue paper money nor amend contracts and creditors could pursue debtors across State lines. The slave States got what they wanted: three-fifths of the total number of slaves counted toward entitlement of the number of Representatives in the House of Representatives. Slave owners got what they wanted: States into which slaves had escaped had to return them to their owners.

Debate over the structure of the new government to protect their property interests took much longer, and what emerged was a republican form—what today we call a representative democracy. The lower body or House of Representatives was to be composed of one representative for every 30,000 people in each state. Voting qualifications were left to each state to decide. A few states had no property qualifications. The rest required various amounts of property to be eligible to vote. Native Americans, slaves and women were excluded. Representatives were to serve for two years. All bills passed were subject to concurrence by the Senate. Although Representatives were popularly elected and there were no property qualifications to be one, it was anticipated that only men of property would be elected.

The upper legislative body, or Senate, was to be composed of two Senators from each state. The state legislatures would select them. The reasoning is set out in *The Federalist*, Number 63, written by either Madison or Hamilton. It was to defend the "people against their own temporary errors and delusions, their irregular passion[s]," and their being "misled by the artful misrepresentations of interested men."

> In these critical moments, how salutary will be the interference of some temperate and respectable body of citizens [the Senate], in order to check the misguided career, and to suspend the blow mediated by the people against themselves, until reason, justice, and truth can regain their authority over the public mind?

By "the people" is meant the popularly elected Representatives of the House. It was believed by the members of the Constitutional Convention that the manner in which Senators would be selected would result in a Senate composed of men of superior character who would preserve the true national interest, i.e., the interests of the rich and powerful, elite ruling class. In the House, then, the upward movement of any democratic faction, say, for paper money, for example, would be effectively blocked by the Senate.

The President was to be elected by an Electoral College, the members of which to be selected by the state legislatures. Each state was entitled to as many Electors as it had Legislators. The President had veto power over all bills sent to him, a veto that could be overridden only by a two-thirds' majority in each of the Senate and the House. These provisions were additional security against any attacks on property rights, which was the Founding Fathers' major concern.

To further block any factional interest detrimental to property rights was a Supreme Court. Its members were to be appointed by the President and approved by the Senate. The Constitution was designed to protect property, so laws adverse to property that managed to surmount the House, the Senate and a President would be declared unconstitutional.

The final block on attempts to adversely affect property rights was the difficult process of amending the Constitution. A two-thirds' majority in both the House and the Senate would be necessary to propose an amendment or two-thirds of the state legislatures would be necessary to call a Convention to propose an amendment. Three-fourths of state legislatures or State Conventions were necessary for adoption of an amendment.

Comments on the Founding Fathers and What They Accomplished

My point is not to be unfairly critical of the Founding Fathers nor to take sides in a partisan debate about them. My point is to show that beneath their political, philosophical, psychological and sociological positions and the Constitution they created was the then-current status of the devolvement of consciousness into unconscious self-awareness. In particular, I'll deal with their low level of selves-in-relationship, their high level of individualism and low level of communalism and their high level of insatiable wants and compulsion for power.

My study of the colonial period, of the Revolution, of the conditions during the period of the Articles of Confederation, of the Constitutional Convention of 1787, of our Founding Fathers and of the Constitution and its ratification has been a revelation to me. I had expected—and found confirmed—the anti-democratic mindset of our Founding Fathers and that the Constitution they formulated was anti-democratic. I hardly expected to discover, however, that they and the Constitution represented so perfectly what I independently discovered about our precursors: the Stage III Indo-Europeans of some 6,000 years ago. Stage III of unconscious self-awareness means insatiable wants, a compulsion for power, individualism, private property, classes and the necessity of a nation-state, primarily to regulate private property.

It does not take being a primal person to make this connection between the characteristics of Stage III unconscious self-awareness and our Founding Fathers. The primal point of view just provides the basis for this clustering of characteristics. The connection can easily be found in the writings of the 17th and 18th century English philosophers and economists and in the writings of our Founding Fathers, which reflect the mentoring of those philosophers and economists.

Why haven't we been taught that our Founding Fathers were not saints but men of their day? Why were we not taught that being men of their day they feared democracy as much as they did monarchy? Why were we taught that we live in a classless society when our Founding Fathers saw that we did and protected their wealthy class from the classes of the poor, of slaves and of Native Americans? Why were we not taught that the Constitution they designed was for the very purpose of protecting their property from any attempts by the masses to equalize wealth?

What we were taught was that our Founding Fathers were idealists when, in fact, they were realists. What we were taught was the same blind patriotism our Founding Fathers used to garner support for a system that would require class struggles to secure rights for all the people, rights not based on property. What we were taught was denial: denial that our Founding Fathers could have base notions of greed and power; denial that our nation could ever have base notions of greed and power in our foreign policies; denial that we could ever be "off base." What each of us was taught was to be so occupied with being idealistically self-congratulatory that we would never run the chance of being a realist.

The Founding Fathers as Men of Their Time

The Founding Fathers were men of their time—what else could they be? Hofstadter says they should neither be castigated as "selfish reactionaries" nor praised as selfless visionaries. Rather, he calls them "realists." Realists they were, but to leave it at that is to miss that they exhibited the current status of some 5,000-plus years of the growth of the condition of insatiable wants and compulsion for power and of the growth of individualism and the decline of communalism. They were selfish reactionaries in that they were reacting against the "leveling" impulses of the poor, laboring many and quite aware that they were consolidating their wealth-related power against the power of majority "factions" to impose any "wicked project." They were selfless visionaries in that for their time they were proposing the first national Constitution that was an accurate manifestation of the then-current status of unconscious self-awareness.

The degree of their individualism is seen in the social contract theories of government of such men as Hobbes and Locke, which they accepted as being true, dating back to even the earliest of human societies. My research does not bear out that individualism goes this far back. As I stated much earlier in this history, when unconscious self-awareness came about, humanity was much closer to being a self-in-relationship and, consequently, communalism was much in evidence and individualism was an aberration. The individualism of the Founding Fathers was also exhibited in their pursuit of happiness which, for them, was success in the acquisition of personal wealth, which provides the means to avoid suffering and to embrace pleasure.

In 1913, Charles Beard published his book, *An Economic Interpretation of the Constitution of the United States*. It caused an outrage because Beard was accused of denigrating the character of the Founding Fathers by falsely attributing to them crass economic motives for what they produced. But Beard merely made clear that, in the worldview of these men, governments were instituted to regulate property interests and that for the common good, men of wealth must be the ones who control government directly or control the laws by which the government operates. This point of view was none other than that of John Locke, their philosophical mentor.

Most of the 55 men who drafted the Constitution were wealthy lawyers. They were owners of large tracts of land and/or slaves, were manufacturers, were import/exporters, were moneylenders and were holders of Confederacy bonds. Together what they wanted was a strong central government to levy tariffs; to prohibit paper money for the payment of loans; to protect land speculators as they appropriated Native American territory; to prevent runaway slaves from finding sanctuary in neighboring states; to guarantee to Confederacy bondholders that the bonds would be paid off at their face value and not at their greatly depreciated market value; and to levy taxes to, among other things, pay off those bonds. When it becomes clear that these economic interests lie behind the political details of the Constitution, it can be seen that our Constitution is not just about "a new nation conceived in liberty," but the product of various segments of the rich and powerful, elite ruling class to consolidate their wealth and power, while reluctantly handing out just enough rights to the masses to buy their support.

The Way in Which the Founding Fathers were High-minded

The Founding Fathers' views of humanity as being innately predaciously self-interested notwithstanding, they were quite high-minded in their efforts to put together a new nation conceived in liberty in which all men are equal. It is just that their high-mindedness was founded on an understanding of human nature in which property is essential to liberty and men are equal only insofar as they are free to make a gift of their personal freedom to form a government for the sake of self-preservation.

The Founding Fathers assumed that it was human nature to want to accumulate property and power. They could see that everyone varies as to faculties (abilities), that inevitably some men will accumulate more property than others, that those with less will try to take from those with more if they can and that government is necessary to protect property rights. With that assumption and those observations, the Founding Fathers were quite high-minded and, in their own view, realistic in creating a new nation that would take into account that assumption and those observations. Thus, in the view of Parenti, "there was nothing in their concept of nation that worked against their class interest and a great deal that worked for it." Their high-mindedness and selfish class interest went hand-in-hand. Their goal was to defend the wealthy few from the laboring many, which goal they honestly saw as being to the ultimate benefit of everyone.

The Founding Fathers on Human Nature

It was the Founding Fathers' experience that historically it had always been every man for himself; humans were not only naturally acquisitive but predaciously self-interested. Governments not only had to be set up to protect the right to acquire and to use property, but to control predacious self-interest as well. The Founding Fathers were correct in their observations of humanity but, having no knowledge of primal pain, they mistakenly attributed acquisitiveness and predacious self-interest to man's nature rather than to primal pain.

In reasoning that the way humans are now is the way we have always been, the Founding Fathers were no different than any of our ancestors, stretching back thousands of years. Previous understandings of humanity about itself have always been looked upon as being either mythological or wrong. The Founding Fathers projected back in time the current status of the devolvement of selves-in-relationship into communalism and individualism. In direct contradiction of the view of the Founding Fathers on human nature, my research shows that the farther back we go the more in evidence is a higher degree of selves-in-relationship and a lesser degree of communalism and individualism. Specifically, with regard to the notion of the Founding Fathers that it was every man for himself, I've found that in the first two stages of unconscious self-awareness, it was far more likely that there was a redistribution of wealth, that there was a "leveling," so that no one suffered alone from want.

Undoubtedly, the pessimistic view of human nature held by the Founding Fathers was influenced by Puritanism which, in turn, was influenced by the theology of John Calvin. Granted that there is a question as to whether the Founding Fathers were Deists or Christians, it is evident that they saw no evidence that being a Christian resulted in a sloughing off of the greed and lust for power that is characteristic of a predacious self-interest. Their experience of humans in general and, perhaps, even of their personal experience, indicated to them that baptism, conversion and sanctification were not effective. The Constitution they wrote took account of a humanity in whom they saw no hope of a change for the better.

Regardless of the generally pessimistic view of human nature held by the Founding Fathers, they also held an elevated opinion of themselves. They felt that governments arose specifically for the purpose of regulating property. Therefore, the people who owned the most property were the best qualified to put together a constitution to run the country and to be the elected and appointed officials of the government. Jay's feeling that those who own the country ought to run it is then not as crass as it appears.

In their elevated opinion of themselves, the Founding Fathers thought of themselves as men of "virtue and principle." But, who are men of virtue and principle? Unlike the propertyless masses, the Founding Fathers would not tread upon the rights of citizens to acquire great wealth, nor endanger the primacy of property rights to liberty. In other words, they saw that property endowed them with superior qualities. This vision, however, blinded them from seeing that underneath what they called virtue and principle was the same old predacious self-interest common to all.

The Founding Fathers and Property Rights and Civil Rights

In the Founding Fathers' experience, humans were naturally acquisitive. Therefore, they believed that humans should have liberty for the unfettered acquisition and use of property. Hence, their view of government was that its purpose was to protect property so that liberty could be maintained.

Since our government was set up to protect the liberty of property rights, the governmental protection of the liberty of civil rights has had to come through class struggle and the threat of class struggle erupting into revolution. Maintaining civil rights is a constant struggle. The rich and powerful, elite ruling class is often successful in rolling back civil rights by claiming that there is a threat to national security that requires curtailing civil rights.

To illustrate how precarious civil rights have always been, eight years had not yet passed under the Constitution and the Bill of Rights guaranteeing free speech when Congress passed the Sedition Act of 1798. That act criminalized any speech, oral or written, that was judged to be either false or scandalous or malicious and was directed against the government or the Congress or the President with the intent to defame, to bring into disrepute, or to cause hatred against them. Ten persons were jailed. The Supreme Court upheld the law. Zinn notes that even though there is no prior restraint, how secure is the right of free speech when it can be punished by imprisonment after the fact? The threat of being jailed is an effective deterrent to free speech.

The Founding Fathers on Power and the Constitution

Richard Hofstadter opens Chapter 1 of his book, *The American Political Tradition*, with quotes from James Madison and John Adams on the subject of power. From Madison—"Wherever the real power in a government lies, there is the danger of oppression. In our Government the real power lies in the majority of the community . . ." From Adams—"Power naturally grows . . . because human passions are insatiable. But that power alone can grow which already is too great; that which is unchecked; that which has no equal to control it."

The Constitution that the Founding Fathers created effectively nullified the real power that lay in the majority of the community. The power that alone could grow, that was unchecked, that had no equal to control it, that was already too great was the power of the rich and powerful, elite ruling class. The Constitution, with its separation of powers, effectively nullified the power of any faction within the government to grow. It did nothing, however, to control the powers of the whole class of the rich and powerful from enriching themselves at the expense of the majority. Therefore, ultimately, Madison's caution about creating a government obliged to control itself has been ignored.

The unwritten alliance of the rich and powerful with all three branches of our government, or their occupation of its offices, has nullified the system of checks and balances. Our Congress and the Presidency are the best money can buy. The Congress has allowed the Executive branch to usurp its power. The Supreme Court endorses the notion, in the name of the constitutional right of free speech, that soft money—the monied alliance between the rich and powerful and the government—does not subvert the Constitution. The recent campaign finance reform bill that the Supreme Court said was constitutional is not going to prevent anyone or any corporation from buying influence in Washington. The Federalist objective to ally government with commercial interests has been eminently successful to this day. Ultimately, the Founding Fathers revealed that the rich and powerful will act in their own predacious self-interest and devise a government that appears to be fair to all but which, in reality, favors the rich and powerful. In general, what I have found is that regardless of the form of government, the wealthy few run their country. Why? Because wealth means power and power is the means for control.

The Founding Fathers were well aware of the connection between wealth and power. Most certainly they were familiar with Adam Smith's *Wealth of Nations*, which was published in 1776. Smith wrote that wealth is the power to purchase "a certain command over all the labor, or over all the produce of labor which is then in the market." It was the preservation of the exercise of this power of their wealth to command labor and the produce of labor to which the Founding Fathers directed their attention.

The Founding Fathers on Class

I have read and am singularly unimpressed with the views of historians such as Benjamin F. Wright who claim that the Founding Fathers were not a "small group of intensely reactionary persons, bent upon establishing an American oligarchy." The Founding Fathers were not trying to establish an oligarchy; they were determined to protect the one they had from the excesses of both monarchy and democracy. An oligarchy already existed in the Colonies and in the nation under the Articles of Confederation. The few who governed were also the wealthy, so it can also be said that a plutocracy existed simultaneously. In the Colonies and in the nation, we had government by the wealthy few. Wright's view represents the propensity of the people for denial, for hero worship and for national self-aggrandizement.

To preserve the existing plutocratic oligarchic state of affairs was an unstated objective of the Founding Fathers. To state that objective would have made it immeasurably more difficult to gain the support of the propertyless populace. Instead, what they had done with the Declaration of Independence, and now proposed to do with the Constitution, was to clothe their own self-serving interests in the language of a patriotic nationalism.

As far as I know, the Founding Fathers did not use the words oligarchy and plutocracy—which imply a class structure—but they were not averse to using the word "class" to describe society as they knew it. Throughout my reading of the Founding Fathers, I found constant references to class. By "class," they meant a society divided by wealth, power and faculties.

Hamilton, for example, said that the rich and well-born are a *class* to whom belongs a permanent share in government. All others are in a *class* who cannot be trusted in a democratic assembly to pursue the common good; they will act imprudently. He wanted a President and a Senate chosen for life. He favored aid to commerce, industry and banking but opposed aid to the poor.

Since our Founding Fathers thought that government existed for the protection and promulgation of property rights exclusively, they had little interest in civil rights. In fact they actively opposed the incorporation of a Bill of Rights in the Constitution. It was only under the threat of revolt that it was agreed upon during the period of ratification that the new Congress would amend the Constitution with the Bill of Rights. From the very beginning of the new nation, the achieving of civil rights has always been, and continues to be, a matter of class struggle and the threat of class revolt—the rich and powerful, elite ruling class making concessions only when they felt they had to.

There are at least two reasons we don't hear of gains in civil and human rights as a class struggle. The first has to do with denial. We are so obsessed with the idea that our society is so perfect that it can't have any real failings. The second has to do with all of us sharing with the rich and powerful the same goal of attaining ever greater wealth. The rich and the poor, the powerful and the weak, alike, are driven by the same insatiable wants and compulsion for power.

Some General Comments on the Constitution

While it is true that the Founding Fathers feared monarchy and a military dictatorship as much as they feared democracy, they had an affinity with monarchy and dictatorship that they did not have with democracy. That affinity was wealth and power. When they spoke of democracy, they meant direct majority rule. This led, they said, to either a tyranny in which there would be rule by a rich demagogue who patronized the mob or an aristocracy composed of the original leaders of the democratic elements. Democracy, they feared, would always end with leveling; the poor majority would always plunder the wealthy few.

Shay's Rebellion was the immediate reference point for the "mob" and leveling as the Founding Fathers met in the Constitutional Convention of 1787. Because of it, the Founding Fathers were going to make sure that only men of good birth and fortune controlled the nation, men who would check the leveling impulses of the propertyless multitude that composed the majority faction.

Madison stated this objective in the Federalist #10: "To secure the public good and private rights against the danger of such a faction and at the same time preserve the spirit and form of popular government is then the great object to which our inquiries are directed." Madison then goes on to say that a Republic, that is, a government of representatives of the people, is the best way to accomplish the goal. What he does not say is that while he wants to preserve the spirit and form of popular government, he wants to provide as little as possible of the substance of popular government. He does not say so, but he means to preserve the existing oligarchic, plutocratic class structure under the guise of democratic forms. With the semblance of a democratic form, he garnered sufficient popular support and left intact the existing class structure. With a strong central, representative government he provided for the insatiable wants of the rich and powerful to increase their wealth, while stifling the leveling, insatiable wants of the laboring poor.

How did the Founding Fathers get away with so openly, jealously guarding their own wealth, power and class, while so openly discrediting the motives of the poor, laboring class? How did a Constitution so flagrantly one-sided get adopted?

First of all, the Constitution did enough for the middle class to secure their support. In that middle class were owners of sufficient property to qualify to vote in most of the states. Also in that middle class were large numbers of men whose jobs were impacted by imports. Provisions in the Constitution for tariffs protected their jobs from foreign competition.

Secondly, the ploy of patriotism and national unity was employed to capitalize on and manipulate the deep-seated urge within all of us to be part of something larger than ourselves. This urge goes all the way back to very ancient times when we were much closer to being selves-in-relationship. If religion is the sacred opiate of the people, then patriotism is the secular opiate of the people, both of which are designed to dull a person's mind to his suffering at the hands of an overbearing rich and powerful, elite ruling class.

And thirdly, they got away with it because of the manner in which the Constitution was to be adopted. It was to be by the ratification of a minimum of nine State Conventions. The members of the Conventions were to be elected by the same men who were qualified to vote in each state. Qualifications varied. It was expected that the same men who were elected to state offices would be elected to the Conventions. There was never a popular vote.

What we wound up with is what Parenti calls "a dual political system": a symbolic one on public display and taught in our schools and a substantive one that makes sure that the rich and powerful are taken care of, one that is usually not heard of nor accounted for.

And now I skip to the modern period to see how, 200-plus years later, individualism, insatiable wants, compulsion for power, nationalism and class struggle are playing out.

CHAPTER 14

THE DEVOLUTION OF CONSCIOUSNESS INTO UNCONSCIOUS SELF-AWARENESS IN THE UNITED STATES IN THE MODERN PERIOD

Introduction

There are many histories of the United States. None, however, has been written from a point of view that has been enlightened by a knowledge of the human psyche, gained through experiencing the pain of suppressed, unmet, infantile needs and of the helplessness in getting those needs met. That pain, those needs and that helplessness underlie all of the greed, all of the compulsion for power and all of the self-centered individualism of contemporary life. That, at least, is my experience.

Other histories generally fall into one of two categories. Either they see consensus among all of our people throughout our history or they see conflict as being the defining feature of it. There is a basis for each in Stage III unconscious self-awareness. It is true that insatiable wants and a compulsion for power infects us all. Whether we be rich or poor, powerful or powerless, underneath we share the same outlook on ourselves as Americans, anyone of whom can become immensely wealthy or President. That is the consensus point of view. It is also true that insatiable wants and a compulsion for power, in combination with differences in abilities, in opportunities and in inheritance, lead to the creation of classes, parochial class interests and to class struggle. That is the conflict point of view.

Together, the consensus and conflict points of view present a balanced picture of our history. Consequently, in my history, I aim, not so much to curse the darkness of insatiable wants turning into just plain greed or the compulsion for power turning into the absolute corruption of absolute power, but to suggest a means of understanding of why we are where we are today.

By Chapter 12, I brought the devolution of consciousness into unconscious self-awareness down through the 1st millennium BCE Essentially, by that time the Stage II Mother Goddess cultures had been taken over by the Stage III

Warrior God cultures. By that time, Buddhism had been around for some 500 years and Christianity was just beginning, both being Stage IV religions of transcendence. Greek philosophy had made its transition into the transcendence of Pure Reason. Basically, nothing has changed since that period except a much further decline into Stage III of unconscious self-awareness.

It was with that justification that I skipped to the colonial period of the history of the Americas. I then proceeded to describe what the current level of insatiable greed and lust for power meant for the formulation of the Constitution of the United States of America. With that foundation, I can skip again from the late 18th century to the 19th century to show how that foundation still determines the way in which greed and power drive unconscious self-awareness.

What also characterizes Stage III unconscious self-awareness today, even more so than during the period of our Founding Fathers, is individualism. To a much greater extent, people are acting as independent selves without regard for the common good of everyone, regardless of class. Also, even more so today, our nation-state is controlled by the rich and powerful, elite ruling class, either by being the elected and appointed officials of the government or by controlling the officials of the government for the purpose of maintaining and enhancing their class interests.

Because my goal is not just to describe what's happening these days with regard to greed, power, individualism, classes, capitalism, private property and imperialism—plenty of other writers are doing that—I restate once again what is behind it all. The inability of parents to nurture their children properly causes primal pain. Primal pain is pain too traumatic to integrate and must be suppressed, first by placation, second by reimmersion and third by denying needs. Together, these three become a child's defense system and, in time, they take over from a child's original consciousness. Together, they form what I call unconscious self-awareness. It is unconscious because the first purpose of the defense system is to block primal pain from consciousness, and the second is to block even the memory of it.

Here, I could devote many pages on how, ever since we stopped placating our parents to be nurtured, we continue to placate to get what we want. Here, I could also devote many pages on how, ever since we stopped diverting ourselves from primal pain as children, we continue to immerse ourselves in TV or work or play or drugs or what have you in order to forget for a while the suffering that would come up if we stopped running. Here, I could write reams on the devastating effects that primal pain has on our mental, emotional and physical health. Rather, here, I'm going to concentrate my efforts on what the denial of needs means for our lives.

Stage III historically and personally for each of us means that a point has come in our childhood when we can no longer hide from ourselves that we are helpless in getting our needs met. Placation and reimmersion have become ineffective. The pain of unmet needs is such that now we must deny our needs if we are to remain viable. After we have done so, we are unaware of the fact that those needs have resurfaced as insatiable wants. We are also unaware of the fact that the control we now seek over our lives is a compulsion for power to compensate for those feelings of helplessness and is a means of satisfying our wants.

In Stage III, if primal pain becomes great enough, insatiable wants become just plain greed. Greed is the primal-pain-driven necessity to continuously expand what one wants in order to keep ahead of primal-pain-laden needs that are ever pushing upwards to become conscious.

Likewise with power. Empowerment is the antidote to feelings of helplessness. If primal pain becomes great enough, absolute power is required to keep pace with overwhelming helplessness and need.

Biologically, when we had to deny our needs, self-awareness had to cut connections between the emotional/sexual brain and the thinking brain and become primarily centered in the thinking brain. One consequence of this change was that self-awareness became far more individualistic and far less communalistic. This is so because the emotional/sexual brain retains a lot of what it means to be a self-in-relationship, while the thinking brain has given up most of it.

The internal mating of insatiable wants with individualism is the basis in the external world for private property. The difference in the abilities of people to accumulate wealth and power and in the opportunities open to them lead to a few achieving great wealth and power and to the many achieving very little. This is the basis for the division of society into classes and for the rich and powerful upper class to institute the nation-state to protect their wealth and power from the lower classes whom they feel are predacious. The mating of insatiable wants with a compulsion for power, with individualism and with private property produces capitalism. With capitalism comes not only a global imperialism but one that extends into space as well. Imperialistic, capitalistic visionaries are already planning for the exploitation of the moon and Mars. This is what Stage III is all about regarding insatiable wants and the compulsion for power.

A brief review here of the clash between the Warrior God and Mother Goddess cultures will help to put into context the current situation regarding the exponential increase in primal pain since that period.

When the Stage III, Indo-European Warrior God peoples invaded the Stage II, Mother Goddess peoples, all Indo-Europeans were more individualistic than communalistic. That is, they exhibited more of the characteristics of independent selves than they did of selves-in-relationship. The Mother Goddess peoples were more communalistic than individualistic. That is, they exhibited more of the characteristics of being selves-in-relationship than they did of being independent selves.

The Indo-Europeans were more individualistic because of the consequences of a certain, critical rise in the level of their primal pain. That level necessitated the blocking of that pain by cutting most of the connections between the individualistic thinking brain and the communalistic emotional/sexual brain. This consigned self-awareness to be located primarily in the individualistic, thinking brain. The people of the Mother Goddess cultures were more communalistic because their level of primal pain still permitted them to retain a self-awareness located primarily in the communalistic, emotional/sexual brain.

Another consequence for the Indo-Europeans because of the necessity to cut most of the connections between the thinking brain and the emotional/sexual brain was a major disconnection between their minds and their emotions. They were now much more likely not to know what they were feeling or feeling what they knew. In contrast, the minds and the emotions of the Mother Goddess peoples were still integrated to a large extent.

This contrast between the ancient Stage III Indo-Europeans and the equally ancient Stage II Mother Goddess peoples highlights the differences between people today. We are all in Stage III today. The basic difference among us is the degree of our primal pain. The degree of each one's primal pain has determined the degree to which each has had to devolve into the characteristics of Stage III. The degree of our primal pain has determined the degree to which each of us has felt helpless in getting our infantile needs met; the degree to which each has had to deny his needs; the degree to which each has had his needs resurface as insatiable wants; the degree to which each has had to compensate for his helplessness by having a compulsion for power; the degree to which each has had to cut connections between one's thinking brain and one's emotional/sexual brain; the degree to which each has had to become more of an individualist and less of a communalist; the degree to which each has lost the beingness of a self-in-relationship; the degree to which one's sense of the common good has become more the society's protection of the individual's inalienable right to the unfettered acquisition and use of private property; and the degree to which one's sense of the common good has become less of society's protection of the individual's inalienable right to the necessities of life. Today, these differences among us have a profound effect on how we think, how we feel and how we act on the social issues of our time.

A basic premise of mine throughout this history has been that our external and internal worlds mirror each other. From here on in this section, I'm going to examine the basic positions and actions people have taken on various social issues and suggest what they reveal about the interior status of one's unconscious self-awareness. I will give attention to four of the variables that indicate a Stage III level of the disconnection between the individualistic, thinking brain and the communalistic, emotional/sexual brain: (1) individualism/communalism, (2) wants/power, (3) mind/emotions and (4) openness to pain and suffering.

Those positions and actions that appear to reflect a greater, rather than a lesser, connection between the thinking brain and the emotional/sexual brain would justify a number of conclusions.

1. They represent a lesser unconscious self-awareness.
2. They represent a greater connection between thought and emotion.
3. They represent being more open to being empathetic to pain and suffering.
4. They represent more of being a self-in-relationship, of being an interdependent self rather than an independent self.
5. They represent less of insatiable wants and less of a compulsion for power.

Those positions and actions that appear to reflect a lesser rather than a greater connection between the two brains would justify opposite conclusions.

Just as throughout our entire past, today, ever-increasing levels of primal pain continue to make our selves ever more unconscious. Ever higher levels of primal pain mean acting more and more as an independent self. It will mean having more and greater insatiable wants and a greater compulsion for power. It will mean an ever wider disconnect between our minds and our emotions. And, it will mean less of the ability to be open to our own pain and suffering and to that of others.

This overall movement toward greater unconsciousness will have a profound effect on our social, political and economic lives. Our communities, from a small town to the whole nation, will deteriorate for lack of people who reflect enough of being a self-in-relationship. Greed will consume our Earth Mother. The lust for absolute power of our national government will absolutely corrupt our country. Our minds, devoid of any significant connection to our emotions, will produce such a cold, logical intellectualism that is so right that it is wrong. And, finally, there will be too few left to make a difference in the fight to make a human right of freedom from need.

All other considerations being equal, in general, the positions women take on social, political and economic issues will reflect less unconsciousness than the position men will take. In the chapter on Communalism and Individualism, under the subheading of Men: Left-Brainers; Women: Right-Brainers, I related the history of why women are less unconscious than men. In the transition from Stage II to Stage III, the characteristics of Stage II were deemed to be feminine by the masculine-oriented Stage III cultures. Consequently, historically in Stage III, women are more communalistic and less individualistic than men. They have fewer insatiable wants and less of a compulsion for power. They have more connections between their minds and their emotions. They are more open to pain and to suffering.

As time goes on, however, and the general level of primal pain goes up, women are becoming more like men as far as communalism/individualism, wants/

power, mind/emotions and openness are concerned. Women who have accumulated the most primal pain are depending less on the emotions and sex as tools of power and more on the intellect, as men do. It is clear that in business and in politics women are becoming more like men all the time.

Today, wherever and whenever the feminist movement has led women into entering any previously exclusively male-dominated area, more often than not women have taken on traits usually associated with men. Those male traits are being highly competitive, emotionally cold, intellectually rigid and inured to pain. Usually, women in business or politics have not made those arenas more sensitive to, or responsive to, human needs. More likely, they have become just as insensitive, or as unresponsive, to human needs as are their male counterparts. This suggests that when women take on traditionally male traits, they have severed as many brain connections as men have.

Concomitantly, some men are attempting to become less unconscious. They are working toward reopening connections between the thinking brain and the emotional/sexual brain. They feel it might very well be the better way to be open to one's emotions and to accept the greater suffering that goes along with that openness. But men, who do try to be more open, face ever-increasing suffering as primal pain increases. Whether or not these men can persevere in being open is a good question. What women are demonstrating in their general movement toward becoming more like men is that the pain and suffering that goes with being open is too great to stay with it.

I am not making the point that men should become like women. I am saying that men should become less unconscious and thus more human. I am also saying that women should not sacrifice their less unconscious and more human self-awareness in the pursuit of equality with men in business, in politics, or in any other arena. To use a Biblical metaphor—"Women, don't sell your birthright for a mess of pottage."

While everyone's level of primal pain places his unconscious self-awareness in Stage III today, the positions one takes on various social issues reveal whether one is closer to or further from the less unconscious state of Stage II. The question is whether or not, on balance, one's choices evidence more or less primal pain; more or less disconnection between the thinking brain and the emotional/sexual brains; more or less of the necessity to deny one's needs to remain viable; more or less of insatiable wants substituting for one's needs; more or less of a sense of helplessness in getting one's needs met; more or less of a compulsion for power to compensate for that sense of helplessness; more or less of acting as an independent self or as a self-in-relationship; more or less of a connection between one's mind and one's emotions; and more or less of an openness to pain and suffering. Differing levels of all these evidences mean honest differences in where people are coming from on any choice. Taking into account all these evidences will sort out which positions exhibit more and which less of a Stage III level of unconscious self-awareness.

Second Liners and Third Liners

In order not to have to continuously use the lengthy phrases "more unconscious self-awareness" and "less unconscious self-awareness," I am going to make use of a device Arthur Janov used. He used the words "1st line," 2nd line," and "3rd line" to distinguish one from each other the functions of the sensing/survival, the emotional/sexual and the thinking brains. The 1st line (sensing/survival brain) functions do not affect us here because we are not concerned with the heart or breathing or digestion, for example. We are concerned with all the evidences of the 2nd line (emotional/sexual brain) and the 3rd line (thinking brain) for clues as to whether particular positions on specific issues represent more or less unconsciousness. Persons who are 2nd liners are more apt to espouse positions that are less unconscious than persons who are 3rd liners. This, again, is a restatement of the givenness that our inner and outer worlds mirror each other.

There are gender differences between 2nd and 3rd liners. Because girls are raised to keep more connections between the thinking and the emotional/sexual brain, women are more likely to be 2nd liners. Since boys are told it isn't manly to cry or to admit to being in pain, men are more likely to be 3rd liners.

Since primal pain is constantly increasing, causing the present always to be more unconscious than the past, the trend is inevitably toward an ever-larger hard core of 3rd liners. This holds true for women too. Politically, while there will be election cycles in which 2nd liners capture enough votes to govern for a while, the length of time and frequency that 3rd liners will be in power increases.

When I say that the movement is ever more toward people becoming 3rd liners from being 2nd liners, I am saying that, among other changes, the movement is ever more toward a lust for power. It is not just a movement toward the Right or Conservatism, per se, which it is, but toward power in the hands of the few. This is true whether it be for control of an organization, of a political party or of some level of government. What distinguishes 2nd liners from 3rd liners is not just being Left Wing or Right Wing, Democrat or Republican or Conservative or Liberal, it is the degree to which power is shared among the many or concentrated among the few. Second liners are democratic, while 3rd liners are oligarchic. All other considerations being equal, this movement will be more pronounced in 3rd line and less in 2nd line organizations because all 3rd liners have a greater compulsion for power.

When an organization has devolved to the point where it is controlled by an oligarchy, the leaders tend to surreptitiously betray the organization's goals. Actively promoting the goals threatens the oligarchs' hold on power. Promoting the goals in actuality encourages activism on the part of the members. Activism, in turn, encourages democracy and challenges oligarchy.

Both the Democratic and Republican parties are oligarchic. Therefore, to understand party politics one must realize that the primary goal of the oligarchs is to maintain their power within the party at whatever hierarchical level and wherever in the country. Anything that threatens that power must be opposed. For example, if a candidate runs in opposition to the oligarchs, he must be defeated—even with the collusive help of the other party. Again, any legislation that puts power in the hands of the electorate must be blocked because that would diminish the power of the oligarchs.

As can be seen from the foregoing, a 3rd line lust for oligarchic power cuts across all ideological lines. Second line democratic power is always on the defensive. For many specific examples of oligarchic power usurping democratic power, see Walter Karp's books, *Liberty Under Siege* and *Indispensable Enemies*.

Both 3rd liners and 2nd liners claim the other's agenda has failed because of inherently fatal flaws. Third liners point to moral decay, the persistence of welfare dependency and the demise of planned economies as proof of their claims. Second liners point to a growing lust for power, to greed, to corporate welfare dependency, to the excesses of "free-market economics" and to a deteriorating environment as proof of their claims.

Not only do 3rd and 2nd liners consider the other's agenda to be flawed, they accuse each other of being inconsistent. While 3rd liners are quick to rail against any governmental restraints on their perceived rights to make any profits the markets will bear, they are only too quick to impose governmental restraints on 2nd liner behavior they deem to be immoral. While 2nd liners are quick to rail against any governmental restraints on what they perceive to be matters of personal choice, they are only too quick to impose governmental restraints on 3rd liner behavior they deem to be greedy, capitalistic excesses.

Both 2nd and 3rd liners are flawed because both are grounded in a Stage III unconscious self-awareness. Because 2nd liners are actually closer to the conscious state of selves-in-relationship, 2nd liners are less unconscious than are 3rd liners.

A Stage III level of unconscious self-awareness makes all 2nd and 3rd liners alike in one regard: We differ only in degrees to which we are unconscious. It is this difference that accounts for liberals and conservatives or Democrats and Republicans. The differences are real, but it is want and power that binds us all together. Want and power create classes, which cut across ideological lines. They are also responsible for class struggle, which is denied by popular mythology. Unequal wealth does mean unequal power in class struggle. It does mean that upward mobility is not equally available to everyone.

Probably there are any number of ways in which 2nd liners and 3rd liners can be contrasted, even though the positions overlap. Here are ten:

1. *Change people versus change society.* As 3rd liners are individualistic, they are more likely to claim that morality can't be legislated. They say that to make society more moral, make people more moral. As 2nd liners are more communalistic, they are more apt to claim that changing society can change people. Legislating a change in behavior can result in a change in morality.
2. *Hard on drugs versus soft on drugs.* Third liners come down hard on drugs; 2nd liners don't. The reason 3rd liners do is that their self-awareness comes more from the thinking brain, which is cut off from the painful emotions that give rise to drug use to quell pain. Conversely, 2nd liners are more tolerant of drug use because their self-awareness comes from the emotional/sexual brain, which is far more open to experience painful emotions. Second liners, therefore, are far more understanding of those who have found it necessary to quell their pain by the use of drugs.
3. *Bleeding hearts versus the hard-hearted.* To 3rd liners, 2nd liners are bleeding hearts because, when it comes down to assessing the cause of poverty, drug abuse, or unwanted pregnancy, for example, 2nd liners are soft and indulgent. For the more individualistically minded 3rd liners, 2nd liners foster irresponsible behavior by treating a suffering person as being a victim of circumstances. For the 3rd liner, it boils down to a matter of bad choices, and the solution is tough love. To 2nd liners, 3rd liners are hard-hearted because they take no account of one's circumstances. For the more communalistically oriented 2nd liners, the solutions to poverty, drug abuse, or unwanted pregnancy begin with an understanding of one's choices within the context of one's total environment. The differences here between 2nd and 3rd liners is again accounted for by the degree of disconnection between the thinking brain and the emotional/sexual brain.
4. *Moral absolutism versus contextual ethics.* A single-minded moral absolutist is one who sees all of human behavior in terms of black and white, right and wrong and good and evil. Behavior that breaks a moral absolute is immoral under any and all contexts.

   There have always been contextual ethics throughout human history because there is always some connection between the individualistic thinking brain and the communalistic emotional/sexual brain. In ancient Stage I and Stage II societies, each person experienced himself much more as a self-in-relationship than as an independent self. Each person acted for the benefit of everyone else. It wasn't necessary for anyone to act in his own best interest because everyone else was doing exactly the same. Everyone's best interest was being looked out for by everyone else. Consequently, it was only marginally necessary for society to "lay down the law" to regulate personal behavior for the welfare of each person and of the society.

When Stage III came about, it was the case that each person experienced himself more as an independent self than as a self-in-relationship. Concomitant with this individualism was such an advanced degree of greed and lust for power that it was crucially necessary for society to "lay down the law" to prohibit behavior that was either self-destructive or destructive of the welfare of the society. Stage III, then, is when such means to harmonize society as customs, mores and taboos had to be supplanted by legally enforceable moral absolutes. Nevertheless, there were always extenuating circumstances, more or less equally codified, that were taken into consideration in the administration of the morally absolute law. The source, then for moral absolutes is to be found in such a Stage III degree of the devolution of selves-in-relationship into individualism that it became necessary to introduce moral absolutes to control greed and a lust for power.

The codification of moral absolutes happens in all kinds of Stage III societies: those dominated by Warlords, democracies, republics, dictatorships, monarchies and theocracies, any one of them or all of them, either with or without a constitution. The danger in any Stage III society has always been, and still is, that since the most powerful rise to rule society, moral absolutes are made into law that reflect whatever are the views of the ruling elite. Then they are enforced upon everyone, regardless of whether or not the society is homogenous.

In addition, there has always been, and still is, in any Stage III society a situation in which men will make moral absolutes into law that discriminate against women. Earlier I described what our linear ancestors, the Indo-Europeans, did to make women into property to be bought and sold. Currently, there is an African country that requires the circumcision of women—the cutting out of the clitoris—to aid in curbing any desire for sex that might make them adulterous. Recently, the U.S. Congress passed a law that was signed by President Bush that is a moral absolute, forbidding absolutely what opponents of abortion call "partial birth abortion." The law makes no provision for exceptions, for example, in the case of a severely deformed fetus who would not survive in any event or in the case where the health or life of the mother was endangered. If the whole Congress and the President were women, it isn't likely that a law would be passed and signed that did not allow for the health and life of the mother to be taken into consideration.

What is it that is revealed about a single-minded moral absolutist who thinks a particular ethical choice is immoral under any and all contexts? It reveals a Stage III, 3rd line unconscious self-awareness devolved in the extreme. It reveals someone who is so individualistic as to have severed all but a thread of connection between the individualistic thinking brain and the communalistic emotional/sexual brain. It reveals someone who is a Stage III 3rd liner who is so ideologically inured to pain that it is an a priori ideology rather than an informed empathy that agonizes over choices that are all equally painful. It reveals a Stage III 3rd liner who sets himself against the collective, historical experience of humankind to make allowances for circumstances.

Since so many of my readers are likely to be Jewish or Christian or Muslim, I want to elaborate on what the Bible reveals about moral absolutism and contextual ethics. I begin with the fourth commandment—a relatively unemotionally laden issue.

"Remember the sabbath day, to keep it holy" (Exodus 20:8) is a moral absolute. Verses nine through eleven go on to state why and to whom it applies. As to why, it is because God labored six days to create the cosmos and rested on the seventh. As to whom, it apparently applies to everyone within an Israelite city, except wives—they are not mentioned—and to cattle. Aha! Wives have known all along that there is no day of rest for them.

The commandment seems simple enough to honor. Yet, by the time of Jesus there were approximately 750 lawful exceptions to the prohibition about working on the Sabbath. This was a recognition that the simple moral absolute had to be applied within the context of complicated human situations.

In Matthew 12:9-14, Jesus himself broke the Sabbath by healing a man with a withered hand. Jesus' comment on his own action of breaking the Sabbath moral absolute was that it was "lawful to do good on the Sabbath." Jesus said that he had come to fulfill the Law. By example, he showed that what that meant was fulfilling the spirit rather than the letter of the Law, that it meant having the Law written upon one's heart. Both fulfilling the spirit of the Law and having it written upon one's heart is to have open connections between the thinking and the emotional/sexual brains.

An emotionally, highly charged commandment is the sixth: "You shall not kill" (Exodus 20:13). Again, the moral absolute seems simple enough, but mentioned throughout later passages are numerous God-ordained exceptions. Perhaps the most startling exception is found in I Samuel 15:3. Here, God instructs Saul to smite the Amalekites and "utterly destroy all that they have; do not spare them, but kill both man and woman, infant and suckling, ox and sheep, camel and ass." It is very likely that some of the women were pregnant, so God's orders included the killing of the unborn. God's justification for the slaughter of the entire population was that the Amalekites were worshippers of false gods.

I do not question God's motives here, but just note that the context justified setting aside the moral absolute not to kill.

The Bible, therefore, makes it clear that neither moral absolutes nor contextual ethics are to be used exclusively in determining what is a moral or ethical course of action.

How then does the Bible instruct believers to find their way? Jesus rose above both a legalistic moral absolution and an anything-goes contextual ethics by saying that one is to love God totally and to love one's neighbor as oneself. But, even here there is no specific ideological direction that predetermines just what one should do in any and all contexts. Paul, too, recognized this when he admonished the Christians in Philippi to "work out your own salvation with fear and trembling; for God is at work in you, both to will and work for his good pleasure" (Philippians 2:12, 13). In other words, believers are to be guided by what is right in an absolute moral sense but will let love determine what is right in any given context. In some cases, the killing of an unborn child will be a justified act and fall within the total Biblical context of what is moral and ethical.

Secular law also recognizes that both moral absolutism and contextual ethics are necessary. It is unlawful to kill someone else deliberately, but allowances are made for justifiable homicide. State and Federal governments justify deliberately executing some criminals. War justifies the killing of combatants. If civilians are killed, including the unborn, it is regrettable but nevertheless justified. And, specifically with reference to the unborn, State and Federal laws allow for the killing of them in various justifiable contexts. Not as long as humanity continues in a state of Stage III unconscious self-awareness will there be a cessation of laws embodying moral absolutes to be administered in specific contexts.

In summary, the Stage III 3rd liner is most likely to be a moral absolutist because of the greater degree of his primal pain, of his individualism, of his disconnection between his mind and his emotions, of the disconnection between his thinking and his emotional/sexual brains and of his overall greater degree of unconscious self-awareness. The Stage III 2nd liner is more likely to be a contextual ethicist because of a lesser degree of all the characteristics just cited.

Philosophers, theologians and the ones to whom the Deities of the various religions have given revelation have all wrestled with what, ultimately, is the basis for morality or for ethical behavior. There is no consensus. From my experience as a primal person, I offer my own explanation. The foundation is to be found in the conscious state of relatively primal-pain-free children before the onset of unconscious self-awareness and—with due caution—in adults who exhibit being a self-in-relationship, regardless of whether or not they are primal persons.

If there are any criteria for judging whether or not a moral or ethical choice has universal application, the criteria must be found to be consistent with what it means to be conscious as a self-in-relationship. No easy task! The discovery will entail an exhaustive study of Stage I societies for historical clues as to what it means. A careful examination of their interdependent relationships of children, parents, extended family, tribe and clan should reveal much of what vastly less unconscious societies than ours exhibited about the moral and ethical behavior of selves-in-relationship. The discovery will entail the collation of the anecdotal primal experiences of primal persons in order to develop a model: It will entail the observations of and by primal parents who are doing the best they can to make a home for their children and who have begun the journey back toward consciousness.

5. *Sins of the spirit versus sins of the flesh.* Third liners, being more into the intellect than are 2nd liners, are more prone to commit sins of the spirit, such as hypocrisy, self-righteousness and pride. Second liners, being more into the emotions and sex, are more prone to commit sins of the flesh, such as infidelity and overindulgence.
6. *Democracy versus Theocracy.* The sixth difference between Stage III 2nd liners and 3rd liners has to do with democracy and theocracy as these words are applied to national governments. "Democracy" comes from the Greek words for people and power. It means that in a democracy the ultimate power resides in the people. "Theocracy" comes from the Greek words for God and power. It means that in a theocracy the ultimate power resides in God.

This difference between 2nd and 3rd liners is a special case because not all 2nd liners are for people power (democracy) and not all 3rd liners are for God power (theocracy). It is the case that when 3rd liners become religious, they are apt to be theocrats and seek to have their religion's moral code become the law of the State. It is also the case that when 2nd liners become religious, they are apt to be democrats (not Democrats), and do not seek to have their religion's moral code enforced upon everyone by a theocratic State.

An early example of theocracy is seen in the worldview of the Indo-Europeans. For them, cattle were the currency of the day, and they wanted all of them. Their leaders—the priests and warriors—said that God had given all cattle to them, so if any other people had cattle they must have stolen them. Their leaders' will and God's will were identified as one and the same.

A perfect modern example of theocracy is Vatican City. God rules the city through his appointed representative, the Pope.

A modern example of a Muslim theocracy that is incrementally working its way toward democracy is Iran. There is now a democratically elected legislative body, but the Ayatollah and the other "high priests" have the final say.

In the United States we have a secular demo (people) cracy (power). In our midst we also have a significant movement toward theo (God) cracy (power). The Protestant, conservative, right wing of Christianity has as its goal a Sacred God Power replacing a Secular People Power. They have aligned themselves with the Republican Party, which was a minority party. Now, they have made the Republican Party a majority party that cannot get its candidates elected without supporting the theocratic agenda of this element in Christianity. Since it would be self-defeating to say that what they want is a theocracy, they just pursue their goal specific issue by specific issue.

In my view, theocracy in its best light today is an effort to end suffering, in its broadest sense, by an abandonment of secular government and by a return to a state of affairs when everything was Sacred and that existed before Secularism ever made its appearance. It is a misguided effort because, as far back as the Indo-Europeans, theocracies have not mitigated suffering any better than have democracies. Instead they've codified the existing level of insatiable wants and compulsion for power as being the will of God, thus ensuring the continuation of suffering.

What is it that makes one a Christian in the first place? It is the experience that one cannot save one's self from sin (suffering) and having the faith that God has done so in the redeeming work of Jesus Christ. What is it that makes some Christians into theocrats? It is the mistaken notion that the saving work of Jesus Christ includes the establishment of theocratic nation-states and that Christians should use political power to work toward that goal. It is a mistaken equation of the Kingdom of God on earth with theocratic political nation-states.

Over and over I've pointed out that the compulsion for power is at the core of Stage III of unconscious self-awareness. The third chapter of Genesis, which relates the fall of humankind, in effect says the same thing. What lured Adam and Eve was the temptation to become like gods. That is, it was a lust for power that was the downfall of all of humanity. Look now at the entry of Jesus into Jerusalem the week prior to his crucifixion.

Jesus rode into Jerusalem on a donkey, a beast of burden, rather than upon a horse, a symbol of political and military power. It was a final announcement that his Kingdom of God on earth was one of humble service to humanity in the alleviation of suffering. It was equally an announcement that his Kingdom of God on earth did not include the use of military and political power to reestablish the old theocracy that included Judah and Israel.

It was this announcement that was too much for Judas to stomach. Judas was a Zealot, that is, he was a member of a Jewish movement that sought the overthrow of the Romans and the reestablishment of the old theocracy in Palestine. It was then he began to plot to betray Jesus to get him out of the way as an obstacle to the Zealots' cause.

Right-wing theocratic-minded Christians take note: Jesus rejected a theocratic political Jewish State. Insofar as Christians use political power to make their nation into a theocracy, they betray Christ as surely as did Judas and make sure that their self-fulfilling prophecy of "persecution" of themselves takes place.

From my viewpoint, a Christian is one who experiences unconscious self-awareness as a sinful self, unredeemable through its own efforts. One then begins a journey to replace unconscious self-awareness with the mind of Christ. Insofar as one is successful, one transcends a Stage III level of insatiable wants and a compulsion for power. Insofar as one fails to make progress, one remains stuck in a Stage III level of unconscious self-awareness. If a Christian's pain level makes him into a 3rd liner, it means that he is a Christian who has a great compulsion for power. The coupling of a mistaken notion of the nature of the saving work of Jesus Christ with a great compulsion for power makes one ripe for the temptation to exercise power in the name of God through the establishment of a theocracy. Make no mistake about it. The hidden agenda of the Christian right today is the destruction of democracy and the construction of a theocracy.

7. *Freedom of choice versus no choice.* Both 2nd liners and 3rd liners lay claim to belief in the freedom of choice as one of the pillars supporting democracy. Both groups will also claim that some choices should be proscribed or at least prescribed. The degree to which the thinking brain is cut off from the emotional/sexual brain determines on what basis a particular choice should be able to be made freely or should be proscribed or prescribed. Yet there is no clear-cut division between 2nd and 3rd liners as to which choices should be permitted and which prohibited.

   With regard to property, for example, one would think that because 3rd liners are the most into the individualistic, intellectualistic, insatiable-wants-dominated thinking brain that all of them would favor unfettered choice to acquire and use property. But there are some 3rd liners who are communalistic enough to know that for the protection of everyone from the excessive greed of some that some prescribing of choice is necessary.

   Likewise, one would think that because 2nd liners are the least into the thinking brain that all of them would favor fettered choice to acquire and use property. But since everyone is in Stage III, some 2nd liners are going to favor unfettered choice.

And, with such issues as assisted dying, abortion and medical marijuana, for example, one would think that most 2nd liners would be opposed to free choice and most 3rd liners would be in favor. The reason is that all these choices are individualistic in nature. The reverse is probably true, most 2nd liners being in favor and most 3rd liners opposed. The reason is that 2nd liners are more open to experience pain and, therefore, are more likely to be empathetic to the people involved. Some 2nd liners will be empathetic but choose alternate solutions. They, however, take it upon themselves to make the choices for the people involved. Since 3rd liners are more inured to pain, their reasons for either being in favor of or against assisted dying or abortion or medical marijuana are going to be intellectual in nature. They will use rational argument one way or the other. Since religious doctrine is intellectual rather than emotional in nature, I include that as part of a 3rd liner's intellectual response, if it is called upon to argue one way or the other.

The issue of States' rights cuts across these lines. Federalism comes into play, not because of any rigidly held beliefs, but to back up what one supports. Claiming States' rights is a convenient fall-back position to try to institutionalize one's position on such matters as assisted dying or abortion or medical marijuana.

8. *Private property versus public property.* The issue today between 2nd liners and 3rd liners is the degree to which an individual's or a corporation's private property should be regulated or deregulated and the degree to which the community's public property should be protected or privatized. A 2nd liner most likely is going to want greater regulation of private property and greater protections for public property, both of which he sees as being for the common good. A 3rd liner most likely is going to want greater deregulation of private property and greater privatization of public property, both of which he also sees as being for the common good. Here are several examples.

Airwave frequencies for television and radio stations are public property. Second liners seek the protection of the airwaves from the monopoly of corporate media giants in order to preserve what remains of the diversity of viewpoints. Third liners seek the privatization of the airwaves because, in general, government shouldn't be in "business" and specifically, the marketplace can do a better job of managing the airwaves.

Many municipalities own and manage their own water public utility. It is more likely that 2nd liners with their greater connections to the communalistic, emotional/sexual brain will seek to preserve and to protect this public utility for the benefit of everyone. It is more likely that 3rd liners with their self-awareness more centered in the individualistic, thinking brain will seek the privatization of this publicly held water utility for the benefit of stockholders. Cities needing aid and seeking federal help are told they must also consider privatization as an option.

In the public interest, 2nd liners see the necessity of regulating the natural gas and electricity industries. Third liners see deregulation of these industries as resulting in greater efficiencies and in greater competition, resulting in lower prices. The recent, fake energy shortage in California that was masterminded by the energy companies is once again proof that 3rd liner greed requires regulation. Deregulation usually means out-of-control rampant greed that results in fiscal fiascoes, the high cost of which is being placed on ordinary taxpayers. Memories are then jolted as to why regulation happened in the first place. Remember the savings and loan taxpayer bailout to the extent of hundreds of billions of dollars.

Our Founding Fathers knew that they—the rich and powerful, elite ruling class—as well as the propertyless masses had a predacious self-interest. They knew, therefore, that they had to be protected from each other as much as they felt they had to protect themselves from the masses. Consequently, they were for governmental regulation carried out through the separation of powers to keep themselves from destroying each other.

Nothing has changed to this day. Yet there are those among the ruling class who have so much greed and so much lust for power that despite all the demonstrated need for regulation, they seek deregulation. They feel they will survive the ensuing self-destructing, unrestricted competition. If deregulation occurs, it eventuates in an economic debacle in which the average taxpayer, investor, or employee is the one to pay for the greed of the rich and powerful.

9. *Private property rights versus human rights.* What is at stake here are opposing views of what is the common good. Overall, one's sense of what is the common good is determined by how connected or disconnected are one's thinking and one's emotional/sexual brains.

From a primal point of view, the more one acts as a 3rd liner independent self, the more one restricts the common good to the government's protection of the individual's right to the unfettered acquisition and use of private property. Since governments are formed by the rich and powerful, elite ruling class for this specific purpose, unfettered property rights are invariably protected, regardless of the form of government. An exception to this are the so-called Communist states in which the government owns everything except personal property. These States are all visionary in that they are attempting to go back to a time when there was more of a status of selves-in-relationship. They are all doomed to evolve no further than the Dictatorship of the Proletariat because all people have devolved to such a state of individualism as to make true Communism impossible.

From a primal point of view, the more one acts as a 2nd liner interdependent self, the more one expands the common good to the government's protection of everyone's natural, human, social and civil rights. Since governments are formed for the specific purpose of protecting 3rd line property rights, it takes successful class struggle by 2nd liners to get natural, human, social and civil rights enshrined in constitutions or codified into laws.

For 3rd liners, so-called human rights are not entitlements in and of themselves; they are derivatives of property rights. If property rights are not protected, then none of the other "rights" are possible. If human rights are put first, then property rights are sacrificed. To a 3rd liner's mind, grave injustices abound because an industrious person's property is confiscated and given to malingerers of every sort.

For 2nd liners, human rights are entitlements in and of themselves. And, since governments set up the conditions to enable individuals to accumulate wealth, to a 2nd liner's mind those who have profited most owe something back to make sure everyone's human needs are met.

Related to human rights are government services, such as education, law enforcement and firefighting. Here, a 3rd liner level of insatiable wants, coupled with acting as an independent self, results in a contradiction that does not get resolved. It is the expectation for government to provide needed services but there is an unwillingness to pay for them. A 3rd liner's level of Stage III makes one so unconscious as to be unable to experience oneself as an interdependent member of a community. Second liners have retained enough of that experience to be willing to be taxed so that these needed services are fully funded.

The foreign policy of the United States and its actions and votes at the United Nations clearly indicate that America supports the right of private property and free trade and consistently opposes human rights. To me, the record shows that the rich and powerful, elite ruling class—who really are in control—exhibit the most extreme form to date of 3rd line, Stage III, unconscious self-awareness.

Article 25 of the U.N.'s charter in 1948 is entitled "Universal Declaration of Human Rights." It states that

> Everyone has the right to a standard of living adequate for the health and well-being of himself and his family, including food, clothing, housing and medical care and necessary social services and the right to security in the event of unemployment, sickness, disability, widowhood, old age or other lack of livelihood in circumstances beyond his control.

The United States has either consistently opposed or voted against the implementation of the human rights listed in Article 25. Examples: In 1982 and 1983, the United States was the only country to vote against a declaration that education, work, health care, proper nourishment and national development are human rights, this despite the fact that these rights are in the U.N. charter. In 1989 at the U.N. Convention on the Rights of the Child, only the United States and Iraq did not ratify it. In 1996, at the U.N.-sponsored World Food summit, the United States objected to the inclusion of the right of everyone to have access to safe and nutritious food. The United States did not accept the notion that there is a right to access to food.

International "Free Trade" is an issue that cannot be separated from private property rights and human rights. "Free Trade" is one cause the United States will pursue—as long as we can protect our own products from being undersold, such as steel, cotton, rice and sugar. In countries struggling financially, the United States—through the World Trade Organization, the World Bank and the International Monetary Fund, all of which we control—enforces the adoption of economic policies that are at the expense of human rights. Some of the loan conditions might include the privatization of publicly held utilities, which invariably has meant hardship for many. It is a 3rd line, Stage III mentality that puts private property rights before human rights.

With regard to health care in the United States, 3rd liners are more likely to favor the continuation of the status quo in which corporations do make millions, and millions make do without adequate health care or have none at all. Second liners are more likely to favor universal health coverage. Again, all the reasons previously cited for the differences between 2nd and 3rd liners account for their differences regarding health care.

10. *Free-market economies versus centrally planned economies.* If we let 3rd liners define what is going on today worldwide in the realm of economics, they would say that history proves that free-market economies are successful, while centrally planned economies are failures. They do reflect the views of the 17th and 18th century English philosophers who said that men are naturally acquisitive. The modern euphemism for "acquisitive" is "entrepreneurial." In primal language, in Stage III, people have insatiable wants. Third liner, free-market economists point to the demise of centrally planned economies and say, "See, we were right after all."

    Third liner, free-market economists, however, are not being forthright when they claim that free-market economies are not being centrally planned. As far as I can tell, there never has been a free-market economy; it has always involved an alliance with government. That alliance includes tax breaks, tariffs, bailouts, anti-union laws and gunboat diplomacy to protect national interests or national security, i.e., the interests and security of multi-national corporations.

What makes U.S. agriculture competitive worldwide is the huge subsidy it gets from the government. The last Farm Bill to pass Congress gave the industry $81 billion, mostly to large corporations. The high-tech industry's subsidy is hidden in the Pentagon budget that pays for research, then gives it to the private sector. The pharmaceutical industry also gets a lot of free research because of public funding through the university system. Market discipline is what is imposed on developing nations; protection from market discipline is what is composed for developed nations.

What 3rd line, free-market economists are looking for in any Third World country is whether the political/economic climate favors individualism, the unfettered acquisition and use of private property and corporate profit or whether it favors communalism, regulated private property and the confiscation of private property through taxes under the guise of filling human rights. Remember, that for free-market economists human rights are based on property rights, and the basic human right is the right to compete for a job.

At the end of his tenure in office, President Eisenhower warned of the dangers to democracy because of the military/industrial complex. What he failed to note was the complicity of government in those dangers, including his own administration. Long before, and certainly after Eisenhower, both Democratic and Republican administrations have been willing partners in the complex. Our economy is a capitalistic, centrally planned alliance between the government, the military and industry. It makes no difference to this alliance what the form of government is in other countries. It relates equally well to similar alliances in other republics or to dictatorships, either of the right or the left. The common ground of these international relations is the priority of corporate profits over human rights. If human rights suffer, well, that can't be helped because there are always winners and losers.

If we let 2nd liners define what is happening today and what history proves about economics, they would say that all economies are centrally planned. They would say that the real question is whether an economy puts profits or people first, whether it puts huge wealth for the few or human rights for the many first or whether it puts environmental exploitation or environmental preservation first.

I find four reasons as to why national economies that have put human rights first usually do not survive. The first is the way in which the World Bank operates as a front for the expansion of markets for multi-national corporations while touting that it fulfills human needs. Initially, the World Bank loans money to these countries for development. The terms of the loan include the opening of the economy to foreign competition. This has the effect of destroying the local economy. Then, when the country needs to be bailed out with another loan, even harsher "restructuring adjustments" are imposed that require the privatization of publicly held industries and an even further opening of their markets to foreign imports. The end result is more profits for the multi-national corporations, more poverty for the people and a more complete takeover by the rich and powerful, elite ruling class of the country.

A second reason is quite simple. If a country resists and persists in a tax structure that reduces corporate profits to produce money for the human needs of the people, there is a flight of capital from the country. It is moved to a country more amenable to the maximizing of corporate profits.

A third reason has to do with outright subversion. The United States was involved in the successful coup of General Pinochet in Chile and in the failed coup against President Chavez in Venezuela. To further its "national interests," the United States has interfered militarily in the internal affairs of Central and South American countries. Invariably, this has been done to protect U.S. corporate interests that were being interfered with by a nation's internal policies.

The fourth reason why planned economies that have placed human rights over corporate profits have failed is because the consciousness of humanity has devolved so far from the state of selves-in-relationship that the bonds no longer exist between people for economies based on human rights to work and to survive. For them to work, they need a Stage II outlook upon life that considers one's social bonds to be as important as one's private interests. For them to work, self-awareness must still have adequate connections to the outside world that enable it to carry out a concern for the welfare of the community. For them to work, self-awareness cannot have devolved to the current level of Stage III's lust for power and insatiable greed that brings forth an individualism that precludes the necessary level of communalism for them to succeed.

Because unconscious self-awareness has devolved to the point where insatiable wants and a compulsion for power predominate, the outcome is the survival of economies that put corporate profits first and the demise of economies that put human rights first. As much as I deplore such a conclusion, unless there is a fundamental shift in self-awareness toward selves-in-relationship, the cycle will continue. That cycle is when the rich and powerful, elite class of rulers denies the human rights of the ruled to a sufficient extent that the ruled rise up in revolution and denies the rulers the right to rule. But, since no fundamental change has taken place, the new rulers become the new despoilers. This is a cycle the Founding Fathers saw in history.

What I have added here is the primal foundation for that cycle. What is needed to break that cycle is for both 2nd and 3rd liners to become less unconscious. The only way I know for that to take place is through the process of primaling away one's insatiable wants and compulsion for power.

2nd and 3rd Line Family Models

As a follow-up to the previous subsection on the differences between 2nd liners and 3rd liners, I turn now to an analysis based on the parenting models produced by being either a 2nd liner or a 3rd liner. Some Stage III parents are at the lower end of the scale of Stage III primal pain. These are 2nd line parents who have retained a greater degree of connection between the thinking brain and the emotional/sexual brain. These parents will *feel* more that they are *being homemakers for their children.* They will *think* a lot less that what they are *doing* is *raising their children.* Children growing up in this kind of a family will have less primal pain and be more of a self-in-relationship—an interdependent self—and less of an independent self.

Some Stage III parents are at the upper end of the scale of Stage III primal pain. These are 3rd line parents who have the least degree of connection between the thinking brain and the emotional/sexual brain. These parents will *think* more that what they are *doing* is *raising their children.* They will *feel* less that they are *being homemakers for their children.* Children growing up in this kind of a family will have greater primal pain and be more of an independent self and less of an interdependent self-in-relationship.

It is the homemaking kind of parenting that promotes all the 2nd line positions explored in the previous subsection. Likewise, it is the raising a child kind of parenting that promotes all the 3rd line positions explored above.

George Lakoff is an expert in the field of cognitive linguistics, which is the scientific study of the nature of thought and its expression in language. Information about his work here is from one of his books. The title is *Don't Think of an Elephant! Know Your Values and Frame the Debate.*

Lakoff's analysis of the difference between conservatives and progressives is the difference between a strict father family model and a nurturant parent family model. I quote in its entirety Lakoff's description of both models, which is found on pages 39-41 of the "elephant" book.

> The nurturant parent family assumes that the world, despite its dangers and difficulties, is basically good, can be made better, and that it is one's responsibility to work toward that. Accordingly, children are born good and parents can make them better. Both parents share responsibility for raising the children. Their job is to nurture their children and raise their children to be nurturers. Nurturing has two aspects: empathy (feeling and caring how others feel) and responsibility (for taking care of oneself and others for whom

we are responsible). These two aspects of nurturance imply family values that we can recognize as progressive political values: from empathy, we want for others protection from harm, fulfillment in life, fairness, freedom (consistent with responsibility), and open two-way communication. From responsibility follow competence, trust, commitment, community building, and so on.

From these values, specific policies follow: governmental protection in the form of a social safety net and government regulation, as well as the military and the police (from protection), universal education (from competence, fairness), civil liberties and equal treatment (from fairness and freedom), accountability (from trust), public service (from responsibility), open government (from open communication), and the promotion of an economy that benefits all (from fairness) and functions to promote these values (from responsibility).

The role of government is to provide the infrastructure and services to enact these values, and taxes are the dues you pay to live in such a civilized society. In foreign policy the role of the nation should be to promote cooperation and extend these values to the world. These are traditional progressive values in American politics.

The conservative worldview is shaped by very different family values.

The strict father model assumes that the world is and always will be dangerous and difficult, and that children are born bad and must be made good. The strict father is the moral authority who has to support and defend the family, tell his wife what to do, and teach his kids right from wrong. The only way to do that is through painful punishment—physical discipline that by adulthood will develop into internal discipline. Morality and survival jointly arise from such discipline—discipline to follow moral precepts and discipline to pursue your self-interest to become self-reliant. The good people are the disciplined people. Once grown, the self-reliant, disciplined children are on their own, and the father is not to meddle in their lives. Those children who remain dependent (who were spoiled, overly willful, or recalcitrant) should be forced to undergo further discipline or should be cut free with no support to face the discipline of the outside world.

Project this onto the nation and you have the radical right-wing politics that has been misnamed "conservative." The good citizens are the disciplined ones—those who have already become wealthy or at least self-reliant—and

> those who are on the way. Social programs "spoil" people, giving them things they haven't earned and keeping them dependent. They are therefore evil and to be eliminated. Government is there only to protect the nation, maintain order, administer justice (punishment), and to provide for the orderly conduct of and the promotion of business. Business (the market) is the mechanism by which the disciplined people become self-reliant, and wealth is a measure of discipline. Taxes beyond the minimum needed for such government are punishments that take away from the good, disciplined people rewards that they have earned, and spend it on those who have not earned it.
>
> In foreign affairs the government should maintain its sovereignty and impose its moral authority everywhere it can, while seeking its self-interest (the economic self-interest of corporations and military strength).

Lakoff's nurturant parent and strict father models overlap. Some parents are going to be mostly nurturers. Some fathers are going to be mostly strict fathers. Most parents/fathers are going to be somewhere in-between. The nurturant parent is going to be the least unconscious from a primal point of view.

Lakoff's nurturant parent model, my making a home for children model and Janov's 2nd line model augment one another for understanding choices that represent more of being an interdependent self-in-relationship. Likewise, Lakoff's strict father model, my raising a child model and Janov's 3rd line model augment one another for understanding choices that represent more of being an independent self.

I take special note here of James Dobson, author of a number of books, head of Focus on the Family and who reaches millions of people through his organization. This survey of Stage III, 2nd and 3rd liners is incomplete without an exposition of Dobson's religious concept of the strict father family model as described in his book, *Dare to Discipline*. What follows here is a condensation of his strict father family model as summarized in Lakoff's book, pages 7-11.

Dobson's strict father family model is based on a number of assumptions:

> The world is a dangerous place because there is evil out there.
>
> The world is difficult because it is competitive, and there will always be winners and losers.
>
> There is an absolute right and wrong.
>
> Children are born bad [original sin]. They want to do what feels good, not what is right, and so they have to be made good.

> What is needed is a strong, strict father who can protect and support the family in a dangerous, difficult world and teach his children right from wrong.

The strict father is a moral authority who knows from the *Bible* what is absolutely, morally right and what is absolutely, morally wrong. What is required of children is obedience to the strict father as the moral authority on the *Bible.* The way to teach obedience to children to do what is right and to abstain from what is wrong is painful punishment, which includes hitting them. Physical punishment leads to the development of an internal discipline that keeps a child from doing wrong. This is the primary purpose for learning self-discipline. Without punishment, there is no morality, and the world goes to Hell.

There is a secondary effect for learning self-discipline. That effect is that it makes it possible as an adult to achieve prosperity and self-reliance in a dangerous, difficult and competitive world. The strict father family model, therefore, connects morality with prosperity. The internal discipline a child needs to be moral allows him as an adult to be prosperous.

The link between being a moral person and a prosperous person is the pursuit of self-interest. The child pursues his self-interest in avoiding punishment by becoming obedient. The adult pursues his self-interest by avoiding poverty and by becoming as prosperous as he can.

Dobson not only makes a connection between the strict father family model and morality and prosperity, he sees one also with free-market capitalism. The link here, as well, is the pursuit of self-interest. He harks back to the 18th century economist, Adam Smith. Smith said that if everyone pursues his own self-interest, then the invisible hand of nature will see to it that everyone's self-interest will be maximized. Pursue your own self-interest and you help everyone. This is what makes the pursuit of self-interest a moral absolute and justifies free-market capitalism.

The corollary to following your own self-interest because it results naturally in the common good is: Don't try to help anyone else because it results unnaturally in skewing the natural order. Those who need help are in that situation because they did not learn to pursue their self-interest and become disciplined. The strict father is not to interfere in their lives.

Lakoff then goes on to discuss what implications the morality of the pursuit of self-interest to become prosperous and self-reliant has for social programs. Since this is what is moral, it is immoral for the government to give people what they have not earned. To do so makes people dependent, which is an immoral state of being. Social programs are immoral.

The way for Christian believers in the strict father family model to counter the immorality of social programs is to make sure there is no money available for social programs. The way to do this is to give large tax cuts to those whose prosperity reveals their discipline and their morality. In this scenario, deficits are a good thing because they lead to cuts in the funding for social programs or even their elimination.

Next, Lakoff considers what the Christian strict father family model has for foreign policy. The nation is the family writ large. The president, then, is the moral authority who says what is right and enforces it. He would be immoral if he did not do so. He tells the world what is right, and since the U.S. has the power to do so, morally he unilaterally enforces it, using any means necessary, including war.

Lakoff continues. Just as individuals do in economic terms—act as rational actors in the pursuit of self-interest—so do nations. However, only nations that follow the strict father family model act rationally. There are rogue nations such as Iraq, Iran, Syria and North Korea who must be dealt with as if they were rebellious teenagers. There are child nations, which are all the nations developing toward industrialization. These nations you tell how to develop, give them rules to follow and punish them when they do wrong. And, since the U.N. is composed mainly of developing child nations, the U.S. does not ask its permission to do anything; it acts unilaterally in the pursuit of the national self-interest.

Next, I offer my critique of Dobson's religious version of the strict father family model. In the first place, it is a sure-fire formula for the creation of maximum primal pain in children. To convey to a child that there is something intrinsically wrong with him just causes such catastrophic primal pain that eventually the child has to give up all of himself in the vain hope that he will be nurtured. That Dobson assumes that a child just wants to feel good rather than to be good is just another way of saying that every child is born with original sin, of which he must be purged. Whether verbalized or not, the child's primal-pain-laden question is: "What's wrong with me?" But, of course, nothing is wrong.

Physically punishing a child and then hugging him afterwards sends a mixed message to the child. The first message is, by far, the strongest and tends to overwhelm the second. The first message is fear. Depending on the degree of buried rage the parent has over his own unmet childhood needs, the fear can escalate to fear for life itself. The second message is one of love and caring and nurture, but it is no match for fear of punishment. Now, piled on top of the primal pain generated by needs not being met is the primal pain generated by the fear that your parents actually will physically, mentally and emotionally hurt you. Even if the punishment is administered dispassionately, it is still only a euphemism for cold-blooded child abuse.

In the second place, Dobson's religious strict father family model produces evidences in adulthood of more, rather than less, primal pain. The pursuit of self-interest to be prosperous is evidence of the substitution of insatiable wants for unmet needs. Recall, that in Stage III, in order to remain viable, the child must deny his needs, only to have them resurface as insatiable wants. The morality of the pursuit of self-interest to be prosperous is the thinking brain's rationalization for insatiable wants.

The pursuit of self-interest to be self-reliant is evidence of the cutting of connections between the individualistic thinking brain and the communalistic emotional/sexual brain. Self-reliance is just another term for individualism and evidences the loss of being a self-in-relationship. Self-reliance is another evidence for a Stage III level of primal pain. Self-reliance implies that society is no more than a collection of isolated individuals who are focused on their own self-interests.

The willingness to use force is further evidence of a Stage III level of primal pain. Recall, that there comes a time in a child's life when he compensates for his feelings of helplessness in getting his needs met by seeking power. Now, in adulthood, there is a compulsion for power and the willingness to use force, if necessary, to keep at bay feelings of helplessness.

Dobson links the strict father family model with free-market capitalism. The linkage is the morality of the pursuit of self-interest to be prosperous and self-reliant. Recall, that it is insatiable want and individualism that produces private property which, in turn, leads to free-market capitalism. Hence, Dobson's support for free-market capitalism is ultimately based on a Stage III level of primal pain. It is the mindset of a Stage III, 3rd line level of unconscious self-awareness that allows a religious person to find a sacred basis for the morality of the pursuit of self-interest, for free-market capitalism and for the use of force in the exercise of power.

As of the date of this writing, the summer of 2005, all government social programs are under attack. It is time to assess what the future might hold if the Christian, strict father family model becomes the norm for the nation. The place to begin is in the late 1700s. Most people were poor. Many were mired in debt too deep to climb out. They were either jailed, sold as indentured work hands or sent to a poorhouse. If they were farm owners, their land was foreclosed, usually just before a harvest. The founding fathers, disciples of Adam Smith, had no interest in "leveling": the redistribution of wealth. Remember my earlier quote from James Madison regarding majority factions. What they want is "a rage for paper money, for an abolition of debts, for an equal distribution of property, or for any other improper or wicked project . . ." That is where the U.S. began as a nation. It wasn't until the 1930s with Roosevelt's New Deal and continuing with Johnson's War on Poverty in the 1960s that class conflict in the U.S. had at last succeeded in achieving some semblance of the responsibility of everyone, by everyone, for everyone. Since 1970—that's when Dobson's book was first published—whether from a sacred or a secular worldview, the strict father family model has mobilized and organized the radical right to eliminate every social program.

Within their own worldview, the believers in the strict father family model do not see themselves as uncaring. Quite simply, they do not think it is right to take money from those who have been disciplined enough by self-interest to become prosperous and give it to those who have not been so disciplined. The problem, as they see it, is not one of physical poverty, but one of a spiritual poverty. People in poverty are there because, in God's estimation, they have not sufficiently atoned for their original sin, they haven't been sufficiently repentant and they are in need of salvation. Therefore, "welfare" should be strictly a private, nongovernmental matter with the saving of souls as its basic expression of caring.

This is what is behind Bush's faith-based program for helping people out of need. What these people need is faith, predictably, Christian faith, to extricate themselves from need. However, it is against the law for people in the church or church-related organizations that are receiving tax money to proselytize while carrying out their mission. Yet, what is one to conclude but that they are proselytizing because, in their view, becoming converted is the spiritual ladder out of the mire of physical poverty.

From everything that Bush has ever said about himself, I am convinced that eventually he will cut off funds for his faith-based initiative. I believe he shares Dobson's views that it is immoral to give money to people who haven't earned it. I believe his ultimate goal is to get the government out of welfare and into promoting Christianity. Dobson is reported to speak frequently with the White House, so it is no stretch to conclude that Bush shares Dobson's views.

In the 1800s in this country, there were no governmental social programs to alleviate poverty. Hence, there was no need for evangelicals with a strict father family model to rail against immoral programs to lift people out of poverty. The situation was different in England and in Ireland, however, during this period. What happened in those countries could happen here. The information that follows here is taken from an article by Gordon Bigelow entitled "Let There Be Markets" that was published in the May, 2005, issue of *Harper's Magazine*.

This was the situation in England in the 1820s. Adam Smith's prediction that free market capitalism would not only enrich the self-interested entrepreneur, but enrich society as a whole was not working. There was great suffering for the new, industrial poor. Those who could not work or support themselves, orphans and the disabled, were cared for by local parish organizations. It was a joint responsibility of church and state to prevent starvation and unavoidable suffering.

Smith, however, scoffed at personal riches. And, David Picardo, another author on the same subject, thought that class conflict was a part of the capitalist world. This created a problem for some free market advocates; they needed a moral justification for their own wealth as well as for the poverty of the masses. That moral justification came with the ascendancy of evangelical Anglicans to positions of power in the government.

The evangelicals believed in a providential God who created a logical and orderly universe. The new, capitalist economy was a fulfillment of God's plan. The free market was God's plan to reward good Christian behavior and to punish the unrepentant. Therefore, it was unthinkable to them to conceptualize that free-market capitalism was causing class conflict or that there was a flaw in free-market capitalism's theory that everyone would benefit from each person's self-centered pursuit of wealth. Class conflict could not be because that would mean God had created a world at war with itself. Poverty could not be the unintended and inevitable fall-out from capitalism because nothing fell outside of God's plan for humanity.

In 1834, the evangelicals eliminated the parish-based system of aiding those in need. In its place they passed the Poor Law Amendment of 1834. It made cash payments to the poor illegal. Their only recourse were local workhouses. Life in them was miserable, but that was of no concern to the evangelicals. Poverty was punishment for a sinful life. Poverty was not a problem to be fixed; it was a spiritual condition. The workhouses weren't supposed to alleviate suffering; they were supposed to save souls.

In Ireland between 1845 and 1850, a similar approach to poverty was taken by evangelicals. This was the time of the potato famine. The government responded by importing cornmeal from the U.S. and selling it cheaply to wholesalers. In 1846, evangelicals won control of the government and dismantled this relief program. Their reasons for doing so were that the program was an artificial interference in the free market and that it would perpetuate the problems of the poor. Besides, they said that it would force the people off the land and into the cities where they would become cheap labor, stimulating the economy. Well, there was no economic boom. A million people died of starvation and another million emigrated.

Bigelow concludes his article, in part, by saying:

> The first evangelicals fought for free trade because they thought it would encourage virtuous behavior, but two centuries of capitalism have taught a different lesson, many times over. The wages of sin are often, and notoriously, a private jet and a wicked stock-option package. The wages of hard moral choice are often $5.15 an hour.

In this subsection, I have given far more space to the connection between Stage III, 3rd line unconscious self-awareness and the strict father family model than I have for the 2nd line, nurturant parent family model. I hope I have made clear why. While there are great gaps in the national pattern for being an interdependent, self-in-relationship kind of society—for instance, no universal health care—the U.S. still has Social Security, Medicare, Medicaid, unemployment compensation, public education and many other programs that exhibit that interdependence. All of these programs are in danger of being eliminated. The basis for doing so is a Stage III, 3rd line level of unconscious self-awareness. That level results in a secular, hands-off, free-market capitalism that writes off the losers as part of the natural order of economic Law—losers who are in no way entitled to having their needs fulfilled through social programs. That level can also result in a kind of Christian theology that enshrines the individualism, the greed and the lust for power characteristic of Stage III, 3rd line unconsciousness—a theology that equates poverty with sinfulness. Whether it be a Stage III, 3rd line secular or sacred strict father family model, the goal is the elimination of all Stage III, 2nd line, nurturant parent social programs that represent interdependence and selves-in-relationship.

Social Class and 2nd and 3rd Liners

Some General Comments About Social Class and 2nd and 3rd Liners

There is no direct connection between one's class and whether one is either a 2nd or 3rd liner.

In each class, 2nd liners are going to be an ever-declining minority as primal pain drives more and more people to become 3rd liners.

While the protection of property rights and the prevention of "leveling" is at the forefront of the interests of the rich and powerful, elite ruling class, they are part of the makeup of all 3rd liners, who are the majority in each class. While the protection of human rights and an equitable distribution of wealth is part of the makeup of all 2nd liners, they will always be a minority in each class in Stage III.

Accumulated Wealth and Power and Class Interests

At every level there are class interests. Accumulated wealth (the degree of satisfied insatiable wants) not only defines the classes, it determines how much accumulated power (the degree of the satisfaction of the lust for power) each class has to advance its interests. Ordinarily, the wealthiest of the wealthy have enough power to rule, regardless of the form of government and as long as they don't get too greedy. If they don't take care of the middle class or throw enough crumbs to the lower class, power can shift so dramatically that revolution occurs.

How 2nd and 3rd Liners Think of Class

Third liners, especially those in the rich and powerful, elite ruling class, are likely to think in terms of class, regardless of whether or not they use that term. In fact, to preserve their class prerogatives, they are likely to deny that there is a class structure and accuse 2nd liners of injecting a fictitious, divisive class struggle into society. Second liners of all classes, while recognizing that classes and class struggle exist, are likely to think in terms of a society of equal and interdependent selves and affirm that a classless society is the goal.

Variables That Affect 2nd and 3rd Liners and Their Class

If one has a 3rd line level of primal pain and is a member of the lowest class and at the same time is having difficulty in securing the necessities of life, there are no lofty thoughts of the common good as being the inalienable right to acquire and use private property. The only thought is to survive. If such a 3rd liner has superior abilities and fortunate circumstances, chances are he will rise to become a member of the rich and powerful, elite ruling class. If such a 3rd liner has ordinary abilities and circumstances, chances are he will be just one more example of the majority in every class in a materialistic, consuming culture which is obsessed with attempting to satisfy insatiable wants.

If one has a 2nd line level of primal pain and is a member of the lowest class and at the same time is having a problem securing the necessities of life, there are no lofty thoughts about the common good being an equitable distribution of wealth. The only thought is to survive. If a 2nd liner has superior abilities and fortunate circumstances, chances are he will stand out in his efforts to bring about a more equitable distribution of wealth, regardless of his class. If a 2nd liner has ordinary abilities and circumstances, chances are he will be one more example of the minority in a materialistic, consuming culture whose wants are relatively low and who are relatively satisfied with what they have.

Color, ethnic background and gender are variables that make the relationship even more complex between the level of one's primal pain and one's class. These three variables, in the main, have confined people to subordinate classes regardless of their degree of primal pain. A fourth variable, inheritance, accounts for many in the top class, regardless of the level of their primal pain. One's birth determines in which class one starts out. It also determines which opportunities are open to one. Abilities determine what one makes of one's birth class and of one's opportunities.

2nd Line and 3rd Line Definitions of the Common Good

Third liners in all classes will espouse a common good for the nation that translates into each individual's right to freely acquire and use his property, based on his abilities, his opportunities and his birth. That right should not be abridged by any redistribution of property for the benefit of others.

Regardless of class, 3rd liners are likely to attribute the redistribution of wealth to the predacious self-interest of people who lack virtue, character and principle. They are right in that there will always be some 3rd liners, regardless of class, who will take advantage of any system that redistributes wealth for human rights because of their greed. Third liners are also quite likely to use a euphemism such as "being naturally an entrepreneur" to explain their own "impeccable" behavior.

On the other hand, a predacious self-interest can hardly be attributed to either those in genuine need or those 2nd liners in the top class who favor a redistribution of wealth to fulfill human rights. An example of the latter is multi-millionaire Bill Gates, Sr. He favors the retention of the Federal Estate Tax because it is a means by which those who have benefited most from the leading nation that fosters the acquisition of wealth can give back to the nation. Bill Gates exhibits 2nd line behavior in this regard, even though he is a member of the rich and powerful, elite ruling class.

Second liners will espouse a common good for the nation that means that everyone has the right to adequate food, shelter and medical care, for example. This holds true for 2nd liners, regardless of class.

These two concepts of the common good are mutually exclusive. In a society of selves-in-relationship, everyone has the human right to food, shelter, clothing, education and medical care. That right inevitably involves the redistribution of wealth because there are always those who do not have the means to secure these fundamental human needs.

The history of the United States has been one of class struggle. Almost all of that struggle is unknown to the public because it has been left out of the textbooks of primary and secondary education. The Anti-Renter movement, the Dorr Rebellion, the plight of millions who were cast aside in the turbulent growth of the nation, the continuation of the Hamiltonian idea that Congress should help business interests but not the lower classes, the trade union movement, the Flour Riot, strikes, the Female Labor Reform Association, a legal system designed to protect property but not persons, reforms in name only, labor conditions, the Haymarket tragedy, Depressions, State Alliances, populism and other indicators of class struggle too many to list have characterized U.S. history. The Mexican-American War, the Civil War, the Spanish-American War, World War I, World War II and the Second Iraq War each interrupted class struggle. In fact, one of the hidden justifications for some of these was to quell class warfare. (For a comprehensive picture of class struggle in the United States, see Chapters 10 and 11 of Howard Zinn's *A People's History of the United States 1492-Present.*)

Today, the gains that have been made through class struggle to make sure no one remains in need are being reversed. Welfare, Social Security, Medicare and Medicaid are under severe attack by 3rd liners who feel, just as our Founding Fathers did, that the government has no business being in the business of confiscating the wealth of the worthy and giving it to the unworthy. Forcing people off welfare without regard to the social consequences of low or no wages, the privatization of Social Security, forcing people off Medicare and into HMOs, the scaling back of Medicaid, the slashing of taxes for the wealthy and wars that create precedent-setting national debt are all policies deliberately followed by 3rd liners to make sure no public monies are available to fund social programs.

What is behind Bush's tax cuts is the complete elimination of taxes on unearned income, that is, on dividends and interest. When completed, it means a giant step toward the goal of ending "leveling": the redistribution of wealth from the rich and powerful, elite ruling class to the wage-earning and unemployed classes. Leveling redistributes wealth in the form of social services. The same goal is behind the privatization of Social Security and welfare reform. And what lies at the bottom of it all is a 3rd line level of unconscious self-awareness with its greed and lust for power.

What is ironic about the goal of ending the taxation of dividends and interest is that it actually represents a huge transfer of wealth from wage-earners to the rich and powerful, elite ruling class. After all, dividends are corporate profits, and profits represent wealth created by wage-earners. So the lower classes, who would ordinarily be receiving back—in the form of social services—a portion of the wealth they created, are denied that portion of the wealth they created by their own labor. Granted, many wage-earners are also stockholders, but dividends are a very small portion of their income. Unlike for the rich and powerful, elite ruling class—who for the most part are neither wage-earners nor self-employed—dividends are earned income for middle and lower class wage-earners.

What is almost criminal in this redistribution of wealth from the wage-earning class to the wealthy stockholding class is Congress's refusal to block corporations from establishing an off-shore address and thus avoid paying any income taxes. Now, even corporate income taxes, that would have flowed back in the form of social services to the wealth-creating wage-earners, instead go to the rich and powerful, elite ruling class in the form of increased dividends.

The Tripartite Attitude of the Rich and Powerful, Elite Ruling Class

What characterizes the mindset of the 3rd line majority of the rich and powerful, elite ruling class is a tripartite attitude that seems almost universally connected to wealth and revolves around the protection of private property. Each part of that attitude can be traced to a Stage III level of insatiable wants and compulsion for power.

The first part of that attitude is that those who are wealthy are more qualified to run the nation than those without wealth. As I pointed out in the last chapter, this was the attitude of our Founding Fathers as they crafted the Constitution. Since the primary function of government is the protection of private property, the nation is equated with property. When it is recalled that want and power are at the center of Stage III unconscious self-awareness, it is easy to reach the conclusion that in the minds of the Founding Fathers great wealth and the power that goes along with it gives the wealthy not only the right to rule, but the means to do it as well.

The second part of that attitude is that those who have great wealth are superior in character to those without wealth. This, too, was part of the mindset of the Founding Fathers and why they felt justified in crafting a Constitution that would screen out those inferiors who had no wealth. Just as our Founding Fathers thought, so today there is the idea that humans are naturally acquisitive. Since that is so, the argument runs, then it must be true that those who are the most successfully acquisitive are superior to those who are the least successfully acquisitive. From my understanding of the nature of the connection between primal pain and insatiable wants, I conclude that those who feel the most superior are the ones who have the greatest primal pain. Therefore, they are the most driven to satisfy insatiable wants and have acquired great wealth.

The third part of that tripartite attitude is the fear that a predaciously self-interested, democratic majority would tax away the wealth of the ruling class and take it for themselves. As with the other parts of the mindset, this fear was also part of the mindset of the Founding Fathers. It accounts for all the stratagems placed in the Constitution to prevent any "wicked and improper" scheme for "leveling." Since, in Stage III, wants are insatiable, one has to clutch to oneself what one has. There is the fear that people will try to take away what you have if given half a chance.

Socialism, Communism and Capitalism

Nineteenth and twentieth century socialism and communism were reform movements that attempted to go back to what was the situation in Stage II when property was communal. They were last-gasp efforts to revive a level of communalism that was natural 10,000 years ago. Not in any so-called communist country has communism ever come about. No communist country has ever gotten past the dictatorship of the proletariat. This is not communism. Communism comes about when the state withers away and the ideal of "from each according to his abilities and to each according to his needs" becomes a reality.

Capitalists are on the right track when they claim that socialism and communism don't work because humans are inherently individualistic entrepreneurs, but that assessment is not of an inherent trait. Rather, it is an accurate statement of the current status of Stage III unconscious self-awareness.

For the same reason, capitalists have claimed that capitalism has survived: Humans are naturally capitalistic. But, as I said, this is not so. Capitalism works because, in the outer world, it is the perfect expression of a want-and-power-driven unconscious self-awareness in the inner world. A Stage III self-awareness that has to deny needs, only to have them resurface as insatiable wants, results in a capitalism based upon an insatiable greed for profit. A Stage III self-awareness that must compensate for being helpless to get needs met by resorting to the use of power results in a capitalism based upon a lust for power. Hence, capitalism is based upon a psychology that is even more flawed than the psychology that was present in Stage II that resulted in socialistic economies.

Modern capitalism has failed because the current status of self-awareness is such that greed and the concentration of power in the hands of the few does not allow the unfettered, individualistic pursuit of economic goals to result in capitalism's ideal that it results in the greatest good accruing to the greatest number. It results rather in the greatest good accruing to the greedy, powerful few *and* the many grubbing for what they can get. As Stage III primal pain continues to escalate, both in the inner world and in the outer world, capitalism will founder on the excesses of individualism, materialism, consumerism, the lust for power and an insatiable greed.

In one sense, capitalism survives because it is the direct outgrowth of Stage III self-awareness. Where can it lead us though, since it is based on power and greed? One place will be to an environment so polluted, so exhausted, so devoid of life forms that we might very well cause our own extinction.

Another place it will lead to is a bunker mentality among everyone in an effort to hold on to what little one might have in order to survive. Each one will be pitted against all others. The struggle for power and the grab for possessions will become the central motif of life. Just as the promises of a glittering future in a communist workers' paradise are ending in failure, so will those same promises fail wherever there is capitalism.

The glittering promises of the powerful few to the population at large are shown up for what they are—just glitter—when the actual goals of capitalism are exposed. Here are five examples of the hypocrisy of capitalism:

1. Capitalism will speak glowingly about a strong economy. What, however, is a strong economy but high consumer spending. In turn, high consumer spending means a low savings rate by the general population. The powerful few know that the way to satisfy their own insatiable greed is to encourage people to spend, spend, spend, all the while knowing that the only way to wealth is to save, save, save. The hypocrisy is shown in the shameless expenditure of billions of dollars to exploit every human weakness through deceptive advertising to manipulate the masses into buying as a means to personal fulfillment. The lending institutions beg us to borrow from them, resulting in the general population shouldering crushing debt at outrageous interest rates.
2. Capitalism claims that the least government is the best government. What it really seeks is an alliance between big government and big business to make sure that the government passes laws and issues regulations that

do not interfere with the maximizing of profits—the public's interests be damned. When deregulation of an industry results in billions of tax dollars being spent to bail out that industry's collapse because of greed, then we remember that insatiable greed was the reason for regulation in the first place.

3. Capitalism claims that competition results in the greatest benefits to the greatest number. If this were so, then why do corporations do everything they can to eliminate their competition? Mergers, unfriendly takeovers and predatory pricing eliminate competition. They lead to poorer service and high prices much of the time. Power and greed account for this hypocrisy.
4. Capitalism's two-faced attitude toward welfare exposes its hypocrisy. Capitalism claims that government welfare for the people destroys individual responsibility. In recent years, government welfare for individuals has been dismantled. In contrast, big business has sought to maintain its own welfare dependence on the government. Capitalism seeks favorable tax breaks and government subsidies but doesn't claim that corporate welfare makes corporations less responsible for their own situations.
5. While decrying the evils of national governments to regulate them for the common good, international capitalism has created the oligarchic World Trade Organization (WTO) that is a super government in itself, which is neither responsible to the United Nations nor to any national state, but only to international corporations. The WTO is not responsible to the people, as is a national state. Under the "restraint of trade" provisions of parallel entities such as the North American Free Trade Agreement, corporations can even sue a country for damages because an environmental law has restrained their trade.

What the international corporations are doing in Third World countries is no different from what the national corporations did in the old and new worlds. They fight against regulations and laws that seek to prevent them from polluting the environment and creating health hazards. They either create or make use of sweatshop conditions to maximize profits. They seek to keep the workers disorganized and weak. They work to prevent union organization. They secure initial tax breaks to the detriment of the local people and then threaten to leave if the tax breaks are not extended. Remember how long it took in this country to outlaw sweatshops, reduce the work week from seventy to forty hours, put in place legal safeguards for union organization and put in place health standards in the workplace. We forget that we had to regulate corporate greed and power in order to force corporations to be environmentally responsible and to treat employees fairly.

Already we are beginning to experience the fallout of the globalization of capitalism and so-called free-market economics. A forerunner of it was the taxpayer bail-out of the savings and loan industry in the 1980s. The powerful few convinced Congress to deregulate savings and loan associations. An insatiable and unrestrained greed for profit followed that ended in the collapse of the industry. Taxpayers, to the tune of hundreds of billions of dollars, had to pay to see to it that the little guy didn't lose what he had placed in a savings and loan institution.

Globalization means that the failure of the economy in one country could bring down economies worldwide. It is a given that markets will fluctuate, so it is possible that a global downturn could produce unprecedented starvation worldwide. How can so-called sound free-market economic policies prevent melt-downs when the foundation of these policies is a self-awareness characterized by a lust for power and by insatiable greed?

The crisis in Mexico in 1994 is an example of the capitalistic greed of the powerful few resulting in an imminent melt-down of the country. The U.S. taxpayers provided the money loaned to Mexico to prevent chaos. Had it not been for the bail-out, the greed of the powerful few would have caused additional untold misery for the Mexican people.

The near failure of Long-Term Capital Management (LTCM) in 1998 is another example of capitalistic greed. In the opinion of economists, its failure could have brought on a worldwide depression. The greed for profit of one mutual fund was great enough to do so. The banks bailed out LTCM, but this means that dividends belonging to all bank stockholders and not just to the powerful few were used for the bail-out. Again, whether it be taxpayer money or small investors' money, the ordinary working person, of whom the powerful really couldn't care less, has to bail out those who are exploiting him.

As this is being written, the Enron/Arthur Andersen debacle is playing out nationwide. The debacle is not an isolated case of wrongdoing. It is symptomatic of a population in Stage III self-awareness, driven by a lust for power and an uncontrollable greed for profit. If previous events are any guide to what might happen now, loud cries will well up to punish the wrongdoers. But, even if Congress and the administration act to make sure effective regulations are put in place to curb the greed that is endemic to the system, the regulations are not likely to work. The powerful few will protect their own, while thousands of hapless employees of these and other companies will be left to fend for themselves when the next debacle occurs.

Unilateralism as the National Expression of Acting as an Independent Self

With the demise of the Soviet Union, the United States is left as the only superpower. It is becoming clear now that it was the counter-balancing power of the Soviet Union that kept the United States from simply riding roughshod over any opposition to its own individualistic, self-interest. One example of unilateralism is the refusal to sign on for the ending of the use of land mines. Another is the refusal to reduce harmful emissions in accordance with the Kyoto agreements. A third is the threat to shut down U.N. peacekeeping missions if U.S. personnel are not exempted from the jurisdiction of the newly operating World Court. The stance on terrorism—that everyone who is not with us is against us—is another example. There are others. On both national and international levels, the most destructive behavior of the common good is to act unilaterally as an independent nation. The same holds true on individual and communal levels.

Summary

As I pointed out early in this chapter, one key to understanding what is happening these days in terms of greed and power is to know that the outer and inner worlds mirror each other. An internal world of Stage III unconscious self-awareness, with its every thought, emotion and deed conditioned by insatiable wants and a compulsion for power, is going to create an external world based on want and power.

Equally important to understanding what is going on today is to know what causes the basic difference between people. That difference is the amount of primal paint that each person has, which determines how many insatiable wants one has and how much one is driven to accumulate and use power. In this regard, earlier I noted that while everyone today is in Stage III, those with less primal pain will continue to exhibit more of the characteristics of Stage II. Those people I labeled 2nd liners, following Janov's lead. Those with greater primal pain will exhibit to a higher degree the characteristics of Stage III. Those people I labeled 3rd liners.

The most important point to consider in this chapter is whether or not the primal worldview resonates with you in accounting for what is happening in yourself and all around you. It is important to avoid getting hung up on the merits or demerits of what is happening in the external world, divorced from what is happening in the internal world.

CHAPTER 15

THE UNITED STATES

A Nation Dominated by Greed, by a Lust for Power, by the Quest for World Domination and by the Willingness to Use Violence and Terrorism to Achieve These Ends

Introduction

As I begin this penultimate chapter, I realize that much of what I'm going to say is not only controversial and will arouse angry feelings, it will be categorically denied. All humans are in a state of denial. U.S. citizens, generally speaking, are farther along in that state of denial than any other people. I believe we have the most primal pain overall and primal pain that is of the highest valence. This means that in order to remain psychologically viable we must deny that we are in pain at all. That denial prevents us from experiencing just how far we have devolved from a state of consciousness into a state of unconscious self-awareness. Richard Hofstadter in the Introduction of his book, *The American Political Tradition*, says that Americans are more interested in a "sentimental appreciation [of our past] rather than of critical analysis." This chapter will brush aside any such denial and explore just how greedy and lustful of power we have become as a nation.

Up to this point, I have repeatedly laid out the connection of primal pain with Stage III's primary motif of insatiable wants and a compulsion for power. In this chapter, I will lay out the connection between primal pain and the use of power to commit violent acts against others. This connection lays the foundation for the willingness of the nation's leaders, who have a lust for power, to use violence in the quest for world domination.

While no direct connection can be assumed, it is reasonable to think that those who have the greatest primal pain, that is, those who as young children felt the greatest helplessness in getting their needs met and felt the greatest rage when they could no longer stand the pain, are those who have risen to the positions of greatest power in government. Those with the greatest pain are most likely to use violence to achieve their goals.

The internal components of those who have an external quest for world domination are primal pain, needs, greed, helplessness, a lust for power, anger and the rational justification of the use of power, whether nonviolent or violent, to achieve that goal. I will try to weave those components into a meaningful whole within the context of a Stage III unconscious self-awareness with its primary motif of needs/wants/power, which is located primarily in the thinking brain.

The *lust for power* compensates for the feeling of *helplessness* that arises when the child realizes that he is powerless to get his *needs* met. The willingness to use *violence* to achieve dominance to satisfy one's *greed* comes from the suppressed anger that arose in the emotional/sexual brain when *primal pain* could no longer be tolerated. The *rational justification* for the use of violence comes from the want-dominated thinking brain, which is cut off from the need-dominated emotional/sexual brain.

U.S. Foreign Interventions 1798-2003

By far, the most dangerous sign of the U.S. government's lust for power and its quest for world domination is its abysmal record in engaging in covert actions or preemptive wars against defenseless countries that dared to free themselves from our control or that resisted coming under our control. In 1962, when the U.S. government sought to justify the use of armed force against Cuba, Secretary of State Dean Rusk presented to a Senate committee a list of 103 instances of the use of U.S. armed forces abroad between the years 1798 and 1895. The list included a brief description of each incursion. (See *A People's History of the United States, 1492-Present* by Howard Zinn, pp. 297-298, for a partial list.) In *Why Do People Hate America?* by Ziaudlin Sardar and Merryl Wyn Davies, pp. 92-101, the authors provide a list of 114 interventions by the military, both domestic and foreign. The following, by presidential listing, are the foreign interventions. In a number of references, the dates given extend into the administrations of ensuing presidents.

Benjamin Harrison: 1889-1893

1890: Argentina
1891: Chile
1891: Haiti

Grover Cleveland: 1893-1897

1893-?: Hawaii
1894: Nicaragua
1894-95: China
1894-96: Korea
1895: Panama
1896: Nicaragua

William McKinley: 1897-1901

1898-00:	China
1898-1910:	Philippines
1898-1902:	Cuba
1898-?:	Puerto Rico
1898-?:	Guam
1898:	Nicaragua
1899-?:	Samoa
1899:	Nicaragua

Theodore Roosevelt: 1901-1909

1901-1914:	Panama
1903:	Honduras
1903-04:	Dominican Republic
1904-05:	Korea
1906-09:	Cuba
1907:	Nicaragua
1907:	Honduras
1908:	Panama

William Taft: 1909-1913

1910:	Nicaragua
1911:	Honduras
1911-41:	China
1912:	Cuba
1912:	Panama
1912:	Honduras
1912-33:	Nicaragua

Woodrow Wilson: 1913-1921

1913:	Mexico
1914:	Dominican Republic
1914-18:	Mexico
1914-34:	Haiti
1916-24:	Dominican Republic
1917-33:	Cuba
1917-18:	World War I
1918-22:	Russia
1918-22:	Panama
1919:	Yugoslavia
1919:	Honduras
1920:	Guatemala

Warren Harding: 1921-1923
- 1922: Turkey
- 1922-27: China

Calvin Coolidge: 1923-1929
- 1924-25: Honduras
- 1925: Panama
- 1927-34: China

Herbert Hoover: 1929-1933
- 1932: El Salvador

Franklin Roosevelt: 1933-1945
- 1941-45: World War II

Harry Truman: 1945-1953
- 1947-49: Greece
- 1948-49: China
- 1948-54: Philippines
- 1950: Puerto Rico
- 1950-03: Korea

Dwight Eisenhower: 1953-1961
- 1953: Iran
- 1954: Guatemala
- 1956: Egypt
- 1958: Lebanon
- 1958: Panama
- 1960: Vietnam

John Kennedy: 1961-1963
- 1961: Cuba
- 1961-63: Vietnam
- 1962: Laos

Lyndon Johnson: 1963-1969
- 1963-69: Vietnam
- 1964: Panama
- 1965: Indonesia
- 1965-66: Dominican Republic
- 1966-67: Guatemala

Richard Nixon: 1969-1974

1969-74:	Cambodia
1969-74:	Vietnam
1970:	Oman
1971-73:	Laos
1973:	Chile

Gerald Ford: 1974-1977

1974-75:	Vietnam
1974-75:	Cambodia
1976-92:	Angola

James Carter: 1977-1981

1980:	Iran

Ronald Reagan: 1981-1989

1981:	Libya
1981-82:	El Salvador
1981-90:	Nicaragua
1982-84:	Lebanon
1983-89:	Honduras
1983-84:	Grenada
1984:	Iran
1986:	Libya
1986:	Bolivia
1987-88:	Iran

George Bush: 1989-1993

1989:	Libya
1989:	Philippines
1989-90:	Panama
1990:	Liberia
1990-91:	Saudi Arabia
1990-?:	Iraq
1991:	Kuwait
1992-94:	Somalia
1992-94:	Yugoslavia

William Clinton: 1993-2001

1993-95:	Bosnia
1994-96:	Haiti

1995:	Croatia
1996-97:	Zaire
1997:	Liberia
1997:	Albania
1998:	Sudan
1998:	Afghanistan
1998:	Iraq
1999-?:	Yugoslavia
2000:	Yemen

George W. Bush: 2001-____

2001:	Macedonia
2001:	Afghanistan
2003-?:	Iraq

Selected Examples of Major Instances of the U.S.'s Quest for "Expansion," Economic Imperialism and World Domination

The purpose of this section is to call attention to the administrations of a number of our presidents to illustrate the U.S.'s greed and lust for power. The absence of any president's name from this section is not meant to imply that he did not further the greed and lust for power of the rich and powerful, elite ruling class.

Thomas Jefferson: 1801-1809

From the time of Columbus, all of the Americas were part of the colonial empires of Spain, England and France. The Native Americans were either killed, enslaved, decimated by diseases new to them, or pushed ever farther west. The United States of America had hardly begun when it began to carry out its own imperialistic ambitions on all of the Native-American-occupied territory west of the thirteen original states, all the way to the Pacific Ocean.

The same rationale for taking Native American land that was used nearly 200 years earlier was still being used during Jefferson's presidency. All land occupied by Native Americans was legally a "vacuum." They had not "subdued" the land, so they had only a "natural" right to it, which carries no legal standing. They did not have the "civil" right to it that had legal standing. Hence, it was perfectly legal for the United States to buy from France in 1803 that huge swath of land through mid-North America known as the Louisiana Purchase. The Native Americans who occupied the land had no legal standing in the matter.

Jefferson wasted no time in furthering his imperialistic goals for the United States. In 1804, the Lewis and Clark expedition was sent west, ostensibly to find a water route to the Pacific and to gather information about plants, animals, geography, Indians and natural resources. Whether or not Jefferson lied, I don't know, but the real reason was to get to the mouth of the Columbia River and to claim it for the United States before the British could. To simply refer to the U.S.'s imperialism as "westward expansion" is to use a euphemism to hide from ourselves the true nature of the U.S.'s greed, lust for power and willingness to use violence to achieve its goals.

James Polk: 1845-1849

Polk had two imperialistic ambitions. The first was to dominate the world's market for cotton. Cotton was to that day what oil is for today. The second was to make California a part of U.S. territory and thus open Asian markets to our products. Mexico was the obstacle to both ambitions.

During the presidency of Andrew Jackson, 1829-1837, the United States aided the Mexican territory of Texas to revolt successfully. In 1836, Texas claimed independence and called itself the Lone Star Republic. The United States and Mexico recognized the Nueces River as the boundary between Texas and Mexico, but Texas said it was the Rio Grande River, 150 miles farther south. That is where matters stood in 1845.

Polk's first move was to convince Texas to accept annexation, which it did in 1845. Polk said he would accept the claim of Texas that its southern border was the Rio Grande River. His next move was to send an army to the Rio Grande, anticipating that it would provoke war with Mexico. It did. Some U.S. soldiers were killed, giving Polk the excuse he needed to invade Mexico.

In his message to Congress, asking for a declaration of war, Polk lied twice. He claimed that the area where the U.S. soldiers were killed was undisputed U.S. territory. Not so. It was territory claimed by Mexico and controlled and inhabited by Mexico. He claimed that it was necessary to send the troops for self-defense. Not so. He sent them to provoke a war.

The war was packaged and sold to the public in terms we know so well today from the Bush administration. The Mexican people were to be given the blessings of liberty and democracy from a superior race. God, himself, was the providential hand who agreeably was making it all happen.

It was at this time that the phrase "manifest destiny" was coined and applied to the United States. The full quote is, "Our manifest destiny [is] to overspread the continent allowed by Providence for the free development of our multiplying millions."

By the Treaty of Guadalupe Hidalgo in 1848, the border of Texas was set at the Rio Grande River and New Mexico and California were ceded to the United

States. We paid Mexico $18 million, $7 million less than the United States offered before the war.

William McKinley: 1897-1901

What was different about McKinley's imperialistic designs was that he thought the United States should have colonies as did the major European nations. He thought it was time the United States became a player in international politics; otherwise, the United States couldn't truly be a great nation. McKinley's goals were pure classical imperialism. He claimed he was being guided by God.

What McKinley needed was a pretext to go to war to gain colonies. That pretext was provided by some Cuban-Americans during Cleveland's administration in 1895 who sailed undetected to Cuba and began guerrilla warfare against Spanish rule. On January 1, 1898, McKinley deliberately sent the battleship *Maine* to Havana, Cuba, to provoke the Spanish into war. Publicly, he said the ship was paying a courtesy visit. On February 15, 1898, an explosion on the *Maine* sunk the ship. The cause has never been determined. The least likely explanation is that Spain was responsible because the last thing it wanted was U.S. intervention in the guerrilla war. If it were not an accident, the most likely explanation is that the guerrillas caused it. Regardless, it was what McKinley needed and on April 20, 1898, Congress declared war on Spain.

In order to justify the war against Spain and to make it seem that it was inevitable, McKinley used the stratagems that the rich and powerful, elite ruling class have always used to garner public support. The first stratagem was to divert the people's attention away from just grievances. The second was to claim that the goal was humanitarian. The third was that this war was to preserve the national honor. The fourth was to stir up a jingoistic patriotism.

What McKinley had to overcome so far as the people were concerned was to preserve the idealistic conception of the nation as being above something so un-American as imperialism, while at the same time following an imperialistic foreign policy. Actually, both the Democratic and Republican parties were indistinguishable in this regard. The real power lay in the rich and powerful, elite ruling class who dominated both parties. The people were fooled into thinking that they were the ones who made the decisions that guided the nation's leaders. The Republican propaganda machine duped the people into approving the invasion of Cuba, Puerto Rico and the Philippines; the colonization of the Philippines; and the annexation of Hawaii. In his book *The Sorrows of Empire*, Chalmer Johnson quotes Teddy Roosevelt, arguing for the annexation of the Philippines: "'There is not an imperialist in the country . . . Expansion? Yes . . . Expansion has been the law of our national growth.'" The Spanish-American War represented the evidence of the reality of a sufficient jump in primal pain that the United States is not only imperialistic but bent on world domination.

Woodrow Wilson: 1913-1921

The historical record is replete with statements Wilson made about himself. This is most fortunate because it permits some conclusions to be drawn about what his childhood must have been like to have produced an adult with his personality.

Early in his life, Wilson wanted to become a great statesman. His mind was filled with great political plans. He dreamt of achieving great national triumphs. Wilson wanted to be president of the United States so that he could use his substantial personal powers to employ the powers of the presidency to attain personal greatness. Coupled with this were his strong will and his sense of being so very right, which meant that those who opposed him must be wrong. He wanted to be president so that he could drive the people to do great things. He felt it was not possible for the people to do so on their own; they needed to be driven by strong leaders. But he also had a fear that the people might turn against him and thwart his dream of personal greatness. Sometimes, even as president, he was frustrated or ill, anxious that his great powers would atrophy and that his calling to greatness would amount to nothing.

While it is not possible to know with certainty how Wilson's parents treated him as a child, I believe they treated him as a nobody. I believe he felt he was never listened to and that he didn't count.

Wilson's father was a Presbyterian minister. Perhaps the young Woodrow felt that God thought of him as a wretched nobody who didn't deserve to be saved but was. Just as his father was called to the ministry, I believe Wilson felt called to be of service to humanity.

I believe that how Wilson's parents treated him, coupled with the religious setting of his early life, formed the inner world that made Wilson into someone who was obsessed with being somebody. This nobody would become a great somebody to whom the people would listen and whom he would greatly serve. This is what lay behind his compulsive political ambition to be a great statesman. Tragically, this blind ambition led the United States into the horrors of World War I, a war in which 116, 708 American soldiers alone were slaughtered. And for what? Overseas markets for our surplus production. Tragically, for Wilson too. His proposed League of Nations was DOA (dead on arrival) in France. In September of 1919, against doctor's orders, Wilson began a desperate nationwide tour to garner support for the Treaty of Versailles and the eviscerated League of Nations. In October he suffered a severe stroke that incapacitated him for the remaining five years of his life. A tragic end for a man driven to be a somebody.

The lead-up to the U.S. entry into World War I is instructive again of the lengths to which presidents and the rich and powerful, elite ruling class will go to further their goals. The president's goal was to get the United States into the war on the Allies' side and to be the main figure in crafting the peace under a

League of Nations. The goal of the elite ruling class was to further the gains made in the Spanish-American War to make the United States into an imperialistic nation by getting the country into World War I. Their aim was not territory but markets.

Wilson knew that the war was one that was of no vital matter to the American people. He had to make every appearance of being neutral, while pursuing a course that would cause Germany to give the United States justification for entering the war. That course revolved around Germany's submarine warfare. The British had blockaded Germany in order to starve every man, woman and child into submission—as it was aptly put by Winston Churchill. Germany, in turn, said it would sink ships bound for Allied ports. Wilson told Germany that Americans had the right to travel unharmed, even on ships bearing arms and bound for England. Various ships were sunk on which were Americans and arms, including the *Lusitania*, but Wilson could not parlay that into getting the United States into the war.

It had been an uphill battle, even after the sinking of the *Lusitania* in May of 1915, for the rich and powerful, elite ruling class to mobilize the people to support going to war. That class included the Republican Party leaders, Wall Street capitalists, the military and President Wilson. This was a war that could mean only grief for hundreds of thousands of American families. This was a war calculated to advance the various agendas of the rich and powerful, elite ruling class and particularly that of President Wilson.

The usual ploys of leaders bent on having their war were employed to "impel the people to greatness." The first of these was to convince the people that the nation's defenses were in a deplorable state. In the interest of national defense, a "preparedness movement" was begun. It really had nothing to do with preparedness, but everything to do with molding public opinion. Preparedness in the avowed interest of peace was manipulated into a crazed crusade to incite a frenzied war fever. Germany was to be feared and hated. The national honor was at stake. Those opposed to preparedness were dupes, cowards, traitors and should be silenced. An invasion was imminent. One Republican, James Beck, a former Assistant Attorney General and an exponent of war, said that it would take Germany exactly 16 days to land exactly 387,000 men on our shores. There were wild claims about a Germany bent on world domination, German surprise attacks and amphibious landing parties. The U.S. Navy, one of the larger of the great powers, staged a war game from Maine all the way to Florida. The "invaders" beat the "defenders." "Staged," I think so. "Moral preparedness" of the people was also pursued. This meant universal military training, patriotic education and a zealous patriotism. Teddy Roosevelt said that all of this was to get the people into a proper framework for war.

The outspoken exponents of war knew that their position was not supportable in a fair debate. Hence, what they sought was to vilify those who advocated genuine neutrality. "Those who are not for preparedness will be responsible when we are invaded." They said that certain hyphenated Americans were a menace. The tone of the country became ugly and repressive. Wilson said that, "Unfortunately, voices have been raised in America which spoke alien sympathies." "Rebuke" and drown them out "in the deep unison of a common, unhesitating national feeling." In December of 1915, Wilson asked Congress to make criticism of his foreign policy a criminal act. Congress refused. Wilson and the elite ruling class did everything they could to slander and discredit those who stood up for genuine neutrality.

Lies. Lies as a ploy. In a speech of October 1916, Wilson lied. "I think the whole Nation is convinced that we ought to be prepared, not for war, but for defense, and very adequately prepared." The lie was his implying that he was not for war when, in reality, he was doing everything he could to get the United States into the war. "Everything" included Americans traveling on armed merchant ships being killed when German submarines sunk those ships. In 1916, a nonbonding resolution was being considered in a House committee that called upon the president to warn Americans not to travel on such ships, and if they did, it was at their own peril. The public supported it. Wilson was successful in keeping it bottled up in committee so that it never came to a vote. In the election of 1916, Wilson lied when he attacked his opponent Charles Hughes for being for war. Again, Wilson was implying that he was for peace. Walter Karp, in his book *The Politics of War*, quotes an anti-preparedness writer in 1916 as follows: "'Perhaps never before were more lies told, more truth suppressed, more insincerity shown' than in the frantic agitation for war carried on under the aegis of 'preparedness.'"

Then, early in 1917, a German message to Mexico was intercepted and decoded. It was an offer to Mexico to enter the war with Germany against the United States when it declared war against Germany. In return, Germany would aid Mexico in getting back Texas, New Mexico and Arizona from the United States. That was all Wilson needed to justify entering the war.

Franklin Roosevelt: 1933-1945

Roosevelt was no different than Presidents Polk, McKinley and Wilson before him in misleading the public about going to war. According to Thomas A. Bailey, an historian who was supportive of Roosevelt, Roosevelt lied to the American public about being neutral before December 7, 1941, when we were not. Radhabinol Pal, one of the judges in the Tokyo War Crimes Trial, pointed out that the U.S. embargoes on scrap iron and oil against Japan were, in effect, provocations for Japan to go to war against us.

Even before World War II was over, the military-industrial-political complex was planning how to make U.S. economic power dominate the world and to back it up with military power. This wartime partnership continued after the war and placed the United States on a permanent wartime economy.

Our leaders knew that England would be so weakened after the war that the United States could fill the ensuing power vacuum both economically and militarily. Our leaders felt it was necessary to do so in our national self-interest because our country would need increasingly bigger overseas markets to absorb our surpluses. They also feared that without the continuation of a wartime economy a new depression would occur. So much for altruism. Even the Marshall Plan—which the American public paid for—had behind it the re-creation of European markets for the private gain of American corporations.

Harry Truman: 1945-1953

The February 2004 issue of *Harper's Magazine* included an article entitled "The Oil We Eat" by Richard Manning. In it, Manning quotes George Kennan, the former head of a State Department planning committee, who explained in a 1948 national security memo how the United States should deal with its "newfound role as the dominant force on earth."

> We have about 50 percent of the world's wealth but only 6.3 percent of its population. In this situation, we cannot fail to be the object of envy and resentment. Our real task in the coming period is to devise a pattern of relationships which will permit us to maintain this position of disparity without positive detriment to our national security. To do so, we will have to dispense with all sentimentality and day-dreaming; and our attention will have to be concentrated everywhere on our immediate national objectives. We need not deceive ourselves that we can afford today the luxury of altruism and world-benefaction. The day is not far off when we are going to have to deal in straight power concepts.

During the depression of the 1930s, part of the answer to the question of how to stimulate the economy was the Works Progress Administration (WPA). Thousands of people were put to work at taxpayer expense to build and rebuild the infrastructure of the country. The billions of tax dollars that were paid to corporations during World War II brought the United States out of that depression. But by 1948, when consumer demand began to fall off, there was concern that the country might slide back into another 1930s' kind of depression. U.S. leaders knew that the way to save capitalism, the economy and the country was to continue taxpayer-funded stimulation of the economy. But should the stimulation take the form of social spending—as was done in the 1930s—or the form of military spending—as was done during World War II?

Noam Chomsky in *Understanding Power*, pages 73-76, says that the nation's leaders decided it had to be military spending and for "straight power reasons." On top of that, Chomsky continues, the public is to be kept from knowing that it is all about power. He quotes Stuart Symington, the first Secretary of the Air Force in 1948, as follows: "The word to use is not 'subsidy,' the word to use is 'security.'" So, if the foreign policy of the United States is to be guided by "straight power concepts" (George Kennan), and if the economy is to be kept profitable through military spending and the public is to be kept in the dark about it all, then the government must, as Chomsky says, "maintain a pretense of constant security threats— . . . whatever's around." For more than sixty years now this has been the plan of the rich and powerful, elite ruling class, Iraq being the latest nonexistent threat to the national security of the United States.

Besides power and subsidies to big business to keep the economy from another depression, there is another reason why military spending was and is the choice of how to stimulate the economy. If the choice had been social spending rather than arms, the people would insist on having a say in how the money was spent. That's a "no no" for the rich and powerful, elite ruling class because, even back to the Founding Fathers, the people are to have as little to do with government as possible. Concessions will be made, but only when sufficient public pressure is brought to bear on the ruling class.

Dwight Eisenhower: 1953-1961

In August of 1941, Roosevelt and Churchill devised the Atlantic Charter, which was a blueprint for the postwar world. In it they said that their countries respected "the right of all peoples to choose the form of government under which they will live." It was the right of nations to self-determination. While any number of U.S. presidents before and after have violated that principle, I mention one here because of what the CIA in the 1950s first called "blowback." Blowback refers to unintended consequences of covert operations that make matters worse in the long run.

In 1953 the Iranian government nationalized the oil industry. The CIA backed a coup to oust Mossadegh, the Prime Minister of Iran, which enabled the Shah to regain the throne. The blowback came during Carter's presidency when a revolution brought the Ayatollah Khomeni to power and the U.S. embassy staff held hostage for over a year. Overall, the right of nations to self-determination has meant for the United States that the U.S. will support any regime, no matter how brutal, as long as it is not anti-America.

Lyndon Johnson: 1963-1969

What I point out here is part of the "how" in carrying out a policy of domination and imperialism. At the time, Robert McNamara was Secretary of Defense and

McGeorge Bundy was Special Assistant to the President for National Security Affairs. A 1965 declassified document of an exchange between them explains how such a policy is carried out. The place of the military in a country is to overthrow a civilian government if it is not furthering the welfare of the country. That welfare is the welfare of U.S. corporations. What the United States does then is to aid the country's military and to destabilize the civilian government in order to overthrow it.

Vietnam. Johnson lied to the American public in August of 1964. He claimed that North Vietnamese torpedo boats had attacked two U.S. destroyers in international waters. It was a lie. Johnson used the lie to push through Congress the Tonkin Resolution that gave him the power to initiate war without a formal declaration of war by Congress. The bombing of North Vietnam began.

Secretly, Johnson had already begun planning for all-out war but, in that election year, he appeared to take a reasonable course. Meanwhile Goldwater was talking about using nuclear weapons. After the election, in 1965 Johnson sent 200,000, troops to Vietnam. In 1966, another 200,000. By 1968, there were 500,000.

Despite the right of the Vietnamese people to self-determination, the United States intervened in a hopeless war of our making to stop that from happening. Why? Because of the domino theory. If one southeast Asian nation turned Communist, they all would. Then, both our military and economic interests would be jeopardized. As usual, power and greed ruled the day.

The U.S. forces suffered 58,000 dead and 303,000 wounded. Not only Vietnam, but Cambodia and Laos were devastated. The United States used chemical warfare. Agent Orange denuded the landscape and caused birth defects for decades. Millions died as a consequence of the U.S. quest for world domination.

Ronald Reagan: 1981-1989

What was new about Reagan's policies of world domination and economic imperialism was that he had to do things illegally because Congress had cut off funding for overt and covert military assistance and interventions. Instead of the United States itself carrying on terrorist actions, the United States hired terrorist nations to carry out the missions. This was brought out in the Oliver North trial. A government-produced summary of what was going on described a "massive international terrorist network run by the United States." (See *Understanding Power* by Noam Chomsky, pp. 4-6.) In my view, this represents a big jump in the level of primal pain, necessitating an even greater obsession with a lust for power.

George W. Bush: 2001-____

The U.S. role in the April 11, 2002, coup in Venezuela evidences that the United States will not tolerate a country following an independent path. This is especially true if that path favors human rights over property rights, and even more true if that country is a major supplier of oil to the United States. Attaches of the U.S. military had been in touch with members of the Venezuelan military by June of 2001 to examine the possibility of a coup. The CIA organized the coup. Our military was stationed at the Venezuela-Colombia border in case there were problems. President Chavez had doubled the royalties charged to foreign oil companies. The Bush administration quickly endorsed the coup leader, Pedro Carmona, a wealthy businessman and a former business associate of George Bush, Sr. Massive public protests forced Carmona to step down two days later.

The foregoing on Venezuela is an example of how U.S. economic imperialism is backed up by the military. Arundhati Roy, author of the six-million-copy best-seller *The God of Small Things*, spoke in Santa Fe, New Mexico, on September 18, 2002. Her subject was "Globalization and Terrorism." With regard to economic imperialism, she quotes from Thomas Friedman's book *The Lexus and the Olive Tree*. "'The hidden hand of the market will never work without the hidden fist. McDonald's cannot flourish without McDonnell-Douglas . . . and the hidden fist that keeps the world safe for Silicon Valley's technologies to flourish is called the U.S. Army, Air Force, Navy and Marine Corps.'" The United States packages its many military interventions in high-sounding motives as being in the defense of democracy or human rights or freedom. Somehow, all these interventions result in more markets for the United States. Usually, they aid a military and a rich and powerful, elite ruling class who are notorious for their dismal record on democracy or human rights or freedom.

An article in the October 2002 issue of *Harper's Magazine* by David Armstrong entitled "Dick Cheney's Song of America" outlines the current shape of U.S. intentions for world domination. Armstrong is an investigative reporter for the National Security News Service. He says that these current intentions began to be formulated in 1989 as it became apparent that the U.S.S.R. was about to collapse.

The chief architects of the plan for how the United States would dominate the world as the sole superpower were Dick Cheney, Secretary of Defense; Paul Wolfowitz, Undersecretary of Defense; and Colin Powell, Chairman of the Joint Chiefs of Staff. On August 2, 1990, President George Bush Sr. unveiled the new plan. Basically, it meant having fewer troops in more bases around the world in order to counter any "regional contingencies" and to be able to dispatch troops on a moment's notice to any "corner of the globe." That day Iraq invaded Kuwait. (George Bush Sr. told the American people that we must retaliate in order to "preserve the American way of life." In this case, the appeal to jingoistic patriotism was to crush the ambitions of a regional power, ambitions the United States was not going to tolerate anywhere if it could help it.)

The name given to the plan for domination was "Defense Planning Guidance" (DPG), and it underwent revisions up through the last days of the Bush Sr.

administration. During Clinton's administration, the focus was more on economic rather than on military imperialism. However, Clinton showed he was willing to use the U.S. military in Somalia, Haiti and Bosnia.

In July of 2002, the latest revision of the Defense Planning Guidance (DPG) was released to the press, with Donald Rumsfeld as the author. It is the vision as well, however, of Cheney, Wolfowitz and Powell. Armstrong says that

> The Plan is for the United States to rule the world. The overt theme is unilateralism, but it is ultimately a story of domination. It calls for the United States to maintain its overwhelming military superiority and prevent new rivals from rising up to challenge it on the world stage. It calls for domination over friends and enemies alike. It says not that the United States must be more powerful, but that it must be absolutely powerful.

Armstrong's article gives a complete history of the various updates of the DPG. One conclusion he comes to is that a policy of domination is likely to "generate backlash." Those threatened with "preemption may themselves launch preemptory strikes." Those "dominated may object and find means to strike back." Such a policy he says "may, paradoxically, result in greater factionalism and rivalry, precisely the things we seek to end."

Vital to the current administration's imperialistic ambitions is the establishment of military bases in Middle East oil-producing countries. Dating even as far back as the first Gulf War, Cheney, Wolfowitz and Powell wanted the United States to oust Saddam, occupy Iraq and establish bases there. They were disappointed when Bush Sr. would not do so. They were also disappointed when Clinton could not be convinced to do so. When Bush Jr. was elected, their time had come. Long before 9/11, they were planning for the invasion of Iraq. What they needed was a new Pearl Harbor, and they got it on September 11, 2001. Now, under the cloak of a war on terrorism, they implemented the imperialistic goals of the Defense Planning Guidance of July 2002. The preventive wars against Afghanistan and Iraq are conclusive evidence that the United States is carrying out its intentions of ruling the world unilaterally.

Before the administration of Bush Jr., the United States acted as other nations in that it acted rationally in its own best interests, without taking undue risks. Bush Jr. changed that rational approach into the apocalyptic idea that the United States is the force of Good, fighting against the forces of Evil. This goes way beyond even his claim that God is on our side. In an article in the June 24, 2003, issue of *Ha'aretz*, an Israeli newspaper, Bush is quoted as saying, "God told me to strike al Qaeda and I struck them, and then he instructed me to strike at Saddam, which I did . . ." This is covered in a July 7, 2003, issue of the *San Francisco Chronicle.*

It is not much of a stretch to say that Bush heads up a Christian jihad, just as much as Osama bin Laden heads up a Muslim jihad. The term "crusade" fits just as easily as does "jihad" into either worldview.

Regardless of whether a nation is constitutionally secular or theocratic, regardless of the particular religion dominant in any nation and regardless of the attributes of mercy, forgiveness and peace-giving of any God, it is still to that Deity's Warrior God attributes that prayer is made to bless the nation's self-justified wars of greed and domination. In the United States, regardless of the majority's pious platitudes about believing in the New Testament God who seeks to end suffering, when it comes to war, loyalties are to the Old Testament Yahweh: the Warrior God of the early Israelites. It wasn't the God and Father of Jesus Christ, the Prince of Peace, who told Bush to invade Afghanistan and Iraq; it was Yahweh the Warrior God.

The real reasons for the U.S. invasion of Iraq have to do with oil and the dollar. By becoming the dominant power in the Middle East, the United States gains control of most of the world's oil reserves. Saudi Arabia, with its great oil reserves, has long been business partners with the Bush family.

The dollar as a reason for the invasion has received very little attention. Yet it might be the more important reason. In 1971, President Nixon took the United States off the gold standard, and from then on the dollar has been the dominant world currency. Now, because of the United States' huge trade deficit, its budget deficits and its huge national indebtedness, the dollar is estimated to be as much as 40 percent overvalued. This makes the dollar vulnerable, as well as it does U.S. economic power generally.

If the United States continues its unilateral course, it is possible that the European Union, Russia and China might band together to challenge the dollar. If so, the same kind of adjustments the World Bank has forced upon Third World countries might happen to the United States, in which case, domestic spending might have to be cut drastically, and the people would have to make some very painful adjustments.

In 2000, Iraq began selling what oil it was allowed to sell for Euros. That put pressure on the U.S. dollar. Other countries, including Iran, considered doing the same. Since the invasion, the United States has returned Iraq to selling its oil for dollars. The reason the people hear very little of this is because the administration doesn't want the people to be aware of its imperialism nor of the danger to the economy that its borrow-and-spend policies have caused.

Earlier I discussed the real reasons why the United States invaded Iraq. In the next section, I list a dozen-or-so statements made by the President, the Vice President, the Secretary of State and the Secretary of Defense to convince the American public that Saddam Hussein had weapons of mass destruction. Without exception, every statement made by our leaders, either before or after the war, regarding Iraq's alleged weapons of mass destruction or connections with al Qaeda has proven to be wrong. A further administration intent was to make a connection between Saddam Hussein and al Qaeda, thus trading upon the fear of follow-up terrorist acts to September 11, 2001. All of it put together was to persuade the public that for reasons of national security the United States must make a preemptive strike now before it is too late. (I use the word "preemptive" here rather than the word "preventive" because of the distinction made between them by international law. A preemptive war is one that is begun in the face of an obvious imminent threat. An obvious imminent threat would be the mobilization of military forces. Such a preemptive war is justified. A preventive war is an aggressive war, regardless of claims that it has been launched in self-defense. The Bush administration lied in order to make everyone believe that Iraq posed an obvious, imminent threat.)

A brief summary of the history of U.N. inspections regarding Iraq's weapons of mass destruction and the status of the inspections and WMDs as of 2003 provides the necessary background for judging the truthfulness of the statements made by the administration before the war began in March of 2003. The main source for this summary is a speech given by Scott Ritter in Santa Fe, New Mexico, on February 1, 2004. Ritter is a former Marine intelligence officer, a veteran of the first Gulf war and served as a U.N. weapons inspector for seven years. He was in charge of intelligence.

Ritter explained that the original inspection teams were composed of international scientists. Simply put, Iraq was to declare what WMDs it had, and then the inspectors would verify that all the weapons had been declared and destroy them. Iraq consistently lied and hid the weapons. So, intelligence officers were assigned to ferret out the hidden weapons. They followed paper trails. They became "forensic archeologists." They checked with Germany, which had provided machines and tools. They did chemical analyses of paint, soil and air. They were successful in their efforts. By 1998, when the inspection teams were withdrawn from Iraq, Ritter estimates that 90-95 percent of all prohibited weapons and the means to produce them had been destroyed. There was no evidence that the remaining 5-10 percent that were unaccounted for had been retained by Iraq. Ritter says that he met with U.S., British, French and Israeli intelligence and "no one said Iraq had weapons of mass destruction in 1998, not a single country."

A secondary source for this summary was the TV program *Frontline*, which aired a BBC program on January 22, 2004, entitled "Chasing Saddam's Weapons." The program drew attention to the United Nations' sending inspectors back to Iraq in the fall of 2002. Hans Blix was Executive Chairman of the team. The team worked into 2003, but found no weapons of mass destruction. So, from 1998 right up through just before the war began in March of 2003, no weapons were to be found, and there were no facilities to produce them. Iraq had no capability to produce WMDs.

Because of the lies Powell told later at the United Nations on February 5, 2003, I include a quote here that was part of the *Frontline* program. On February 24, 2001, Powell said, "He [Saddam] has not developed any significant capability with regard to WMDs. He is unable to project conventional power against his neighbors." Powell spoke the truth, but that was before the administration needed trumped-up charges of WMDs to support its decision to make war on Iraq, regardless.

Also, with regard to what Powell said and did at the United Nations in February of 2003, I include here what Ritter had to say about the kind of anthrax Iraq developed. Iraq, he said, produced only "liquid bulk agent." What did Powell do? He held up a vial of white powder and said that if Iraq had this white powder form that a few teaspoons spread out over a city could kill thousands. So, what was in that vial? Perhaps it was dry, powdered anthrax. Ritter says that the only country to produce that kind of anthrax was the United States!

The preponderance of evidence shows that at no time after 1998 did Iraq have any WMDs or the means to produce them. This was true when the administration began its propaganda blitz in August of 2002. It was true in October of 2002 when the CIA presented its National Intelligence Estimate, regardless of what was contained in that report. It was true on March 19, 2003, when preventive war was unleashed on Iraq over nonexistent WMDs. And it remains true to this day in March 2010.

The claims made about WMDs before the war but after October 2002 were supposedly based on the National Intelligence Estimate (NIE) provided by the CIA in October of 2002. In a speech at Georgetown University on February 5, 2004, CIA Director George Tenet assessed that NIE. He said that their analysts differed on the status of Iraq's programs for missiles, nuclear weapons and chemical and biological weapons. He said that the analysts' debates were spelled out in the NIE. He said that the NIE never claimed that Iraq posed an immediate or imminent threat to the United States. So what are we to make of the carefully qualified statements in the NIE and the unqualified charges made by administration officials that Iraq had weapons of mass destruction?

I believe, first of all, that the administration put tremendous pressure on the CIA to make the analysts' views coincide with the case the administration was already placing before the American people. That case was justification for a war on Iraq that had already been decided upon months before. On August 29, 2002, Bush signed the executive order for Operation Iraqi Freedom. This was months before Bush went to Congress for authorization for war against Iraq. I believe that Vice President Cheney did go to the CIA to put pressure on the CIA to produce an NIE favorable to the administration's aims. And secondly, I believe that administration officials deliberately manufactured a threat to the United

States by Iraq in order to justify what they were going to do anyway: invade Iraq. This manufacturing of an imminent threat constituted lying to the public. The administration knew full well that the NIE of October 2002 did not indicate an imminent threat. And after the war, all of the claims of having found WMDs were outright lies.

In Project Censored's recently published *Censored 2005*, there is an update of their lead story in *Censored 2004*: "The Neoconservative Plan for Global Dominance." The update is on pages 135-139, and it lists the sources behind the update. The update was written by Christopher Robin Cox. The update makes clear that the administration created secret organizations to develop evidence of Iraq's connection to 9/11 and of its WMDs. These organizations were separate from the CIA and the weapons inspectors. Two of these were the Office of Special Plans and the Counter-Terrorism Evaluation Group. They were organized by Under Secretary of Defense Douglas Feith and Donald Rumsfeld. According to Cox, these organizations chose the "worst-case scenarios" due to a lack of "actionable" evidence.

The Pentagon's Defense Policy Board (DPB Group), chaired by Richard Perle, worked closely with the Office of Special Plans. The DPB Group met with Ahmed Chalabi, head of the Iraqi National Congress (INC). Chalabi and the INC fed "misleading intelligence" to Bush. (Chalabi had his own agenda in that he wanted the United States to invade Iraq and to install him as head of an interim government.)

When the war was over, the Office of Special Plans and the Counter-Terrorism Evaluation Group quickly disappeared. Cox says that little mention of them has been made in the mainstream media.

Publicly, the administration and David Kay, the first head of the U.S./Iraq Survey Group of inspectors, have laid the blame for "intelligence failure" on George Tenet, then head of the CIA. No on failure. Yes on fibs. But fibs with tragic consequences for democracy, for world peace, but most of all for those whose lives have been lost and continue to be lost in the lost cause of global dominance.

One specific lie of the President deserves attention here because of the ongoing furor over whether or not what he said was the truth. The statement was made in his State of the Union address on January 28, 2003. In it, Bush said, "The British government has learned that Saddam Hussein recently sought significant quantities of uranium from Africa." Well, the British report didn't say "recently." It said that Iraq tried to buy uranium from Niger in 1999. That was four years before Bush's address to the nation in January of 2003. It appears that Iraq did make some inquiries about purchasing uranium in 1999, but that was hardly a recent event. Nor were those inquiries of any danger to the United States. France heads an international consortium that controls the uranium mines in Niger.

The government of Niger could not have sold any of that uranium to Iraq, even if it wanted to. The citing of the British report was a lie because it was designed to make the people believe as true something Bush knew to be untrue—that Iraq was an imminent threat to the United States. It was a lie because, as of the date of Bush's speech, the CIA believed the British report was not true and had so informed Bush's speech writers as early as October of 2002.

In the *New York Times* article by David Sanger and James Risen dated July 12, 2003, George Tenet, Director of the CIA, accepted blame for the "slip-up" in letting this claim be included in Bush's address. Tenet was the designated fall guy.

In that same article, the authors pointed out that according to administration officials who were involved with drafting a speech Bush would give on October 7, 2002, they removed the African uranium claim from the speech "at the CIA's behest." So four months before the State of the Union address, the White House knew the claim was questionable. Yet it was still included in the address. All the backtracking by administration personnel to place the blame on Tenet was nothing more than a blatant cover-up for a bald-faced lie.

The PBS program *NOW* of October 29, 2004, further rounds out what was known about Iraq's alleged pursuit of uranium from Niger prior to Bush's State of the Union address. In October of 2002, George Tenet made one phone call and sent two memos to the National Security team at the White House. In them he said, ". . . the evidence is weak . . ." "The Africa story is overblown." In addition, *NOW* stated that in the NIE of October 2002, State Department experts said, "The claims of Iraqi pursuit of . . . uranium in Africa are . . . highly dubious." And finally, *NOW* quotes from a Senate Intelligence Committee report in 2004. The CIA had investigated as far back as 2001 and concluded that "[t]here is no corroboration . . . that such an agreement [to buy uranium from Africa] was reached or that uranium was transferred."

An article written by Bob Drogin and Greg Miller for the *Los Angeles Times* and appearing in *The Bulletin* [Bend, OR] on October 7, 2004, states what might be the last word on this matter. Drogin and Miller are reporting on Charles Duelfer's testimony before the Senate Armed Services Committee on October 6, 2004. Duelfer is David Kay's replacement as head of the Iraq Survey group. The following is a quote from the article:

> . . . Duelfer specifically refuted many of the Bush administration's most dramatic claims before the war, basing his findings in part on extensive information gleaned directly from interrogations of Saddam and his top aides.
>
> Duelfer said, for example, that there was no evidence that Saddam sought to import uranium from Africa, as Bush claimed in his 2003 State of the Union speech.

Administration Lies Regarding Iraq's Weapons of Mass Destruction (WMDs)

I am piling the following lies justifying the war on Iraq one upon the other to show the extent to which President George W. Bush, Jr., Vice President Dick Cheney, National Security Advisor Condoleezza Rice, Secretary of State Colin Powell and Secretary of Defense Donald Rumsfeld are driven by an advanced 3rd line level of Stage III unconscious self-awareness. They have had to deny so many needs that insatiable wants have turned into an insatiable greed. They have experienced so much helplessness in getting their infantile and childhood needs met that a compulsion for power to compensate for that helplessness has turned into a lust for power. The spontaneous anger that arose in them to strike out against the pain of their unmet needs has turned into a calculated willingness to unleash pent-up "shock and awe" violence in a futile attempt to satisfy their greed and cover up their pain.

Cheney: August 2002

"Many of us are convinced that Saddam Hussein will acquire nuclear weapons fairly soon." Cheney took that information from an NIE report, but he left out the crucial words that only "if left unchecked" could Saddam acquire nuclear weapons. It was clear in the NIE that Saddam was not being left unchecked.

"Simply stated, there is no doubt that Saddam Hussein has weapons of mass destruction. There is no doubt he is amassing them to use against our friends, against our allies and against us." According to Scott Ritter, Cheney also lied in August of 2002 when he claimed that Hussein Kamel, Saddam's son-in-law—who defected in August, 1995, said that Iraq was hiding WMDs. Ritter had spoken with both U.S. and British intelligence about Kamel's debriefing. They said that Kamel said that all the weapons had been destroyed.

Bush: September 7, 2002

"I would remind you that when the inspectors first went into Iraq and were denied, finally denied access, a report came out of the atomic—the IAEA—that they were six months away from developing a [nuclear] weapon." The IAEA is the International Atomic Energy Agency, and it did not issue any such report.

Bush: September 12, 2002, at the United Nations

"Saddam Hussein's regime is a grave and gathering danger." Bush claimed that aluminum tubes, which U.S. energy experts determined could not be used for enriching uranium, were going to be used to make a nuclear weapon within a year.

Bush: September 26, 2002

"The danger to our country is grave. The danger to our country is growing. The Iraqi regime possesses biological and chemical weapons."

Rumsfeld: October 3, 2002

"The U.S. knows that Iraq has weapons of mass destruction."

Bush: October 7, 2002

Iraq "possesses and produces chemical and biological weapons. It is seeking nuclear weapons." "Satellite photographs reveal that Iraq is rebuilding facilities at sites that have been part of [Saddam Hussein's] nuclear program in the past."

"Iraq has attempted to purchase aluminum tubes and other equipment needed for gas centrifuges which are used to enrich uranium for nuclear weapons."

"Facing clear evidence of peril, we cannot wait for the final proof, the smoking gun that could come in the form of a mushroom cloud."

Condoleezza Rice: October 8, 2002

"Our first sign might be a mushroom cloud."

Victoria Clarke: October 9, 2002, spokesperson for the Pentagon

"Our first sign might be a mushroom cloud."

On October 10 and 11, 2002, the U.S. Congress voted to give its authority to declare war over to President Bush.

Rumsfeld: January 2003

Saddam Hussein "has an active program to acquire and develop nuclear weapons."

Rumsfeld: January 7, 2003

"There's no doubt in my mind that they currently have chemical and biological weapons."

Ari Fleischer, White House Spokesman: January 9, 2003

"We know for a fact that there are weapons there." [He was referring to weapons of mass destruction.]

Bush: State of the Union Address, January 2003

"The British government has learned that Saddam Hussein recently sought significant quantities of uranium from Africa."

Iraq has "materials to produce as much as 500 tons of mustard and VX nerve agent."

Iraq has "30,000 munitions capable of delivering chemical agents."

"Our intelligence sources tell us that [Saddam] has attempted to purchase high strength aluminum tubes suitable for nuclear weapons production."

These are four of eight "facts" Bush used in his speech to make the case for preemptive war against Iraq. In *Worse Than Watergate* by John Dean, pages 199-205, Dean cites what is in the public record to discredit these facts. His conclusion was that "it is apparent that Bush provided conspicuously distorted, deceptive, and false information." I call that lying. Dean was counsel to President Nixon. He wrote *Blind Ambition*, a best-seller. Currently, he writes and lectures full-time.

With regard to the aluminum tube claim in Bush's address, Dean made the following case for the claim to be false. Within the NIE of October 2002, there was disagreement as to whether the tubes were for uranium enrichment or for conventional weapons. By January 20, 2003, the International Atomic Energy Agency (IAEA) had concluded that, as Iraq had claimed, "[t]he tubes had nothing to do with nuclear weapons; rather, they were part of a conventional rocket program." The IAEA indicated that while it was "'possible to modify such tubes for the manufacture of centrifuges, they are not directly suitable for such use.'" Dean concludes that Bush's claim that the tubes were suitable for nuclear weapons production was false.

The aforementioned *NOW* program of October 29, 2004, sheds additional light on how the administration misrepresented the intelligence on the subject. The *New York Times* quoted government officials who said, "'. . . it was the intelligence agencies' unanimous view [that the tubes] are used to make centrifuges . . . that will enrich uranium to make nuclear weapons . . . the best technical experts and nuclear scientists supported [that] assessment.'" *NOW* quoted an Associated Press source that said that Cheney claimed it was "'. . . irrefutable evidence . . . [that Saddam] . . . once again set up and reconstituted his programs.'" *NOW* also quoted Rice on CNN that the tubes are "'. . . only really suited for nuclear weapons programs.'"

Greg Thielmann spent twenty-five years in the Foreign Service. He retired in 2002. He was a member of the State Department's Bureau of Intelligence and Research. According to Bill Moyers in the PBS *NOW* program of October 29, 2004, "The work of Thielmann's office analyzing the Iraqi threat would later be singled out by a key oversight committee of Congress for being more accurate than that of the CIA or any other intelligence agency." Thielmann's office's report in the NIE of October 2002 said that, "The activities we have detected do not . . . add up to a compelling case . . . [that Iraq is pursuing] an integrated comprehensive approach to acquire nuclear weapons." In that *NOW* program, Thielmann said that the people of America were misled by how senior officials used the intelligence information.

In the *NOW* program, Thielmann was astounded that Bush would make such a claim because Thielmann witnessed an extended debate within the intelligence community about what the tubes could be used for. He said it became more and more obvious that the tubes were suitable only for conventional weapons.

NOW noted that the U.S. Department of Energy disputed the White House position.

In addition to what Dean said about the NIE of October 2002, *NOW* further quoted the NIE that it found "'. . . unpersuasive that the arguments . . . that [the tubes] are intended for that purpose, meaning nuclear weapons . . . the tubes are not intended for use in Iraq's nuclear weapons program.'"

On March 7, 2003, the IAEA made its report to the Security Council of the United Nations. In addition to its earlier conclusion that the tubes in question were for conventional weapons, it also concluded that, "There is no indication that Iraq has attempted to import aluminum tubes for use in centrifuges.'" So ends that segment of the *NOW* program. So, weeks before the United States invaded Iraq on the pretext that it had reconstituted a nuclear weapons program and was an imminent threat to the United States, the evidence clearly indicated that Iraq was not a "grave and gathering danger" (Bush: September 12, 2002, at the United Nations).

Powell: February 5, 2003, at the United Nations

"Our conservative estimate is that Iraq today has a stockpile of between 100 and 500 tons of chemical-weapons agent."

"There can be no doubt Saddam Hussein has biological weapons and the capability to rapidly produce more, many more. And he has the ability to disperse these lethal poisons and diseases in ways that can cause massive death and destruction."

These are but two of some fifteen "facts" of Saddam's WMDs that Powell listed in his speech. Everyone of Powell's claims have been found to be without basis. See *Worse Than Watergate* by John Dean, pages 143-145, for the complete list and why these claims were lies.

The NIE of October 2002 said that Iraq had 100 metric tons of chemical agents. This was a belief by the CIA because they could not independently verify the existence of the chemical agents. Hans Blix's U.N. inspectors went back into Iraq in the fall of 2002 and were there until early in 2003. They found no stockpiles of chemical or biological weapons. Therefore, the claim in the NIE of October 2002 was most likely in error. Yet, Powell, at the United Nations on February 5, 2003, continued to claim that Iraq not only had 100 tons of chemical weapons agent but perhaps as much as 500 tons. At the best, Powell's claims were a gross exaggeration of the estimate and at the worst were lies because of Blix's report.

Bush: February 8, 2003

"We have sources that tell us that Saddam Hussein recently authorized Iraqi field commanders to use chemical weapons—the very weapons the dictator tells us he didn't have."

Bush: March 1, 2003

In a letter to Congressional leaders, Bush linked the invasion of Iraq to September 11, 2001. In the fall of 2003, Bush admitted, "We've had no evidence that Saddam Hussein was involved in September the 11th."

Cheney: March 16, 2003, on Meet The Press

"We believe he [Saddam Hussein] has in fact reconstituted nuclear weapons."

Bush: March 17, 2003

"Intelligence gathered by this and other governments leaves us no doubt that the Iraq regime continues to possess and conceal some of the most lethal weapons ever devised . . . the terrorists could fulfill their stated ambitions and kill thousands or hundreds of thousands of innocent people in our country or any other."

The preventive, not preemptive, war against Iraq began on March 19, 2003.

Rumsfeld: March 30, 2003

"We know where they are [WMDs]. They're in the area around Tikrit and Baghdad and east, west, south and north somewhat."

Bush: In a pre-war press conference, quoted in The Bulletin [Bend, OR] *on May 25, 2003*

Referring to chemical weapon agents, Bush said that "in some cases these materials have been moved to different locations every 12 to 24 hours or placed in vehicles that are in residential neighborhoods."

Bush: May 31, 2003, on Polish television

"We've found the weapons of mass destruction. You know, we found biological laboratories . . . And we'll find more weapons as time goes on. But for those who say we haven't found the banned manufacturing devices or banned weapons, they're wrong. We found them."

Cheney: September 14, 2003, on Meet The Press

When confronted with what he said on *Meet The Press* on March 16, 2003, Cheney said, "Yeah, I did misspeak . . . We never had any evidence that he had acquired a nuclear weapon." Misspeak or lie. Tim Russert's own bias wouldn't allow him to accuse Cheney of lying.

Ronald Kessler is a best-selling author of a dozen-or-so books on the Washington scene. In 2003 he wrote *The CIA at War* and updated it in 2004.

Kessler blunts the gross misrepresentations of the administration about WMDs. Even though the updated edition could have corrected erroneous "facts," it did not. One claim that went uncorrected was that the U.N. inspectors were thrown out of Iraq by Saddam in 1998. In fact, they were withdrawn by the United Nations when it became known that there were U.S. spies among the inspectors and Saddam refused the inspectors access to some of his palaces. Another claim that could have been corrected, but wasn't, concerned the mobile trailers that were found after the war was officially over. The erroneous claim was that they could only be used for the production of biological weapons. In his speech on February 5, 2004, at Georgetown University, George Tenet said that there was no consensus on whether the trailers were used for biological weapons or for producing hydrogen for artillery balloons. Subsequent testing showed no residue of biological agents.

Kessler indicates that G. W. Bush was interested not only in reading the President's Daily Brief, which is "a compilation of intelligence reports prepared overnight by the CIA," he wanted a "face-to-face" daily meeting with CIA Director George Tenet or with other CIA briefers. This makes nearly impossible any possible misunderstanding by Bush of the CIA's estimate of Iraq's WMDs. This makes the conclusion nearly inescapable that Bush, Cheney, Powell, Rumsfeld and Rice so grossly misrepresented what they were told by Tenet or other briefers on a daily basis that their statements constituted lies. Iraq had no tie-ins with al Qaeda. Iraq was not responsible for 9/11. And Iraq had no WMDs.

These five persons (Bush, Cheney, Powell, Rumsfeld and Rice) are the main spokespersons for the rich and powerful, elite ruling class. As to why they and their class felt it necessary to lie to the public about the reasons for going to war against Iraq, there are at least three: (1) they have a hidden agenda for world domination that they know would be repudiated if they acknowledged it. It would be exposed as being for the benefit of the rich and powerful, elite ruling class, not only in the United States but in Iraq as well. (2) As I pointed out about our Founding Fathers, this class feels that the people are not qualified, as they are, to make decisions for the common good. That good is defined as what is good for the rich and powerful, elite ruling class is good for everyone. (3) As I pointed out about Woodrow Wilson, the people have to be "impelled to greatness" for themselves and for the nation. The people, in the minds of this class, possess neither the virtue, nor the character, nor the principles to rule wisely in their own best interests.

Bush, Cheney, Powell, Rice and Rumsfeld are not to be condemned because of their greed, their power, their violence, nor of their lies. In my world, their behavior is accounted for by their primal pain controlling their every thought, their every emotion and their every act. They violated their oaths of office and should have been removed from office. An interim solution is to restore the balance of power between the executive and legislative branches of government. The people must see to it that this is done because, by and large, our legislators are part of the rich and powerful, elite ruling class and knowingly and unconstitutionally gave up the legislature's power to declare war over to the executive branch. The ultimate solution is one that will take many generations and that is to put foot on the primal path toward lesser unconsciousness. Whether full consciousness is possible, I don't know.

When the administration's stated reasons for going to war—WMDs and Iraq's tie-in with September 11, 2001—had been debunked as lies, the justification changed back to regime change: The United States has removed an evil dictator, and now the Iraqis can have a democratic government. This, too, is a cover-up for why the administration was going to invade Iraq, regardless, that there was no defensible reason for doing so.

The United States just doesn't remove dictators because they are "evil," we remove those who are weak AND who attempt to pursue a course independent of U.S. corporate interests. The record shows that we will not attack an "evil" dictator who is strong and who follows an independent course. It also shows that we will aid and abet any "evil" dictator who cooperates with U.S. corporate interests.

The next change in the administration's justification for the preemptive war was that Iraq had the possibility to resume production of WMDs at any time.

That is what Bush said on February 8, 2004, on *Meet The Press*. It now becomes clear what the strategy was in having Tenet, the head of the CIA, say what he said on February 5, 2004, at Georgetown University. Once, early in Tenet's speech assessing the NIE of 2002, he slid so fast over the words that Iraq did not pose an imminent threat that if one were not listening closely, one would have missed them. The balance of his speech was devoted to possible intentions, possible capabilities and possible new discoveries for WMDs. He counseled patience until all the facts were in. Patience is exactly what was counseled before the war by the United Nations, by U.S. allies and by other countries. So the real reasons for the war—oil, protection of the U.S. dollar and the reconstitution of Iraq as a corporate utopia—are still not mentioned.

Up to this date—the spring of 2010—no weapons of mass destruction have been found. The Bush administration lied that it had spared no effort to find WMDs; it knew there were none. The U.S. Iraq Survey Group had come up empty-handed, however. It had, because by 1998, Iraq's WMDs no longer existed.

Congressional committees were set up, ostensibly to discover the truth behind why the administration's claims about Iraq's WMDs were so wrong. The committees' reports said that there was an "intelligence failure." They placed the blame on the entire intelligence apparatus for overstating the status of Iraq's WMDs. My investigation shows that there was no "intelligence failure." What the CIA knew as of October 2002 of Iraq's WMDs was summed up in its National Intelligence Estimate. That report did not give unequivocal support to any information that suggested that Iraq had WMD programs in place, let alone claims that any WMDs actually existed. Therefore, I conclude that the real reason behind claiming that there was an "intelligence failure" was to justify the administration's unsupportable assertions that Iraq had WMDs and was ready to use them now.

On February 5, 2004, George Tenet, spoke at Georgetown University. His topic was to assess the CIA's National Intelligence Estimate of October 2002. I video-taped that speech in its entirety. I have reviewed that tape at least four times. I used the "pause" and "rewind" features of the VCR Remote as often as needed to listen again and again to specific portions of it and to make notes. I compared Tenet's assessment of the intelligence regarding the status of any programs for WMDs and for the existence of any WMDs with the administration's unequivocal claims that Iraq had biological, chemical and nuclear weapons of mass destruction. I came to the following conclusion. The administration not only grossly exaggerated the findings of the NIE, not only grossly misrepresented the NIE, it stated as fact that which the NIE said were only possibilities or probabilities or intentions. The discrepancy between the NIE of October 2002 and the claims of the administration is so blatant that the one inescapable conclusion is that the administration lied. It lied over and over again to convince the United Nations, the Congress and the American people that Saddam Hussein was such an imminent threat that it required the U.S. to initiate a preemptive war in the name of national security.

Throughout the time period in September and October of 2004 when the Iraq Survey Group under Charles Duelfer was reporting on its findings, the administration continued to assert that Iraq had the *capability* to make WMDs. As reported by Colum Lynch in *The Washington Post* on September 18, 2004, Bush said on the 17th, "But Saddam Hussein had the *capability* of making weapons . . ." Lynch also reported that on September 17 Colin Powell on Fox News Channel said that Saddam "clearly had the intention of having such weapons, he had the *capability* of having such weapons, . . ." Lynch also quoted a senior State Department official as follows: "Our view is . . . that no stockpile existed but there was a clear *capability* and clear intent." Bush and Powell were following the time-tested strategy of repeating "talking-point" lies as often as possible until they are accepted as fact.

In the aforementioned article by Drogin and Miller, they report on a "comprehensive CIA report" released on October 6, 2004. This was the report of the Iraq Survey Group. The CIA report said that ". . . the Iraqi regime had no formal, written strategy to revive the banned programs after sanctions, and no staff or infrastructure [*capability*] in place to do so, the investigators found." This is exactly what Scott Ritter said was the case in 1998 and which was confirmed by all subsequent investigations right up through October of 2004. (I italicized "*capability*" in all the quotes.)

On April 1, 2005, The (Bend, Oregon) Bulletin's lead article was one written by Walter Pincus and Peter Baker of The Washington Post. The article was commentary on a report issued March 31, 2005, by the Commission on the Intelligence Capabilities of the United States Regarding Weapons of Mass Destruction. Bush was pressured to appoint this Commission in February of 2004 because of the certainty of the administration's claims that Iraq had weapons of mass destruction and posed an imminent threat and because of the fact that no WMDs were found. The Commission's report was a whitewash for the many lies of the administration regarding Iraq's nonexistent WMDs. The report repeated once again the lie covering up all the other lies that it was faulty intelligence that the administration relied upon that Iraq had WMDs. The information I presented in this chapter more than adequately supports my claim that the report was a whitewash. There is no need to repeat that proof here.

What is worth adding is that Bush did not authorize the Commission to explore how Bush used the information he was given. If it had explored that subject, it would have been forced to report that regardless of what information Bush was given, he had already decided to invade Iraq on the pretext of nonexistent WMDs.

In addition, Pincus and Baker quote the Commission's report that ". . . it is hard to deny the conclusion that intelligence analysts worked in an environment that did not encourage skepticism about the conventional wisdom." That statement is in direct contradiction of George Tenet's statement of February 5, 2004, that the analysts' debates about WMDs were spelled out in the National Intelligence Estimate of October 2002 and provided to the administration. While this contradiction might be placed in the context of who lied and who is telling the truth, the preponderance of other evidence supports my view that the Commission—a creation of Bush—lied to cover up the lies of Bush, Cheney, Powell, Rumsfeld, and Rice.

In June 2005, new evidence came to light that Bush had decided by the summer of 2002 to invade Iraq. Ray McGovern served as an analyst for the CIA for twenty-seven years. He wrote an article that first appeared at TomPaine.com that I read in the June 1, 2005, issue of *The Progressive Populist.* McGovern makes reference to a leak to the London *Sunday Times* of a briefing on July 23, 2002, by Richard Dearlove, head of Britain's equivalent to the CIA, to Prime Minister Tony Blair and his national security advisors. The briefing covered consultations in Washington on Bush's plans to make war on Iraq. Dearlove tells Blair that Bush has decided to "remove Saddam Hussein by launching a war that is to be 'justified by the conjunction of terrorism and weapons of mass destruction.'" Dearlove adds that "'[t]he intelligence and facts are being fixed around the policy.'" According to McGovern, Blair does not "dispute the authenticity of the [briefing] document."

An article by syndicated columnist Molly Ivins in the June 15 issue of *The Progressive Populist* provides further details on the briefing. The date of the London Times' article was May 1, 2005. The memo of the briefing by Dearlove was written by Matthew Rycroft, a foreign policy aide. Ivins states that the memo "has been confirmed as legitimate."

Events concerning the "Downing Street memo" continued to unfold in Washington. On May 5, 122 Congressional Democrats sent a letter to The White House about whether or not there was an effort to "fix" the intelligence and facts around the policy for war. The White House refused to respond. On Thursday, June 16, 2005, several House Democrats urged Congress to conduct an official inquiry to determine whether Bush intentionally misled (lied to) Congress. Misleading Congress is an impeachable offense. Source: The Associated Press, June 17, 2005, by Pete Yost.

As events continue to unfold in Iraq, an updating of the duplicitous actions of the U.S. regarding its goal of bringing democracy to Iraq will shed more light on U.S. hypocrisy and lies in this regard. On January 30, 2005, elections were held in Iraq for an interim government. Its job is to produce a constitution and to arrange for an election of a permanent democratic government. On the surface, the elections seemed to justify the invasion of Iraq, regardless that it was based on lies about WMDs and a nonexistent connection between al Qaeda and Saddam Hussein. That, at least, is what the administration and most of the media want us to accept—that elections free of U.S. interference justified the invasion. A deeper look, however, belies the claims Bush made in his inaugural address on January 20, 2005. In it he said that "it is the policy of the United States to seek and support the growth of democratic movements and institutions in every nation and culture, with the ultimate goal of ending tyranny in our world."

In the first place, U.S. support for tyrannical dictatorships is unquestioned fact. Whether it be for the forward deployment of military bases, for access to oil or for favorable conditions for U.S. corporations, the U.S. will turn a blind eye on tyranny when it suits U.S. objectives.

In the second place, when the U.S. says that its policy is to promote democracy, it is the form but not the substance of democracy that it seeks. This was true for our founding fathers (see Chapter 13). The U.S. has always been a plutocratic oligarchy—government by the wealthy few. It is what the U.S. seeks to promote in Iraq and elsewhere.

And, in the third place, the January 30, 2005, elections in Iraq, rather than being a vindication of U.S. policy, represent a resounding defeat of U.S. goals. A step-by-step review of the U.S.'s retreat from its original tyrannical, imperialistic plan shows that whatever degree of actual democracy that exists in Iraq today, the U.S. cannot take credit for it.

The following sequence of events leading up to the January 30, 2005, elections was gleaned from the June 2005 issue of *Extra*, the magazine of FAIR—For Accuracy In Reporting. The article was entitled "Defeated by Democracy" and was written by Seth Ackerman. The subtitle of the article is, "Reported as triumph, Iraq elections were really Bush's nightmare." Ackerman's contention is that

> From the very start, the administration was determined to install its handpicked favorites in positions of power in Baghdad and to exclude Iraqis with broader public support. For nearly a year, it watched helplessly as that strategy came unglued. Only after its preferred game-plan decisively collapsed—in the face of an armed Sunni insurgency, the popular rejection of U.S.-supported Iraqi elite, and crucially, the threat of a massive Shiite uprising—did the Bush administration reluctantly bow to pressure from Islamists and allow a free vote."

In late 2002, the first Pentagon plan for Iraq was to set up a "provisional government" of "hand-picked Iraqi exiles" even before the war was over. The provisional government would be headed by exiles such as Ahmed Chalabi, head of the Iraqi National Congress in the U.S. and which received funding from the U.S. for almost a decade. This plan was discarded shortly before the invasion. It was decided that the exiles did not have sufficient support in Iraq.

In April of 2003, the Pentagon initiated a new plan for setting up the INC and Ahmed Chalabi as the head of a "democratic Iraq that was amenable to our wishes and desires." The Pentagon estimated that it would take two to three months to accomplish the changeover. The Pentagon airlifted Chalabi and several hundred Pentagon-trained, exile militia into the Iraq town of Nasiriyah. There, Chalabi tried to get the local population to support him. In Baghdad, a "'general'" of the Free Iraqi Forces—the name for the exile militia—and who was an aide of Chalabi declared himself mayor of the city. In Najaf, a group called the Iraqi Coalition of National Unity entered the town on U.S. special forces vehicles and briefly took over the city. The commandeered homes and cars, looted and terrorized the people.

In May of 2003, the next phase of the occupation began. Ambassador Paul Bremer was named head of the Coalition Provisional Authority. I insert here excerpts from a speech by Naomi Klein for what the U.S. intended to accomplish in Iraq to consolidate its imperialistic objectives.

Naomi Klein, an award-winning Canadian journalist, spoke in Seattle on October 9, 2003, at the University of Washington. The title of her speech was "Economic Warfare: From Argentina to Iraq." I summarize the main points she made about what the United States is doing in Iraq.

> Downsizing is also part of the plan. Bremer fired 400,000 state employees. Taxes will be lower with no state services. High unemployment will keep wages low.
>
> The snail's pace of reconstruction caused many Iraqi businesses to fail, while the market was being flooded with imports, which caused more Iraqi business failures.
>
> All restrictions on taking profits out of Iraq have been removed.
>
> Iraq is where, because there is no public input, all the textbook policies of a fully privatized, downsized, deregulated market economy will be put in place. Rumsfeld said that Iraq "will have some of the most enlightened and inviting tax and investment laws in the free world."
>
> All of this so-called reconstruction will take place before the people have any chance to vote on it. And afterwards, if the people want to change things back, that would be expropriation for which there would be retaliation.
>
> Bush wants all of this in place by the summer of 2004 so that Iraq can't be used as a minus election issue against him.

> Most of the world outside of the Arab world has been sold off. Twenty-two of the Arab League countries are not part of the WTO. Their governments own the oil and most of the economy. Oil wealth has kept them outside of the WTO's trading system.
>
> Bush has stated he wants to end that. In ten years he says the Middle East will be a free-trade zone. A foothold is needed and Iraq provides the wedge.
>
> The U.S. is acting like an auctioneer, selling off Iraq to U.S. and British multinational corporations. Reconstruction money is awarded to private U.S. education companies, for example. Contracts have been given to them to print textbooks in the U.S. A British firm is printing Iraq's currency. Reconstruction jobs are being filled mostly by Americans.
>
> The same corporations that are doing the rebuilding will be the ones in the best position to bid for the purchase of Iraq's assets. Bush admits that Iraq is to be remade into a deregulated free-market economy. Paul Bremer, who runs Iraq for the U.S. and who appointed the Iraqi Council, told the Council that it needs to "pry open most of its industries for foreign investment." Two hundred state firms are ready for privatization. Bremer has told Congress Iraq needs to privatize its oil. It is privatization disguised as reconstruction.
>
> New Bridge Strategies is a new company headed by Bush's former campaign manager. This company helps companies further their investment opportunities in Iraq. One of the partners in the firm said, "Getting the rights to distribute Proctor & Gamble products would be a gold mine. One well-stocked 7-Eleven could knock out 30 Iraqi stores. A Wal-Mart could take over the country."

So, what lies under the surface is much, much more than oil; it is about the wholesale transfer of all of Iraq's assets to American and British multi-national corporations. In U.S. history there has never been a more greedy or a more lustful lunge for power than the war on Iraq. It is the most egregiously graphic example to date of Friedman's point that "the hidden hand of the market will never work without the hidden fist."

A year later, writing in the September, 2004, issue of *Harper's Magazine*, Klein updated the overall economic situation and specifically regarding the privatization of some 200 Iraqi state-owned firms. She went to Iraq in March of 2004 to see for herself what was happening. Essentially, nothing is happening, she writes. What little is being rebuilt is with U.S. taxpayer money. Iraq is still so chaotic, investors have been reluctant to risk their own money in reconstruction. The U.S. plan to sell off the state-owned firms was illegal from the start. The next plan to get a Constitution in place before the June 30, 2004, deadline for transfer of authority to the Iraqis failed. That plan would have made legal the sale of the state-owned firms. To date, the Iraqi interim government has been able to resist privatization of the state-owned firms. Klein went on at length to describe the ill-fated attempt by the Coalition Provisional Authority, headed up by Paul Bremer, to rebuild Iraq from "ground zero" into a "corporate utopia." (Concurrently with what Klein was reporting on, the U.S. began construction of over a dozen permanent military bases.)

Bremer's plans were railroaded through the Coalition Provisional Authority by U.S.-appointed Iraqi ministers. The plans were bitterly opposed by trade unions and business leaders who faced ruin if the nation's state-owned businesses were sold off to U.S. and U.K. multi-national corporations. One business leader labeled the policies as "'a recipe for disaster,'" while another said that it was a "'world occupation'" that would make Iraqis "'immigrants in their own land.'" Klein's report of her visit to Iraq in March of 2004 showed that U.S. intentions of rebuilding Iraq into a "corporate utopia" had been successfully resisted.

By June of 2003, a key assumption of the Bush team proved to be wrong. They believed that radical Shiite groups would not have significant followings once Saddam was gone. That was not the case. There was a growing popularity of Islamist political parties among the majority Shiite sect. During Saddam's reign, the Supreme Council for the Islamic Revolution in Iraq was headquartered in Iran. Now, with Saddam gone, the SCIRI had offices across Iraq. Seen as a threat to U.S. objectives, their offices were raided and its leaders were arrested. U.S. military commanders halted all local elections and self-rule in towns and cities. Rather than let SCIRI candidates win elections, U.S. commanders installed their own hand-picked mayors and administrators.

For the next six months, the Bush administration retreated step by step until it had to permit free elections. In June of 2003, "the leading Shiite cleric, Ayatollah al Sistani issued a fatwa [an edict] against Bremer's plan to have U.S.-appointed Iraqis write a constitution and insisted only freely elected Iraqis be involved." Bremer ignored the fatwa and sought to have secular, former exiles back Bremer's plan. That didn't work. Then Bremer tried to get other ayatollahs to warn of the dangers of early elections. That didn't work either. Next, Bremer put forth having partial elections. Neither was that acceptable to Sistani.

Sistani's resolute insistence on free elections caused a crisis for the Bush administration. Bremer flew back to Washington for emergency consultations. The proposed new plan was to speed up the transfer of sovereignty to Iraq. The constitution, however, was to be written by Iraqis selected through "caucuses." While publicly claiming that the U.S.'s opposition to elections was "motivated solely by logistical concerns," the U.S. privately "vetoed a detailed Iraqi technical plan to hold an early vote." In November 2003, Noah Feldman, Bremer's advisor on constitutional matters, revealed the real motive for opposing free and early elections: "'Simply put, if you move too fast, the wrong people could get elected.'"

Sistani declared the new plan to hold caucuses to be illegitimate in "'its totality and its details.'" By January of 2004, there were demonstrations of tens of thousands of Iraqis to support Sistani's insistence on free elections. The Bush administration conceded and set elections for January of 2005.

Nevertheless, the administration continued to install its proxies in positions of power. The U.S. "strong-armed the U.N. into appointing Iyad Alawi interim prime minister. Alawi is a former Baathist with ties to the old Iraqi army. According to a Shiite close to Sistani, "'nothing could be done without U.S. approval.'"

The elections were held in January of 2005. The results showed why the administration didn't want them at all. "The winning slate was a coalition led by the two Shiite parties, SCIRI and Dawa, that had been most feared by the Bush administration." Ackerman concludes: "Looking at the Bush administration's strategy since the invasion, designed to keep power in U.S. hands while marginalizing Islamist parties, the elections can only be considered a massive defeat for the administration."

Jim Hightower, writing for *The Progressive Populist* in its June 15, 2005, issue, exposed how the U.S. has compromised Iraq's supposed sovereignty. He pointed out that the Iraqi Intelligence Service does not report to the newly elected government but to the CIA. Even the head of Iraqi Intelligence, Mohammed Abudullah Shahwani, was chosen by the U.S. Right after the elections, the U.S. moved Iraq's national intelligence archives into U.S. headquarters and put them off-limits to the newly elected officials. This was done because the U.S. doesn't trust the new leaders nor real democracy. The U.S. claims that the new government is too friendly with Iran. Also, the U.S. has done a lot of spying on the new leaders, and the U.S. wants to keep this information from the people and their chosen leaders. Hightower quoted one of the new lawmakers. The Iraqi Intelligence Service "'is not working for the Iraqi government; it's working for the CIA. I prefer to call it the American Intelligence Service of Iraq.'"

A further indication of the Bush administration's fear of a theocratic Islamist government and of losing out on Iraq's oil was a condition it placed on the elections. Although the Kurds represent only about 15% of the population, they were to be guaranteed 25% of the seats in the new government. This move was to aid the U.S. for at least gaining control of the oil in areas controlled by the Kurds.

With regard to the elections, it simply won't do for the Bush administration to claim that, see, we were right after all and for a compliant mainstream media to obligingly go along. The pretext for a preemptive war was built on a foundation of lies. The war, in actuality, was an illegal preventive war to advance U.S. goals for world domination. And, with regard to the elections, what the U.S. really wanted was a subservient, secular state, headed by someone like Ahmed Chalabi, whom we had bought and paid for. Instead, the U.S. might very well have been the cause of another theocratic rather than democratic nation-state coming into being.

Why is there not a national public groundswell of repudiation of the nation's leaders when they lie to the public about issues so serious as war? We expect them to lie, but why no repudiation? I think it is because, to whatever extent, each of us has an underlying feeling of helplessness about life that is compensated for by a compulsion to seek power. We are led to believe, in vain, that a successful war will end that primal, substrata level of insecurity we all share. Thus, despite our disbelief, we believe.

Diversion and Patriotism as Ploys of the 3rd Line Rich and Powerful, Elite Ruling Class to Further Their Greed and Lust for Power

The 3rd line rich and powerful, elite ruling class in Colonial America acted the way the upper class does when it needs to preserve its own class interests. Our Founding Fathers and the class they represented diverted the lower classes' attention away from what were grievous injustices perpetrated by the upper class and toward a common enemy: England. They clothed their predacious self-interest in patriotic garb. They were successful in enlisting a sufficient number of the lower classes to revolt and, with crucial help from France, won independence.

Right down to 2003, the same scenario played out in the 3rd line Bush administration's mobilization of support for the war on Iraq. The people have been distracted from a languishing economy, from the administration's trashing of the environment, from the administration's selling out to big business, from huge transfers of wealth from the middle and lower classes to the upper class, from the cutting back or cutting out of social programs and from the administration's weakening of the Security and Exchange Commission's enforcement of new rules for the accounting industry—to hit the highlights.

The war against Iraq was justified on the patriotic grounds that it was a matter of national security to effect a "regime change" in a dangerous dictatorship. Actually, Iraq was no military threat because of a decade of trade sanctions and disarmament. Iraq possessed no weapons of mass destruction.

The ploy of distracting the public from just grievances against the domestic agenda of the Bush administration, coupled with the ploy of demonizing Iraq, a country that would not do our bidding, effectively obscured the foreign policy of the administration. That foreign policy is world domination through control of the world's oil. The bogus threat of a nuclear attack was the perfect cover for the United States to gain control of Iraq's oil.

A quote from Hermann Goering during the Nuremberg trials on April 18, 1946, highlights the ploy of claiming the national security is at stake if a nation's leaders want war when they know the people don't. Goering was Reich Marshal and head of the Luftwaffe in Nazi Germany. The Goering quote is from a speech given by Ray McGovern, an ex-CIA analyst, on October 26, 2003. McGovern is quoting from notes made by Gustav Gilbert, Goering's interrogator. Gilbert has just said that the common people were not thankful for leaders who brought them war and destruction. Goering responded, "That's understood. But, after all, it is the leaders of the country who determine the policy. And it is always a simple matter to drag the people along, whether it is democracy, whether it is a dictatorship, whether it's a parliamentary or a fascist regime." Gilbert injects at this point that in the United States only the elected representatives of the people in Congress can declare war. Goering ends by saying, "Oh, that is well and good, but voice or no voice, the people can always be brought to do the bidding of their leaders. That is easy. All you have to do is tell them that they are being attacked and denounce the pacifists for lack of patriotism and exposing the country to danger. It works the same way in any country."

It certainly worked for Bush. Most people felt we were threatened by a mushroom cloud. Bush said so on October 7, 2002. Condoleezza Rice, National Security Advisor, said so on October 8, 2002. Victoria Clarke, Pentagon spokeswoman, said so on October 9, 2002. Congress voted for war on October 10 and October 11, 2002.

A 3rd line level of greed and lust for absolute power accounts for the rich and powerful, elite ruling class's domestic and foreign policies. It accounts for why that class feels that it alone knows what is the national interest and has the right to exclude all lower classes from the decision-making process. The lower classes are to keep mouths shut, "watch out what you say" (Ari Fleischer, Bush's White House Spokesperson), stay in line, don't rock the boat, be diverted in brainless activities and buy, buy, buy to stimulate the economy and to satisfy insatiable wants.

A Few Measures of the U.S. Greed and Lust for Power

One measure of the U.S. greed is the percentage of gross national product that is given as foreign aid. Of the twenty-two most developed nations, the United States is last in the percentage of foreign aid to gross national product: 0.1%. Most of what we give goes to Egypt and Israel, and that is in the form of military aid. The United States is like a spoiled child who says, "What's mine is mine, and you can't have it." How insatiable is the U.S. greed? The United States consumes over half of all the goods and services of the world, while being less than 10 percent of the world's population.

One measure of the U.S. lust for power is the growth of the military budget. When the U.S.S.R. fell apart, the military budget was $260 billion. Now it is $400 billion. It keeps growing even though no country would dare provoke the United States militarily. Well, how much military power does it take for the United States to be secure, even though it is the sole superpower? Apparently no amount is sufficient. Why? Because there are billions of people around the world who are 2nd liners and need to be kept in line. Why? Because in some countries there is a 3rd line, rich and powerful, elite ruling class who want their country to go its own independent way. And why? Because ever-increasing levels of primal pain cause ever greater feelings of helplessness that must be compensated for by accumulating ever more power in a vain attempt to feel secure.

An intangible measure of the greed that characterizes the United States is it being called "the land of opportunity." This is the country that encourages greed. The United States is the country of choice to which to emigrate of those whose level of insatiable wants cannot be met in their home country. Granted, there have been many who have emigrated out of need.

Why the United States is Hated Over Much of the World

Long before September 11, 2001, the United States was hated throughout the world. September 11, 2001, however, forced the United States to focus on why. Unfortunately, the answer most widely given—they hate us for our freedoms—was so far off the mark as to preclude any meaningful national self-examination of our foreign policy being responsible for that hatred. A good, comprehensive source on the subject is *Why Do People Hate America?* by Ziauddin Sardar and Merryl Wyn Davies. Here, I will make brief references to a number of reasons they give as to why the United States is so hated.

Military intervention is high on the list. As I noted earlier, in all of U.S. history, we have militarily intervened over 200 times. Many of them have been to protect U.S. corporations from any interference from foreign governments. Many of them have been to effect regime change, and that usually meant a compliant right-wing dictator who crushed an emerging populist movement. Declassified National Security Council reports indicate that the main thrust of our foreign policy in the Third World is to prevent the rise of nationalistic governments that seek to improve living standards for the people because that interferes with U.S. corporations and the country's wealth flowing to the United States. Third World countries are to be sources of cheap labor, natural resources and markets for U.S. businesses.

A major source of hatred of the United States is our Middle East policy and strategy. Despite the United States' avowed commitment to peace between Israel and the Palestinians, the United States has consistently sided with Israel and blocked the creation of a viable Palestinian state. This is so, even though Israel has illegally occupied for decades territory outside its legal borders, including the West Bank and the Gaza Strip. A National Security Council memo of 1958 says that what we don't want is "radical Arab nationalism," which means countries that will not submit to U.S. power.

Another source of hatred is the U.S. insistence that its model for economics, for culture and indeed for anything that we can export for profit is the only acceptable model. Among other consequences, it results in the disintegration of indigenous cultures throughout the world.

Hypocrisy is another major reason for hatred of the United States. Now, more than ever, the U.S. claims for Goodness have reached cosmological proportions: God is on our side. That automatically means that there is Evil with a capital "E" out there. But the United States says one thing and does another. The United States says it's for human rights, then votes them down at the United Nations or supports dictators who crush them. The United States says it is committed to the right of a people for self-determination, then engineers a covert CIA coup to replace a democratically elected leader.

The problem of hatred of the United States is not Osama bin Laden and al Qaeda. The problem is the underlying causes that drive people to commit terrorist acts. The cause is not that they are jealous of our freedoms. They are angry at the way the United States has prostituted its freedoms in the cause of military, economic, ethnic, racist and religious imperialism. It shouldn't be difficult to understand Islamic fundamentalist terrorism. The United States has exhibited Christian fundamentalist terrorism in the bombing of abortion-providing clinics and in the murder of doctors who perform abortions. All one has to do to understand religious fundamentalist terrorism is to listen to their rationale for claming that it is God telling them to kill the Evil Ones.

Actually, what is being forced upon the rest of the world by a United States bent on world domination is not Americanism as such, as both its proponents and opponents claim. Rather, what is being exported and foisted on people worldwide is the most advanced Stage III, 3rd line level of unconscious self-awareness to date. Since a Stage III, 3rd line rich and powerful, elite ruling class can be found in every country, they all work together for the common good of their class. The difference between this class in the United States and abroad is the immense wealth and political and military power at the disposal of the U.S. class to aid this same class in other countries to impose the rights of private property investors at the cost of sacrificing human rights.

The U.S. class does not always have to act unilaterally. The U.S. class domination of the World Trade Organization, the World Bank and the International Monetary Fund enables it to carry out its goals without calling attention to itself. It helps in that these organizations carry out their business in secret.

The WTO as the Government of the Future

While the United States continues to pursue its goals of economic imperialism and world domination, the United States might become as irrelevant as it has made the United Nations. The United States might create such a degree of worldwide hatred for itself that retaliation against our policies worldwide could result in the collapse of the U.S. economy. In which case, that would leave the WTO as the de facto world government. In the long run, the United States might only be a transitional Stage toward a world run by multi-national corporations.

One indication of how even the United States as *the* superpower must allow its internal politics to give way before WTO policies regards steel tariffs. Bush imposed steel tariffs to enhance his electoral chances in steel-producing states. The WTO countered by threatening to impose tariffs on goods produced by states crucial to Bush's re-election. Bush rescinded the tariffs. That is a sign of what is to come.

Over time what is coming about is the fulfillment of the dream of the rich and powerful, elite ruling class the world over. It is the emergence of government on the national and international levels that truly insulates policy from politics. On the international level, it is the World Trade Organization, the World Bank, the International Monetary Fund, the Inter-American Development Bank, the European Economic Community, the G-7 and the international trade agreements such as G.A.T.T., N.A.F.T.A. and the General Agreement on Trade in Services that are the means by which the people are effectively blocked out from any meaningful participation in the decisions that affect every aspect of their lives. The Founding Fathers' view that the people should have as little to do with government as possible and that those who own the country should run it is coming true in a way they wouldn't believe. It is technology that enables the ruling class in every country to conduct business without regard for national borders. It is, according to the World Bank, technocratic insulation.

What is coming to pass on the international level is government that is solely devoted to protecting and enhancing private property. The WTO is working toward the end of dismantling and privatizing all government-provided services, including education, health care, child care, energy, water, postal service, libraries, museums, power and transportation. For example, it has hired a private company—Global Division for Transnational Education—to single out and pressure countries that want to keep out foreign educational providers and keep their public educational systems from being open to the global, privatized, educational marketplace. Under WTO regulations, a foreign corporation would have the right to establish itself and to compete for public funding. Countries would be prohibited from favoring their own corporations. No regulations inhibiting free trade in education would be allowed. Once a service had been privatized, a country wouldn't be able to go back to a nationalized service without the threat of sanctions. The WTO is arriving at the place where the United States' Founding Fathers began: Government is not in the business of providing social services. Worldwide, a Stage III, 3rd line level of unconscious self-awareness with its focus on greed and a lust for power is taking over.

CHAPTER 16

FINAL THOUGHTS

. . . My Purpose and the Means Used to Fulfill It

My basic purpose was to lead you to realize that human consciousness has devolved into an unconscious self-awareness. Further, it was my intention to guide you into a personal experience of your own primal-pain-driven self-awareness such that you would seek to restore your own pre-self-aware childhood consciousness.

As a means to those ends, I laid out much of my own experience with my primal-pain-driven self-awareness to illustrate how I became unconscious and how I've begun the process of restoring my own pre-self-aware childhood consciousness. Equally important as a means, I used the history of religious ideas to reveal the progression of unconsciousness throughout the world, but mainly in those areas antecedent to our Western and Eastern cultures. I pointed out that the first three stages of religion follow the first three stages in the development of self-awareness: placation, reimmersion and power which, in turn, follow the sequence of the maturation of the sensing, emotional/sexual and thinking levels of the brain.

. . . *My Education*

I had no idea when I started to write this book just how deep into every level of our national life that greed and a lust for power had penetrated. The history books I read in elementary and high schools described a United States of America that was democratic, that was fundamentally idealistic, that had equality of opportunity, that pursued justice and that cultivated a well-placed patriotism. It wasn't until a few years ago when I began reading histories and critiques that exposed the darker underside of U.S. history that I grasped the extent to which a rich and powerful, elite ruling class has run the United States for its own benefit at the expense of the general public.

. . . the Darker Underside of the United States Today

Best Congress money can buy.

Power lies in the hands of those who control the wealth of the country.

Bent on world domination.

Control oil and control the world.

Just enough concessions to the general population to keep them in line.

Bust unions.

Harass and repress all popular movements, if possible.

Resist proportional representation in order to resist populism.

Create fear, uncertainty and insecurity among the people to keep them in line and to convince them to acquiesce in the restriction of their civil rights.

When necessary, divert the people's focus on matters of concern to them by going to war and furthering the goal of world domination.

Maintain the illusion of democracy so that it is easy to stir up a jingoistic patriotism in support of the hidden goals of the ruling class.

Present the façade of encouraging debate on national issues but quash any debate that questions the authority, motives, goals, or actions of the elite ruling class.

Control the media so as to control what the people see, hear and read.

Pretend that the elite are for everyone exercising his right to vote when actually a large nonvoting public that feels their votes make no difference makes it easier to maintain control.

Maintain the Third World as a source of raw materials, cheap labor and a market for finished products.

. . . the Nature of Government in the United States

The real power in the United States lies not in the elected representatives, except if they are among those who own and control the great concentrations of wealth and property in the country. This rich and powerful, elite ruling class would have the general public believe that in substance the United States is a republic or a representative democracy, but in reality the United States is a combination of plutocracy and oligarchy. The United States is run by the wealthy few. The history of the United States as, indeed, it has been for all nation states is one of the ever-increasing concentration of wealth and power in the hands of the few. And, as right-wing Christianity continues to exercise greater and greater power in the Republican Party, the danger is that the United States will be taken over by a theocratic, plutocratic oligarchy.

. . . on the Republican and Democratic Parties

Up until perhaps the end of World War II, the Republican and Democratic parties stood for clearly marked principles. By the administration of Clinton, the Democratic party had become so much like the Republican party that many today see little or no difference between them. This has happened because, as primal pain has increased—resulting in greater individualism, lesser communalism, greater insatiable wants and a greater lust for power—everyone has moved closer toward exhibiting the principles of the Republican party. This means that maybe as many as half the population—those who are in the lower classes—are now left without adequate representation in government.

A third party is needed, but both the Republican and Democratic parties have made it extremely difficult for any third party to get people into the national government. The winner-take-all rules that govern national elections ensures that only Republicans or Democrats are going to be elected. Proportional representation among parties is not allowed.

Yet, third parties or third-party candidates that exhibit more of the 2nd line characteristic of selves-in-relationship are relatively ineffectual. This is so because power lies with the 3rd line rich and powerful, elite ruling class. And, even if a 2nd line President and Congress started to carry out policies that lowered corporate profitability, there would be a flight of capital, crippling the economy. Again, I go back to my basic point that there must be a movement back into childhood consciousness for any real change to take place.

. . . Being Prisoners of the Past

All of us, some more, some less, are acting out a past that won't let go of us. Whatever the valence of our primal pain, to that extent we are locked into the past. Although we survived, we are still in a survival mode, placating others by sacrificing our real selves in the hope of being accepted as we are. We continue to immerse ourselves in countless ways to divert ourselves from suffering. We try to fill the void within us by vainly trying to satisfy insatiable wants. And we still compensate for that sense of helplessness in getting our infantile needs met by compulsively seeking power over others.

. . . the Old and the New Inner and Outer Worlds

The old world is dying. A new world is being born. That's the way it is for me, both in the outer and inner worlds. The old world and the old me dies hard. The new world and the new me are not having the easiest of births. What I do know is that there is a new me inside who seeks to shed the old me. That's the way I experience the world outside me. What I do know is that there is an ever-increasing number of primal persons who seek to shed the old world of unconscious self-awareness and to usher in the new-old world of childhood consciousness.

. . . *the Primal Answer to a Society Based on Greed and Power*

The answer of consciousness to the question of what to do about a society based upon a lust for power and an insatiable greed cannot be to seek power, even for a grassroots political party. To do so would be to eventually achieve power and be corrupted by it. No. The answer must lie in a life-long commitment to the primal maxim on a personal level and to the transformation of society based upon power and greed into one based upon the meeting of real needs. The primal maxim is to go for what one wants in life and to primal one's pain as it arises. What happens when one "goes for what one *wants* in life" is that it is likely that the pursuit of wants will cause personal suffering. If one does not repress the suffering, but gives full expression to it, the way is open to feel the pain of the underlying, unmet infantile and childhood *needs*. That is how the primal maxim works. That is how primaling incrementally reverses unconscious self-awareness back into childhood consciousness. Our real needs are natural—to have enough to eat, to be safe, to be stimulated to grow and to develop at our own pace, to be accepted and loved and to be touched.

What would such a society look like? I don't know. It will probably take hundreds of generations to get there. Primaling has been around for only thirty-some years and its effect to date has been miniscule. A fresh examination from a primal point of view of the raw data of indigenous cultures gathered by anthropologists would certainly give us models as to how peoples with far less primal pain and with far less unconsciousness attempted to meet real needs.

. . . *What I See for the Immediate Future*

Right now, I can't see any farther ahead than changing the inner landscape by promoting primaling. Primaling is particularly important for adults in their early twenties before they have children, and even after they have children and are trying, not to raise them, but to make a home for them. (There is a profound difference between raising children and making a home for them.) Parents who are primal persons will cause less primal pain in their children. The children will have less need to placate their parents by sacrificing their consciousness. They will have less need to divert themselves from themselves to defend against their pain. They will not feel as helpless in getting their needs met. They will not feel so compelled to compensate for that helplessness by acquiring power. They will not have to suppress their need as much, only to have it resurface as insatiable wants. Over generations, this will make a tremendous difference on the outer landscape from the village, to the nation, to the world.

. . . Why I've Persevered on This Project

Over the ten years it has taken for me to write this book, I knew that if someday I should find myself on my deathbed and had dropped the project I would feel that my life went unfulfilled. This understanding has kept me at it.

Periodically, I have felt overwhelmed with the task and been tempted to drop it. Then, I remind myself that I can paint the inner landscape that is the perfect mirror of the external landscape of greed and power. I remind myself that perhaps I can make a positive contribution to reversing the growth of primal pain and, thus, the growth of insatiable wants and a compulsion for power. Perhaps I can help to recreate the conditions for a communalism and an individualism that more closely reflect selves-in-relationship.

. . . Being a Work in Progress

No matter that at some point I felt this book was ready to be published, it remains a work in progress. I, too, remain, as a primal person, a work in progress. This is also true for all those who share an evolving childhood consciousness and who add their own contributions to fostering a primal way of life.

. . . on the Primal Solution

What is there to hang on to in a world crazy with primal pain, a world unconsciously careening toward personal, social and environmental disaster, compulsively lusting after power and driven in vain to satisfy insatiable greed? What is there to hang on to but those moments when one connects the pain of one's early past with the suffering of one's present and exclaims, "Aha, I was asleep and now I'm awake. Aha, now I know who I am and why I am the way I am. Aha, I'm more free from the past than I was, more free to create a new, less unconscious world."

Don't take my word for it. Who the hell am I but one more person trying to do the best for myself and for all others. Figure it out for yourself why greed and power account for 99.9 percent of what's going down these days, and that bad breath and body odor account for the remaining 1/10 of 1 percent.

FOR FURTHER READING

Beard, Charles A. *An Economic Interpretation of the Constitution of the United States.* 1913. New York: The Free Press, 1966.
Bonheim, Jalaja. *Goddess: A Celebration in Art and Literature.* New York: Stewart, Tabori & Chang, 1997.
Campbell, Joseph. *The Hero With a Thousand Faces.* 1949. Princeton: Princeton University Press, 1972.
Chomsky, Noam. *Hegemony or Survival.* New York: Henry Holt & Co., 2003.
—. *The New Military Humanism.* Monroe, ME: Common Courage Press, 1999.
—. *Power and Terror.* New York: Seven Stories Press, 2003.
—. *Towards a New Cold War.* 1973. New York: Pantheon Press, 1982.
—. *Understanding Power.* Eds. Peter R. Mitchell and John Schoeffel. New York: The New Press, 2002.
Dean, John W. *Worse Than Watergate.* New York: Little, Brown & Co., 2004.
Durant, Will. *The Story of Civilization: Part 1.* 1935. New York: Simon & Schuster, 1954.
Eliad, Mircea. *A History of Religious Ideas, Vol. 1.* 1978. Chicago: The University of Chicago Press, 1981.
—. *A History of Religious Ideas, Vol. 2.* 1978. Chicago and London: The University of Chicago Press, 1982.
—. *The Myth of the Eternal Return: or Cosmos and History.* 1954. Princeton: Princeton University Press, 1954.
—. *Shamanism: Archaic Techniques of Ecstasy.* 1964. Princeton: Princeton University Press, 1974.
Ferry, David. *Gilgamesh: A New Rendering in English Verse.* New York: Farrar, Strauss & Giroux, 1992.
Flowers, Betty Sue. *Joseph Campbell: The Power of Myth with Bill Moyers.* New York: Doubleday, 1988.
Fiszman, Joseph R., ed. *The American Political Arena.* Boston: Little, Brown & Co., 1962.
Gimbutas, Marija. *The Goddesses and Gods of Old Europe.* 1974. Berkeley: University of California Press, 1982.
Halifax, Joan. *Shaman: The Wounded Healer.* New York: The Crossroad Publishing Company, 1982.

Hofstadter, Richard. *The American Political Tradition.* 1973. New York: Vintage Books, 1974.
Janov, Arthur. *The Anatomy of Mental Illness.* 1971. New York: Berkeley Publishing Corporation, 1974.
—. *The Biology of Love.* New York: Prometheus Books, 2002.
—. *The Feeling Child.* New York: Simon & Schuster, 1973.
—. *Imprints: The Lifelong Effects of the Birth Experience.* New York: Coward-McCann, 1983.
—. *The New Primal Scream: Primal Therapy 20 Years On.* Wilmington: Enterprise Publishing, 1991.
—. *The Primal Revolution: Toward a Real World.* 1972. New York: Simon & Schuster, 1973.
—. *The Primal Scream.* 1970. New York: G. P. Putnam's Sons, 1980.
—. *Prisoners of Pain: Unlocking the Power of the Mind to End Suffering.* New York: Anchor Press/Doubleday, 1980.
—. *Why You Get Sick and How You Get Well.* West Hollywood, California: Dove Books, 1996.
Janov, Arthur, and E. Michael Holden. *Primal Man: The New Consciousness.* New York: Thomas Y. Crowell, 1975.
Johnson, Chalmers. *The Sorrows of Empire.* New York: Henry Holt & Co., 2004.
Karp, Walter. *Indispensable Enemies.* New York: Franklin Square Press, 1993.
—. *Liberty Under Siege.* 1988. New York: Franklin Square Press, 1993.
—. *The Politics of War.* 1979. New York: Franklin Square Press, 2003.
Kessler, Ronald. *The CIA at War.* 2003. New York: St. Martin's Griffin, 2004.
Kiiwaczek, Paul. *In Search of Zarathustra.* New York: Alfred A. Knopf, 2003.
Lakoff, George. *Don't Think of an Elephant! Know Your Values and Frame the Debate: The Essential Guide for Progressives.* White River Junction, Vermont: Chelsea Green Publishing Company, 2004.
Leeming, David, and Jake Page. *Goddess: Myths of the Female Divine.* New York: Oxford University Press, 1994.
Levi-Strauss, Claude. *Totemism.* 1962. Boston: Beacon Press, 1963.
Lincoln, Bruce. *Death, War, and Sacrifice.* Chicago: The University of Chicago Press, 1991.
Loewen, James W. *Lies My Teacher Told Me.* New York: The New Press, 1995.
Mallory, J. P. *In Search of the Indo-Europeans.* 1989. New York: Thames & Hudson, Inc., 1992.
Mann, A. T., and Jane Lyle. *Sacred Sexuality.* New York: Barnes & Noble, Inc., 1995.
McEvedy, Colin. *The Penguin Atlas of Ancient History.* Hong Kong: Penguin Books, 1967.
Miller, David, ed. *Tell Me Lies.* London: Pluto Press, 2004.
Motz, Lotte. *The Faces of the Goddess.* New York: Oxford University Press, 1997.

Palast, Greg. *The Best Democracy Money Can Buy*. 2002. New York: Penguin Group, 2003.
Parenti, Michael. *Democracy for the Few*. 5th ed. New York: St. Martin's Press, 1988.
Parrinder, Geoffrey, ed. *World Religions*. 1971. New York: Facts on File, 1985.
Phillips, Kevin. *Wealth and Democracy*. New York: Broadway Books, 2002.
Phillips, Peter, ed. *Censored 2004*. New York: Seven Stories Press, 2003.
—. *Censored 2005*. New York: Seven Stories Press, 2004.
Rampton, Sheldon, and John Stauber. *Weapons of Mass Deception*. New York: Jeremy P. Tarcher, 2003.
Sardar, Ziauddin, and Merryl Wyn Davies. *Why Do People Hate America?* New York: The Disinformation Company Ltd., 2002.
Shlain, Leonard. *The Alphabet Versus the Goddess*. New York: Penguin Putnam, Inc., 1998.
Sklar, Holly, ed. *Trilateralism*. Boston: South End Press, 1980.
Smith, Adam. *Wealth of Nations*. 1776. New York: Prometheus Books, 1991.
Solomon, Norman, and Reese Erlich. *Target Iraq*. New York: Context Books, 2003.
Stone, Merlin. *When God Was a Woman*. New York: Barnes & Noble, Inc., 1976.
Turner, Alice K. *The History of Hell*. New York: Harcourt Brace & Co., 1993.
Wright, Benjamin F., ed. *The Federalist*. New York: Metrobooks, 1961.
Zaehner, R. C. *The Dawn and Twilight of Zorastrianism*. 1961. London: Phoenix Press, 2002.
Zinn, Howard. *A People's History of the United States 1492-Present*. 1980, 1995, 1998. New York: HarperCollins, 1999.